Gulf Publishing Company
Book Publishing Division
Houston, Texas

The Symbolic Profile

Ruth Thacker Fry, Ph.D.
Joyce Hall

THE SYMBOLIC PROFILE

*Library of Congress
Catalog Card Number 76-5085
ISBN 0-87201-815-6*

Edited by Tim Calk/Designed by Susan Corte

Acknowledgements

We wish to acknowledge the assistance and encouragement
to proceed with the manual given by Ethel Kurth and Mary
Eileen Dobson. A very special thanks to Dr. LaBerta Hatwick
for the many helpful discussions during the early days of the
Profile's use.

We wish to express our sincere appreciation to Carolyn Fay for
sharing her creative interpretation of the Profile through
her body movement class.

Our thanks also go to Irene Corbit for her help in editing
and preparing the manuscript.

Finally, thanks to the thousands of people who have so willingly
shared their material with us through their Profiles and especially
to those few whose Profiles were used in the manual.

The Authors

Contents

Preface

This manual came into being through the insistence of psychiatrists, psychologists, counselors, ministers, and teachers, who became acquainted with the Profile and were interested in learning to use it in their own practices. They expressed the need for an instructive manual which would give them a guide to administering and analyzing the Profile. During the past twenty years literally thousands of Profiles have been added to my files, and it is from these we have selected representative cases to analyze and amplify.

The Ruth Fry Symbolic Profile was developed to fulfill a special need in the counseling situation—that of becoming more quickly and easily acquainted with the client. In time it was found to show the personal growth of counselees and students as they made further use of the Profile.

An objective of any counseling situation, aside from the stated purpose of the healing process, is to help the person know where he is confined in his own psyche and to enable him to see the multiplicity contained in life and the world in which he lives. New ways of thinking, feeling, and perceiving help him to find his own reality, bringing the total personality into play—the beauty and ugliness, the dark and light, his own limitations and potentials. People need a new direction of interest as well as tools to help them face their problems.

Because the Profile utilizes projective testing methods, it is suitable for counseling requirements. The possibilities of the Profile are unlimited.

A creative body movement class at the Jung Center used the Profile as a starting point to learn more about themselves. The class members felt this method to be very helpful in developing increased awareness. This was accomplished by concentrating on one square during each session for six weeks, and acting out their individual Profile drawings in body movement.

One student had drawn a peacock (see Case 29 in the Ego Square (#1). In trying to experience himself as a peacock, he visualized a path strewn with jewels. But, as a peacock, he could not walk on the path and had to become himself in order to tread a new way and gather the jewels. This work gave him the opportunity to look at his peacock attitude which had been limiting his psychological growth. When asked what the peacock meant to him, he said, "Peacocks are proud and try to show off, and I don't know that side of myself at all."

Included in this manual is one counselor's experience in using only the Profile on a short-term basis as a means of working with a person on a particular troubled area.

If a client is familiar with the techniques of active imagination[1] or other meditative processes, he can use the drawings as a way of working through his fantasies about himself and discovering where development can take place. The creative possibilities of the Profile are available to anyone wishing to explore new ways of personal awareness.

The Profile is not a test. The late Dr. Bruno Klopfer suggested that it be called The Ruth Fry Symbolic Profile "because to see it as a test would take the heart out of it."

Because my orientation is primarily Jungian, the symbolic approach in the counseling situation is the one I naturally follow. However, any counselor, no matter what his persuasion, will find this aid a useful adjunct. The knowledge of the meaning of symbols would be a valuable asset in analyzing the Profile as would the prior knowledge of the techniques of the Rorschach, the Wartegg-Zeichentest, and the Thematic Apperception Text. A distinct advantage to using the Profile is that it can be completed in a short period of time, and there is no scoring problem as in the aforementioned tests.

Ruth Thacker Fry

Introduction

The Ruth Fry Symbolic Profile has proven over the years to be a valuable counseling aid for the many people who have used it. The Profile is designed not as a test, but as an opportunity for the unconscious to speak.

The small symbols in the six squares elicit responses from the person doing the Profile, as they stimulate the unconscious.[2] There are no "right" or "wrong" responses. The drawings are an expression of the unconscious psychological condition of the client. The statement completions are based on more conscious attitudes, but can be strongly influenced by the unconscious, especially if a word touches upon a sensitive area in the person's psyche.

The style of the Profile allows the client to express his own uniqueness in a situation where he might otherwise be inarticulate. It uses symbolic language, as " . . . a word or an image is symbolic when it implies something more than its obvious and immediate meaning."[3] In this way, the Profile can be a bridge on which two people, the counselor and counselee, can meet.

The Profile is especially useful when the client is unfamiliar to the counselor because it quickly highlights the client's real problems. It also interests a reluctant counselee who might otherwise be unwilling or unable to become immediately involved in the counseling situation. One woman refused to do a Profile and then felt compelled to fill it out because "it looked so lonesome." She had projected her own loneliness onto a piece of paper.

The design of the Profile allows the person to follow the natural order of thinking about himself. A person's usual reaction to a situation is, "How do I think and/or feel about this?" In the first square, the Ego Square (#1), the person draws how he thinks and/or feels about himself. After expressing his own ego standpoint, the person goes on to the Fantasy Square (#2). His fantasy would be the anticipation of possible ways to handle a situation, usually a type of wishful thinking. Having first put down the way things are as he sees them (Ego Square) and then as he wishes them to be (Fantasy Square), he is then free to move on to the Family Square (#3), as this tends to be the next social unit beyond the self. Here the person may express his place in and his concerns with regard to the family unit.

In the Self-Determination Square (#4) he is able to consider his own aspirations, his willpower, so to speak.

Having taken a stand on his goals and aspirations, the person then seeks an understanding of the meaning of his life, which is presented in the Religious Square (#5). The individual is now able to symbolize his potential or resources available for his own fulfillment in the Potential Square (#6).

The meaning of the six symbols used in these squares follows the pattern of the individual's approach to life. In *A Dictionary of Symbols*, J.E. Cirlot says, "In short, there is nothing arbitrary about graphic symbolism[(59)]; everything obeys a system which develops out of a single point and expands into more complex forms in which shape, rhythm, quantity, position, order, and direction all help to explain and define the pattern."[4]

The symbol in the Ego Square (#1) is the quaternary, a small square, an earth form having to do with the material and passive.[5] The ego " . . . forms, as it were, the centre of the field of consciousness; and, in so far as this comprises the empirical personality, the ego is the subject of all personal acts of consciousness."[6] The ego is the means by which adaptation to outward reality is experienced.

The wavy line in the Fantasy Square (#2) is a symbol for air[7] and could represent imaginative thoughts or ideas floating around, the possibilities of solutions which are still up in the air. These would be elusive, indefinite contents of the unconscious.

The "unity of origin"[8] symbol, a small dot, is in the Family Square (#3). The family is the most instinctive, fundamental social, or mating group—the seed of individual origin. This social unit is the first place in which we begin to experience ourselves in relationship to others.

The Self-Determination Square (#4), with the diagonal line, contains the symbol for the "active dynamic principle."[9] The development of the diagonal line would be an indication of the person's search for direction in his life.

The symbol of the Religious Square (#5) represents "Infinity, the universe, the All."[10] This symbol would help to express the universal instinctive need to be in touch with that which is more than we. The relationship, or lack of relationship, to a god-image, either personal or impersonal, is where we seek the ultimate meaning of life. From our perception of this image, reflecting life's meaning, we derive our ethical behavior and/or moral attitudes.

The arc in the Potential Square (#6) is part of a circle. The circle, symbolizing wholeness, denotes the totality of the personality.[11] The symbol is left open on the Profile for the purpose of stimulating the person to find his own potential.

The Profile is not usually discussed at the first interview between counselor and counselee. It may be presented at the first meeting, but the second interview would be used to discuss its meaning. By the third interview some real groundwork should be established.

~~~ THE RUTH FRY SYMBOLIC PROFILE ~~~

NAME: _____   DATE: _____

SEX: _____   MARRIED: _____

AGE: _____   SINGLE: _____

Directions:

1. Draw something in each square below
   using the symbol presented. Label each square.
2. After the pictures are completed, finish the
   sentences using the key words - a quick,
   first response.

(Copyright 1961 by Ruth Thacker Fry)

□	~	•
Ego Square (#1)	*Fantasy Square (#2)*	*Family Square (#3)*
/	o	⌒
Self-Determination Square (#4)	*Religion Square (#5)*	*Potential Square (#6)*

Blank Profiles may be ordered from the Jung Institute, Houston, Texas

1. I like _____

2. I want _____

3. My family _____

4. I must _____

5. Church is _____

6. I hope _____

7. I love _____

8. I feel _____

9. Children are _____

10. People think of me _____

11. God _____

12. I often _____

13. I hate _____

14. Someday I _____

15. My father _____

16. I can not _____

17. I fear _____

18. I wish _____

19. I failed _____

20. My greatest success _____

21. My mother _____

22. I need _____

23. I believe _____

24. My worst fault _____

25. Women _____

26. Love _____

27. Sisters are _____

28. I regret _____

29. I was happiest when _____

30. People _____

31. Men _____

32. Sex _____

33. At home _____

34. I miss _____

35. I think _____

36. Marriage _____

37. Brothers _____

38. A spouse _____

39. I think of myself as _____

40. My dreams _____

The statement completion part of the Profile refers to the symbolic drawings. A person may, however, be touched in a sensitive area and digress from the specific word stimuli set forth in the statements. He may, for instance, have a train of thought started by a statement concerning the parent, and continue pursuing the thought through the following sentences. A temptation always present, which should be avoided, is that of drawing conclusions from one symbol or statement which the counselor feels to be significant and to pursue that, not taking into account the whole picture as presented on both parts of the Profile.

It should be noted that the statement completions appear just as the clients responded to them, without corrections or alterations to spelling or grammar.

Since a symbol can mean different things on different levels the counselor must not insist upon a particular interpretation of a symbol. If the counselee is unable to accept the counselor's view, if it does not "click" with him, then the point should not be pressed. If the interpretation is valid and yet is rejected, the opportunity for recognition will come again at a time when the individual is perhaps better able to deal with it.

To summarize, the Profile is a tool to help the counselor begin to know the counselee. It is not a test, but a means of encountering another person on a level otherwise reached only by long and intensive counseling.

The suggestion is made that anyone wanting to use the Profile in a counseling situation will gain skill and facility by first familiarizing himself with the form through Profile analyses of friends or family. In going over the Profile of someone well-known, it is possible to check Profile observations against the facts of the person's life and personality.

The Symbolic Profile is not a toy or a parlor game. As a tool, it can be of real value to counselors, teachers, and clergy who have the background to use it with wisdom and integrity.

Description

The Ruth Fry Symbolic Profile is printed on an 8½ x 11-inch piece of paper in black and white. The front page of the Profile asks pertinent information about the person doing the Profile, gives directions, and provides six squares, each of which contains a symbol. Each of the squares in the Profile bears a relationship to the different areas of a person's life. The second part of the Profile presents forty short statements containing key words meant to elicit a quick response from the individual filling out the Profile.

Purpose

The Profile is a tool to be used by the participants in a counseling situation as a means of communicating on a personal as well as psychological level.

It is not meant to give concrete conclusions and none should be deduced from it. The purpose is to get a quick, overall, almost intuitive feeling about the person doing the Profile.

As will be shown, it may be used in many forms of counseling: pre-marital, analysis, family relations, etc. The primary purpose is that of "building a bridge" and establishing a relationship between two people. It must be emphasized that the counselor should not try to place the person in any particular "complex" niche at any time.

There is no limit to the times a person may fill out the Profile, as the record of several Profiles written at different times will show changes or growth in attitudes on the part of the counselee.

Procedure

The counselor usually gives the Profile to a client after the first interview. He hands it to the subject after folding the paper from top to bottom, giving no instructions, but pointing out that directions are on the front of the Profile.

The counselor informs the client there is no time limit. Different types of media (pencils, crayons, pen, ink) are provided, and the subject is given complete freedom in their use. The counselor may suggest that the person take the Profile home to complete. Also, Profiles can be given to the client for other members of his family, if requested, as these could help to give a more complete picture of the individual's life situation.

Approach to Analysis

When a client presents any material—fantasy (visual or written), drawings, dreams, visions—he is telling the counselor about himself in symbolic language. The Profile serves this same purpose only in a more complete and easily accessible way. The counselor can then take the material presented on the Profile as if someone came to him and said, "Last night I had a dream, I dreamed _____."

The first Profile is usually drawn with pencil or pen, rarely in color, no matter what media are available for his use. Dr. C.G. Jung says, " . . . from a certain moment on the patients begin to make use of colour, and this is generally the moment when merely intellectual interest gives way to emotional participation."[12] Later Profiles are often done in color. If the counselor receives one in black and white from a client who has been doing them in color, it is advisable to question what media were available at the time. If the different media were available for his use, the counselor might suspect a depression or a cutting off from feelings in some way which he may wish to pursue further.

To receive a Profile with bizarre or eccentric statements confirmed by drawings of an exceptional nature could be a clue to a severe disturbance in the counselee. If the counselor feels there is an indication this person is out-of-touch with reality, and not simply in a rebellious or resistant mood, then the client would need to be referred to a psychotherapist.

There will be times when the counselor may receive a Profile specifically displaying a strong emotion, and he would need to be alert to such drawings. Case 2 is a good example of repressed or unconscious anger.

Ordinarily the person would begin with the first square, the Ego Square (#1), but occasionally he may start with another square. This would not change the significance of the individual squares, as the symbols themselves touch upon certain areas of a person's psychology. (The order in which he does them is not of paramount importance.)

Occasionally a subject will dislike doing the Profile and may react in an unexpected manner, such as turning the form upside down. This may be an act of rebellion at following directions or he may resent the Profile itself.

The counselor questions the personal associations of the subject to the six drawings, asking the "w" questions—who, what, why, when, where, and also how. Since the drawings are symbolic, it is necessary first to determine their personal meaning to the subject. Suppose the counselee draws a fish; the counselor may know the fish as an old Christian symbol, but upon questioning, the subject may point out it is brain food. Does the counselee feel he needs brain food? How does he feel about his own brain power? Here we have an example of an objective and a subjective meaning applied to the same symbol. The counselor also notes the drawing's appearance; i.e., is the fish husky, lean, fierce, meek?

At times the person will be unable to amplify the drawings. When this happens, the counselor may find it helpful to ask the subject to have a fantasy or tell a story about one of his drawings.

In one case, a woman was unable to amplify, associate, or even talk about her drawing of Indians sitting around a campfire in front of a tepee. The counselor asked if she could tell a story about the picture. She told of an old wise chief who was in the tent and what he meant to her. Later she reported several important dreams about this old man which held personal meaning for her.

The drawings in the squares may all seem to be in good order except one, such as the Family Square (#3) in Cases 1 and 14. This may be an indication that something is wrong in the marriage or family. One of the first persons to use the Profile put a question mark in the Family Square (#3). When asked why, he said he didn't know. When told it was the Family Square, he replied he and his wife were trying to reconcile after a long separation and he wasn't too sure it would work out.

What if the counselor receives a Profile in which only one square gives a sense of order or strength (Case 3)? What do the statement completions say about this person? What are the qualities (fragmented, hostile, depressed, etc.) expressed in the drawings? What positive and stable area or areas may be emphasized to the client as a point of reassurance and encouragement? On one Profile a young man filled the squares with fragmented and hostile drawings with the exception of his Religious Square. In this he drew a game of tic-tac-toe, which he won. Amazingly, people often draw the tic-tac-toe game in a square only to find themselves losers.

The person who relates in an extroverted manner as a rule uses all of the space (Case 4), while an introvert may need to have room around him (Case 5). Attitude-type may show in any drawing, but is particularly evident in the Ego Square (#1). Extroversion is defined by Jung as an "attitude-type characterized by concentration of interest on the external object."[13] Introversion is an "attitude-type characterized by orientation in life through subjective psychic contents."[14]

Sometimes a person will be unable to stay in the boundaries of the squares; he seems to spread into the other squares in the paper. Could this be a need to enlarge his world (Case 6)?

If the subject has not incorporated the symbols presented into his drawings, he may not be using what he has available and may not be living up to his potential. (Case 1)

Cirlot's A Dictionary of Symbols points out several factors of importance when approaching graphic symbolism. " . . . in order to decide upon the significance of any graphic figure, we must bear in mind the following factors: (a) its resemblance to figures of cosmic beings; (b) its shape, whether open or closed, regular or irregular, geometric or biomorphic; (c) the number of component elements making up the shape, together with the significance of this number; (d) the dominant 'rhythms' as the expression of its elemental, dynamic potential and its movement; (e) the spatial arrangement, or the disposition of its different zones; (f) its proportions; (g) its colours, if any."[15]

The statement completion portion of the Symbolic Profile is helpful in understanding the six drawings. The statements present a portrait of the subject as he sees himself or as he wishes others to see him because this material is closer to consciousness.

Although there is no hard and fast rule, the user of the Profile will find some relationship between certain statements and squares. As an example, if the counselor receives a Profile with a disturbed or scattered drawing in the Family Square (#3) he would need to check any statements relating to family and/or marriage. The composite of the statements and drawings combine to give a more complete picture of the person's family situation. The statements and the drawings seem either to compensate or complement each other.[16]

What is the self-image presented in the statements? Do the drawings confirm this image? Or is it perhaps a persona the person presents to the world?

The counselor would look for the repetition of a word (Case 7); one-sidedness, either all positive (Case 8), or all sad (Case 9), etc; one question starting a whole train of thought (Case 6). Was there a statement to which the person could not respond, and if not, why?

Statements containing the words "should" or "ought" would be considered evidence of opinionated, rigid attitudes, lacking an individual viewpoint. These "shoulds" frequently revolve around a troubled area in the person's life, usually verified by the drawings.

Analysis

The Ego Square (#1) shows the center of consciousness. The ego standpoint, as Jung defines it, is ours by virtue of experience, both collective and personal. What is the feeling that goes with the symbols used? Is it a friendly open drawing? Is it connected or scattered? What does it say about the person? If it is a house, is it a friendly house? Is there a doorknob on the door, a path, flowers or trees, and is smoke coming out of the chimney (Case 4)? The robot, office buildings, etc. would indicate an ego built largely on collective values or morals (Case 10 and Case 11). In dream interpretation, we would say that a house resembles the personality of the person. This would be especially true of a drawing in the Ego Square (#1). It usually indicates how approachable a person is on the ego level and something of

how the person feels about himself. If the person has drawn a large, overlapping figure (Case 6) there is the temptation to think he is self-assured. However, this could be a defense mechanism. The counselor might do well to look for confirmation in the other drawings in the Profile and in the statements. The person in reality might be very shy and feel he has to appear this way, or he may be trying to expand his awareness of other areas of his life.

The Fantasy Square (#2) can sometimes be seen as compensation to one of the other squares. By talking with the counselee the counselor may be able to determine that the fantasy symbol brings up a conflict of opposites (Case 12). This fantasy might be compensation to an ego attitude (Case 13), or a way of dealing with a family situation (Case 14). Jung says, in speaking of fantasy, " . . . most fantasies consist of anticipations. They are for the most part preparatory acts, or even psychic exercises for dealing with certain future realities."[17] What is the solution offered in the Fantasy Square (#2)? Is the person unable to have a fantasy suggesting a way to handle his conflicts? When fantasy is blocked, and it often is, there is nothing of substance drawn in this square (Case 15).

The Family Square (#3) deals with either the past or present family, and how the subject fits into it. An adolescent, or adult with an adolescent attitude, frequently thinks he is the center of the family (Case 16). The counselor can normally tell if it is an unfriendly family (Case 14), a harmonious family (Case 17), or a disconnected family (Case 18). The counselor should determine if all the members of the family are represented, or is someone left out or added? The counselor's questions can help the person to express his feelings about where he sees himself in relation to the rest of the family.

Sometimes when the same person does several Profiles over a period of time, the counselor will notice that symbols appearing in the Self-Determination Square (#4) in previous drawings have moved into the Ego Square (#1). For instance, a child in a time of distress drew a house *inside* the small symbol in the Ego Square (#1), showing that the child felt very small. In the Self-Determination Square (#4) she drew a big house, expressing her will to move into the big house. Although several years later she drew the big house in the Ego Square (#1), showing the development of a stronger ego, her original feeling of helplessness was evident in the tiny house of the earlier Profile. The goal of the psyche is sometimes drawn here as a scale, seesaw, etc., expressing the balance of opposites (Case 19). A way to travel or move, a path, or a road (Case 20) is another common symbol illustrating determination.

The individual's religious needs and his own religious point of view are expressed in the Religious Square (#5). Do the symbols drawn in this square show his feeling on the natural level (Case 27)? Is it cosmic (Case 2 and Case

13), connected (Case 21), or scattered (Case 16)? Does it give light to his life (Case 22), or is it underground (Case 6)?

The Potential Square (#6), or future, is often rewarding because frequently the symbols manifest a form of wholeness. A mandala, a symbol of wholeness, will emerge as a circle (Case 9), or even a face (Case 16). Nature symbols are also common, possibly reflecting new growth (Case 18) or the instinctive level (Case 4). The "ups and downs" of life may be drawn as a roller coaster ride (Case 23). Men as well as women have drawn a pregnant woman, suggesting the possibility of the birth of something new in the person's life (Case 24). An example of symbols carrying possible negative feeling might be a sunset (Case 25), suggesting a need to go into the depths of the unconscious, or perhaps a depression.

An area of strong interest—politics, family, social causes, etc.—expressed, either in drawings or statements, may provide an opening to begin communicating with the client.

The statements of the Profile are of help in understanding the symbolic drawings. Is there too wide a divergence between the drawings and the statements, or do they tend to confirm and supplement one another?

Case 1
Unused Potential

Female, Age 25, Single
Drawn with pen and blue ink

When a person does not use the symbols presented in the squares, he is usually underliving himself. Often there is a need to become meaningfully involved in some job or project as a part of the therapy. The young woman who did this Profile had many fears and was deeply concerned about her mental health due to her family background. She had suffered severe abdominal pains from the age of five months and had been hospitalized for them. She came to the C.G. Jung Educational Center of Houston, Texas for assistance and was referred to a counselor after she filled in the Profile. The counselor suggested that she enroll in classes, in addition to the counseling, for which she would do volunteer work at the Jung Center, as she had no money. There were several reasons for this suggestion. First, she needed to find an interest which at the same time would help her gain insight into her problems. Second, she needed to contribute in some way toward the cost of the counseling and classes made available to her. The third, and perhaps the most important, reason is that by doing the volunteer work she valued herself enough to expend energy to help herself.

After the first interview the counselee was asked to write down what she saw in the Profile, and it was her own idea to add a few later thoughts and insights. The counselor has also contributed notes about the drawings and statements. The client was from France and had difficulty with the English language, but only where necessary for clarification have her words been changed.

This particular presentation of a Profile emphasizes the importance of a client's amplification of drawings and statements.

Ego Square (#1)

"... I did not want a plane square, I wanted a square in perspective ... Consequently I ... prolonged it in perspective. It has no end. This is suggested by the lines issuing from the box ... it is like a tunnel; made in air. I am inside and walking." (Note: See statements 13, 19, 25, and 39.)

Later ...

"Cube of ice. (Note: She refers to the drawing of the tunnel.) One hour ago I wanted to be in the refrigerator to preserve me! ... There is more than a channel

(Text continued on page 10)

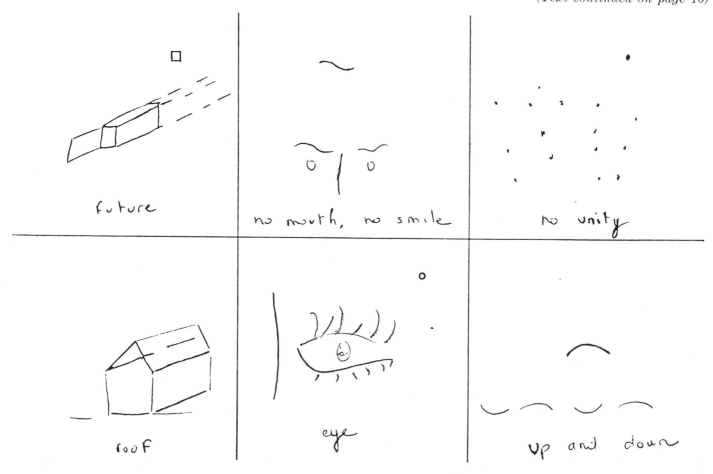

future

no mouth, no smile

no unity

roof

eye

up and down

1. I like _everything_
2. I want _to be truly alive_
3. My family _is a problem_
4. I must _change my relationship with the life_
5. Church is _nothing for me_
6. I hope _to get rid of my past_
7. I love _the sun_
8. I feel _sick_
9. Children are _in becoming_
10. People think of me _I don't know what they think of me_
11. God _was created to give a sense of security_
12. I often _eat!_
13. I hate _myself_
14. Someday I _shall succeed to build myself_
15. My father _was supposed to be schizophrenic_
16. I can not _build my life from what I saw_
17. I fear _to not succeed to live something different from my past_
18. I wish _somebody can help me, I feel like a hole, robbed._
19. I failed _to set up my mind about my stay, or if I leave the states_
20. My greatest success _was to separate my parents_
21. My mother _is neurotic_
22. I need _to know what is the life with people not sick_
23. I believe _that I have great potential in myself_
24. My worst fault _nothing. I don't feel guilty_
25. Women _have much trouble to be free than men_
26. Love _is something impossible for me now_
27. Sisters are _in my girlfriends_
28. I regret _I can not be balanced to enjoy my stay here_
29. I was happiest when _I was very thin_
30. People _try to find themselves or forget them in working_
31. Men _where are they?_
32. Sex _is a part of life_
33. At home _I always thought of somewhere else_
34. I miss _nature_
35. I think _too much_
36. Marriage _has no meaning--a happy couple has meaning_
37. Brothers _I don't like this word_
38. A spouse _"   "   --too similar to the word "to possess"_
39. I think of myself as _a big problem_
40. My dreams _I don't remember them_

between the States and France, more than a channel between my sickness and my health."

Fantasy Square (#2)

"After drawing the right eyebrow I knew that it was an eyebrow and I drew lighter the second one. Then the eyes, then the nose. The nose is not finished because I was wondering how I could draw the mouth. I didn't want it to smile because I don't feel like smiling, but why looking farther? There is no mouth! There cannot be a smile . . . (Note: The counselee identified the face with her mother.)

"The glance is very stern. On my drawing the eyes have no colors. When I finished all the Profile I remarked that I had many pens and I had used only a dark one. I had not thought about colors. (Note: See statements 2, 8, and 14. A person needs a mouth and the colors of emotion to effectively participate in life.)

"The drawing is low in the square, like if something heavy refrain it to be upper. Great asymmetric. The right eye, left on my drawing, seems to be not true and screaming that it is right. The other is true but it is too shy and look both the right eye and in front of itself. But my drawing has not a crossing eyes! These eyes think a lot. It is like it were relief, geographical relief, behind the paper in a big cube of . . ." (Note: See reference to cube under Ego Square.)

Later . . .

"I thought in English. 'Iron' in my mind was a tiner (meaning steel) cube, but I could not look for the translation because the word 'iron' was very strong and I could not do anything before writing it. Iron = haïr (French word) = to hate. Haïr is in the box. She hates me and is ambiguous, but she has not crossing eyes so I cannot be sure that she hated me." (Note: She has associated ice, iron or steel, and hate with her mother. Also, she would preserve herself in the refrigerator. Was this her mother's way of dealing with life problems? Is the client continuing this pattern of coldness and hardness? There appears to be some ambivalence as to whether the eyes, her mother's eyes, see straight or not.)

Family Square (#3)

"I have not many ideas about it. Spattered dots . . . like . . . but they bursted in spite of their will." (Note: See statements 3, 6, 15, 16, 17, 20, 21, 22, 25, 33, 36, and 38.)

Later . . .

"I separated my parents in spite of his (the father) wishes. He was smiling and whistling before. He seems to be died. Could I have acted in an other way? (Note:

See statement 24. She might be questioning her statement that she does not feel guilty.) At this point I went to the refrigerator saying 'I don't care. I drink' and poured a glass of milk. I guess that this is the sentence he (the father) used to say when he went to the cafe more and more. Now he is fat and I become fat. My conscious wants to be thin, my unconscious does not want to. (Note: She has unconsciously identified with the father who 'went to the cafe' as a way of avoiding conflict.)

"Hello, Mother! I am fat and ugly and my face is covered with pimples because of you. I hate you.

"I hate you because you never let my father becoming a human being. He said that only his dog loved him, and he made himself as low as an animal.

"I know you are not responsible. I know the law forced you to stay married with him . . . Sometimes I feel I am near the madness.

"HELP! I don't know if I am ready to look at my past, it is like one hundred horror movies . . . Where am I born? In madness, no wonder why I want to reborn . . . absolutely different from the past." (Note: See statements 4 and 6.)

Later . . .

"I am pregnant with myself. So I am fat. After the delivery I would be . . . I was thinking that you asked me some money. My ugliness is already something I pay to reborn, and my first reaction is how much do I have to pay to be reborn. (Note: She then had a fantasy about six dots, identifying them as herself and the parents, each as two dots—the old personalities and the reborn ones. She reached the conclusion that she was the only one able to be reborn.)

"Am I destroying myself because my father is destroyed? Or because I know no man to think about? No man who thinks about me. Sexuality problem." (Note: The client is in reality sexually active.)

Self-Determination Square (#4)

"I wanted to draw only a roof but to know that it is a roof we have to see the walls. (Note: She said at the first interview that the roof was rising in the air with her sitting on it.)

"It's a wooden house, only the walls of the facade touch the soil. I am on the top of the roof, cold and unafraid." (Note: Again she refers to the cold as a way of handling her life problems.)

Later . . .

"I called this drawing 'Roof.' Today I would like to call it 'House in Erection.' Erection because the house is excited by what it sees around it, all the details of life, and it channels (Note: See the reference to channel under

Ego Square.) all its energy to be connected with them." (Note: To erect a house is to build an individual personality.)

Religious Square (#5)

"My eye. At least I have beautiful eyes. They are my security. I am my own security. I don't believe in a religion, I try to find my strength in myself." (Note: See statements 11, 16, and 23.)

Later . . .

"Like a shoe. Shoes we wear to go fishing because it is muddy. When I was little I had to go fishing with my father and I hated it."

Potential Square (#6)

"Up and down. Life a time span. If it is my life so far, I can explain it. (Note: The client tells what the broken curved lines mean in the Potential Square, describing them one by one.)

(Up)	⌣	"Early until I was 11, and not conscious of my father's troubles.
(Down)	⌢	"I was, often, not sure my mother loved me. Big family troubles.
(Up)	⌣	"Up because men were like a shield or umbrella helping me. (Note: The line depicting men is in the down position.)
(Down)	⌢	"Now. I broke with my boy friend and I am conscious of all the negative points in my life.

"Up and down are not connected . . . and the line I imagine further is not connected with them and it is a straight line. I know that I am down now and that it is the first time I can go very down and after that build myself on solid basis." (Note: See statements 6, 18, and 30. Also, the "up" lines are containing, and the "down" lines do not contain.)

Comments by Counselor

The client is intelligent and well-educated. She is an attractive person with beautiful eyes, and there is no evidence of a serious weight problem. She had recently broken what had been a close and intimate relationship with a young man. The drawings and statements are not at variance with each other, and she is well aware of conflict.

All the drawings in the Profile are specifically connected with one another by her amplifications, but the Fantasy Square (#2) and the Religious Square (#5) offer interesting symbolic connections between the undrawn mouth and the eye.

At the first meeting the counselee identified the partial face in the Fantasy Square (#2) as her mother. She said there was no mouth because there was no communication between her and her mother. Cirlot says that in Egyptian hieroglyphs the mouth stands for the "power of speech," the "creative word."[19] He continues, "Very closely connected with this hieroglyph [of the mouth] is another showing a mouth with a solar disc inside. This disc, primarily standing for the sun, is connected, but not identical, with the eye."[20]

In regard to the eye, Cirlot states, " . . . the Egyptians defined the eye—or rather, the circle of the iris with the pupil at the centre—as the 'sun in the mouth' (or the creative Word).[21] He then says, "Finally, to come back to the pure meaning of the eye in itself, Jung considers it to be the maternal bosom, and the pupil its 'child.' Thus the great solar god becomes a child again, seeking renovation at his mother's bosom (a symbol, for the Egyptians, of the mouth).[22] The sun often symbolizes, in the simplest terms, the heroic consciousness, and in Jung's viewpoint is "a symbol of the source of life and of the ultimate wholeness of man."[23]

The counselee liked the eye, but did not think she drew the line to the left in the Religious Square (#5). The counselor wondered, although not saying so, if she did not want to see that her determination was to float up in the air, thus leaving the earth and her reality. The tunnel in the Ego Square (#1), entitled "Future," is also in the air. Resistance is often conveyed by denial and/or forgetting.

When the counselee was asked why she did not like the word "brothers" (statement 37), she replied that she associated the word with the Algerians who call everybody brother. Her father's brother, with whom she had felt some positive relationship as a child, had gone to Algeria as a soldier. When he returned their relationship had changed. She felt rejected by her father again through the brother.

The client's decision to start a straight connected line after the broken curved lines in the Potential Square (#6) is hopeful. Statements 6, 18, 23, and 30 express verbally her need to begin a new life, and to believe in her own potentials.

Case 2
Unconscious Anger

Female, Age 19, Married
Drawn with pencil

There is anger in the drawings in this Profile, and yet the statements are positive and cheerful. The church in the Ego Square (#1) expresses the collective viewpoint of her ego. The young woman is expressing "anger" in the Fantasy Square (#2). Are the attitudes of the collective ego functioning as her defense against the repressed anger?

The Family Square (#3) is a "kite killer." Who or what kills her ambition in the family? Since the kite seems to be caught on electric or telephone wires there could be a problem of communication. As all statements pertaining to the family are positive, the counselor might wonder what is being repressed.

The Self-Determination Square (#4) pictures a sword, "Arthur's Excalibur." The counselor might suspect that the client's determination is to swing the sword to right whatever she feels is wrong. This could be a most destructive way to handle the problem. The sword is also, however, a weapon of discrimination in its more positive sense.

The cosmic symbols in the Religious Square (#5) are remote, suggesting little relationship with her religious feelings. She does make an attempt to bring the earth and moon together in this drawing. But with a church in the Ego Square (#1), the cosmic symbols in the Religious Square (#5) would seem to be even more significant.

The counselor would find it worthwhile to inquire about what in the Potential Square (#6) she is saying "I can" in shorthand.

"Our House"

"ANGER"

"Kite · Killer"

"Arthur's Excaliber"

"Can You Imagine This?!"

Full Moon

Earth

Shorthand Symbol meaning "I Can"

1. I like _to dance_
2. I want _to learn_
3. My family _is loving and giving_
4. I must _see the light_
5. Church is _a place to worship God_
6. I hope _for peace_
7. I love _everyone_
8. I feel _great_
9. Children are _carefree_
10. People think of me _as too young to be married_
11. God _is within us_
12. I often _daydream_
13. I hate _mustard_
14. Someday I _will write a book_
15. My father _is understanding and good_
16. I can not _sit still very long_
17. I fear _lightening_
18. I wish _I took more time to read_
19. I failed _German III_
20. My greatest success _is my homelife_
21. My mother _is generous and loving_
22. I need _to be understood by more people_
23. I believe _in God_
24. My worst fault _is sometimes criticising others_
25. Women _are supposed to be feminine_
26. Love _thy neighbor_
27. Sisters are _nuns_
28. I regret _that my relatives cannot live closer_
29. I was happiest when _I was a new bride_
30. People _are fun to watch_
31. Men _are supposed to be masculine_
32. Sex _appeal_
33. At home _I relax_
34. I miss _my husband when he is not with me_
35. I think _constantly_
36. Marriage _is a big step to take_
37. Brothers _are nice to have around_
38. A husband _is comforting_
39. I think of myself as _responsible_
40. My dreams _are meaningful_

Case 3
Order or Strength
Portrayed in Only One Square

Male, Age 18, Single
Drawn with pencil

The counselor needs to seriously examine the statements of the Profile. The counselee drew in only one square. Why? The statements speak for themselves—the young man is depressed (statements 4, 6, 8, 10, 14, 17, 18 and 19)! Does he need someone to talk to?

The counselor noticed that this young man had originally drawn something in the Ego Square (#1) and the Self-Determination Square (#4), but had erased his drawings. Why? Why was he unable to complete the five squares? He could be blocked, his defenses might be up, or he might be out-of-touch with himself.

The flower, however, in the Potential Square (#6) would be a hopeful symbol, particularly in this square. The flower is a mandala form, a symbol of wholeness, although in his drawing it is without roots. The counselor would need to encourage the counselee's positive potential. The young man might be helped to find his own motivation through the activities indicated in statements 2 and 4.

The age of the client is always important. Young men of this age often dislike their family (statements 3, 15, 21, 27, and 33) and want to escape (statements 2, 12, 14, and 16). Boredom, too, could possibly be a problem.

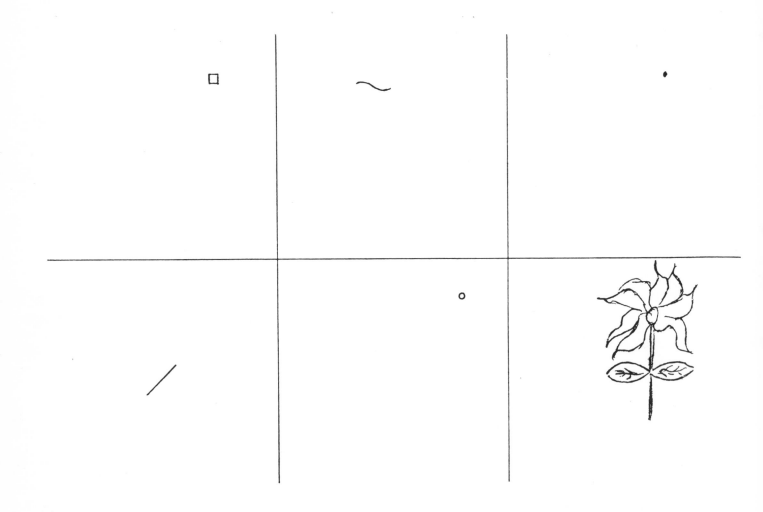

1. I like *everyone*
2. I want *paint-oils   play the guitar   go to Brazil*
3. My family *is screwed*
4. I must *do a lot of things in a very short time*
5. Church is *weird but ok once in a while*
6. I hope *to die before I get old*
7. I love *everybody*
8. I feel *depressed*
9. Children are *far out*
10. People think of me *as a nice person but a little strange*
11. God *is a long ways off*
12. I often *sit under big trees and look at the things around me*
13. I hate *people who think they are better than everyone else*
14. Someday I *hope to travel all around the world*
15. My father *is a fool*
16. I can not *decied what to do or where to go*
17. I fear *I won't live as long as I want*
18. I wish *my life would change*
19. I failed *to do a lot of things I should have*
20. My greatest success *VOID*
21. My mother *is one of the biggest fools I know and someday she will regret it.*
22. I need *time and money*
23. I believe _____
24. My worst fault *not being able to talk to people*
25. Women *are fantastic*
26. Love *is the most important thing in life*
27. Sisters are *hell*
28. I regret *to say I'm not satisfied with the world today*
29. I was happiest when *first fell in love*
30. People *are what life is about*
31. Men *are crazy*
32. Sex *is very nessesary*
33. At home *I get bored*
34. I miss *a lot of old aquaitances I made a few years ago*
35. I think *a lot*
36. Marriage *sounds ok but not now*
37. Brothers *never had any*
38. A husband *no thanks!*
39. I think of myself as *friendly person*
40. My dreams *hopefully will come true someday*

Case 4
Extroverted

Female, Age 41, Married
Drawn with pen and blue ink

This Profile is on a very extroverted level. The woman, extroverted and active, had five children and was deeply involved in her family life. The elephant in the Family Sqaure (#3) is a mother symbol, and motherhood was her dominant role in life. The Self-Determination Square (#4) is well-balanced and whole. The "pearls in a necklace" in the Religious Square (#5) are connected, showing a wholeness in her religious attitudes. The "home" in the Ego Square (#1) is large and friendly with smoke coming from the chimney, a door with a doorknob, and a tree growing in front of it. The "turtle and friends" in the Potential Square (#6) may show a need to pull back a little with her thoughts (the "friends").

Animals, as images of the instinctual life, signify symbolically a particular movement of energy. Birds often represent thoughts and flights of fancy, and they quickly dart here and there. The turtle is slow and carries his shell on his back for protection. The turtles in her drawing are going toward the left. The left side, since ancient times, has been equated with the dark unknown, the unconscious. Are the birds also going to the left? The client may be living on too extroverted and active a level and needs to find an unknown aspect of herself. See statements 1, 2, 6, 12, 24, 28, 34, and 35.

The statements of this Profile are in agreement with the drawings. When this occurs, the counselor may conclude that the person is in harmony with herself. Such is not always the case, but the whole tone of this Profile does give such an impression. However, the Potential Square (#6) indicates possible new ways of meeting the world yet to be integrated.

1. I like _and dislike my life_
2. I want _an inner peace_
3. My family _means a great deal to me_
4. I must _discipline myself in mundane matters_
5. Church is _an outward expression of an inward need_
6. I hope _is an aspiration_
7. I love _a great many persons_
8. I feel _different each day of my life_
9. Children are _life-continuing_
10. People think of me _the way they want to_
11. God _is a word_
12. I often _wonder_
13. I hate _hate and the stupidity of it_
14. Someday I _will die_
15. My father _was my friend_
16. I can not _do a lot of things_
17. I fear _what I don't understand_
18. I wish _is the same as I hope_
19. I failed _at more than one thing_
20. My greatest success _is living and trying_
21. My mother _is the same as always_
22. I need _love_
23. I believe _because I must_
24. My worst fault _self doubt_
25. Women _and men_
26. Love _is forever_
27. Sisters are _female relatives and women of the future_
28. I regret _the passing of time with so much to be done_
29. I was happiest when _yesterday can be tomorrow_
30. People _are different_
31. Men _and women_
32. Sex _a definitive word_
33. At home _is a kitchen and people we love_
34. I miss _what I have not known_
35. I think _more than I should at times_
36. Marriage _(man's name)--the mutual way!_
37. Brothers _the opposite of sisters_
38. A husband _man and (man's name)_
39. I think of myself as _woman_
40. My dreams _are mine and dreams of many others_

Case 5
Introverted

Male, Age 28, Single
Drawn with pencil

This Profile was drawn by a Roman Catholic priest, an introverted and careful person, as reflected in his drawings. The Profile seems to imply a need to find wholeness in the family area as evidenced by the face in the Family Square (#3). Feelings expressed in the statements regarding family are positive (statements 7, 9, 15, 21, 25, 27, 31, 32, 33, 36, 37, and 38). Yet statement 3 gives the address of an apartment that he shares with his fellow priests, not his natural family. Perhaps this is where he needs to look for his wholeness. (He later left the priesthood and married.)

The truck in the Ego Square (#1) is small but looks to be a strong vehicle. Often in dream symbolism a vehicle will represent the ego. A cross is in the Self-Determination Square (#4). Is he at the crossroads of his life? Is this the time to hold the tension of the opposites? The cross could also express his determination to hold onto the religious meaning of his life. The Fantasy Square (#2), "an ice cream cone," presents a union of opposites with the curved and straight lines coming together. The ice cream cone is a symbol commonly drawn on the Profile. Could the cone reflect immaturity in his fantasy life? In the Religious Square (#5) there is again something to eat, "a bunch of grapes," but this drawing seems on a different level from the ice cream cone. Grapes are a symbol of the Holy Eucharist, as well as of the Dionysian element. Statement 17 says he fears "making a fool of myself." The drinking of wine made from grapes sometimes releases inhibitions. Is it a letting go which he fears? A turtle in the Potential Square (#6) indicates a need to deal with the material world in some way. This turtle is in his shell. Is it by withdrawal he will handle his fear?

a truck

an ice cream cone

a face

a Chi-Rho

a bunch of grapes

a turtle in his shell.

1. I like _to ski_
2. I want _to go to the Jung Institute of Analytical Psychology_
3. My family _Lives at (address)_
4. I must _answer these questions or--finish these sentences_
5. Church is _good_
6. I hope _to go to Heaven_
7. I love _my mother_
8. I feel _tired_
9. Children are _delightful_
10. People think of me _as a good person_
11. God _is love_
12. I often _say Mass_
13. I hate _hatred_
14. Someday I _want to go back to school_
15. My father _is kind_
16. I can not _seem to think of anything to write here_
17. I fear _making a fool of myself_
18. I wish _I were smart_
19. I failed _Greek_
20. My greatest success _was directing a difficult play._
21. My mother _is completely herself._
22. I need _to be loved._
23. I believe _in God._
24. My worst fault _is my sharp tongue._
25. Women _are good_
26. Love _is necessary_
27. Sisters are _are fun._
28. I regret _not having studied harder in school_
29. I was happiest when _I really helped someone._
30. People _are friendly._
31. Men _are strong._
32. Sex _is good_
33. At home _I can relax_
34. I miss _my friends in the seminary and their companionship_
35. I think _deep_
36. Marriage _is holy._
37. Brothers _are a comfort._
38. A husband _is a provider_
39. I think of myself as _well balanced._
40. My dreams _are fewer._

Case 5: Introverted   19

Case 6
Unable to Stay in Boundaries

Male, Age 33, Married
Drawn with pen and black ink

The man who drew this Profile has a well-developed ego (#1) which seems determined to touch the personal side of his life in the Self-Determination Square (#4), "home," as well as his fantasy of "infinity" (#2). His maze could be not only a place in which to get lost, but also a defense of the center of his being. He seems to be cut off from his own feelings (statements 35 and 39).

In statements 11 through 19 it is as though he is telling a story about God, death, and his father. The figure holding a cross in the Family Square (#3), called "beads," might prompt the question, "Is the figure gay or sad?" One person saw this figure as gay and another saw it as sad, but how does the subject himself see it?

The underground tunnel in the Religious Square (#5) shows a great deal of active thinking. However, it is well-contained. This tunnel is man-made, not a natural formation. As an underground passage it would not be easily accessible. Who constructed the tunnel? For what reason? Where does it go?

This Profile might be an expression of the counselee's need to understand his own feelings about life and death and their meaning to him.

The Potential Square (#6) is a "sunrise" showing the possibility of a new day of light.

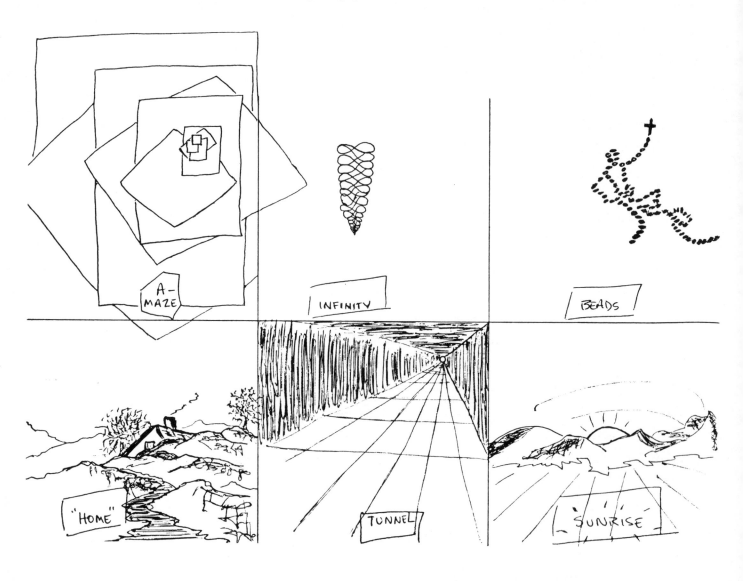

1. I like _reading_

2. I want _love_

3. My family _loves me_

4. I must _love them_

5. Church is _safe_

6. I hope _to go somewhere_

7. I love _my wife_

8. I feel _good and wondering, curious_

9. Children are _great_

10. People think of me _hardly at all_

11. God _lives_

12. I often _think of him_

13. I hate _myself_

14. Someday I _hope to write professionally_

15. My father _is dead_

16. I can not _see him_

17. I fear _death_

18. I wish _to live_

19. I failed _to succeed in reaching my father_

20. My greatest success _was marrying_

21. My mother _is alive_

22. I need _warmth_

23. I believe _in myself. (?)_

24. My worst fault _is fear_

25. Women _are attractive_

26. Love _is what this is all about_

27. Sisters are _alive (2 of them)_

28. I regret _not seeing them more often_

29. I was happiest when _I was younger_

30. People _sometimes threaten my privacy_

31. Men _are friends_

32. Sex _interests me_

33. At home _I am alone a lot_

34. I miss _company_

35. I think _too much, feel too little_

36. Marriage _is the way_

37. Brothers _never lived_

38. A husband _supports his family_

39. I think of myself as _not very successful at self-honesty_

40. My dreams _are constant and interest me continually_

Case 7
Repetition of One Word

Female, Age 12, Single
Drawn with pencil

A twelve-year-old girl drew this rather humorous Profile showing a youthful feminine propensity—that of falling in love with a horse. An adolescent girl, before she is old enough to fall in love with a man, often substitutes falling in love with a horse, as though the unconscious is preparing the way toward her maturity. Her feelings about sex and marriage seem to be negative in statements 26, 32, 36 and 39. Also, why, when she loves her dog (statement 7), does statement 24 say her worst fault "is my dog"? She has drawn a dog in the Ego Square (#1). Why? The horse is in the Family Square (#3), perhaps telling the counselor her instinct and energy are contained within the family, a situation not inappropriate for someone her age. However, the back half of the horse is missing—the part containing the sexual organs. Her parents were later divorced and perhaps she reflected her attitude toward marriage or her parents in this drawing.

1. I like _horses_
2. I want _a horse_
3. My family _is small_
4. I must _get some money_
5. Church is _(name of church)_
6. I hope _to get a horse_
7. I love _my dog_
8. I feel _silly_
9. Children are _swell_
10. People think of me _as a kid_
11. God _is the best_
12. I often _wish for a horse_
13. I hate _nothing_
14. Someday I _will get a horse_
15. My father _is old_
16. I can not _stop wishing for a horse_
17. I fear _that I wont get a horse_
18. I wish _I can get a horse_
19. I failed _nothing at school_
20. My greatest success _is to get a horse_
21. My mother _is fun_
22. I need _a horse_
23. I believe _that I will get a horse_
24. My worst fault _is my dog_
25. Women _are O.K._
26. Love _is stupid_
27. Sisters are _nuts_
28. I regret _not getting a horse_
29. I was happiest when _I had a horse_
30. People _are stupid_
31. Men _are fine_
32. Sex _is messy_
33. At home _I have fun_
34. I miss _not having a horse_
35. I think _of many things_
36. Marriage _is stupid_
37. Brothers _are silly_
38. A husband _is dumb_
39. I think of myself as _a horse lover. Don't you?_
40. My dreams _____

Case 7: Repetition of One Word   23

Case 8
One-Sided Statements

Female, Age 34, Married
Drawn with pen and black ink

The statements of this Profile are very positive. The drawings on the front page are not positive, however. Statement 18 gives a clue to this inconsistency. Why must she move, and where would she like to go? Her fantasy (square #2) is one of "movement"; the Self-Determination (#4) is "danger"; and the Potential Square (#6) is "boring." This woman has unused potential (the unincorporated symbols in squares #1, #2, and #3). The Family Square (#3) is labeled "contentment" and would be on the natural level, as illustrated by the flower. One might wonder if the unused potential in the psyche is the source of "movement," "danger," and boredom.

It would be helpful to encourage this woman to find new areas of interest which would stimulate her personal growth.

Equality

movement

contentment

danger

Dipper

boring

1. I like _people_
2. I want _lots_
3. My family _is lovely_
4. I must _be patient_
5. Church is _good_
6. I hope _for the best_
7. I love _my family_
8. I feel _well_
9. Children are _people_
10. People think of me _nicely, I hope._
11. God _is love_
12. I often _read_
13. I hate _injustice_
14. Someday I _will be old_
15. My father _is special_
16. I can not _do nothing_
17. I fear _sometimes_
18. I wish _to move_
19. I failed _when I lose my patience_
20. My greatest success _is my marriage_
21. My mother _is beautiful_
22. I need _love_
23. I believe _in God_
24. My worst fault _is impatience_
25. Women _are strong_
26. Love _is beautiful_
27. Sisters are _wonderful_
28. I regret _hurting the people I have hurt._
29. I was happiest when _now._
30. People _are people_
31. Men _are interesting_
32. Sex _is great_
33. At home _is family_
34. I miss _my Mother and Father._
35. I think _a lot_
36. Marriage _is good for me_
37. Brothers _are brothers_
38. A husband _strengthens his wife_
39. I think of myself as _a complex person._
40. My dreams _sometimes upset me._

Case 9
All Sad Statements

Female, Age 37, Married
Drawn with pencil

At the time this woman filled out her Profile she was in a state of severe depression. Depression can be the result of inflation; a person can be depressed and inflated at the same time. Inflation would be the consequence of the ego (the center of consciousness) being overwhelmed or flooded by unconscious contents which the ego is not yet able to handle. The depression, as depicted by the drawings, is confirmed by the statements on the reverse side. Her statement (statement 8), "I feel empty and yet about to burst," is portrayed on the front as "a lopsided ballon," "an elongated heart," and "a rotten apple"—all of which would be prone to burst. She also says in statement 18, "I wish I could explode."

She expresses her need to talk (statement 2) about her feelings of emptiness (statement 8) and yet she wishes to explode (statement 18); statement 24 says her worst fault "is my need to talk." Why is she blocked in the expression of her emotions? Who says she should not verbalize her feelings?

This Profile gives the impression of emptiness—the emptiness of the circles and the unfinished statements. However, all the drawings show the struggle for wholeness in the mandala form.

In the Potential Square (#6) she has a ball with which to play. Does she feel a need for play in her life? Playing ball in primitive times was a sacred rite signifying the game of life.[18]

There is more order in the bottom half of the Profile. The "x" in the Religious Square is the St. Andrew's Cross—a dynamic sign denoting intercommunication between the upper and lower worlds.[24] Communication seems to be one of her major concerns (statements 2, 3, 24, and 25).

The Profile reveals troubled relationships in the counselee's inner and outer worlds.

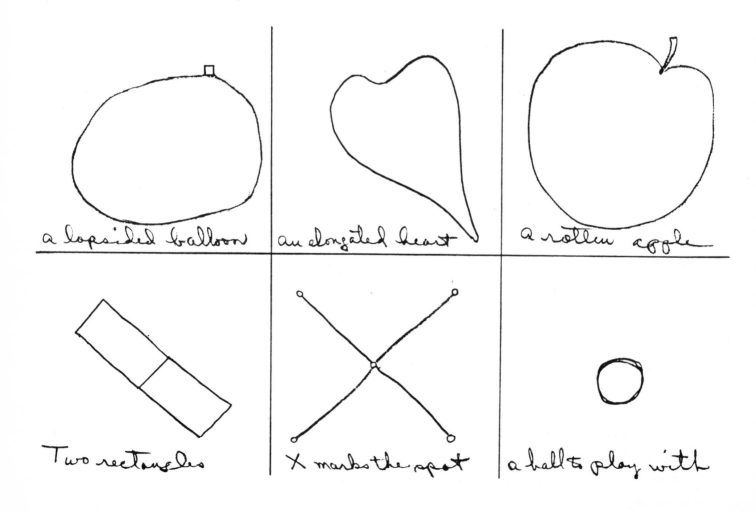

a lopsided balloon

an elongated heart

a rotten apple

Two rectangles

X marks the spot

a ball to play with

1. I like _nothing_
2. I want _to talk_
3. My family _won't talk_
4. I must _be free of the feelings_
5. Church is _nothing_
6. I hope _to understand_
7. I love _what?_
8. I feel _empty and yet about to burst_
9. Children are _prisoners_
10. People think of me _how?_
11. God _is nowhere_
12. I often _feel lost_
13. I hate _being lost_
14. Someday I _might find myself_
15. My father _is gone_
16. I can not _find him, either_
17. I fear _everything_
18. I wish _I could explode_
19. I failed _continuously_
20. My greatest success _I can't remember_
21. My mother _is far away_
22. I need _her_
23. I believe _she could help_
24. My worst fault _is my need to talk_
25. Women _are to talk to_
26. Love _I can't finish!_
27. Sisters are _____
28. I regret _____
29. I was happiest when _____
30. People _____
31. Men _____
32. Sex _____
33. At home _____
34. I miss _____
35. I think _____
36. Marriage _____
37. Brothers _____
38. A husband _____
39. I think of myself as _____
40. My dreams _____

Case 10
Collective Symbol in Ego Square

Male, Age 31, Single
Drawn with pen and red ink

The man who filled out this Profile is a Roman Catholic priest. Since he did not fill out the statements, the counselor would have only the drawings with which to work. The counselor would have to begin by asking questions, seeking confirmation of what appears in the drawings. This man saw himself as a robot, and his fantasy of the "hippie on a Honda" was obvious compensation! The counselor might wonder if the young man always ended up in the "dog house" when he tried to break out of the "robot" ego. Also, the "sinister young man" in the Potential Square (#6) shows an unconscious part of his personality about which he needs to know—his shadow side.

1. I like _____

2. I want _____

3. My family _____

4. I must _____

5. Church is _____

6. I hope _____

7. I love _____

8. I feel _____

9. Children are _____

10. People think of me _____

11. God _____

12. I often _____

13. I hate _____

14. Someday I _____

15. My father _____

16. I can not _____

17. I fear _____

18. I wish _____

19. I failed _____

20. My greatest success _____

21. My mother _____

22. I need _____

23. I believe _____

24. My worst fault _____

25. Women _____

26. Love _____

27. Sisters are _____

28. I regret _____

29. I was happiest when _____

30. People _____

31. Men _____

32. Sex _____

33. At home _____

34. I miss _____

35. I think _____

36. Marriage _____

37. Brothers _____

38. A husband _____

39. I think of myself as _____

40. My dreams _____

Case 11
Collective Symbol
in Ego Square

Female, Age 44, Married
Drawn with pen and blue ink

The Ego Square (#1) shows an ego built largely on collective values, the city "skyline." This contrasts with her determination to have a "home" which reflects her personal or individual standpoint. The counselor might wonder if this person sees herself as a "portrait of a lady." Is this her way of dealing with her life? Also, the "toys" in the Family Square (#3) might lead the counselor to ask to whom the toys belong. Did she feel like a toy in her childhood family or is this how she sees *her* children or herself in the present family?

The "still life" of flowers and a book in the Religious Square (#5) is something pretty to look at and something to read. Flowers are a natural symbol, but these are cut and without roots and the book's title is not clear. This person felt that she was at a standstill in her religious life (statement 5). She had left the institutional church and when told this was the Religious Square (#5) said the "still life" was the way she felt. When a small insect such as a "ladybug" is drawn, as in the Potential Square (#6), the counselor might wonder if the instinctive life is very small. Also, is there a connection between the "portrait of a *lady*" and the "*lady*bug"?

1. I like _lots of things_
2. I want _to live fully_
3. My family _is my life_
4. I must _grow_
5. Church is _? a very confused area in my life at present._
6. I hope _to find deeper and deeper areas of myself._
7. I love _to think_
8. I feel _confused about my feelings_
9. Children are _an extension of parents in many ways_
10. People think of me _differently, depending upon who the people are_
11. God _is in everything_
12. I often _worry about many things_
13. I hate _to grow old and rigid in my thinking._
14. Someday I _will die_
15. My father _was a good man_
16. I can not _answer this question_
17. I fear _not doing my Best_
18. I wish _I knew myself better_
19. I failed _to live up to my best potential_
20. My greatest success _is in seeking_
21. My mother _is difficult for me to love_
22. I need _to learn more about my needs_
23. I believe _I will find answers as I go on_
24. My worst fault _is judging--myself and others_
25. Women _are different than men_
26. Love _is difficult to define_
27. Sisters are _interesting--somewhat like a reflection_
28. I regret _not being a better mother_
29. I was happiest when _even I found new areas to explore_
30. People _need each other_
31. Men _are great_
32. Sex _is marvelous sometimes, difficult other times_
33. At home _is where I like to be most_
34. I miss _the energy of my youth or younger years_
35. I think _all the time about many things_
36. Marriage _is quite an adventure_
37. Brothers _make life interesting for sisters_
38. A husband _would be hard to live without tho' sometimes hard to live with._
39. I think of myself as _striving for the best in life_
40. My dreams _I find extremely interesting_

Case 12
Conflict of Opposites in Fantasy Square

Male, Age 49, Married
Drawn with pen and blue ink

Fantasy is a form of wishful thinking as well as a preparation to deal with disturbing factors. Also, fantasy is usually a passive activity, indicated here by the curved lines of the "flying carpet" (Fantasy Square #2). The man who drew this Profile was a clergyman who said he felt trapped and "fenced in" by the church structure (Religious Square #5). He felt a strong need to enlarge his ministry. To go on a flying carpet would

release him from what he feels to be a frustrating situation. The magic carpet was also a means to fly to another city where he hoped eventually to become an analyst. Because at the time he did the Profile he could see no way to fulfill this desire, a magic carpet seemed to be his only solution. Statements 2, 8, 14, 16, and 20 show his awareness of this desire.

The man identified the ladder in the Family Square (#3) as the Biblical ladder of Jacob. What does it mean to him? Is it related to the "flying carpet?" Both of these symbols go up into the air.

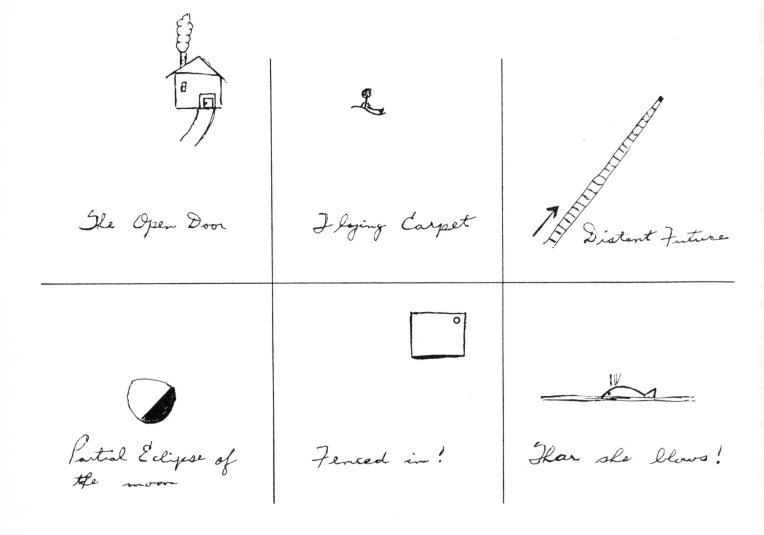

I like _life_

I want _self-understanding_

My family _are a joy to me_

I must _persevere_

Church is _a collection of religiously-oriented people_

I hope _that I will make a contribution to man_

I love _people_

I feel _sensitive towards my fellowmen_

Children are _nice_

People think of me _as caring_

God _is wonderful_

I often _talk to God_

I hate _pettiness (my negative anima)_

Someday I _hope to be an analyst_

My father _was kind and good_

I can not _find my niche in life_

I fear _snakes_

I wish _I could begin at 18 knowing what I know now._

I failed _many times_

My greatest success _is counseling and the healing ministry_

My mother _is old and cold_

I need _confidence_

I believe _in man_

My worst fault _is self-condemnation_

Women _are gentle and nice_

Love _is the most powerful force in the universe_

Sisters are _nice_

I regret _so many changes in my life_

I was happiest when _I first me my wife (beautiful anima projection)_

People _are basically good_

Men _are strong_

Sex _is the maximum relationship between man and woman_

At home _we have our sanctuary_

I miss _my wasted years_

I think _most often of helping others_

Marriage _is the highest compliment one partner can pay the other_

Brothers _are nice but rivals too_

A husband _should treasure his wife_

I think of myself as _being a person with a contribution to make to mankind_

My dreams _are very interesting and I wish I understood their message._

Case 13
Fantasy Compensating Ego

Female, Age 38, Married
Drawn with pen and blue ink

One might feel in looking at this Profile that the ego structure in the Ego Square (#1) is well-organized, but possibly there is a need for this drawing as a means of holding together the main aspects of the personality. (Holding together is one of the values of the mandala.) A large sword is drawn in the Fantasy Square (#2). The sword has a double symbolism—of wounding and of being wounded. Does the woman who drew the sword feel wounded or does she want to use the sword? A positive aspect of the sword is discrimination. Following the drawing of the "rose window," the sword in fantasy might be a compensation. The Ego Square (#1) contains the feminine or curved lines and the Fantasy Square (#2) the masculine or straight lines.

The Family Square (#3) is a picture of a good location for a picnic, but there are no people present. The branches of one tree are straight lines, frequently depicting aggressiveness and anger. Does the tree represent a person or a situation in the family? Statements 13, 19, 28, 31, 32, and 38 would be helpful in discussing this square. In the Self-Determination Square (#4) is the "cross and book." One would wonder if she is having difficulty with the words in the Bible, if this is a Bible, and with the symbol of the cross. In fact, do the words of the Bible on marriage have anything to do with the Family Square (#3)? The Religious Square (#5), having all cosmic figures in it, might prompt the question, "Is this a continuation of the conflict between the cross and the book, or is it cosmic consciousness?"

The Potential Square (#6) showing the "heart's door" is positive. Does the picture suggest the possibility of finding her own feeling side? The straight lines around the heart would suggest energy available in this area. Statements 12 and 24 might be of help here, as she says she pushes herself too hard and doesn't take time for herself.

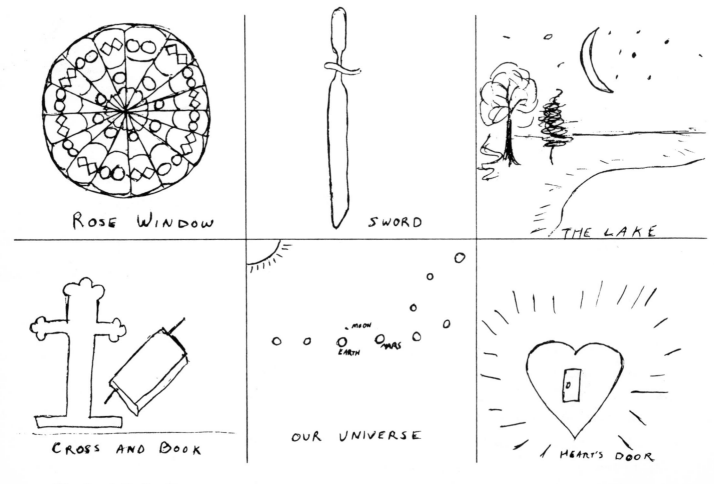

ROSE WINDOW

SWORD

THE LAKE

CROSS AND BOOK

OUR UNIVERSE

HEART'S DOOR

1. I like _being here_
2. I want _to study more deeply the entire field of Psychology_
3. My family _need me still._
4. I must _finish this profile before I fall asleep_
5. Church is _people_
6. I hope _to take a relevant course in Psychology or Sociology this winter_
7. I love _life._
8. I feel _good_
9. Children are _renewing._
10. People think of me _as friendly, but not always._
11. God _is._
12. I often _push beyond the limit of my energies._
13. I hate _my husband's childish bouts._
14. Someday I _want to help others find Jungian Psychology in the way that I have been helped_
15. My father _loves me._
16. I can not _think of anything to say here._
17. I fear _the awesome rightness of the new direction my life is taking_
18. I wish _I could study in Houston some day_
19. I failed _every time I was a door mat._
20. My greatest success _is right now_
21. My mother _loves me._
22. I need _me._
23. I believe _all will be well._
24. My worst fault _is not taking more time to set myself right._
25. Women _are a many faceted wonder_
26. Love _is._
27. Sisters are _good friends_
28. I regret _being a doormat so long_
29. I was happiest when _I realized we were nearly in Houston_
30. People _are wonderful_
31. Men _are much less formidable._
32. Sex _should be shared not taken_
33. At home _is a new direction_
34. I miss _the children_
35. I think _the birth of the rebirth is occuring to me now_
36. Marriage _is sharing_
37. Brothers _can be spoiled brats_
38. A husband _can be so frustrating_
39. I think of myself as _generally extraverted and intuitive_
40. My dreams _are an area I would like to delve into, in depth._

Case 14
Fantasy as Way of Handling Family Situation

Female, Age 33, Married
Drawn with pen and turquoise ink

The appearance of the upper portion of this Profile differs considerably from the bottom three squares. The drawings in the lower half appear to be of a different quality in style and on a more positive level.

The three balloons in the Ego Square (#1) would indicate that this woman's ego is not in a particularly stable condition at this time, as balloons are filled with air.

Fantasy is an anticipation of ways in which to solve problems. How does the tombstone relate to her family situation, or to the Religious Square (#5) (death and new birth)? Who or what lies under the tombstone? And what do the bells mean to her?

The Family Square (#3) with skull and crossbones identifies the pirate attitude and may contain possible destruction. The counselor could begin with the counselee's thoughts about her family and her fantasy about them (statements 3, 6, 7, 9, 15, 21, and 25). Is there a need for this woman to deal with her own cruelty or the cruelty of another family member? The problem (statements 36 and 38) seems to be in the marriage itself (statements 26, 28, and 34). Her chief concern centers around her children (statements 6, 7, and 39).

The Religious Square (#5) shows Christmas—the time of new birth, of the Christ Child. Statement 12 says she often "sits and stares out of the window." For what is she waiting in life?

1. I like _to live_
2. I want _to grow up_
3. My family _confuses me_
4. I must _make a lot of money_
5. Church is _not satisfactory_
6. I hope _my children will be better people than I_
7. I love _my children_
8. I feel _helpless sometimes_
9. Children are _a lot of work_
10. People think of me _very little_
11. God _is where?_
12. I often _sit and stare out the window_
13. I hate _for people to bother me_
14. Someday I _would like to travel around the world_
15. My father _is dead_
16. I can not _endure being bored_
17. I fear _being alone late at night_
18. I wish _I were sucessful_
19. I failed _to take advantage of opportunities offered to me._
20. My greatest success _is that I have managed to stay married._
21. My mother _gets on my nerves_
22. I need _to understand myself_
23. I believe _there is a God somewhere_
24. My worst fault _is belittling myself_
25. Women _are cruel_
26. Love _is hard to find_
27. Sisters are _related_
28. I regret _that I married at 18_
29. I was happiest when _I was dancing_
30. People _are everywhere_
31. Men _are people_
32. Sex _is powerful_
33. At home _I can be myself_
34. I miss _the freedom I had when I was younger_
35. I think _someday I'll find myself._
36. Marriage _is a bother, sometimes_
37. Brothers _fight a lot_
38. A husband _is in the way_
39. I think of myself as _wanting to provide a way for my children to live in this world._
40. My dreams _getting hard to remember_

Case 15
Blocked Fantasy

Female, Age 48, Married
Drawn with pen and blue ink

The Fantasy Square (#2) poses difficulty for some people. That this one is labeled "grey" would indicate little fantasy activity. Statements 2, 8, 14, and 20 tend to confirm an inability to find solutions for her feelings of being without meaning and direction in life.

The triangle in the Religious Square (#5) is labeled "abomination." Since statement 5 says church is a "dilemma," the counselor might wonder if there is a religious problem. The Potential Square (#6), "easy fall," could signify coming to earth and reality. She is, however, prepared with a parachute. This would be a hopeful potential, even though the "fall" might be a painful one. Statements 6, 24, and 30 could offer some clues to the reason for the fall.

Why does she "bury" her dreams (statement 40)? In what way are they threatening?

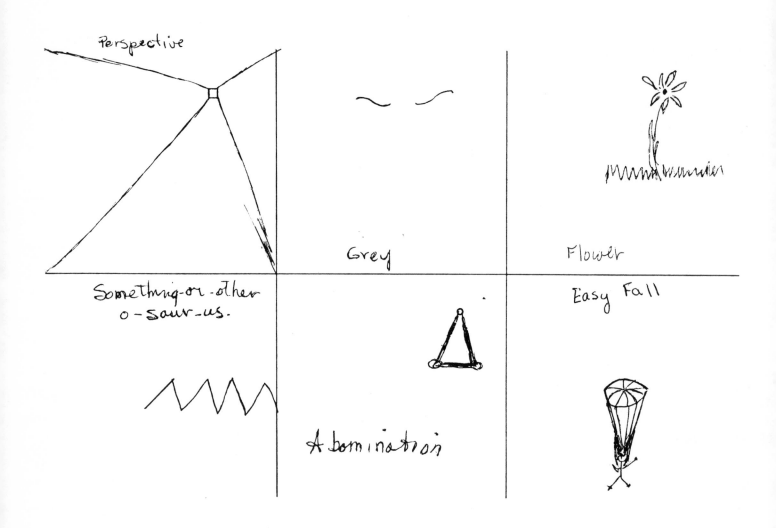

1. I like _being thinner_
2. I want _to do something well--my job, preferably._
3. My family _takes a lot of time_
4. I must _be more useful_
5. Church is _a dilemma_
6. I hope _for some kind of self-realization eventually._
7. I love _it when things work out well._
8. I feel _very neuter_
9. Children are _always there_
10. People think of me _no kidding!_
11. God _church_
12. I often _miss_
13. I hate _being late and/or un-put-together_
14. Someday I _wonder what--_
15. My father _is an interesting unknown_
16. I can not _seem to change my pattern of doing things_
17. I fear _I shan't accomplish a whole lot._
18. I wish _we were all happier_
19. I failed _to try to meet things_
20. My greatest success _escapes me._
21. My mother _lives alone._
22. I need _more patience and a little excitement, too._
23. I believe _there must be something more to do than I'm doing_
24. My worst fault _isn't something I want to write down_
25. Women _are OK_
26. Love _is talked about a lot_
27. Sisters are _sisters._
28. I regret _lots of things_
29. I was happiest when _I could be out playing_
30. People _change_
31. Men _are OK, too._
32. Sex _gives me problems if it's public_
33. At home _I'm a drag_
34. I miss _wanting things_
35. I think _there must be something to do that's both interesting and useful_
36. Marriage _endures_
37. Brothers _are rare in my life_
38. A husband _husbands_
39. I think of myself as _disorganized_
40. My dreams _are non-existant, I bury them_

Case 16
Adolescent as Center of Family

Female, Age 24, Married
Drawn with pen and blue ink

The drawings in this Profile seem to be on an immature level, not displaying many resources for a woman of 24 years. She did not title the drawings, which would have been of help to the counselor. The jack-o-lantern in the Ego Square (#1) might be a symbol of the persona, the mask we all wear in our different roles. But since a jack-o-lantern is really empty inside, the counselor might wonder if this person has a functioning ego structure. Too, the question might be asked as to whether she felt empty inside.

The subject drew herself in the Family Square (#3), a typical adolescent attitude—always the center of the family. The statements express some anxiety about the marital situation (statements 14, 17, 18, 22, 38, and 39).

She drew a kite in the Self-Determination Square (#4) and no one is holding the string. Is her ambition threatening to fly away with her, or is she going to let go of it? See statements 4, 14, 16, 24, and 35.

When the counselor sees bubbles in the Religious Square (#5) he might suspect that the person does not have much contact with the spirit and meaning of his life. The statements pertaining to this square (statements 5, 11, and 23) seem to be on a collective level.

The Potential Square (#6) also has a face in it, but on a more human level, showing a struggle for wholeness in her life. The baby could portray the birth of a new attitude (statements 6, 12, 18, 24, and 35).

1. I like _life_
2. I want _to be a good wife and mother_
3. My family _is delightful_
4. I must _be more patient_
5. Church is _my means to salvation_
6. I hope _become a better person_
7. I love _(man's name) and (woman's name)_
8. I feel _tired_
9. Children are _Delightful trouble_
10. People think of me _as a nice person_
11. God _is love_
12. I often _brood too much_
13. I hate _bickering over trivials_
14. Someday I _hope to achieve an intellectual compatability with my husband_
15. My father _is a wise and loving man who teases_
16. I can not _do everything my husband expects_
17. I fear _divorce_
18. I wish _my husband understood himself_
19. I failed _somewhere I'm sure but I don't remember_
20. My greatest success _I can't remember_
21. My mother _is just right_
22. I need _more confidence in my ability as a housewife_
23. I believe _in God_
24. My worst fault _impatience_
25. Women _are my friends for the most part_
26. Love _can solve many problems but not all_
27. Sisters are _wonderful things to have_
28. I regret _don't know_
29. I was happiest when _many many times--there is no happiest_
30. People _are interesting_
31. Men _are nice to be with_
32. Sex _is Delightful_
33. At home _is peaceful and happy; at home we have a good time_
34. I miss _not a thing_
35. I think _I will eventually succeed_
36. Marriage _is a wonderful challange_
37. Brothers _are nice to have_
38. A husband _must help his wife_
39. I think of myself as _lucky (though happy first) but hairey problems_
40. My dreams _Ramble on and on but I never remember them_

Case 17
Harmonious Family

Female, Age 38, Married
Drawn with pencil

This woman's family feeling seems to be harmonious, even to the point of drawing harmony in the Family Square (#3). Or is there a need for harmony in the family? The tempo is in 4/4 time, a double quaternary, a symbol of wholeness. Interestingly, she emphasized the lines around the squares, as though to frame the drawings. One gets the feeling from the whole Profile that she has a "together" personality.

In the Ego Square (#1) and the Fantasy Square (#2) are symbols of new things, "beginning" and "but-terflies," emerging. The unconscious could be preparing her for her quest of the "truth" of the Self-Determination Square (#4), a new understanding and knowledge of life and herself (statements 2, 6, 18, and 20). Perhaps this is the meaning of "silhouettes at sunset" in the Potential Square (#6)—she is prepared to go into the unconscious to find whatever her need may be. What is the meaning of her husband and son in the drawing? Or *is* it her husband and son?

Within two years after completing this Profile, she and her husband were divorced.

1. I like *living*
2. I want *to understand myself more*
3. My family *consists of a husband and son.*
4. I must *be more patient*
5. Church is *another place of worship*
6. I hope *to become a whole person.*
7. I love *life.*
8. I feel *happy most of the time.*
9. Children are *the hope of the future.*
10. People think of me *as I think of them.*
11. God *is love.*
12. I often *go for long walks in the woods.*
13. I hate *some of my actions.*
14. Someday I *will go to Europe.*
15. My father *is living in (name of state)*
16. I can not *stand to see people hurt.*
17. I fear *snakes.*
18. I wish *to understand more.*
19. I failed *in learning self control*
20. My greatest success *is in the future.*
21. My mother *is living in (name of state).*
22. I need *some quiet time each day.*
23. I believe *in myself.*
24. My worst fault *is talking too much*
25. Women *are nice*
26. Love *is people.*
27. Sisters are *someone I didn't have*
28. I regret *my mistakes.*
29. I was happiest when *I married and became a mother.*
30. People *are varied.*
31. Men *are nice.*
32. Sex *is sharing self with your mate.*
33. At home *we share responsibilities.*
34. I miss *old friends*
35. I think *of different things*
36. Marriage *is working together*
37. Brothers *are a help to sisters.*
38. A husband *is a human being, who you share life with*
39. I think of myself as *a nice person.*
40. My dreams *puzzel me at times.*

Case 18
Disconnected Family

Female, Age 29, Married
Drawn with pen and black ink

The Ego Square (#1) is a "city," indicating a collective viewpoint. The freeway, Self-Determination Square (#4), is another collective viewpoint, but might also be seen as a play on words—a "free way." The vehicle (a car is often a dream symbol ego) is going down and into the unconscious. Her Fantasy Square (#2) shows a kite "flying high," symbolizing ambition.

Is the lad in the Religious Square (#5) the kite flyer? He is angelic looking with some kind of light over his head, but one wonders what is going on inside of him. Also, he is whistling. Cirlot says, "Whistling is, to follow Jung, like clacking the tongue in so far as both are archaic ways of calling to and attracting the attention of theriomorphic dieties—or totemic or deified animals. This explains the social taboo upon whistling."[25] Is this the youth she speaks of in statement 23?

The Family Square (#3) is a "puzzle." Could she connect the dots and make a picture from them? Her statements about her family (statements 3, 9, 15, 31, 32, 36, and 38) seem to be on a collective and positive level. What is puzzling her about the family? The Potential Square (#6) shows "growth" (her growth) of a flower from among rocks. Her use of time seems to bother her (statements 6, 12, 24, 25, and 39.) She also seems to have a poor opinion of herself at this time (statement 39).

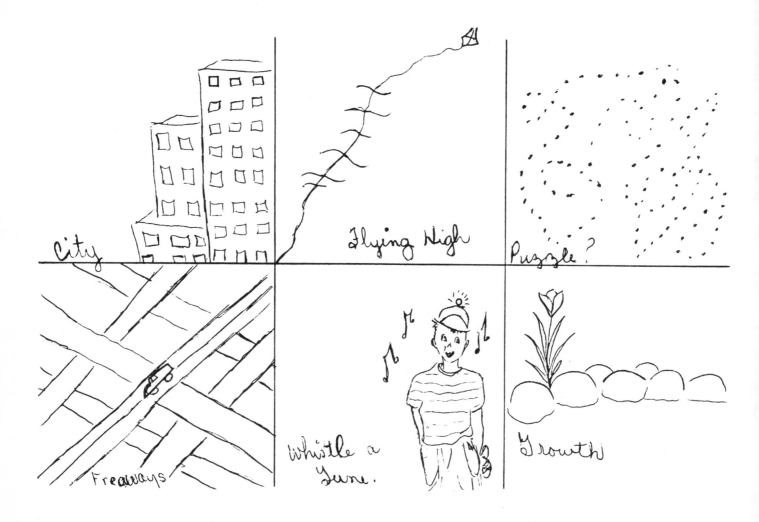

1. I like _to eat_
2. I want _a Coke_
3. My family _is happy_
4. I must _discipline myself_
5. Church is _a group worship_
6. I hope _I can do my washing today._
7. I love _my children and husband_
8. I feel _like traveling._
9. Children are _a blessing._
10. People think of me _as assistent pastor._
11. God _is Good and Great._
12. I often _get too many things started and not finished._
13. I hate _mices._
14. Someday I _hope to teach._
15. My father _is a good man._
16. I can not _impose on people._
17. I fear _snakes._
18. I wish _I had no debts._
19. I failed _myself._
20. My greatest success _____
21. My mother _is sick_
22. I need _self confidence_
23. I believe _there is potential leadership in youth._
24. My worst fault _is to be a good steward of my time._
25. Women _are changeable as the weather._
26. Love _is undefinable in words._
27. Sisters are _ones helpers_
28. I regret _loosing opportunities_
29. I was happiest when _I felt a sense of accomplishment._
30. People _are different in Character._
31. Men _are important._
32. Sex _has its place._
33. At home _I am myself more than in public--(relaxed)_
34. I miss _my family_
35. I think _flowers are mircles_
36. Marriage _is a holy institution_
37. Brothers _have strong ties._
38. A husband _is a wifes helper in so many ways_
39. I think of myself as _a poor organizer._
40. My dreams _are far and few between._

Case 19
Balance of Opposites
in Self-Determination Square

Female, Age 28, Married
Drawn with pencil

A balance symbol of any kind, be it scales, see-saw, or balance, as this woman has drawn in the Self-Determination Square (#4), shows determination to achieve balance in her life. In statements 4, 10, 16, 22, and 35 she speaks of searching for new ways in which to express herself. She feels that she lacks motivation.

The Family Square shows her to be troubled. Does she see trouble in the family? She has spots before her eyes. The counselor, after reading statements 31 and 38 might ask her if in some way her needs are not being met? What are her expectations? Maybe this is where she needs balance in her life. The remainder of the squares in the Profile are well-balanced.

The horn-of-plenty in the Religious Square (#5) is an unlimited source of nourishment. This attitude is confirmed by statements 5, 11, and 23.

The counselor might inquire what the "mask of tragedy" in the Potential Square (#6) is meant to cover? Is she wearing it or discarding it? Is there a connection between the eyes in the Family Square (#3), which are rather comedic, and the "mask of tragedy"?

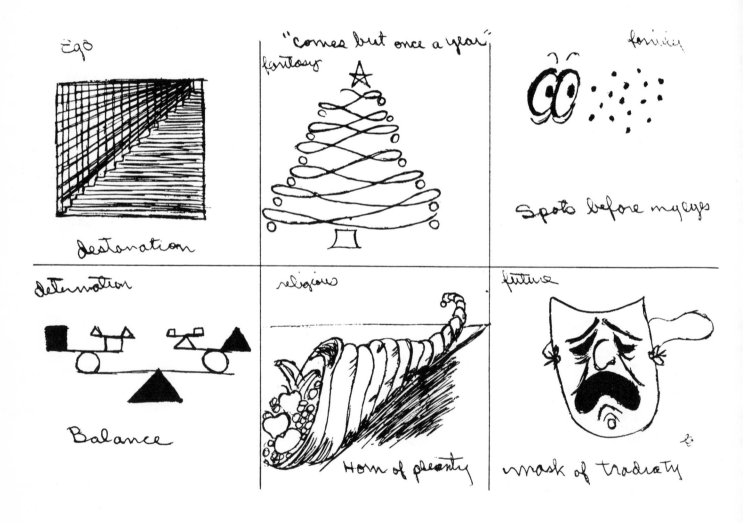

1. I like _feeling good, blue skies, cool water and a lot to do._
2. I want _to understand life, myself and be happy._
3. My family _is an average family about the same as anyones._
4. I must _learn to express myself so people will understand me._
5. Church is _many things to many people._
6. I hope _that everything will be O. K._
7. I love _my family._
8. I feel _very uncomfortabel inside not knowing what to expect._
9. Children are _little grownups that are wise beyond their years._
10. People think of me _as just another face in the crowd, they don't care to know me._
11. God _is always with me and watches over me._
12. I often _do things and say things I wish I had thought over first._
13. I hate _to be emposed upon continuously._
14. Someday I _will reach 35._
15. My father _really means well and he tries the best he knows how._
16. I can not _always make myself do what I must do._
17. I fear _that people will disregard me completely._
18. I wish _to have another healthy baby._
19. I failed _third grade_
20. My greatest success _has not yet happened_
21. My mother _thinks a lot about herself and her life._
22. I need _more understanding and more motivation._
23. I believe _there is a reason for everything that happens._
24. My worst fault _is lousing my cool._
25. Women _seem to be smart, have good times and do for others._
26. Love _is something all living beings need._
27. Sisters are _nice to have._
28. I regret _only one mistake at a time._
29. I was happiest when _we were in (name of state) by ourselfs with friends._
30. People _are unpredictable individuals._
31. Men _are grown up little boys until they are 40._
32. Sex _is a drive all people have but differently._
33. At home _I feel comfortable and relaxed._
34. I miss _the good times I had on vacation._
35. I think _that I don't always try as hard as I could._
36. Marriage _is good for people, they need it._
37. Brothers _will usually do a lot for you._
38. A husband _should be someone you can count on to back you up._
39. I think of myself as _someone who has always managed._
40. My dreams _mean a lot and confuse me._

Case 20
Path or Road
in Self-Determination Square

Female, Age 50, Married
Drawn with pencil

The "road" in the Self-Determination Square (#4) could be the road this woman needs to travel to enlarge her world. Statements 2, 4, 6, 14, 17, 22, 34, 35, and 40 seem to emphasize her need to participate in the world more and contribute to it. There is no pathway to her "home" in the Ego Square (#1), but plants grow around the foundation, and there is a doorknob with which to open the door. The "road" may be the means to go in and out of her own ego.

In the Family Square (#3) there is a path on which to travel from birth to death, although the lines are neither strong nor well-connected. The woman who drew this Profile begins at "birth" and stops at "death." The Fantasy Square (#2) might be compensation, for "infinity" is endless. The "eye," frequently drawn in the Potential Square (#6), may indicate the counselee has the potential of seeing what needs to be seen, perhaps in a more objective way. Also, the eye symbolically can be "the eye of God."

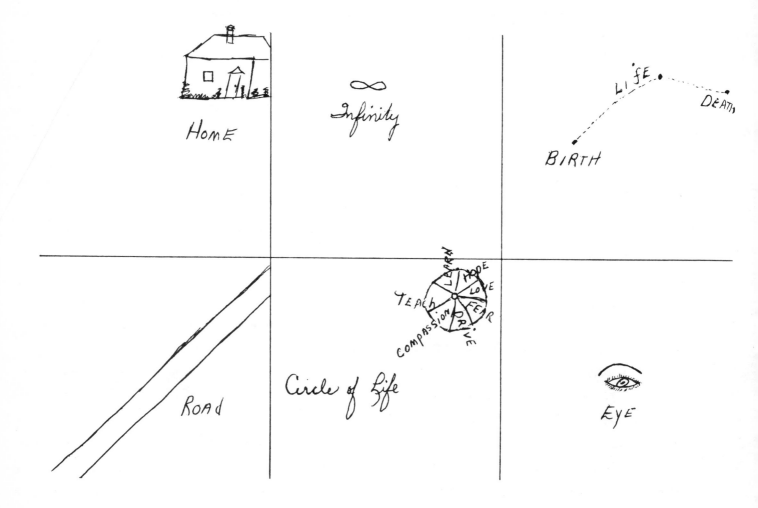

1. I like _being a part of this world._
2. I want _to strive to discipline myself; less emotional about life._
3. My family _we all love each other in our way and help when needed._
4. I must _find worthwhile activities and let my sons live their own lives._
5. Church is _another place to have communication with God._
6. I hope _I can each day improve myself and contribute to life._
7. I love _my husband, my children, all who have contributed to our lives._
8. I feel _I have many blessings, God has been kind to me._
9. Children are _like unfolding flowers._
10. People think of me _as happy, confident, responsible._
11. God _has given me strength to live thru difficult situations._
12. I often _procrastinate in making decisions._
13. I hate _to be involved in a situation which I do not believe right._
14. Someday I _would like to travel and see more of our world._
15. My father _I have always felt close, although thru divorce away from him._
16. I can not _tolerate malicious gossip; deliberate unkindness._
17. I fear _being old and not being able to care for myself._
18. I wish _I could see myself as others see me._
19. I failed _in learning how to deal with people who try to manipulate me._
20. My greatest success _over coming inferiority complex by realizing I am important to God._
21. My mother _has never been close to me, but I have love and concern for her._
22. I need _to feel accomplishment in my daily life._
23. I believe _in God, myself, my country and my fellow man._
24. My worst fault _too sensitive; I wish I could more passive._
25. Women _I like some and love others very much; enjoy companionship._
26. Love _basic human need, we reach for it in different ways._
27. Sisters are _I have one, we are closer now that we are older._
28. I regret _not overcoming an inferior feeling earlier in life._
29. I was happiest when _I was helping guide two wonderful boys to grow._
30. People _I enjoy the many facets of different personalities & viewpoints._
31. Men _I like them, although I do not always know how they think._
32. Sex _God's way of making two people one._
33. At home _I enjoy keeping a good home clean, happy, comfortable._
34. I miss _being a part of the world outside my home._
35. I think _life is what we make it, but we must strive each day._
36. Marriage _most intimate relationship between man and woman._
37. Brothers _I have one, to this day I do not understand him._
38. A husband _someone to love, care for, understand, & be responsible._
39. I think of myself as _intelligent, most of the time happy, thoughtful of others._
40. My dreams _are to make myself acceptable to God & contribute to mankind._

Case 20: Path or Road in Self-Determination Square 49

Case 21
Connected Feelings
in Religious Square

Female, Middle-aged, Married
Drawn with pencil

Many people draw a rosary in the Religious Square (#5), not knowing the significance of this square. This woman was not a Catholic, but was religious in her view of life. She attended church regularly, but was not involved in the workings of the institution. She was a shy person and had built her ego block by block, as shown in the Ego Square (#1). This shyness shows through in the Self-Determination Square (#4) in that her determination seems to have no goals or drives. She is just an observer of life with a basket of food, sitting here under a tree, which might be the same tree as in the Family Square (#3).

Interestingly, the acorn in the Family Square (#3) grows into what might be the symbolic "tree of life." Her growth would possibly be in this area. Concern about her health is expressed in statements 4, 6, 8, 18, 22, and 39. Perhaps her physical condition is the reason she must sit under the tree by the side of the road. "The all-seeing eye" (Potential Square #6) could be the ability to see where growth lies in her own life.

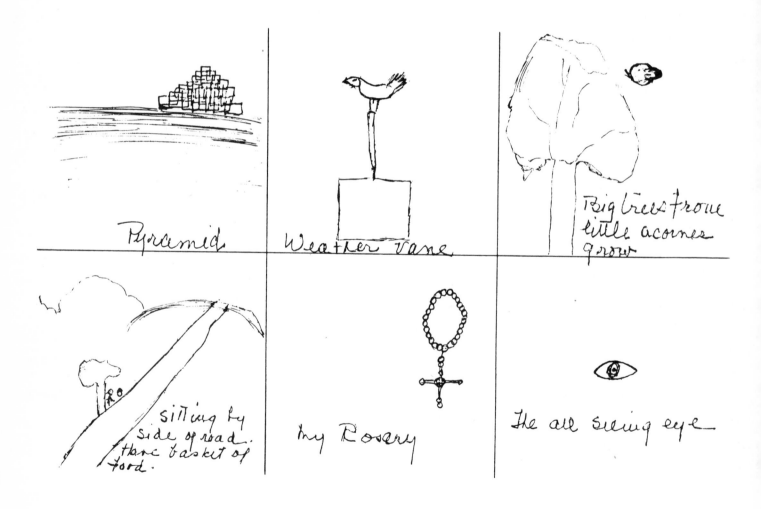

Pyramid

Weather Vane

Big trees from little acorns grow

sitting by side of road. have basket of food.

my Rosary

The all seeing eye

1. I like _Harmony_
2. I want _Harmony_
3. My family _Is dear to me_
4. I must _Be Strong_
5. Church is _Necessary_
6. I hope _I am growing stronger--physically--spiritually_
7. I love _(man's name)_
8. I feel _Weary_
9. Children are _Loving and complex_
10. People think of me _As good._
11. God _is all_
12. I often _Day dream_
13. I hate _Drunkedness_
14. Someday I _Hope to be a whole person_
15. My father _Was generous_
16. I can not _Read fast_
17. I fear _Failure_
18. I wish _I was well and strong_
19. I failed _My son_
20. My greatest success _Marrying (man's name)_
21. My mother _Was a whole person_
22. I need _Health_
23. I believe _In God_
24. My worst fault _Procrastination_
25. Women _Are good and Bad_
26. Love _Is selfish and unselfish_
27. Sisters are _Loving & Tedious_
28. I regret _Not studying more_
29. I was happiest when _I was studying psychology and putting it into effect_
30. People _Complex_
31. Men _Are boys grown tall_
32. Sex _Is satisfying_
33. At home _Is safe and comforting_
34. I miss _Gayiety in myself & a Pack of joy in life_
35. I think _Life is hard to live fully_
36. Marriage _Is the happiest and unhappiest state_
37. Brothers _Are dear and loving_
38. A husband _Has given me everything & a hasband has given me nothing_
39. I think of myself as _Complex and Frail_
40. My dreams _Have meant much to me._

Case 22
Light In Religious Square

Male, Age 46, Married
Drawn with pencil

A Protestant clergyman, this man's religious feelings (Religious Square #5) appear to give him a place to live and the proverbial "light in the window." Statements 5 and 11 seem to confirm this drawing. The Ego Square (#1) shows a well-developed ego, but is called "the beam in my eye." What does he not see? In looking at the statements 7 and 13, which often go with the Ego Square (#1), the question might arise as to what death means to him and why he feels the need to be reborn. The "butterfly" in the Self-Determination Square (#4) is an ancient symbol of rebirth and new life, and also a symbol of psychic development.

The Potential Square (#6) shows a "snowman melting." When a subject draws a snowman or snow, the counselor knows there is a coldness somewhere in the person's life. In this drawing the snowman is being melted by the light and warmth of the sun. The sun, a source of light on a different level from the candle in the window, is for many people a religious symbol.

The lines in this man's drawings are predominantly curved. Cirlot's *A Dictionary of Symbols* says, "... straight lines are always expressive of activity, compared with curves which denote passivity."[26] The counselor might wonder if this man has dealt with his own passivity. Statements 3, 9, 15, 16, and 21 might help the counselor enlarge upon this subject with the counselee.

THE BEAM IN MY EYE

WOMAN, THE ETERNAL MYSTERY

BULLSEYE!

BUTTERFLY

LIGHT IN THE WINDOW

SNOW MAN MELTING

1. I like _to travel in exotic lands--_
2. I want _to know all about me--_
3. My family _places too many demands on me._
4. I must _fulfill my destiny._
5. Church is _for helping us be who we are_
6. I hope _I will always be as alive as I feel now._
7. I love _people._
8. I feel _great._
9. Children are _tragic._
10. People think of me _as being much more than I am._
11. God _frees us to be human._
12. I often _reach beyond my reach._
13. I hate _dead people who don't know they are._
14. Someday I _will write a novel._
15. My father _let me be a real person._
16. I can not _be at ease around my mother._
17. I fear _what?_
18. I wish _for more of what I am._
19. I failed _my family by ignoring their needs._
20. My greatest success _is in knowing myself._
21. My mother _is a cosmic marshmallow._
22. I need _love and praise._
23. I believe _in humanity._
24. My worst fault _is being self-centered_
25. Women _are wonderful_
26. Love _makes the world technicolored._
27. Sisters are _something I never had._
28. I regret _very little_
29. I was happiest when _I realized I was me._
30. People _are terrific_
31. Men _are great_
32. Sex _is here to stay--and I'm delighted._
33. At home _I'm not often enough._
34. I miss _some old friends._
35. I think _all the time._
36. Marriage _is passe_
37. Brothers _are something else I never had._
38. A husband _is for wives._
39. I think of myself as _life-giving to those who aren't afraid of it._
40. My dreams _are almost impossible to capture._

Case 23
Ups and Downs of Life in Potential Square

Female, Age 15, Single
Drawn with pen and black ink and titled in blue ink

This young girl drew a picture of a family problem in the Ego Square (#1), drawing her ego structure as the "typical husband." She seemingly identified with her father who was an alcoholic. The Self-Determination Square (#4) may be her own self-portrait as a "stupid fisherman." She is fishing where there are no fish, but there *are* fish in the stream.

She is at the proper age to be having fantasies about boys, and in the Fantasy Square (#2) is "a rock musi-cian," one of her generation's cultural heroes. The Religious Square (#5) contains "a snowman." A snowman is neither human nor warm! It is also one of three masculine figures she has drawn on the Profile. In fact, the Profile appears to be mainly concerned with the problem of her relationship with men—fathers, husbands, and boyfriends. Note that the rock musician in her fantasy wears a cross, an ancient religious symbol. The Potential Square (#6) shows a "fun roller-coaster" which is how her life is in the family situation—up and down.

1. I like _boys_
2. I want _money_
3. My family _is very difficult_
4. I must _work_
5. Church is _a farse_
6. I hope _to get a call from (boy's name)_
7. I love _(boy's name)_
8. I feel _negleted_
9. Children are _always good to me_
10. People think of me _as what they want to think_
11. God _lives_
12. I often _get depressed_
13. I hate _school_
14. Someday I _hope to have my own home_
15. My father _drinks too much_
16. I can not _do Math well_
17. I fear _that I am wasting my life_
18. I wish _that I knew what (boy's name) is up to._
19. I failed _please (boy's name), I guess._
20. My greatest success _is myself._
21. My mother _is my best friend_
22. I need _love_
23. I believe _in honesty_
24. My worst fault _is conceit_
25. Women _are much more dependent than men_
26. Love _conquers all & will find a way_
27. Sisters are _people you can't stand_
28. I regret _that I lost (boy's name)_
29. I was happiest when _(boy's name) and I were together by the sea._
30. People _are self-centered._
31. Men _are basically more insecure than women_
32. Sex _must be complemented by love_
33. At home _I am my laziest_
34. I miss _(boy's name)_
35. I think _of (boy's name) all the time_
36. Marriage _isn't easy_
37. Brothers _are great people to have around_
38. A husband _should be a one-woman man_
39. I think of myself as _easy-going_
40. My dreams _are that (boy's name) will come back to me._

Case 24
New Birth in Potential Square

Female, Age 44, Married
Drawn with pencil

The woman who filled out this Profile did not use the symbols presented in the Ego Square (#1) or in the Fantasy Square (#2). A friendly house is drawn in the Ego Square with smoke coming out of the chimney. In statement 33 she says "at home there is a fire," and perhaps there is fire in her ego structure. Fire could be a symbol of transformation. In the Self-Determination Square (#4) she again draws a house, this time incorporating the symbol, only there is no chimney and she titles it "part of roof of house." The counselor might wonder if there isn't a need to develop her thinking function, as this would be symbolized as the "roof" of the personality. It would also be worthwhile to ask who "you" is in statements 22 and 34.

The Family Square (#3) does not seem to be brought together and is in a state of movement. What is at the center of all the movement? When a woman, considering herself to be beyond childbearing years, draws a pregnant woman, as in the Potential Square (#6), one feels that something new is coming into her life and the prognosis is generally healthy.

1. I like _everything_
2. I want _something_
3. My family _is great_
4. I must _do something_
5. Church is _O K_
6. I hope _for something_
7. I love _people_
8. I feel _O K_
9. Children are _sweet_
10. People think of me _as "sweet"_
11. God _is good_
12. I often _gravitate_
13. I hate _something_
14. Someday I _will go_
15. My father _swell_
16. I can not _hear. . .?_
17. I fear _something_
18. I wish _I would. . .?_
19. I failed _to do it_
20. My greatest success _is smashing_
21. My mother _hated me_
22. I need _you_
23. I believe _it's O K_
24. My worst fault _is laziness_
25. Women _are good_
26. Love _is kind_
27. Sisters are _sweet_
28. I regret _nothing_
29. I was happiest when _I was little_
30. People _are good_
31. Men _are great_
32. Sex _is wonderful_
33. At home _there is a fire_
34. I miss _you_
35. I think _somethings_
36. Marriage _is love_
37. Brothers _are good_
38. A husband _is tired_
39. I think of myself as _good_
40. My dreams _are worthwhile_

Case 25
Sunset in Potential Square

Female, Age 39, Married
Drawn with colored pencils

This Profile contains the color orange, symbolic of fire and passion, in both the Fantasy Square (#2) and the Potential Square (#6). The use of color would be an expression of this woman's feelings or emotions, her emotional involvement with the unconscious.

An extreme amount of pressure had built up within this woman, indicated by the volcano in the Fantasy Square (#2), and confirmed by statements 8, 12, 17, and 22. She says that her worst fault is her bad temper (statement 24). The fact that the fire in the volcano occurs in the Fantasy Square (#2) indicates that the counselor needs to be aware of suppressed tensions and the possibility of an emotional explosion. An erupting volcano is destructive. A counselor who thoughtlessly exposes this much emotion could precipitate a psychotic episode in the client.

The statements seem to indicate difficulties with her family. What causes the pressure within her? Letting the balloons out of Pandora's box in the Self-Determination Square (#4) could be another indication that pressures need to be released.

Judging from her statements (statements 3, 9, 25, 26, 28, and 36) this woman feels imprisoned by marriage. The counselor could ask if the flower in the Family Square (#3) is too large—overshadowing the house—or is the house too small? Why is there a size discrepancy? She mentions in statements 25 and 26 that "women are caged" and "love is a cage." Is this tiny house her cage?

The clouds in the Potential Square (#6) probably denote anxiety. Is there a relationship between the three symbols in the Family Square (#3) (there are three members in her family) and the three clouds in the Potential Square?

A sunset, or a valley between two mountains, (Potential Square #6) often implies the possibility of a depression or of sinking into the unconscious. Statement 1 says that she "likes to sleep." Is this escape from her problems? Could there be a need for introversion?

1. I like _to sleep._
2. I want _to be left alone for a while._
3. My family _always seems to need me._
4. I must _be there._
5. Church is _nowhere._
6. I hope _to go someplace._
7. I love _quiet._
8. I feel _desperate._
9. Children are _needing._
10. People think of me _as strong._
11. God _is nowhere._
12. I often _feel desperate and lonely._
13. I hate _to feel that way._
14. Someday I _understand my feelings._
15. My father _is a gardener._
16. I can not _be a gardener._
17. I fear _many things._
18. I wish _I didn't._
19. I failed _to understand._
20. My greatest success _?_
21. My mother _is having her problems._
22. I need _to know my own problems._
23. I believe _sometimes._
24. My worst fault _is my bad temper._
25. Women _are caged._
26. Love _is a cage._
27. Sisters are _like me._
28. I regret _getting married._
29. I was happiest when _--who knows?_
30. People _are people._
31. Men _don't understand women._
32. Sex _is too much with us._
33. At home _is sex, sex, sex._
34. I miss _quiet._
35. I think _of many ways to get it._
36. Marriage _is harder than Hell._
37. Brothers _are men._
38. A husband _is a man._
39. I think of myself as _a woman._
40. My dreams _come and go._

Case 26
Lack of Direction
in Self-Determination Square

Male, Age 30, Married
Drawn with pencil

The young man's drawing in the Self-Determination Square (#5) is composed of many lines going in different directions. There is no attempt to put it into form. A very masculine drawing—nothing but straight lines—it does not have any direction.

The statements of the Profile confirm this drawing (statements 2, 4, 14, 16, 17, 18, 19, 24, and 28) he wants "many things," he must "succeed," he fears "failure," he failed "never," his worst fault "snobbism," etc.

The Profile is not, when considered as a whole, scattered. The conflict seems to lie mainly with his inability to decide on a specific goal or direction in his life. Perhaps the fact that the statement completions are done in capital letters emphasizes his need to establish a pattern or goal in his life.

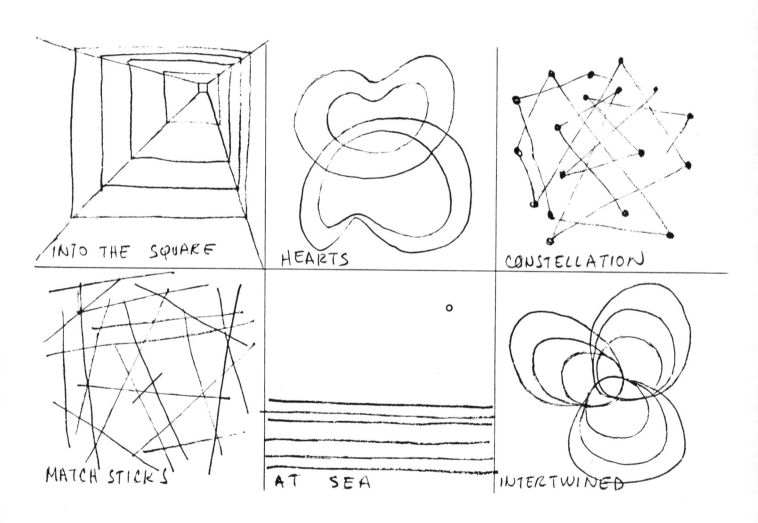

INTO THE SQUARE

HEARTS

CONSTELLATION

MATCH STICKS

AT SEA

INTERTWINED

1. I like ___ME___
2. I want ___MANY THINGS___
3. My family ___IS NOT STARTED YET___
4. I must ___SUCCEED___
5. Church is ___A PLACE TO WORSHIP___
6. I hope ___TO ENJOY LIFE___
7. I love ___(WOMAN'S NAME)___
8. I feel ___VERY GOOD___
9. Children are ___DELIGHTFUL LITTLE PEOPLE___
10. People think of me ___HIGHLY___
11. God ___IS WITH ME___
12. I often ___DAY DREAM___
13. I hate _____
14. Someday I ___HOPE TO BE FAMOUS___
15. My father ___IS VERY ALIVE___
16. I can not ___KEEP FROM BRAGGING___
17. I fear ___FAILURE___
18. I wish ___FOR TOO MANY THINGS___ ___(NOT REALLY)___
19. I failed ___NEVER___
20. My greatest success ___HAS NOT HAPPENED YET___
21. My mother ___IS SICK___
22. I need ___PEOPLE___
23. I believe ___MOST PEOPLE ARE HONEST___
24. My worst fault ___SNOBBISM___
25. Women ___HUMAN BEINGS___
26. Love ___MARRIAGE - SHARING___
27. Sisters are ___NOTHING___
28. I regret ___I DON'T HAVE THE MONEY TO DO ALL THE PROJECTS___
29. I was happiest when ___NOW___
30. People ___ARE DIFFERENT___
31. Men ___MUSCULAR___
32. Sex ___INTERCOURSE___
33. At home ___RESTFUL___
34. I miss _____
35. I think _____
36. Marriage ___JOY - LOVE - LIVING TOGETHER - BEING TOGETHER___
37. Brothers ___TALL___
38. A husband ___IS THE PROVIDER___
39. I think of myself as ___PRETTY GOOD___
40. My dreams ___TELL ME THINGS___

Case 26: Lack of Direction in Self-Determination Square   61

Case 27
Religious Feeling
on the Natural Level

Female, Age 25, Married
Drawn with pencil and pen and blue ink

The Ego Square (#1) shows a "building," probably indicating an ego built on collective values. The Family Square (#3) is "a dot board (a game)," and nothing is connected. Fifteen of the statements on the reverse side (statements 2, 3, 16, 19, 22, 23, 28, 31, 32, 33, 35, 36, 38, 39, and 40) show great concern for her marriage. The counselor might find it helpful to discuss her expectations of marriage and of her husband. The "baseball diamond" in the Self-Determination Square (#4) is a symbol of completeness as all sides are equal. Baseball is, however, typically a masculine game.

This woman's religious feeling (Religious Square #5) is on the natural level, and the counselor might wonder if there isn't a need to eat one of the apples. Is it the "face of Eve" in every woman, drawn in the Fantasy Square (#2), which is looking at the forbidden fruit? The Potential Square (#6) is the "sun" which brings light and warmth with its energy (the lines radiating from the sun). The circle of the sun is also a mandala, a symbol of wholeness.

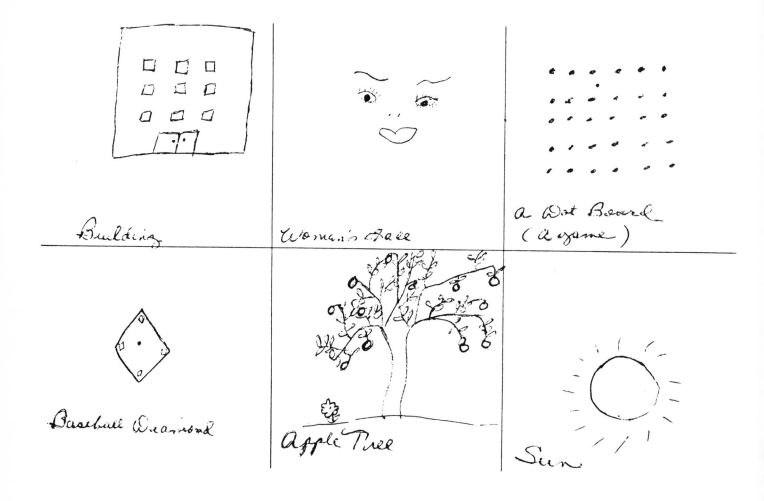

1. I like _to go to church_
2. I want _a happy marriage_
3. My family _is the most important thing to me_
4. I must _Finish this test_
5. Church is _a place I enjoy going to._
6. I hope _I can learn to be completely happy_
7. I love _my family_
8. I feel _fine today_
9. Children are _noisy, but I love mine_
10. People think of me _when they want a cup of coffee_
11. God _is good_
12. I often _feel depressed_
13. I hate _it when I miss church_
14. Someday I _would like to do something big for the Community and God_
15. My father _is good to me_
16. I can not _seem to make my marriage work_
17. I fear _someday I will get out of fellowship with God_
18. I wish _I were happy_
19. I failed _at making my husband happy_
20. My greatest success _hasn't come yet_
21. My mother _is good to me and very helpful_
22. I need _to learn to understand my husband better_
23. I believe _someday I'll probably get a divorce_
24. My worst fault _is worrying about things I can do nothing about_
25. Women _gossip to much_
26. Love _is to love and be loved._
27. Sisters are _O.K. I guess, I never had one_
28. I regret _not making my husband happy_
29. I was happiest when _I was in (name of state)._
30. People _are doing more wrong everyday_
31. Men _are unfaithful_
32. Sex _Female_
33. At home _I feel depressed_
34. I miss _going to church_
35. I think _I might can make my marriage work_
36. Marriage _is wonderful, if both parties are happy_
37. Brothers _are helpful_
38. A husband _is not happy_
39. I think of myself as _a good wife and good mother_
40. My dreams _are to have a Christian home._

Case 28
Development of Symbols

Female, Ages 39 and 48, Married
Illustration A—drawn with pencil
Illustration B—drawn with pen and blue ink

Both Illustration A and Illustration B were done by the same person over a period of nine years. No statement completions were done for either of these Profiles; Illustration A, the Profile first drawn, is quite simple with apparently little going on in this person's unconscious. Yet the basic structure in Illustration A is carried over into Illustration B, as though first only the framework of a house had been laid and later built upon.

In the Ego Square (#1) of Illustration A she has drawn expanding boxes; in Illustration B the same boxes are there with lines radiating out from the center in all directions.

The Fantasy Square (#2) of Illustration A is a bird (or perhaps a snake up in the air) while the fantasy in Illustration B is rich with a bird, a nest in a well-rooted tree, and growing flowers.

A large flower is now growing in the Family Square (#3) in Illustration B while only a circle was drawn in this square in Illustration A.

The circle was again drawn in the Religious Square (#5) in Illustration A, while Illustration B repeats the circle theme, greatly enlarging upon it with lines radiating out into the different areas of her life.

A circle is again drawn in the Potential Square (#6), but in Illustration A it is unadorned. Illustration B shows a rolling circle, down on the earth and moving out, with arrows pointing in the direction of consciousness.

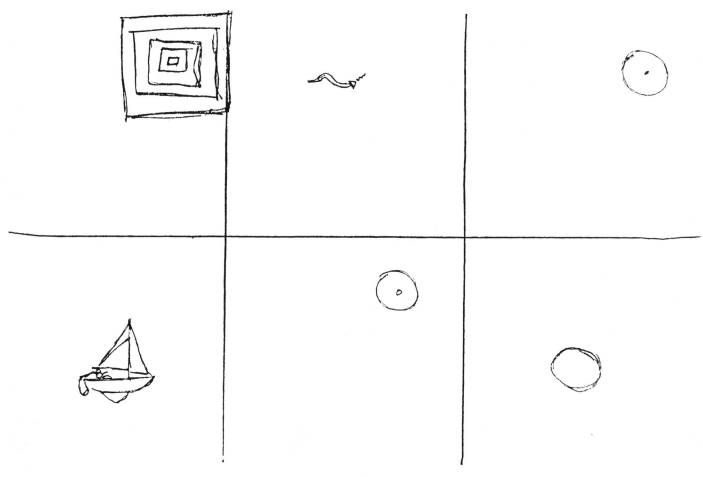

Illustration A

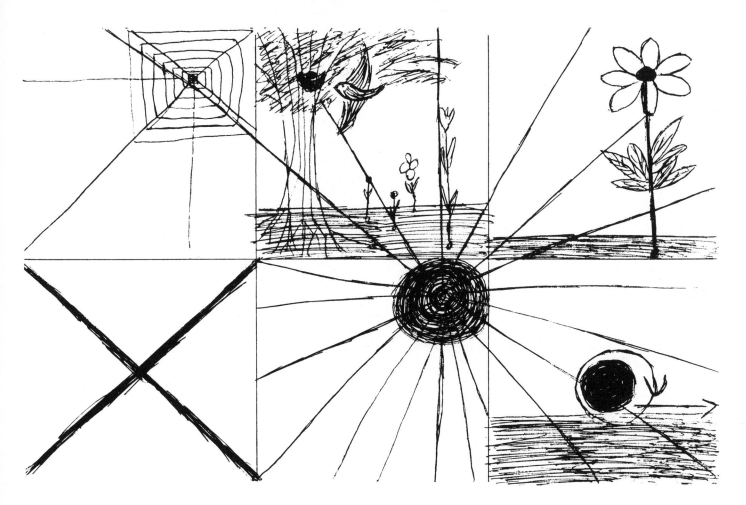

Illustration B

Case 29
Child's Profile
with Story of Drawings

Male, Age 10, Single
Drawn with pencil

Children usually do not object to doing Profiles and they will sometimes tell a story to accompany the drawings.

The young boy who did this Profile had severe vomiting spells and had developed a school phobia. His mother was in analysis at the time she asked him to do the Profile.

Often the parent's and the child's lives become so entangled on an unconscious level that the child can become unconsciously involved in the parent's problem.

When the mother asked her son to tell her about the squares, he said that he had drawn a dream. He said that in the Ego Square (#1), which he titled "the lonely square," he was a circle but different from the other circles.

In the Fantasy Square (#2) is an apple. He said he was hungry and someone had given him a rotten apple. A strange woman named Jill gave him the rotten apple in the dream and she was mean. He met her in a house on _____ street and he walked home eating the rotten apple. His house was empty when he arrived home. When he bit into the apple he found the spider and it made him sick.

In describing the spider in the Family Square (#3), he told his mother, "This spider wears earmuffs and is blue. It is a house spider and lives in your bed. It kisses you, but the kiss tastes terrible."

His mother then asked him whether the spider was a boy or a girl, and he said, "It has no sex and it kisses with its feet." He continued, "I don't know if the spider loves or not, it comes only at night, and I don't like to go to bed."

He then said, "It is my friend. He likes me, but he makes me nervous, and I like him. The name of the spider, also, is Jill."

When asked about the Self-Determination Square (#4), he said that he didn't want to talk about the line—it was only to divide the chapters, as though he were telling a story in two parts.

His comments on the eye in the Religious Square (#5) were, "The spider's eye was watching something—it was watching me. He is my guard. I have to keep him in a pen so that Elmer won't eat him. Elmer and the spider don't like each other. Elmer and the spider used to live

(Text continued on page 68)

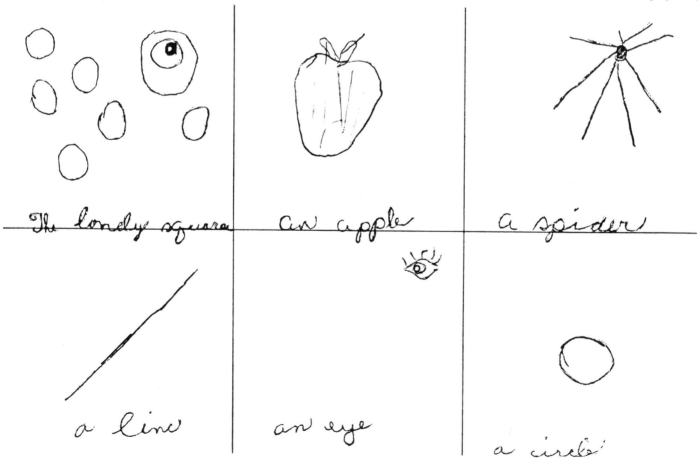

1. I like _you_
2. I want _to be well_
3. My family _is nice_
4. I must _get well._
5. Church is _I don't know_
6. I hope _I get well_
7. I love _my family_
8. I feel _terrible_
9. Children are _I don't know what they are. Some are fun and some aren't._
10. People think of me _as (boy's name)_
11. God _is in heaven._
12. I often _feel bad_
13. I hate _feeling like this_
14. Someday I _I'll get well_
15. My father _is nice_
16. I can not _think_
17. I fear _sickness_
18. I wish _I'd get well_
19. I failed _in getting well_
20. My greatest success _(dog's name)_
21. My mother _I love_
22. I need _myself_
23. I believe _in getting well_
24. My worst fault _getting sick_
25. Women _are nice_
26. Love _is beautiful_
27. Sisters are _I don't know_
28. I regret _getting sick_
29. I was happiest when _I was well_
30. People _I don't know_
31. Men _are big_
32. Sex _is male and female_
33. At home _is here_
34. I miss _(dog's name)_
35. I think _always_
36. Marriage _I don't know_
37. Brothers _is (dog's name)_
38. A husband _I don't know. I'm not married._
39. I think of myself as _(boy's name)_
40. My dreams _are pleasant._

together in a cave in the forest. Elmer used to lie on the spider. Elmer also hunted all day."

Next he went back to the Self-Determination Square (#4) and said, "This line is Elmer's friend, another snake." (Elmer now is identified as a snake.)

The boy then gave what he termed his "summary." He said, "It ended up in a circle. Elmer was happy because he and the spider made up and the eye finally saw. The spider had a place to live because the apple was not rotten anymore and now I am a circle like the other people."

Analysis

At the time the boy did this Profile his parents were experiencing marital difficulty. The problem was not dealt with consciously by both parents. Children in such a situation often carry the burden unconsciously.

Also, the boy was at a stage preceding the onset of puberty, having sexual feelings with which to become acquainted plus the dawning realization of his parent's sexual activity.

The correlation between mother and son is interesting in that the mother was trying to integrate her own "devouring spider" side (a negative side of mothering) in analysis (although the boy had no knowledge of this fact.)

This Profile gave the mother an understanding of how deeply her son was involved in her own problems.

Case 30
"The Happy Mutt"

Male, Age 38, Married
Drawn with pencil

A creative body movement class at The C.G. Jung Educational Center in Houston, Texas recently completed a six-week session wherein they worked through their personal Profiles. The first session consisted of drawing the Profile and working with the Ego Square (#1).

For the next five weeks the members of the class moved into and related with the symbolic ramifications of their drawings using the technique of active imagination[1] through body movement.

This Profile was drawn by a man, a computer programmer—a rational and logical thinking person. His experience in relating to the symbol in the Potential Square (#6) helped him to integrate the "happy mutt" within his personality, and seemed to give him a broader basis for relationships which could involve feelings. The following is his own interpretation of his experience.

In my Potential or Future Square I drew a happy spotted "mutt" dog looking toward the right. So I started out being the dog. I got on my hands and knees and turned my attention to my right. But as the situation began to take shape, the form of a dog quickly became transparent and dropped from me. I saw a thin, dark gray veil in front of me. I rose to my feet before it, and parted it with my hands. I stepped through the opening, but the area was still very dim on the other side (because this was the future, I supposed).

I came to the stones of the fireplace [there was in reality a fireplace in the room], but to me they seemed like the smooth faces of a huge diamond pyramid. It seemed to me to symbolize the hardness and sharp edges of logic. I moved into it and sat down, but as I put my forehead against the stones their coldness seemed to bother me. I guess somehow I expected a fire within this diamond fireplace, but there was none, only a deep black hole where one used to be.

I decided that I needed the warmth of people so I went out of the diamond fireplace and began crawling very carefully out into the middle of the room where the people were, with my eyes still closed. I traveled a long way and relished the gentle brush of my hand against another or the very smooth feeling of someone's hair. After a while I noticed the small brown and white dog I had drawn walking beside me on the right. I walked over close to the windows of a sunroom. The light was dazzling even through my closed eyes and I was drawn to the source of this illumination (for mental illumination is what I

Ego

Fantasy

Family

(determined) will

religious

future

assumed it meant). But then I noticed that the dog wouldn't follow me into this sunroom. I asked him why he didn't want to come in, but he didn't answer. He only sat on the other side of the threshold. I walked over to him, looking back into the room. It appeared to be filled with flames. I assumed that this alluded to strong, overpowering emotions.

I withdrew from the room and followed the little dog the way a blind man follows his dog. I was even holding onto the same type of leash. We stopped and sat down. At this point the music began to sound almost like a cross between a howl and a (mythical) siren's call. The dog began to howl, reproducing the music. I finally joined in, too, and it was then I realized I was being like a fountain. I was gushing forth not water, but words and I had to be careful to keep my words as pure and as true as water. After a while I became embarrassed at the quality of what was coming forth from me. I stopped and thanked God for the privilege of having such an experience. Crossing my arms before my forehead, I bent over to face the ground. After a while I resumed my gushing position, but this time it did not last long. I got up shortly and faced the center of the room with the dog beside me. I felt that I had to say to not only the women present but to many more, "Love, . . . Love, it is the only thing really worth doing. Please, Love . . ." I repeated this a number of times in this fantasy.

At this point the music was beginning to reach great crescendos. A sack of rough-cut jewels appeared at my left side and I repeatedly threw handfuls of them, spreading them among all the women in the room. Previously, in fantasy, when women touched the jewels, the jewels changed into roses. After throwing the jewels, I began to make circles with my right hand, and following my hand appeared at least two beautiful rainbows which glittered with a broad outside edge of gold. That was the end, but I felt so good about it that I had to go over to the instructor and thank her for giving me the chance to go through this session.

Case 31
A Profile Series

The following six Profiles were done by a young woman over a period of nine months. She was attending a class in Jungian Psychology at the time the first one was completed (October 9, 1970). She was also at that time seven months pregnant.

In May of 1971 (she was no longer attending the class at the Jung Center) the subject asked if someone would help her with a problem of jealousy which was threatening to become more than she could handle. With this view in mind the counselor met with her for six weeks, trying to help her find a sense of her own identity and strength. During these six weeks the counselor and counselee talked about her feelings, expectations, and goals. The counselor helped her think of ways in which she could experience her own autonomy. This was done by setting small goals for herself each week on which she would then report back to the counselor at the next session. As an example, she needed a new pair of shoes but could not seem to summon the will and energy to buy them.

Analysis in depth was not attempted, and dreams and fantasies were not brought into the discussion. Each week's session was begun with the Profile drawings and statements.

The following is an account by the counselee, in her own words, of what these sessions meant to her and what she gained from them. After her account the counselor gives a general analysis of the Profiles.

The Profile is a useful tool for beginning discussions about one's feelings and problems. In my particular case I was suffering from overwhelming feelings of jealousy, coupled with feelings of inadequacy and almost total dependence on my husband for ego reinforcement. In short, I was in bad shape.

In an effort to thwart my feelings of jealousy, I had tried becoming friends with the girl of whom I was jealous. That didn't work because I really don't like her and had tried to repress my dislike. The discussions that evolved from the Profiles made me realize that negative feelings toward people are not to be repressed. Rather, they really need to be brought out into the open, looked at, and talked about. In learning that jealousy is from a weak ego, we started correcting that by setting up small obtainable goals on a weekly basis. It is amazing how much this improved my feelings of worth! As a further aid I kept an "Ego Aides" book containing my accomplishments—both major and minor ones. Whenever I feel the negative animus[27] moving in, I pull out my "Ego Aides" and this helps considerably in regaining the proper perspective. Getting involved in my pottery as a business has helped in breaking away from total dependence on my husband for ego reinforcement. Now, I'm not as demanding on him. My pottery gives me the satisfaction that I so desperately need for my ego. One more thing I forced myself to face is that I don't use what I have. I'm still not functioning at maximum level, but I'm much better organized than before the talks around the Profiles.

Drawing the pictures on the Profile was difficult for me initially. But gradually I loosened up and was quite surprised how helpful they are in expressing the feelings one has and is not aware of.

(The six profiles begin on the following page)

Profile #1—10/9/70
Female, Age 29, Married
Drawn with pen and blue ink

Often a person will rationalize the fact that he has not incorporated the symbols in his drawings by saying he has misunderstood the directions. The counselor would be wise to check the statements in this case to see if they verify the unused potential. Statements 2, 4, 8, 19, 22, 28, 29, 35, and 39 all point to this young woman's feelings of insecurity and lack of self-worth. There is little with which to relate in the drawings on the human level, but the Family Square (#3) might be the clue to her need of perspective in the family situation. Statements 18, 19, 21, and 38 would help to formulate the questions. Statement 18 particularly gives a clue to her expectations of the marriage relationship.

The rectangular shape of the "brick fence" in the Ego Square (#1) is a "disturbed mandala,"[28] according to Jung. "The predominance of the horizontal over the vertical indicates that the ego-consciousness is uppermost, thus entailing a loss of height and depth."[29] Also, a fence or wall is to keep something in or out, and this fence is built brick by brick. What is being hindered here in either integration or expression? Too, the oblong shape would be on a material level, lacking the spiritual aspect of life. The "bird in flight" in the Fantasy Square (#2) may be compensation for the brick fence, in that it soars in an effort to reach the heavens.

In the Potential Square (#6) is an incomplete face—the features are not contained. Is this a part of her personality she does not yet recognize?

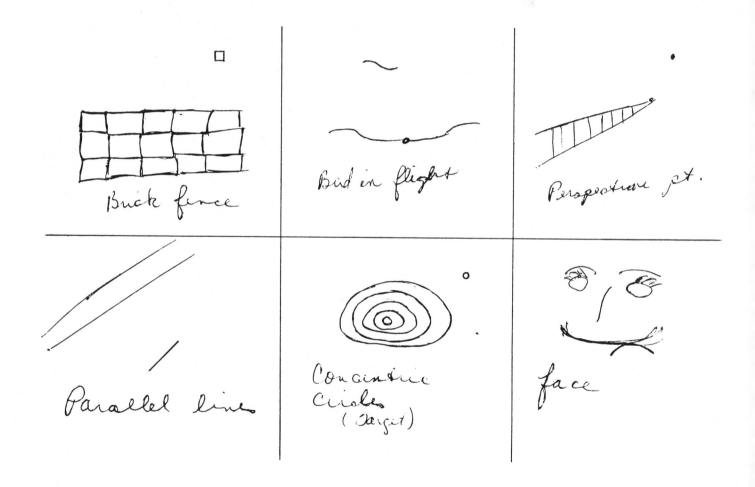

1. I like _people_
2. I want _financial security_
3. My family _is dispersed_
4. I must _be less clumsy_
5. Church is _boring_
6. I hope _to find happiness_
7. I love _the feeling of clay_
8. I feel _insecure sometimes_
9. Children are _refreshing_
10. People think of me _as quiet_
11. God _'s what you want him to be_
12. I often _wish I lived in a small town_
13. I hate _greens (the edible ones)_
14. Someday I _hope to have a potter's wheel_
15. My father _was a kind man_
16. I can not _stand traffic lights_
17. I fear _lonliness_
18. I wish _for a complete marriage relationship_
19. I failed _my man on several occasions_
20. My greatest success _was making a good pot_
21. My mother _must be unhappy_
22. I need _acceptance_
23. I believe _in honesty_
24. My worst fault _is being hard headed_
25. Women _have a good thing going._
26. Love _is good._
27. Sisters are _great to have as friends_
28. I regret _some things I have done._
29. I was happiest when _I was in the womb, I'm sure!_
30. People _are interesting, some of them._
31. Men _are alright_
32. Sex _is great_
33. At home _I enjoy sewing._
34. I miss _some of my friends_
35. I think _I'm lacking in firm beliefs_
36. Marriage _is a full time job_
37. Brothers _are good to have._
38. A husband _should be a loner_
39. I think of myself as _unable to get a clear picture of myself._
40. My dreams _are funny_

Profile #2—5/29/71
Female, Age 30, Married
Drawn with pencil

This is the Profile returned to the counselor at the second week of the counseling sessions. As stated before, the apparent problem was one of jealousy of another woman in relationship to her husband. The drawing in the Ego Square (#1) is titled "shadow," but is a much stronger ego drawing than that drawn nine months earlier. Her Self-Determination (#4) is to have a "home" which would be on a personal and individual level. The road in front of her home is drawn with the same lines she drew in the first Profile which she titled "parallel lines." Statement 4 gives the feeling she wants to resolve her problem in her own personal way. However, the lines in the Self-Determination Square (#4) are not as definite and connected as in the other drawings. Perhaps she entertains doubt.

The drawings in this Profile are on a more human level, an easier level on which to communicate. The "happy" face in the Family Square (#3) is a mandala, expressive perhaps of her need to find wholeness in the family situation. During this discussion the idea of obtaining small goals each week was presented.

1. I like _to take saunas_
2. I want _to resolve my problem of jealousy_
3. My family _is important to me._
4. I must _resolve my problem of jealousy_
5. Church is _part of my childhood_
6. I hope _that my child will be physically sound_
7. I love _my husband_
8. I feel _insecure at times._
9. Children are _so beautifully innocent_
10. People think of me _as easy going._
11. God _is the whole universe._
12. I often _eat ice cream_
13. I hate _greens_
14. Someday I _would like to run a pot shop_
15. My father _was a very kind man_
16. I can not _draw_
17. I fear _lonliness_
18. I wish _I understood why people are prejediced_
19. I failed _a math course_
20. My greatest success _is a good pot_
21. My mother _was born 100 years late._
22. I need _a friend_
23. I believe _in accepting people on an individual basis._
24. My worst fault _is lack of motivation_
25. Women _take advantage of men._
26. Love _should be experienced by everyone._
27. Sisters are _great_
28. I regret _not pursuing the piano_
29. I was happiest when _I was a child._
30. People _generally need more of a sense of humor._
31. Men _are nice to have around_
32. Sex _is great_
33. At home _I need some organization._
34. I miss _my friends_
35. I think _I can resolve my problem._
36. Marriage _is a full time endeavor._
37. Brothers _are fun._
38. A husband _can be a friend as well._
39. I think of myself as _capable but lacking in direction._
40. My dreams _are very interesting to me._

Profile #3—6/7/71
Female, Age 30, Married
Drawn with pencil

One must take into account that this person has begun to learn about the symbolic meaning of the different squares in the Profile. A great deal more consciousness has gone into the drawings, particularly in the Ego Square (#1), and in a determined way she has empha-sized the outlines of the house. Even with this knowl-edge of the Profile, why did she choose the particular symbols drawn, such as "boots on a line" in the Family Square (#3)? There is one boot for each member of the family—the husband, herself, and the baby. The boots are all strung on the same line, as though saying she is determined to keep them together. The subject began to discuss the woman of whom she was jealous, ending by saying that they were a great deal alike in many ways.

HOME   WINE SACK   BOOTS ON A LINE

PIECE OF CHEESE   SUMMER DAY   CRADLE

1. I like _hand made items_
2. I want _to be a good potter._
3. My family _is fun_
4. I must _relate my expectations about (man's name) & me to (man's name)._
5. Church is _a source of happiness for many people._
6. I hope _to always be aware of life._
7. I love _my husband._
8. I feel _happy most of the time_
9. Children are _fun_
10. People think of me _as honest._
11. God _is a nebulous thing._
12. I often _don't finish what I'm doing_
13. I hate _(name of city)_
14. Someday I _would like a mountain cabin_
15. My father _could not handle responsibility._
16. I can not _cope with my jealousy_
17. I fear _drowning_
18. I wish _I was more daring._
19. I failed _(am failing) at gardening_
20. My greatest success _was a perfect score on a math final._
21. My mother _doesn't discuss her feelings_
22. I need _to establish a seperate identy from my husband._
23. I believe _man must learn to be kind._
24. My worst fault _is lack of incentive._
25. Women _'s lib is for the birds_
26. Love _is a deep emotion._
27. Sisters are _good to have._
28. I regret _having been so poor as a child_
29. I was happiest when _I wasn't feeling jealous_
30. People _can be very nice at times_
31. Men _need some liberation._
32. Sex _is great_
33. At home _I do lots of things_
34. I miss _my sister_
35. I think _I need to read more._
36. Marriage _is a two way street._
37. Brothers _are fun_
38. A husband _can be_
39. I think of myself as _not very creative_
40. My dreams _are usually a jumble of the previous day_

Profile #4—6/14/71
Female, Age 30, Married
Drawn with crayon

This Profile is so different from the preceding drawings that one feels something important has happened in the inner world of the counselee as she tried to understand her feelings. This was the first Profile done in color, and the subject said it had been difficult for her to draw. The drawings have moved from the abstract to the human and personal level. Even viewed as a possible regression, there is much on the level of the child, the counselor felt it to be a healthy sign that the young woman was able to begin to express her feelings.

Although the subject was unable to amplify the man's face in the Ego Square (#1) the counselor felt that the subject's masculine thinking was directing her ego at this time, even coloring the eyes a bright blue. The Self-Determination Square (#4), "cobblestone walk," is a warm brown picture with curved lines, expressing her determination to walk on the earth in a more feminine way. The "cobblestone walk" goes into her Ego Square (#1), her Fantasy Square (#2) and her Religious Square (#5), which could express her determination to deal with her fantasies and the meaning of her life in a more feminine way. The figure in the Fantasy Square (#2) wears a green dress, the color of Venus. The counselee said that the woman of whom she was jealous was constantly flirting with her husband, and was "sexy." The discussion then began to center about her own sexy and flirtatious side. Did she know this side of her femininity or was she projecting it all onto the other woman? The subject's decision was to try to find this part of herself, even adding new clothes to her wardrobe.

The figures in the Family Square (#3) were done in red and the swing set in black on greenish-blue grass. The "vendor in carnival" in the Religious Square (#5) wore a red hat and his wares were pink. The balloons were different colors. The "sno ball" in the Potential Square (#6) was pink. The "sno ball," although something cold, is a union of the masculine and feminine lines.

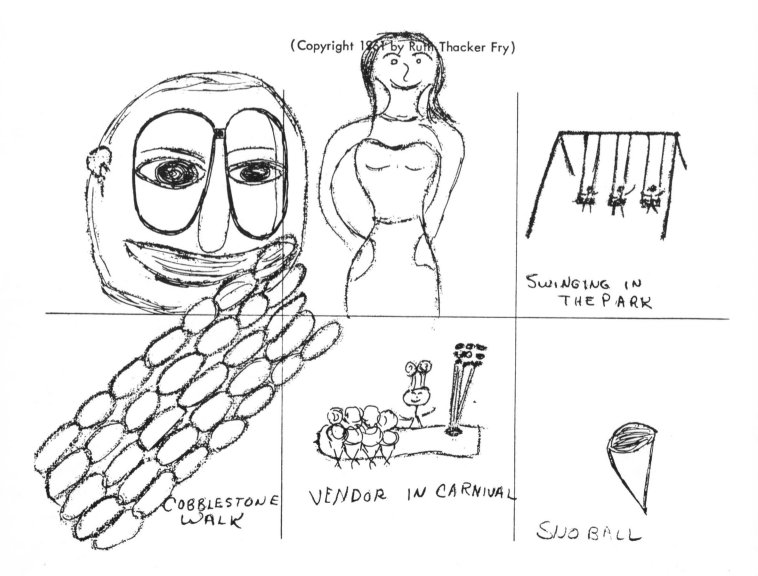

(Copyright 1961 by Ruth Thacker Fry)

SWINGING IN THE PARK

COBBLESTONE WALK

VENDOR IN CARNIVAL

SNO BALL

1. I like _french food_
2. I want _to be a whole person_
3. My family _is a source of happiness_
4. I must _determine why I'm jealous._
5. Church is _not for me._
6. I hope _to live with (man's name) for the rest of my life._
7. I love _to feel clay_
8. I feel _a completness when I hold my baby._
9. Children are _fun_
10. People think of me _as intelligent_
11. God _is something I'd like to believe in._
12. I often _laugh_
13. I hate _being so dependent_
14. Someday I _would like to be wise_
15. My father _was a kind man_
16. I can not _cope with my jealousy feelings_
17. I fear _I might drive (man's name) away with my jealousy_
18. I wish _we didn't have to worry about money_
19. I failed _to see that I'm selfish at times_
20. My greatest success _will be overcoming jealousy feelings_
21. My mother _and I have different values_
22. I need _to give (man's name) more freedom_
23. I believe _in kindness_
24. My worst fault _is trying to treat emotions with logic_
25. Women _are O. K._
26. Love _is a warm feeling for another person_
27. Sisters are _fun_
28. I regret _____
29. I was happiest when _in the last two years (with my husband)_
30. People _are difficult to understand._
31. Men _are nice to be around._
32. Sex _is a wonderful experience_
33. At home _I do lots of things_
34. I miss _my friends_
35. I think _I can solve my problems_
36. Marriage _causes a lot of problems for a lot of people_
37. Brothers _are good to have._
38. A husband _is usually a breadwinner_
39. I think of myself as _a kind person_
40. My dreams _are interesting_

The counselor had suggested the subject use the colors red, blue, green, and yellow, in this Profile hoping it might furnish clues as to how she functioned. (Ordinarily, no instructions are given as to use of different media. However, the counselor was using the theory of the color red relating to values, blue to thinking, yellow to intuition, and green to sensation, as presented in Jung's theory of the basic personality types.[30]) The subject had a degree in math. Evidently the Ego Square (#1), drawn with blue and yellow, relates to her most developed function—that of thinking. She felt the "road map" expressed the function of her ego as a way to get around. The curved lines of this drawing also show a development of her feminine ego. The "feather" in the Self-Determination Square (#4) is drawn in yellow and red—the yellow being uppermost in the drawing, touching into three other squares.

The feather is possibly from the "bird in flight" drawn in the first Profile in the Fantasy Square (#2), as though she is determined to catch the thought expressed by the symbol of the bird.

The "baby with toy" in the Fantasy Square (#2) is green and holds a red toy. The client was unable to title the drawing in the Religious Square (#5), but it is a quaternary which is a symbol of completeness. She ap-pears to be struggling to find completeness in the meaning of her life. The dots are green and the rest of the drawing is in blue.

The "flower" in the Family Square (#3) is blue with a yellow center and a green stem. This drawing seems to say the family feeling is now on a natural level in the unconscious, and it appears to be a healthy flower.

The "silo on a farm" in the Potential Square (#6) is an example of the creative phallus emerging from the unconscious. She has used all of the colors in this drawing. The silo is red brick (refer to the brick fence in her first Profile) and looks as though it has come up out of the ground. It is outlined with green and black. The house and the barn are blue. She identified yellow corn growing behind the buildings. The sky is blue and a yellow sun is shining. From the way in which she used the colors in these drawings the counselor felt her need was to know her own creativity, perhaps a new way of valuing her life.

In the discussion arising out of this Profile, the counselee brought up her ambition to enlarge her skills in pottery making and possibly open a small shop. She needed only $50.00 in order to begin this project, and began to see her goal was not impossible. This was the week, also, that she set herself the immediate goal of buying a new pair of shoes, symbolizing a new way to walk.

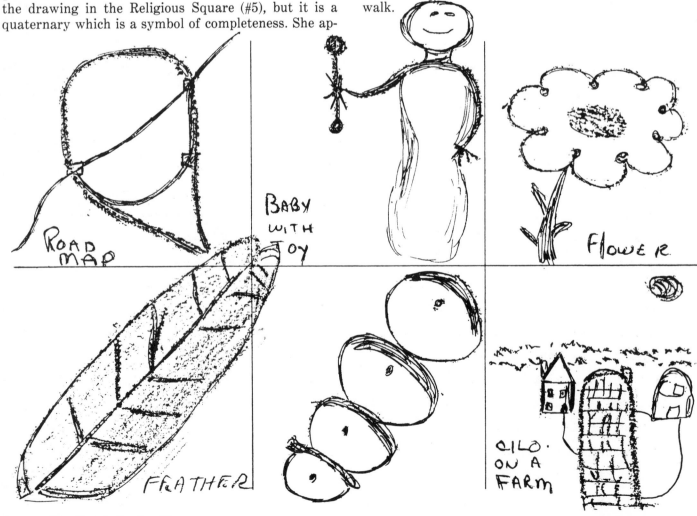

ROAD MAP

BABY WITH TOY

FLOWER

FEATHER

SILO. ON A FARM

1. I like _the forest_
2. I want _a better world for our children_
3. My family _is my main responsibility_
4. I must _accept my emotions as such_
5. Church is _____
6. I hope _____
7. I love _my child_
8. I feel _very close to my husband_
9. Children are _refreshing_
10. People think of me _____
11. God _____
12. I often _dream_
13. I hate _____
14. Someday I _would like to live in the country_
15. My father _was an escapist_
16. I can not _____
17. I fear _____
18. I wish _there was no need for war._
19. I failed _____
20. My greatest success _____
21. My mother _lives in a different world._
22. I need _to know myself better._
23. I believe _coming to the Jung Center is fruitful_
24. My worst fault _not being able to see my worse fault_
25. Women _have a greater sexual capacity than men_
26. Love _is a growing feeling._
27. Sisters are _____
28. I regret _____
29. I was happiest when _____
30. People _are not very nice sometimes_
31. Men _____
32. Sex _____
33. At home _____
34. I miss _____
35. I think _____
36. Marriage _____
37. Brothers _____
38. A husband _____
39. I think of myself as _____
40. My dreams _____

Profile #6—6/28/71
Female, Age 30, Married
Drawn with crayon

The counselor felt moved by this Profile, seeing that the subject had begun to pull the parts of her life together. The background was done in soft orange, the color of fire and transformation in its more positive sense. The subject had by this time started her "Ego Aides" book and this book was the symbol drawn in the Ego Square (#1). The counselor was aware that the "Ego Aides" book was not a permanent answer. The need for ego strength and a sense of self-worth were, however, important at this time. The book had been of great value in reminding her who she was when negative emotions threatened to overcome her. In this last session the counselor felt the subject looked more relaxed. Her appearance had changed as though she had become more aware of herself, although it was not a drastic change. Possibly this change would not have been apparent to a casual observer.

There are numerous containers drawn in this Profile as though the unconscious is showing her that she has the capacity to hold her life. She still has some "nuts to crack" in the Family Square (#3), but there is a tool (the nutcracker in the bowl) with which to work. The red candle perhaps shows that her values could give her light for this task in the area of family feeling. Also, this square contains both the masculine (candle) and feminine (bowl). The bowl containing the nuts is green and the nuts are brown. The Potential Square (#6) contains a yellow cup and green teapot. The subject still had to deal with feelings of jealousy, but felt she had gained some understanding of the problem and was beginning to experience herself as a separate person.

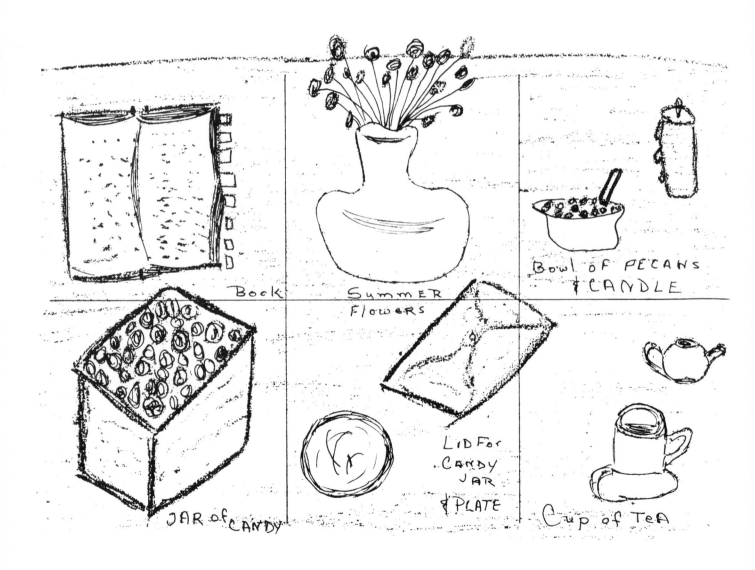

1. I like _fresh flowers_
2. I want _to be financially secure_
3. My family _is my source of completness_
4. I must _develop friends apart from (man's name)_
5. Church is _something I don't think about_
6. I hope _to be an excellent potter_
7. I love _air conditioning_
8. I feel _inept at certain things_
9. Children are _a test of one's patience_
10. People think of me _as a good cook_
11. God _I would like to believe in._
12. I often _don't finish projects_
13. I hate _not finishing projects_
14. Someday I _would like a garden of flowers_
15. My father _and sister were always fighting_
16. I can not _quell my jealousy feelings_
17. I fear _I will kill myself accidently_
18. I wish _I had some more money_
19. I failed _to get involved in my career._
20. My greatest success _having a man replace me when I quit my job._
21. My mother _is proud of her children_
22. I need _to accept my bad qualities_
23. I believe _I'm making progress_
24. My worst fault _I'm not sure as yet._
25. Women _are alright_
26. Love _is a beautiful & trying experience_
27. Sisters are _helpful_
28. I regret _some things I've done_
29. I was happiest when _I was a child_
30. People _are hard to understand_
31. Men _are great_
32. Sex _is great_
33. At home _I do lots of things_
34. I miss _my friends_
35. I think _I should accept myself as is_
36. Marriage _is a full time job._
37. Brothers _are friends_
38. A husband _can be a friend_
39. I think of myself as _clumsy_
40. My dreams _are hard to remember of late_

Afterword

Convincing people that the Profile is not a test on which they will receive a score or grade is sometimes difficult. Counselors new to the Profile are often uneasy because there is no scoring. The Profile asks of the counselor only that he meet a person and start to build a creative relationship without judgement as to what should or should not be. If there is a message in this book, it would be that the Profile is a "just-so" story presented to the counselor and the continuing episodes of a person's story grow from that point.

People do not always need or want therapy or counseling in depth. Perhaps they are bored or blocked in a certain area of their life. This is shown in their drawings. Those who do not incorporate the symbols in the drawings usually make uninteresting pictures, and those who are blocked by a particular problem in certain areas of their life will give this information in the drawings and statements. Helping these people to explore new areas of life will many times start them on the way to finding and developing their own potential and creative means of solving their problems within their own psyche. Unused or blocked energy can turn negative, often destroying lives that could be productive and meaningful. The Profile is a simple means of getting a person in touch with his own psychology.

The most casual meetings over the Profile are sometimes sufficient to change a person's whole direction in life. In Profiles done by five members of a family the three children drew almost identical pictures as the father had drawn. All the drawings were small and without much detail. When the parents saw the children's drawings, they realized how identified the children were with the father. They were not developing their individual personalities in any way. The family was not in counseling, but the drawings alone convinced them of the necessity of helping their children to find interests of their own.

A university professor of law talked with a counselor about his Profile in one meeting and recognized his own angry and sulky inner six-year-old child. This inner child still held the man's parents to blame for his life problems. When the counselor discussed the Profile with him the impact of its meaning hit him so hard he was able to forgive his parents for their cruelty toward him as a child. He then had a strong impression, in fact almost a visionary encounter, that the parents (who had been dead for a number of years) stood before him and said "now we can be at peace." As he set his inner parents free, he too became free of a strong regressive element in his personality. Such experiences of "awe" are healing moments in the therapeutic art.

A woman brought a Profile drawn by her teenage daughter who was never seen by the counselor. All of the drawings emphatically depicted her psychological condition. The lines she used were going in different directions and the titles of the drawings were "Reign" in the Ego Square, "Psycomatic" in the Fantasy Square, "Danger or Hypocritical" in the Family Square, and "Wipe Out!" in the Self-Determination Square. The Religious Square was unused. In the Potential Square she drew a picture of herself riding a horse entitled "Me Breaking the Horse's Back!" The following day the girl was hospitalized with a breakdown. She had certainly followed through on her determination to "Wipe Out!" Her statements also confirmed the feelings expressed in the drawings. A hopeful note expressed in the statements was that she wanted to be happy and to start over. Perhaps the breakdown and subsequent hospitalization would offer her the opportunity for renewal.

The Profile does not measure intelligence. Members of MENSA (an organization composed of people with extremely high I.Q.'s) have used the Profile, and no difference was found between their drawings and those of the average person. Drawings on the Profile by educable retarded persons have not shown their retardation. A counselor can relate to their drawings as easily as to those in any Profile.

People are usually quite receptive to working with the Profile because it contains what *they* have drawn and said about *themselves* in different areas of *their* lives. They tell the counselor what the Profile drawings mean to them. In this way, they participate on a more conscious level in their own psychological processes.

The Profile is not harmful to anyone. Self-knowledge may hurt at times, but it also releases energy needed to live a fuller and more creative life.

References

[1]Active imagination is a meditative process, developed by C.G. Jung, of concentrating on fantasy or dream images and permitting a confrontation to occur between the conscious and unconscious, thereby producing a third or centering point in the psyche.

[2]Carl Jung, *The Collected Works of C.G. Jung*, 2nd ed., Vol. 8, *The Structure and Dynamics of the Psyche*, trans. R.F. Hull (Princeton: Princeton University Press, 1969), p. 185.

[3]Carl Jung et al., *Man and His Symbols* (New York: Doubleday, 1964), p. 20.

[4]J.E. Cirlot, *A Dictionary of Symbols*, trans. Jack Sage (New York: Philosophical Library, 1962), p. 126.

[5]Ibid. p. 117.

[6]Carl Jung, *The Collected Works of C.G. Jung*, 2nd ed., Vol. 9 II, *Aion*, trans. R.F. Hull (Princeton: Princeton University Press, 1969), p. 3.

[7]Cirlot, op. cit. p. 125.

[8]Ibid. p. 117.

[9]Ibid.

[10]Ibid. p. 118.

[11]Carl Jung, *The Collected Works of C.G. Jung*, Vol. 9 I, *The Archetypes and the Collective Unconscious*, trans. R.F. Hull (Princeton: Princeton University Press, 1968), p. 304.

[12]Carl Jung, *The Collected Works of C.G. Jung*, Vol. 14, *Mysterium Conjunctionis*, trans. R.F. Hull (Princeton: Princeton University Press, 1963), p. 248.

[13]Carl Jung, *Memories, Dreams, Reflections*, ed. Aniela Jaffé and trans. Richard and Clara Winston (New York: Random House, 1963), p. 394.

[14]Ibid. p. 396.

[15]Cirlot, op. cit. p. 124.

[16]See dictionary definition of compensate and complement.

[17]Carl Jung, *The Structure and Dynamics of the Psyche*, p. 410.

[18]Joseph Epes Brown, ed., *The Sacred Pipe*, (Norman: University of Oklahoma Press, 1970).

[19]Ibid. p. 211.

[20]Ibid.

[21]Ibid. p. 95.

[22]Ibid. p. 96.

[23]Ibid. p. 304.

[24]Cirlot, op. cit. p. 228.

[25]Ibid. p. 353.

[26]Ibid. p. 126.

[27]Carl Jung, *Memories, Dreams, Reflections*, p. 391.

[28]Carl Jung, *The Collected Works of C.G. Jung*, 2nd ed., Vol. 12, *Psychology and Alchemy*, trans. R.F. Hull (Princeton: Princeton University Press, 1970), p. 193.

[29]Ibid.

[30]Cirlot, op. cit. p. 50.

A GOOD KILL

John McMahon

A GOOD KILL

G. P. PUTNAM'S SONS
New York

PUTNAM
— EST. 1838 —

G. P. PUTNAM'S SONS
Publishers Since 1838
An imprint of Penguin Random House LLC
penguinrandomhouse.com

Library of Congress Cataloging-in-Publication Data

Names: McMahon, John, 1970– author.
Title: A good kill / John McMahon.
Description: New York : G. P. Putnam's Sons, 2021. |
Identifiers: LCCN 2021012338 (print) | LCCN 2021012339 (ebook) |
ISBN 9780593328361 (hardcover) | ISBN 9780593328378 (ebook)
Subjects: GSAFD: Mystery fiction.
Classification: LCC PS3613.C5843 G665 2021 (print) |
LCC PS3613.C5843 (ebook) | DDC 813/.6—dc23
LC record available at https://lccn.loc.gov/2021012338
LC ebook record available at https://lccn.loc.gov/2021012339

Printed in the United States of America
1st Printing

BOOK DESIGN BY KATY RIEGEL

This one's for Hank.
We miss you every day.

A GOOD KILL

In times of reflection, I find that my chosen profession isn't one that I'd recommend to others. Homicide is a lonely division in a police department, filled with a particular type of person—as comfortable with the dead as with the living, and often able to suppress their emotions in ways that cannot be healthy.

My partner, Remy Morgan, had arrived at Falls Magnet Middle School about twenty minutes before me and was hunkered down behind one of six patrol cars that littered the school's front lawn.

I grabbed a Remington 870P from a patrolman and ran in a crouched position, the shotgun clasped under my right arm. Dropped behind the black and white where Remy was.

"One gunman," my partner said, catching me up. "Three students and two teachers hostage. One of the teachers is injured. A shot to the gut is what we hear."

I borrowed Remy's binoculars, placing the Bushnell L Series to my face.

"The hostages are in the art room, P.T.," she said. "Back of the building. Far right. All the rest of the staff and students are accounted for. Fifty-nine adults. Three hundred and ninety-four kids."

I scanned the school grounds. To the right of the main building was a rectangular sports field, currently dressed for football and not a soul on it. To the left was a concrete area with two deserted basketball courts and a cluster of orange metal lunch tables.

Backpacks and Coke cans lay abandoned on the ground in the lunch area. Even farther left was the new library, no longer under construction but not yet open. A vinyl banner was strung across the front, announcing the date of an upcoming ribbon-cutting.

"There's something else," Remy said. "Avis Senza may be one of the three girls inside."

I pulled the binoculars down and made eye contact with my partner.

Avis Senza was a budding thirteen-year-old artist who attended the magnet school. She was also the daughter of our boss, Police Chief Dana Senza.

"Bullshit," I said. But Remy's face was dead serious.

My partner wore gray Kevlar over a white blouse and tan pants. The outfit contrasted with her dark brown skin.

"Vest," she said to me, tapping at her own protection.

I grabbed mine. Pulled the straps tight around my chest. "The first report came in at 1:57," Remy said. "A student saw a man in the art room with a gun. The kid did a one-eighty. Pulled the fire alarm and hightailed it."

From there, whispers and texts moved through the school faster than summer lightning. Soon, four hundred kids were racing across the parking lot.

Kids streamed into the nearby forest, Remy explained. Flooded into adjoining neighborhoods.

I turned and reexamined the campus.

Falls Magnet Middle School was only two years old, built on land that locals once called the Sullivan farm. When I was a kid, I'd ridden my dirt bike here with friends—a six-foot-long frog gig duct-taped to the handlebars, the metal pole of the tool sticking up into the air.

Where the main building stood was once a pond that overflowed from Cleric River. Back when I was ten, you could catch two silver perch and a bullfrog here on a good Saturday.

I leaned on the butt of the Remington. "You got an I.D. on the weapon, Rem? So we know what we're up against?"

Remy turned to a patrolman, crouched just the other side of her. My partner had the sharp cheekbones of a fashion model, and her long hair was flat-ironed and cut at an angle at her shoulders. She could be intimidating.

"The students who ran out of the school," she said to the rookie. "You got 'em in a safe area in the parking lot?"

"Maybe half of them, Detective Morgan," he said. "We've been releasing them to parents."

"Find me the boy who saw the gun," Remy said.

The patrolman took off, sprinting out of the area in a crouched position.

My name is P. T. Marsh, and Mason Falls, Georgia, is my town. Lately we top out at around 130,000 souls. So we're not so big that there's more than two Walmarts in town. Then again, we're not so tiny that it won't make national news when a school shooting happens.

In the distance a hundred feet behind us, a white pop-up tent had been erected by patrol. A planning area. Farther back, in the visitor's parking lot, a CNN van was unloading camera equipment, an unfortunate circumstance of being ninety minutes from Atlanta. There was always a CNN van on some highway nearby.

I tapped at the bullhorn by Remy's side, and she explained how she'd tried to make contact with the gunman before I arrived.

"Patrol also called the cell numbers of both teachers held in the school," she said. "No answer."

"And Chief Senza?"

"He's probably twenty minutes out," Remy said. "Protocol is clear, though, P.T. Talk the shooter down. Make sure no one else gets injured or worse."

I took this in, realizing the extra sensitivity with the chief's daughter in play. Still, I'd overseen last year's active shooter training, so I knew the statistics better than anyone else in the department. In seventy percent of these scenarios, the ordeal ends only when the gunman is confronted or killed by police or himself.

"You remember a D.A.R.E. talk we did here last year?" I asked.

Remy shook her head. We'd been partners for a year and a half. Slightly less if you counted the time this summer when she took a three-month shift working in County.

"The kids weren't paying attention," I reminded her. "So the teacher decided to take the class outside?"

"Yeah." Remy nodded. A look of familiarity came to her face.

I motioned over the top of the one-story brick building where the shooter was. "Those pine trees to the right curve around back. There's a maintenance shed, tucked under a hedge of ironwood."

"What are you thinking?" my partner asked.

"I'm gonna circle back there," I said. "See if I can get a different angle on this guy. Maybe climb up on the roof of that shed."

I grabbed the Remington.

"You got your walkie?" Remy asked.

I looked down. It was clipped to my belt. "And my cell in case you want to stay off the radio."

"If you get the shot . . ." Remy said.

"I thought we were trying to talk him down."

"We are," she said. "But if conditions change and you get a good look . . ."

Remy hesitated, her eyes searching mine. "Do you want *me* to go instead?" she asked.

I took off without answering, making a beeline back toward the police tent. When I was almost there, I ducked left into the forested area that ran between the school and State Route 903.

Four months ago, I'd had a guy in the sights of my gun. A killer who'd taken out a dozen innocents. I'd pulled the trigger and missed him. Then missed again. If my partner hadn't been there, I'd be dead now. Hence her question.

I dodged around thick rows of sugar maple, the silver gray bark of the trees five or six feet from each other. Above me, their green and brown flowers hung in clusters.

In the world of policing against an active shooter, there's pre-1999 and post.

Before the '99 shooting at Columbine, the response to shooters at schools was always the same. Talk the gunman down. Call in SWAT. And wait.

Post-Columbine, all the rules changed. Go in hard and fast. And if need be, kill the shooter before he can hurt any kids.

But when a gunman takes hostages, all bets are off and patience is needed. Prayer doesn't hurt either.

I felt sweat building up under the Kevlar, and my walkie chirped. I pressed the button two times to signal Remy that I was all right.

"We just heard something from the media," Remy's voice squawked.

As I glanced back, I saw our SWAT van pulling in beside the E-Z UP. "What've you got?" I asked into the walkie, slowing to a stop and breathing heavy.

"A student talked to CNN. Apparently he saw the car the gunman came out of. A reporter ran the plates."

Jesus, I thought. *We're already playing catch-up to the media?*

"The gunman's name is Jed Harrington," Remy said. "He's thirty-six. A local."

I glanced through branches of wood fern at the parking lot, now far in the distance. In the last four minutes, two other media vans had pulled in, farther away from the school, behind the E-Z UP.

A CNN reporter stood in front of a camera, and I could see cars backing up onto the highway. More parents arriving. Panic setting in.

"Did someone pull his jacket?" I asked. "Any history of violence?"

"He's got no record, P.T.," Remy said. "Stay tuned, and I'll find out more."

Re-clipping the walkie, I hustled for another hundred yards. The forest curved to my left, bending around the shape of the school.

I thought of Avis Senza, who I'd chatted with three or four times at the precinct. A good kid and the only child of my boss. I knew from personal experience what losing a child could do to a man. The hole that Senza might fall into.

I found the small maintenance shed and moved around the back side. Scrambled up onto an air-conditioning unit.

Our SWAT team had a guy named Pierce who'd trained in talking to hostage-takers. If I could be Pierce's eyes, maybe we could end this standoff with no loss of life.

From atop the AC, I pulled myself onto the roof and scooched my six-foot-two-inch frame to the edge, my stomach flat against the surface. Trees from the forest hung overhead, and branches caught my tufty brown hair and scraped along my back.

At a hundred feet, I could see an eight-by-ten window that looked out from the art room onto the back lawn of the school.

I put the binocs to my face, and the art space came in clear.

The room was large, with students' paintings covering every wall. Four black industrial work tables were spread throughout. High tops with stools around them. But no one sat at the stools.

I scanned left and counted. One, two, three students. All girls, twelve or thirteen, in white blouses and blue-and-red plaid skirts. They huddled in one corner; at the front of the group, my boss's daughter. To her right was a brunette in her thirties, the art teacher presumably.

I saw the injured teacher too, but the shot he'd taken wasn't to the stomach. It was to the chest, and his blood had soaked through a pile of white smocks until they were brick red.

He was dead.

The shooter himself was white and stood near the teacher, close to the window.

Six foot tall and midthirties, Jed Harrington had a face the shape of an egg and sunburnt skin. He was handsome in a rugged way and wore a green-checkered flannel, faded jeans, and hiking boots. He looked more like a dad bringing his kid's forgotten permission slip to school.

My cell buzzed, and I slid it close to my ear. I was lying prone, on my stomach, with the shotgun laid out in front of me. I held the binocs with my free hand.

"You're not gonna believe what I can see from here," I said to Remy.

No sound came back at first, so I pulled the phone up and glanced at the screen. The number was blocked.

"Good afternoon, Detective Marsh," a man's voice came back.

A voice I knew.

The man on the other end was the highest-ranking public official in the state of Georgia, a man named Toby Monroe. *Governor* Monroe to folks who saw him on the news or punched his name at the ballot box.

"I assume you're at this scene?" Monroe said. "The one I'm watching on TV?"

"I am."

"Thank God," Monroe said. "Someone I can trust."

But the governor and I didn't have what I'd call a trusting relationship. Ours was one in which favors were traded. And I was in arrears—owing him a big one.

"What do you need?" I asked.

"I'm calling to expedite anything *you* need," he said. "To make sure no children are hurt at that school."

My eyes tracked the gunman, pacing near the window.

I hadn't seen his weapon yet, but the man's left hand was below the sill. *Was he a lefty? Or had he put the weapon down?*

"No children *have* been hurt," I said.

"So let's keep it that way," Monroe replied. "From what I hear-tell, your job in an active shooter situation is to take out the gunman. No questions asked."

The governor's voice could shift from sophisticated to down-home in a flash. A politician's trick.

"Unless the gunman takes hostages," I said.

My walkie clicked, and I told Monroe to hold on. I put the phone aside, on mute.

I depressed the button on the walkie. "This is Marsh."

"I just talked to the kid who was in the art room," Remy said. "The one who saw the weapon."

"Yeah?"

"P.T.," she said, "he told me the guy only had one gun. A .38 Smith & Wesson."

A school shooter with a single weapon ran contrary to every constant that law enforcement knew of these situations. Even stranger, a revolver. A six-shooter.

"Did he see a duffel?" I asked. "Maybe some bag with—"

"Just the .38," Remy said. "But that doesn't mean he's not packing other weapons or explosives."

Exactly, I thought.

"SWAT wants to know what you see," Remy said. "They're gonna run a phone over to this guy. Pierce thinks he can talk him down."

"Is the boss there yet?" I asked.

"Five minutes out," Remy said. "Stuck behind a glut of parents' cars."

I stared at the female teacher, talking to the gunman. She was petite, with light brown hair that fell to her shoulders. The gunman put his hand on her forearm, and she looked down at it. He pulled his hand back.

"Get right back to you," I said, and Remy clicked off.

When I un-muted the phone, Governor Monroe was still there.

"How are the teachers?" he asked.

"One is dead," I said.

"Shit." His response came back.

I used my binoculars to examine the building at the far end of the school grounds. The structure that had just finished construction.

"I read in the *Register* that you're coming here," I said to Monroe. "To dedicate the new library."

"Yes," he said, his voice quieter now.

I scanned the vinyl banner strung across the front of the library, and my eyes stopped on something etched into the stone above the banner. The governor wasn't just speaking at the dedication.

"Your name," I said, sliding over the Remington so I was ready. "It's on the building?"

"That's not why I'm calling," Monroe said.

But it couldn't be good. The Monroe family name on a building after *this*? Whatever *this* was about to become.

"Mason Falls isn't known as a place where schools get shot up," Monroe said. "Those cities become infamous. But you and I can change that, Marsh. In Georgia, we act strong and fast. We protect children."

I stared down the barrel through the sights of the Remington, laid out across the roof. Sap drippings smeared across my forearms.

"What is it you want?" I asked.

"We can't wait until this psycho hurts a child," Monroe said. "Take him out. Now."

"SWAT wants time," I said.

Monroe's voice got gruffer. "For Christ sake, you just said he killed a teacher."

"They're running a phone line," I explained.

"And next they'll form a committee," he said. "Marsh, you owe me one."

I exhaled, my nose making a whistling noise. This was what I'd been dreading since I heard Monroe's voice.

In May, the governor had supplied me with the name and address of a man who I'd been searching for. A man who'd run my wife and son off the road two years ago. Who'd killed them.

In exchange for that information, he told me that he'd call at some point—for a no-questions-asked favor. And I'd agreed.

I stared across at the gunman.

"I'm not gonna *make* you do this," Monroe said, his voice calming again. "But I think every parent in the state would breathe a sigh of relief if you took out that killer."

I hesitated.

I'd read that Monroe was only one point ahead in the polls. One point ahead of an unknown competitor was a narrow margin for an incumbent governor. If a school shooting went bad, he might fall ten points behind.

"Just know that if you pull that trigger," he said, "you and I are square. All debts settled."

The phone went dead then, and I put my cell down. Focused on the art room.

The teacher said something to the gunman, and Harrington shook his head at her—vehemently, from left to right.

He grabbed the teacher by the shoulders then and swiveled her in my direction, staring out the window.

Had the gunman seen me?

I stayed completely still. Found Jed Harrington in the center of the Remington's scope and waited. He held his weapon to the woman's neck, and I confirmed it was a .38.

The gunman moved closer to the window, dragging the art teacher in front of him. He was forty yards away. Fifty at most.

Slowly, I chambered a slug. Found the release lever and pulled back on the action, pumping the gun to the ready.

The teacher wriggled free from the man's grasp, and he let her go. Then he glanced out at the forest, his .38 resting against the glass.

It was a moment of calm. *Was he reflecting on something? Still searching for some movement?*

I'd spent the last decade of my life trying to understand the machinations of the criminal mind. Why they take the risks that others don't. Their carelessness with the things that I hold dear. And the truth was that my understanding hadn't grown deeper. In the end, they just made me doubt the existence of a higher power.

My walkie came alive with Remy's voice.

"P.T.," she said, "phone line's ready to get walked over."

I stared at the gunman, my index finger resting against the trigger and then drifting away. Hesitating. Shaking.

The Remington 870P isn't a long-distance weapon. It's a short-stock shotgun that's great for clearing a house and hard for bad guys to pull out of a cop's hand. Still, when hunting, I've found that a twelve-gauge can be effective to about eighty yards. Twice this distance.

I eyed the red dot on the Remington and found the gunman.

Harrington had killed one teacher already.

And as I watched, he turned back toward the girls and the art teacher, his Smith & Wesson in hand. Held out in their direction.

Over his shoulder I could see my boss's daughter, Avis, at the front of the pack. She put out her hand, palm facing him, as if to say no.

"P.T.," Remy's voice chirped.

I took aim. Inhaled and squeezed.

2

A gunshot rang out. And the three seventh-grade girls who'd bunched together in the corner of the art room shrieked.

"Stay down!" Kelly Borland yelled.

The art teacher dove across the room and landed atop the girls, her arms pulling them into a clump of hair and tears and uniform blouses.

Keep the girls safe, Borland thought. That's your only job right now. Keep them safe.

The room went silent then, and Kelly Borland's eyes found Leaf Tanner. "Mr. T" to the kids. "Beloved" is how the thirty-one-year-old science teacher was often described.

But today, his body lay still against the far wall, his five-foot-ten-inch frame propped up on a pile of painting smocks. The fabric of the smocks was soaked in the same red that coated Tanner's shirt.

Kelly Borland glanced down at her hands. A spatter of blood covered her forearms. Hers? One of the girls?

She looked across the room.

The gunman who had been threatening them was on the ground. His body, motionless.

Kelly stood up. Ran her fingers along her blouse and skirt to confirm she wasn't hurt.

Then she stumbled over to the window.

Something moved outside, and she stared through a hole in the glass.

A snow goose emerged from the trees and lifted its head. Stared at Kelly Borland.

Was the ordeal over? she wondered.

Was it over that fast?

3

"Shooter is down," I hollered. "I repeat. Shooter is down."

The walkie immediately sprung to life.

"Ten-one-oh-one," Remy hollered. Asking my status in a way that the media would be slow to follow if they were listening.

"Ten-one-oh-six," I answered, letting her know I was safe.

I used my binoculars to scan the art room. The female teacher was staring out the window, which now had a hole the size of a peach pit in it.

"Hold your fire," I said. "Three students and one teacher are clear. Imminent danger occurred, and the shooter is down."

"Ten-four," Remy said.

I watched as the teacher pushed at the gunman's body with her high heels. He didn't move, and she glanced at him funny, as if surveying an animal found hit by a truck on the roadside. She motioned for the girls to get up.

A moment later, three SWAT officers dressed in black entered the art room. They moved the teacher and the girls out in a single huddled mass, their guns on the dead man at all times.

I clicked the walkie again. "I discharged," I said. "So I'm gonna wait here for Fuller."

"Copy that," Remy responded.

Cornell Fuller was the single police officer who'd worked every Internal Affairs case in Mason Falls since I was a rookie detective. He'd recently rebranded his "department" as "Force Investigation Unit," or F.I.U., and demanded that we all use that acronym now. Most of us refused.

I sat on the roof for twenty minutes then, waiting for the shakes to leave my body. They didn't.

My phone rang, and it was Remy.

"I just heard what happened from SWAT," she said. "Jesus, P.T."

I recounted how the gunman had grabbed the teacher. "He had a .38 to her neck," I said. "Dragged her to the window."

"Did he see you?"

"I dunno," I said. "The teacher got loose, and he just stood there for a moment. Then he turned and pointed his gun toward the kids. I took the shot."

My partner said nothing, and I watched SWAT move from classroom to classroom, hand-signaling and clearing each area as they searched for additional weapons or explosives.

"I gotta go," I said, noticing movement through the trees ahead. "Fuller is coming."

I hung up, and the head of Internal Affairs appeared through the hedge.

"Detective Marsh," Fuller said.

"Bird," I answered.

People called Fuller "Big Bird" because he has this scruffy patch of wavy blond hair up on the top of his head. He's unusually skinny, and has a good four inches on me.

"The cops I see . . . I see often," Fuller proclaimed in this nasally voice he's got. The sentence was a reference to him having investigated me before. An investigation I was cleared of.

I ignored the remark. Pointed to the back of the shed. "You wanna come up here, or do you want me to come down?"

"I'll come to you," he said.

Fuller scrambled up the same way I did and crouched, the branches all around his shoulders. He took a photograph of me from that angle. Then a wide shot of the whole roof. He lay down prone beside me and shot a photograph of the art room from my vantage point.

"Your weapon," he said, gloving up and collecting it.

"It's Gattling's," I said. Referring to the blue-suiter whose Remington I'd borrowed. "There's a slug still in there." I motioned at the weapon, which I'd reloaded.

Big Bird opened the action and rolled the shotgun over, popping the unused shell from it. He swabbed my hands. "You have binoculars?"

"My partner's," I said. "Not the department's."

He waited, and I produced them. As I did, I thought of the call from Governor Monroe. *If Fuller asked for my cell phone, did I have to oblige?*

"I just want to see what you saw," Fuller said, looking through the binocs. He held on the classroom window for a beat and then handed them back. Bagged the slug from the rooftop and told me to go to the ambulance. Get checked out.

"And don't talk to anyone," he said.

I climbed down from the shed and walked back to the front of the school, threading my way across the playing field this time, instead of through the forest. The ground was artificial turf, and tiny black beads of rubber had come loose from players' cleats digging in and were scattered everywhere.

The adrenaline surged in my system, and the sound of an eastern kingbird chirping in the nearby trees was crisp. My hands shook for what must've been five minutes.

When I got out front, three ambulances were pulled onto the lawn beside the cruisers. I sat on the back lip of one of them, a tech in her twenties running me through a basic exam.

An EMT walked over, a kit in hand to draw blood.

"We can do this here or at the hospital," the guy said. This was standard practice in an officer-involved shooting. My blood would go to toxicology, where they'd examine it for alcohol or drugs. Anything that could've impaired my judgment when I took that shot.

"Here's fine," I said, and let him get started.

Chief Senza walked over during the exam. He had been at a hearing in court and was wearing his formal blues.

"How you feeling, Marsh?"

I would go to psych tomorrow. A new requirement in Mason Falls. Two visits minimum when you discharge a firearm in the line of duty.

"I'm okay," I said.

Senza was white and had the wide chest of an S.E.C. lineman. Which he was, twenty-five years ago at Auburn. He looked a little piqued, a natural response for a man who'd probably imagined the worst about his daughter thirty minutes earlier.

"Fuller said not to talk to anyone," I said.

"Well, I'm not anyone," the chief answered. He motioned at the next bus over. "I just spoke with the art teacher, Miss Borland. She said that one minute Harrington had a gun at her throat. The next moment he turned to shoot the kids and was on the ground."

I nodded at Senza, because this was true, regardless of what Governor Monroe had asked.

The boss stared at me. "How this ended," he said, "with no kids hurt. My family thanks you, Marsh. My ex-wife, who never thanks anyone . . . she already texted to thank you."

Before I could respond, Remy came over, along with the other two detectives who handle homicide in Mason Falls: Abe Kaplan and Merle Berry.

Abe had been my partner before Remy. A no-nonsense cop who was like a brother to me. Merle is Abe's partner: an older, heavyset guy who needed to retire five years ago. Merle wore a gray suit, and his hair was nuclear white around the temples. A handful of cookie crumbs were stuck to his suit jacket.

"You okay, podna?" Abe asked, slipping into the diction of his youth from back home in Louisiana.

I nodded, and Merle hiked up his dress pants with one hand. He glared at the paramedic, who was done with the blood test, holding a stare until the kid walked away.

Abe had been in the same courtroom as the chief and sported a two-piece suit. He was half Black and half Russian Jew and had broad shoulders and curly hair that grew funny in places.

Abe glanced at me, Remy, and Merle. "It might not be the perfect time," he said. "But we're all here, so can we talk about who's covering what? With the amount of interviews to do and 911 calls that students made, we're gonna be stretched pretty thin."

"Good idea," Senza said.

When I got demoted four months ago, Abe took over the job of setting all of our schedules. He determined who caught what cases. And with only four detectives in homicide, we'd be working sixteen-hour days after an event like this one. That would be even harder with me about to go on leave because of the shooting.

"Well," Abe said. "F.I.U.'s not gonna want P.T. working at all right now. But I don't know how we cover this if he doesn't. What's your thoughts, boss?"

I looked to the chief. Surprised that the idea of me going back to work was even a consideration.

"You want time off?" Senza asked me.

I held my right hand down to keep it from shaking. "I can work," I said.

"I was guessing you'd say that," Abe answered.

He motioned around us. "But you can't be walking around here after taking that shot, P.T. So I propose Remy and Merle stay on-site. Interview kids and teachers the next couple days. Go through the art room. Track how this guy navigated the campus."

"And us?" I said to Abe.

"P.T. and I will find out where this Harrington guy came from. What he does for a living. Family. Relatives. Military experience. How and why he got here today."

Abe looked at the four of us and then around at the mess of ambulances and uniforms.

"You need more bodies?" Senza asked him.

"It'd be great to pull one guy from patrol right away," Abe said. "Help round up witnesses."

"What about Gattling?" Remy asked.

Darren Gattling was a patrolman I'd mentored years ago, the one whose shotgun I'd borrowed. He was smart and mature, good with people.

"I'll talk to patrol about him," Senza said. "I'll also get two detectives from robbery to help starting tomorrow." The boss looked at me and Remy. "But you two are in charge of all the additionals. Abe's got enough on his plate."

Cornell Fuller arrived, and all conversation stopped.

He stared at me, frustrated that I wasn't sitting by myself.

"Staffing discussion," Abe said by way of explanation.

Fuller turned to Senza, incredulous.

"Chief," Fuller said, "you're not thinking of having Marsh work right now, are you? He just killed a man. He should be on paid administrative leave."

Senza glared at Big Bird. "He didn't kill a man, Fuller. He killed a killer."

"Chief," Fuller pleaded.

"We got *this* shooting, Fuller. And two straggler cases. And I got four detectives in homicide. So if you got budget for another man burning a hole in your pocket—please, let me know."

Big Bird looked stumped, and the chief looked from him to me.

"I gotta talk to the media in fifteen minutes," Senza said. He pointed at me and Bird. "I advise that you two chat fast—and then P.T. leaves with Abe."

Fuller nodded begrudgingly, and Abe said he'd wait for me in the car.

I walked with Big Bird around to the window outside the back lawn, where I studied the hole the bullet made.

Through the glass I also saw Harrington, in a pool of blood on the floor inside. Ten feet from him was the teacher, Leaf Tanner, and no one was touching either body until the M.E. got here.

But a smart uniform had taken a pile of clean art smocks and made a dam of white fabric between the two men, so their blood didn't comingle, in case the room's elevation was off.

"Jesus," I said.

"Yeah," Bird agreed.

He gave me an appointment to talk to a shrink first thing the next morning and went back over the details again. What time I got to the school. What made me hike around the back. And why I took the shot.

He told me a shooting board would convene within a week. To confirm if it was a good kill.

"The rule about you not working," Fuller said to me. "It's not to jam you up, P.T. It's to give you time to process. To heal."

At another time or from another person, I might've appreciated this. Might've nodded in understanding or even taken time off voluntarily.

But nine months ago, Fuller had sat at my bedside and accused me of being a dirty cop. He told me I was gonna rot in jail.

"Go to hell, Bird," I said.

4

The sun was going down, and the sweet smell of lilacs from the nearby forest was strong in the air.

Abe had an address on a piece of property that our shooter, Jed Harrington, owned in the foothills south of town. He'd gotten a patrolman at the station to write up an affidavit, and it had been hand-carried to a judge.

When I got into Abe's SUV, he showed me the signed warrant on the screen of an iPad.

Abe had always been old-school. White lined legal pads. Yellow number-two pencils.

"When the hell did this happen?" I motioned at the tablet. "You caught up with 2010 technology?"

Abe rolled his eyes. "Yeah, I guess it must've been during one of your suspensions."

I grinned at him. Touché.

We headed out then, moving slowly around a gaggle of media vans and black and whites, spread throughout the school's overflow parking lot. The place was a zoo, and it was good to put it in our rear-view mirror, at least for the night.

Out on 903, traffic was light. We drove through a rural area called Ridge Creek, where my best friend had lived when I was a teenager. I stared over at a Dollar General we'd rode our bikes to every week to buy junk food. In Mason Falls, we have all the dollar brands. Dollar General. Dollar Store. Dollar Tree.

As we got closer to Harrington's house, the conversation shifted to me and Remy.

We'd been a team for eighteen months, but circumstances and a suspension had split us apart. Then last week, I got off desk duty and Remy finished up her time with County and transferred back to homicide.

"Out of the furnace and into the fire," Abe said. "You and Rem ready?"

"Like riding a bike," I said.

We pulled into Harrington's neighborhood, and media vans clogged the residential street. I flicked on the portable police light that Abe kept on the dash of his old Lexus.

"Obviously you're not the only one who knows this guy's address, Kaplan," I said.

Abe laid on the horn, and the folks in the street separated, revealing two squad cars trying to handle crowd control.

I'm always surprised with the atmosphere after a shooting. Concern and panic fade when a bad man with a gun is taken down, and the succeeding hours are often filled with a sense of morbid jubilation. "Circus-like" is how Remy once described the mood.

We pulled into the driveway at 2944 Bluehaven and got out. Badged a couple journalists who were set up on Harrington's lawn. The news guys acted giddy and pointed at the house like bookies examining a horse.

I pointed at their camera gear. "On the sidewalk or the parkway, guys," I said. "Otherwise, I gotta get patrol to arrest you. Impound your equipment."

Abe had found a house key in the gunman's pocket at the school, and patrol had already cleared the home.

"How about a comment on the shooting, Marsh?" a reporter named Raymond Kirios from the *Mason Falls Register* asked. I ignored him, and Abe closed the front door behind us.

Inside the house, Abe flicked on the lights. The noise of the media was muffled, and Abe and I pulled our Glocks, just to be sure.

"Police," I announced, always double-checking in a situation like this. "Anyone home?"

No response.

We stood in a tiled entryway. A few lights on inside. We'd been told Harrington was single and lived alone, and patrol had verified this with a neighbor before going room to room ten minutes ago.

To our left was a hallway that led to the bedrooms. Off to our right, we could see into the living room and kitchen, which were both empty.

The house was a two-bedroom ranch style. The first room faced onto the front lawn and was the master. A simple bedroom. Nothing on the dresser except for a digital clock and a black cradle for an iPhone. A set of golf clubs leaned against one corner, and the bed was unmade.

The second room was the spare, and the walls were lined in an old-timey wallpaper. In the closet, we saw women's clothes. Two or three outfits in a small size. Two casual skirts and a blouse. Nothing else.

I flicked the label on one of the skirts and saw the words "Rebecca Taylor." I wasn't a fashion snob, but could guess they each fell in the range of three to four hundred dollars. Someone hip, with good taste, but not loaded.

Did Harrington have a girlfriend? A female roommate?

We heard a noise and moved through the living room toward the back of the house. Through a sliding door, I saw a dog scratching at the glass. He was a mixed breed. Part retriever and part husky. Maybe thirty-five pounds. Tan with a white stripe circling his neck.

I opened the door a few inches. The dog whined and wagged his tail. He had white paws and a smear of white on his nose. "What's your name, bud?" I asked.

I couldn't let the animal inside the scene, so I stepped outside. Leaned over and checked his I.D.

Beau, a bone-shaped metal tag read, along with a phone number.

Standing up, I noticed a backhouse behind the place. The sun had fallen, and the evening was getting chilly. A light was on inside the small structure, and the door was left ajar. I wondered if patrol had cleared the casita.

"Abe," I hollered, and moved toward it. The dog followed me, and I kept my Glock out.

"Mason Falls Police," I announced. Wandering across a wide square of dirt and crabgrass.

"On your six," Abe said, coming up behind me.

I pushed open the door with my dress shoe, scanning the place with my Glock. It was empty, but a TV had been left on, the volume muted. The place was small, but enough space for one person. That is, if you removed the fifty banker's boxes that were piled in the middle of the room.

"There's an episode of *Hoarders* waiting for their next location scout," Abe said.

I stepped around the boxes, which were stacked in layers, three high. The room sported a pullout couch, an oak rolltop desk, and an upright wooden gun rack with five weapons behind a glass door.

On the local Fox channel, the news played.

Governor Toby Monroe yapped away, his face pained—a look that he'd probably practiced in front of a mirror. I saw a shot of Falls Magnet Middle School and tapped up the volume so I could hear what Monroe said.

"And although we mourn the loss of a great educator," the governor said, "we are fortunate to have policemen like Detective P. T. Marsh. He saw this madman almost kill three young girls and did his job to keep them safe."

I glanced at Abe. It wasn't good public policy to call out a cop by name. Especially the day of.

"Did you hear that?" I squinted.

"Your buddy." Abe shook his head. "Still has a man crush on you."

Abe knew about some of my past interactions with Monroe over the last two years.

But he didn't know about the incident in May, when I'd asked the governor to use his influence to help find the address of the man who killed my family. No one except Monroe and I knew about that.

The TV displayed a picture of me. A photo from five years ago. I stood outside the court building on 5th Street in slacks and a tweed jacket with patches on the elbows.

"You look good," Abe said. "Young. Ripped." He patted my stomach. "What happened?"

I flicked off the TV and walked over to the gun case. Through the glass we could see two Rugers, one AR-15, and two pistols.

"You got those keys still?" I asked.

Abe moved through Harrington's key ring, getting to the right one.

He unlocked the case, and I reminded Abe that with a school shooting, the Feds would be called in. And that maybe we should wait on going through the weapons.

"Why don't we send a picture to Senza," I said. "Find out who he's already contacted."

We texted the boss. Then we decided that Abe would inspect the bedrooms while I went through the common areas in the house and the room back here in the yard.

Our goal was simple.

The killer was dead already, and there'd be no trial. But school shootings fall into a category that requires meaning. The question of "why" was still unanswered.

Did Jed Harrington have some beef with the school?

Or was it with this science teacher, Leaf Tanner, and the school was simply the location for their standoff?

Abe and I walked back to the house, and I started in the kitchen.

I examined the pantry cabinets, moving my gloved fingers around cans of chili and spaghetti sauce and canisters of Pringles.

As I moved into the living area, I found no notes of any plan Harrington had to enter the middle school. No diagrams or pictures of the school. A handful of magazines covered the coffee table, and the bookcase held fiction hardbacks: the latest from B. J. Graf and Karen Dionne.

Before I moved to the backhouse, Abe poked his head in.

"Anything?"

"So far, zilch," I said. "You?"

He shook his head. "No pictures of middle school kids. No relatives or family that appear to go to Falls Magnet."

I had been away from my phone, and I saw Abe's iPad set up on the dresser in the bedroom. "Did Remy or Merle send us something?"

"Yeah." Abe nodded, grabbing the tablet. "You wanna hear?"

"Absolutely."

"The gunman's full name is Jedidiah William Harrington," he read. "Grew up in Macon. Went to high school there. After that, got a degree in journalism."

"From where?"

"Tulane," Abe said. "He worked in Atlanta at the *AJC*. Then made a leap to *The Washington Post*."

"Impressive."

"They embedded him," Abe continued. "On and off for four years with the troops in Afghanistan."

"Four years is a lot," I said. "I had a friend who was embedded. After twelve months he couldn't take it. He started seeing ghosts, you know?"

"How do you mean?"

"The faces of dead people," I said. "But on those around him. Strangers in the street. Except their faces were changed."

Abe took this in, nodding.

"Where was Harrington working lately?" I asked.

"He wasn't," Abe said. "Unemployed, last two years."

Abe scrolled down through other notes. "Guy's never been married. Co-owns the house with his sister, Maryanne."

I thought of the clothes in the spare bedroom. "Those are her things?" I asked. "In the closet?"

"Figured so," Abe said. "I went onto Facebook. She's petite, and the dresses were all smalls. Merle's contacted her. She lives in Oklahoma and is flying in tomorrow."

Abe put down his iPad. He had defined cheekbones that sat high on his face, and each one was home to six or seven tiny red freckles. Back when we were partners, I once heard a call girl compliment him on those cheeks. In fact, she offered her services for free. Which my partner turned down, at least in front of me. Maybe he circled back later.

"All right," I said. "I'm headed out back. You need anything, shout."

I walked into the backyard, where Beau, the dog, was waiting for me. He had one blue eye and one brown.

Over the top of the one-story house, I could see the lights of news cameras and hear the murmur of reporters, still out front.

Standing at the threshold of the casita, I stared in at the four dozen banker's boxes in the middle of the room. I wondered if Harrington did his research and writing out here.

I started at his desk first, sitting down and pulling open each drawer.

In the top one, I found an old-style Rolodex, with individual index cards, loosely attached on a center spindle. I pulled one card out and stared at the chicken scratches on it. The writing was a combination of numbers and letters. Some code probably used to hide the names of Harrington's sources. A reporter's system, old-school and secret.

I continued flipping through them.

Not every card was like this. On one I found his sister's name, Maryanne Harrington Liggins, along with various phone numbers, some of them crossed out over the years. The index card was sun-faded, and I wasn't even sure if this was a recent system Harrington was using.

I moved to the second drawer and found a molded ceramic picture frame made of two letter *B*'s at the bottom and a big square at the top. The glass inside the frame had been cracked, but underneath was a picture of Jed Harrington, along with his dog, Beau.

In the picture, Harrington donned a Tulane T-shirt and overalls and leaned on a long Ruger. I recognized June Lake in the background.

I wondered who took the photo. Who went hunting or camping with Beau and Jed? Was it his sister? Would she be able to tell us what set her brother off?

In my experience, the families of criminals are often as confused as the rest of us as to the evolution of their criminal sons or daughters. A mother sees her kid's life in flashes: her son as an infant, crawling on a rug. Then a boy in third grade, excited to go to school. And suddenly a nineteen-year-old, held without bail for killing his best friend over twenty dollars.

I took more items out of the drawers. Pads of paper and pens and little tchotchkes collected over the years. None of them led to any connection between Harrington and the school. No reason for him to be at Falls Magnet.

I moved to the boxes next, which were full of file folders that corresponded to various stories that Harrington had written over the years. They ranged from research on corruption to drug trafficking to pieces he'd written about soldiers' lives, adjusting after a return from the Middle East.

I thought of the teacher who'd died, and I texted Remy to find out if Harrington and Tanner knew each other. The answer came back fast:

> No evidence to show that. And no one in the school
> recognizes Harrington.

After working my way through the grouping of boxes on the right, I inspected the left dozen, closest to the door. Each had the same initials on the box tops: *G.U.*

Those boxes were all empty. No manila file folders in them. No papers at all.

I walked over to the Rolodex and looked through the *G*'s.

An index card read *G.U.* in the upper corner, written in red Sharpie. But there were no other markings on the card, other than a chicken scratch of two paw marks.

I glanced at all the file boxes, now spread throughout the room. Among all the investigative pieces Harrington had done, I'd found no articles about corruption at any school board. Nothing about science education to tie him to the dead science teacher.

I heard a noise and stepped into the yard.

The dawn smelled like night-blooming jasmine, and the cobalt sky showed pops of yellow. It always shocks me how much time passes at a crime scene. Now, at almost six a.m., a familiar face was coming toward me.

Mandelle Clearson was an Atlanta PD detective who I knew from two previous cases.

In the first one, I'd helped him find a murder suspect who was hiding in Mason Falls, thinking the area was too rural for APD to chase him. Then earlier this spring, Mandelle had returned the favor and helped me with a case down in Little Five Points, his home precinct.

"Mandelle," I said as he approached. He was nearabout fifty and my build, with salt-and-pepper hair. "What are you doing here?"

Mandelle explained that he was one of a dozen detectives in Atlanta who was a liaison for the ATF, the Bureau of Alcohol, Tobacco, Firearms and Explosives, a division of the Justice Department.

"When a high-profile case involving a gun comes up," he said, "they cover my O.T. and send me around the state."

"So you heard the shooting was in Mason Falls?" I asked.

"I did." Mandelle nodded. "Figured you'd appreciate a friendly doing the gun trace."

"Absolutely," I said.

Mandelle told me he'd just come from my precinct, where he'd inspected the .38 that Harrington had used to kill Leaf Tanner. Now Chief Senza had sent him here, to go through the rest of the reporter's armory.

I showed Mandelle the gun case, and he explained that once he had the serial numbers, he'd work with ATF staff in Martinsburg, West Virginia. They'd liaise with the gun manufacturer, who'd supply the store or distributor who peddled the weapon.

"From there, everything is old-school," Mandelle said. "On a piece of paper in the gun store. The 4473."

"What's the timing on a trace like that?" I asked. "Start to finish?"

"Normally two weeks," Mandelle said, laying the guns atop the white banker's boxes as he spoke. "But in a school shooting, we'll have results back in twenty-four hours."

My phone pulsed.

Staring at the screen, I saw a group text to Remy, Abe, Merle, and me. The sender was Chief Senza, and it demanded that we all be at the precinct in an hour.

"Looks like you guys got lucky, though," Mandelle said.

"How's that?" I asked.

"With this stockpile." He motioned in particular at the AR-15. "If he'd brought any two of these to that school, a lot more people could've been hurt. Kids. Teachers. Cops."

"Yeah," I said.

Which made me wonder: *Why hadn't Harrington armed himself better?*

I told Mandelle I had to get in to work, and grabbed a blue-suiter from out front to sit on the backhouse. Make sure no journalist snuck over a fence and started snapping photos.

Before I left, I walked back into the casita. Mandelle was jotting down serial numbers. "That twenty-four hours on the gun trace," I said to him. "Any way you can make it twelve?"

"I'll do my best," he said, and I nodded in thanks, dialing up Remy as I walked back outside.

An electric line ran across the yard and fed power to the backhouse. A red-tailed hawk sat on the cable, sagging the middle of it and staring at me.

My partner picked up on the first ring, and I could tell that she was driving. "I saw the text," she said. "Just running home for a quick shower."

I'd been up for twenty-three hours straight and was pretty ripe myself.

"Listen, there's a dog here, Rem," I said. "Real nice pup. With your work in County with animals—anyone you could call to pick him up?"

My partner had spent the last ninety days as a humane enforcement officer working in a temporary division that was formed after a dog-fighting scandal broke in May.

"I could ring up one of my buddies," she said. "But the place is overcrowded, P.T. Odds are, the dog's gonna be euthanized within a couple days."

"See what you can do?" I asked, and she agreed.

I filled up a water bowl, grabbed food for the dog, and found Abe inside. He dropped me at my house, and I walked right into a freezing-cold shower.

No rest for the weary.

No sleep when there's a crime to be solved.

5

I got to the precinct by seven forty-five a.m. and grabbed a coffee
from the kitchen, heading into the main conference room before
anyone else showed.

Someone had left a pink box of donuts there, and I flipped the top
open. Two crullers and a jelly. The sugar had crystalized, signaling
they were yesterday's leftovers.

Out the window, the sky was blue and windswept, but the banana
palms in the grassy area outside were like statues, so the wind must've
died overnight.

Remy came in, dressed in black pants and a yellow blouse, her
Glock in a shoulder holster under her jacket. Lately my partner had
begun wearing contacts, but since she'd been up all night, she sported
her old glasses, black-framed numbers that made her look bookish.

Abe and Senza rolled in at the same time. The chief explained that
he'd blocked off one hour, after which he would have a call with Mayor
Stems, who wanted to know exactly where we stood.

"To start." Senza looked down at his notebook. "I asked Merle and
Remy to build out a timeline last night—from the moment Harrington
first showed up at the school. Then let's hear about his background, his

family, and the weapon. In forty-eight hours, the GBI's gonna take possession of this case," Senza said, referring to the Georgia Bureau of Investigation. "So let's get to the bottom and fast."

Merle Berry rolled in late and got a look from the chief. He grabbed a jelly donut with a square white napkin, and the grease stained through the paper before he could take his first bite.

"I'll start with an update on the school," the chief said. "Falls Magnet is temporarily closed. We got the area cordoned off and a cruiser outside. So if you got a lead and need to be there, coordinate with Gattling and he'll liaise with patrol."

"'Til when?" I asked.

"Right now the mayor's working that out with the school board," the chief said. "They're probably gonna reopen in ten days. They're bringing in counselors. Planning a prayer service. An assembly."

I shook my head. I couldn't believe this was happening in Mason Falls. But at the same time, it could've been worse. Much worse.

"When the school reopens, we'll be staffing two SROs," Senza said. "Those are school resource officers. Essentially rookie patrolmen to oversee the new metal detectors in the morning and function as security during the day."

"How long does that go for?" Remy asked.

"Throughout the school year at least," Senza said. "The real end date depends on what we find out about Harrington. If people understand why he did this . . ."

The chief's voice faded, but we all got it. This crime was over. But the chief wanted a motive. And not just him. The community needed it too. A reason Jed Harrington came to Falls Magnet Middle School with a gun.

Senza looked to Remy and Merle. "You two ready?"

Remy plugged her laptop into an outlet, and an image flickered onto the conference room TV. A yearbook photo of a pasty-looking kid. Maybe eleven, with black hair and freckles.

"At 1:44 p.m., Gavin Kinsey came onto campus," Remy said. "Gavin's a sixth grader, and was coming to school late from a dentist appointment."

"His mom or dad drove him?" Abe asked.

"Neither." Remy shook her head. "Mom dropped him off at the dentist, but then went to work. She set up one of those Uber services for kids. They brought him to school."

Merle jumped in. "We've all seen the one road leading in and out of campus. Gavin noticed a car behind the one he was being driven in. It was a Dodge Magnum station wagon. Black. This is the first reported moment that Jed Harrington is on campus."

"Did we talk to the Uber driver?" Abe asked.

"Yeah, but she doesn't remember a thing," Merle said. "Dropped the kid off and moved on to her next ticket."

Merle looked to Remy, who clicked forward to a shot of Harrington's station wagon, parked at the middle school.

"Next moment we're aware of," Remy said. "Harrington exits his car." She pointed at the screen, where an overhead map of the campus was projected. A red X appeared over the parking lot, and my partner walked over. Touched the TV.

"He parked here," she said. "He's now on campus for three minutes. It's 1:47."

"A mom who volunteers at the school passed Harrington," Merle said, and Remy pointed at a second X.

"He crossed the parking lot from here to there." She motioned from west to east.

"How's Harrington acting?" I asked.

"From Mom's memory—normal," Merle said. He glanced down at

a jelly stain on his shirtsleeve, clearly not sure when it had left the do-nut and arrived on his cuff. "Mom didn't think anything of it 'til his picture hit the news," Merle continued.

"How was he concealing the weapon?" Abe asked.

This was a good question. A .38 Special was a revolver with a bulky profile. Tough to hide.

"The mom saw no weapon," Merle said. "So we reckon it was shoved in his waistband or at his back. Harrington was wearing an untucked flannel."

I looked at Remy and Merle's diagram. Harrington had parked fairly close to the art class and was moving directly toward it. "Looks like he knows where he's going."

"Merle and I thought the same thing," Remy said without adding another word.

This was the approach I'd taught her. When you're building a timeline, your job is to itemize the facts. It's everyone else's job to theorize.

"When's he spotted next?" the chief asked, moving things along.

"That's where accounts vary depending on who you talk to," Remy said. "But let's walk through the most likely scenario."

"Around this time, a class ends if you're in seventh or eighth grade," Merle said. "It's 1:50 p.m. The bell rings. Students move around. Harrington's now been on campus for six minutes, and no gun has been pulled, from what we know. He's just another adult walking."

Remy clicked on her computer, and a picture of a room came up. "This is a storage room attached to the art room," she said. "It's got a kiln. Some sort of small printing press. A cordless sander."

"Minor power tools," Merle said. "Stuff the kids need adult super-vision to work with."

Remy clicked again, and beside the same picture appeared a hand-drawn overhead diagram, showing two doors entering this storage area.

"There's two ways into this storage room," she said. "One is through an outdoor courtyard not far from the teacher's lounge. That's a locked door that only teachers have access to. The other is through the art room itself."

We all nodded, waiting for Remy and Merle to explain why their focus had shifted to this storage area.

"Leaf Tanner was shot in this area," Remy said. "There's blood spatter on the east wall."

Remy touched the TV again. "So it looks like he was shot near the door that led in from the courtyard. Then he stumbled across the storage area and into the main art room, where P.T. first saw his body."

"So we're assuming what?" I asked. "The science teacher came into the storage area from the courtyard?"

"Hold that thought," Merle said. "We're going chronological. We'll get back there."

Remy clicked forward, and another kid's photo came up. Olive skin. Teenager, but a big frame. Could pass for eighteen as easy as fifteen.

"Falls Magnet has a zero period early in the morning," Remy said. "So if you're an eighth grader and you go to that, you end up with a free period from two to three p.m. at the end of the day. Meet Easton Pappas."

"Easton goes to this zero period in the morning," Merle said. "Which leaves the time between two and three p.m. as his free period. Like a couple other kids, he goes to the art room during that time."

"Kids paint in there," Remy said. "Or sculpt. Whittle wood. There's no class in there between two and three."

I studied the diagram as Remy continued.

"Now it's 1:54," she said. "Harrington's been on campus ten minutes, and here's our next account of him. This Easton kid opens the door from the hallway to enter the art class. He looks across the art room and into the attached storage area. Sees Jed Harrington holding a .38 and Leaf Tanner on the ground. Already shot."

Abe raised his hand. "Wait—Easton opens the door from the courtyard into the storage room? I thought only teachers could do that."

"No," Remy said. She walked us through her diagram again, explaining that there were two ways into the art room. The first was in from the hallway. This is how students got to class. The other was through the storage room.

"This Easton kid opened the door from the hallway," Remy said. "The main way kids go in for class."

"And what happened next?" Abe asked.

"Easton sees a couple girls working on their canvases. But he also sees *through* the art room and *into* the attached storage area. He sees Harrington with the gun. Standing over Leaf Tanner."

"What's Easton's reaction?" I asked.

"He lets go of the door and splits," Merle said. "He's the same kid who pulls the fire alarm a minute later."

"The three girls who got taken hostage," Abe said. "How come they don't see what this kid Easton sees? How come they don't hear the gunshot?"

"They've got earbuds in," Merle said.

"One of them had an early bootleg of the new Zac Brown album," Remy explained. "They're all plugged into the same phone and the volume is cranked while they paint."

"And Easton's got a vantage point that the girls don't have," Merle added. "A straight view into the storage area from the hallway door."

Remy clicked back to her overhead drawing of the art room and how it was laid out, relative to the storage area. The table that the girls sat at was tucked around a corner, out of sight.

"Sure," I said. "But those girls must've come into the room at some point, just like Easton did. How come they didn't see Harrington when they entered?"

Remy nodded, seeing where I was going. "Yeah, so those girls were already inside, P.T. They had art class the period before, from one to two. So they've been in their same seats for almost an hour. Continuing on with their projects, heads down, and listening to music while they paint. It's their free period too."

"So Easton opens the door," Abe said. "Freaks outs and closes it. Runs the other way. Leaving the girls inside, who can't see what he's seen?"

"Or even hear," Merle said.

"What happens next?" the chief asked.

"Leaf Tanner gets up. Braces himself against the wall here." Remy motioned at her diagram. "He backs into the classroom. The girls see Tanner stagger out, bleeding. Harrington with the gun. The art teacher shrieking."

"Tanner gets to where the smocks are hung," Merle said. "Grabs them and collapses onto the floor."

Abe and I nodded then, understanding the sequence now.

This was where I'd picked up things, from my vantage point atop the maintenance shed. By this point, it was about an hour later, and Leaf Tanner had bled out onto the smocks.

"The thing we're not clear on," Merle said, "is how Harrington got *into* the storage area in the first place. None of the students saw him enter through the hallway door where Easton came in. Which means Harrington must've come in through the courtyard door. But that should've been locked."

"You talk to the art teacher?" Abe asked. "What's her name?"

"Kelly Borland," Merle said, grabbing at his belt to hike up his slacks. "She's a wreck. Can't remember half this shit. She saw the gunman standing near Tanner. The rest is in pieces."

"In pieces how?" I asked.

"Big holes of time she can't recall," Remy said. "She remembers trying to talk Harrington down. The girls screaming. Then she heard the shot, and he's dead."

"She ever seen Jed Harrington before?"

"No," Remy answered.

We all went quiet for a moment, processing the details.

"So we're figuring that the two men both came into the storage area from the exterior door that led in from the courtyard?" I asked.

"Check," Merle said. His face had grown puffier in the last year in that way that you see in guys in their fifties. Their necks expand to the maximum PSI, and the excess air moves to the cheeks.

"Do all teachers have a master key to that door?" Abe asked.

"They do," Remy said.

"So Harrington comes onto campus," I said. "He spots a random teacher he doesn't know. Forces him to open a random door. And shoots him. Is that likely?"

"It's what the facts bear out," Merle said.

This would scare the hell out of me if I was a parent or a school administrator. Because it meant that there was no reason this happened. A crazy man wandered onto a school campus. Shot the first man he saw. And now I understood why Mayor Stems and Chief Senza were so concerned.

"What was the science teacher doing near the art storage room anyway?" Abe asked.

"We don't know," Remy said. "Tanner had a free period at the same time."

"Were the art teacher and the science teacher friends?" I asked.

"According to her, yes," Remy said.

"Were they more than friends?" Abe asked.

"The two weren't seeing each other," Merle said. "We asked students, teachers, close friends."

The chief shifted in his seat, and Merle looked to Remy, who clicked forward.

A picture of Leaf Tanner's body came up. Not at the scene, but in the medical examiner's office. Tanner's chest was muscular and pale, laid out atop a steel gurney. He had a black goatee, and the same color hair, thick like a bath mat, on his chest.

"You want to talk forensics?" Merle looked over.

Abe stood up. "Sarah Raines is going to issue a report in an hour," he said, referring to the medical examiner. "But there's not much we don't know from observation. C.O.D. is arterial bleeding from ballistic trauma. GSW with a .38 Smith & Wesson."

I reported what we knew of the weapon. As I spoke, Remy clicked forward to a picture of the .38 Special, laid out on the ground in the art room where Harrington had gone down.

"Atlanta PD is working with ATF," I said. "We already have confirmation that the .38 is Harrington's weapon. Within the day we'll know when and where he bought it. Also about his other guns."

"Ballistics come in yet?" Abe asked.

"A half hour ago," I said. "One bullet was fired. Five still in the gun, 158-grain lead round-nose. American Eagle brand."

"And no other ammo with him?" the chief asked.

"Nope," Merle said.

"What about his car?" the chief asked.

"We're towing Harrington's Dodge Magnum into the mod yard now," Abe answered.

The mechanical mod yard was the place where MFPD patrolmen brought their black and whites to get fixed or upgraded. It also served as an investigative area for crimes involving a vehicle.

"We left the car at the school yesterday to have the bomb squad inspect it," Merle said. "They gave us the okay to move it this morning, so we took it over to Carlos at six a.m. We'll see if there's anything relevant inside."

The chief ran a hand along his tie, tightening it at the knot. "What haven't we touched on yet?"

"Harrington's got a sister," Merle said. "Maryanne Liggins is her married name. Lives in Oklahoma and is arriving today. P.T. and Abe saw her clothes in the house, but it was only a handful of things. Harrington lived there by himself."

"Any open interviews we didn't get to?" the chief asked.

"Leaf Tanner was married," Remy said. "His widow is coming in today. Also the oldest girl among the three hostages. An eighth grader named Allie D'Antone. Her parents didn't want her talking to us yesterday. She's agreed to come in now."

"I talked the family into that," Senza said. "Allie's a good girl and a friend of Avis. Her parents were just scared yesterday."

"We still need to go through police transmissions and 911 calls," Remy said. "There were forty-one calls made by students as they ran out. We got through twenty-six so far."

The conference room went quiet then, and Senza stood up. Exhaled loudly.

"Well, not that everyone isn't hustling," he said. "But all this hasn't told us a goddamn thing about why. *Why* was Harrington at the school? He had to have *some reason* to do this. The state's gonna take this over in forty-eight hours. The Feds will be involved too. It'd be great if we didn't look like a bunch of local yokels."

Senza looked to me and Abe. "Did you tear his place apart?"

"To the studs," I said. "Not a scrap of anything to indicate he was headed to this school. Or knew anyone at it."

"Is he on social media?"

"Nope," Abe said. "I heard from those two detectives from robbery an hour ago. I sent 'em out to Harrington's place to go through it again. The guy had fifty banker's boxes full of notes and articles he wrote. I'd like to spend some time digging through his writing."

"Good." Senza pointed. "He's a journalist. Out of work. Let's find out if he's got a manifesto sitting around."

Senza tapped at the table. "Someone knows this lunatic, guys," he said. "Someone's his buddy. His boyfriend. His girlfriend. Find them. Find out what beef he had with the school or with this science teacher."

The chief swiveled his gaze. "He's part of the friggin' media, Merle. They love taking down one of their own—almost as much as they love taking down cops. Did you reach out to any places he'd worked?"

"Initial calls," Merle said. "He wrote for the *AJC* years ago. I'm supposed to hear back from them this morning."

There was a lot we hadn't gotten to yet, with just the four of us on the case since three p.m. yesterday.

"Find me something I can tell the mayor," Senza said. "You and you." He pointed at me and Remy. "Pair together again. Same with you and Merle," he said to Abe. "Partners have shorthand. Instinct. I need something and fast. Go."

We all hurried out. We knew a lot, sure, but the chief was right.

When it came to what quelled the public's anxieties and fears, to what answered the question of "why the hell did he do it" . . . we didn't know a damn thing.

6

The man paced the art room.

In his left hand was a .38, so his right hand was free to smack at the right side of his head.

"Stupid, stupid, stupid," he said.

About eight feet away, in the northeast corner of the room, three girls in plaid uniform skirts and white blouses sobbed violently.

"Why did I come here?" he muttered, shaking his head. "If it's gone, it's gone."

"Why don't you put down the gun," the teacher said, her voice low and calm.

The man stopped pacing. "Don't you tell me what to do."

He put his free hand on her arm, and she froze. Looked down. He removed it.

The gunman's head whipped around then, glancing out the window. "Did you see that?"

The female teacher squinted. Took a step toward the window.

"Something moved," he said. "Out by the tree line."

"Nothing moved," she promised.

But he grabbed the teacher, pulling her body in front of his. As he held her, the forest was still.

"Get off of me." She broke free of the man.

The girls started sobbing again, and their cries echoed through the room.

"Shut! Up!" the gunman screamed at the girls.

The teacher turned. Took a step toward her three most promising art students.

"Let's stay nice and quiet," she said to them, her voice suddenly soft and smooth. "We'll get through this, but we need to be calm, okay?"

The girls stopped whimpering. One even managed a nod at Miss Borland.

Then the man turned to face them, his gun in hand.

That's when they heard a cracking noise.

A single pop, like thunder.

7

Abe and I met in my office after Chief Senza left. We carved out what he and Merle would focus on and what Remy and I would pursue. We set a time in the afternoon for the four of us to regroup.

Then Remy marched in with her laptop and two coffees, and it felt like old times. The band before the breakup.

"All right," I said. "We got the weapon, the car, and the dead teacher's wife. That's our morning."

I made some calls to Mandelle Clearson at Atlanta PD, and Remy walked over to meet with Carlos Esqueveda, who ran the mod bay where Harrington's Dodge Magnum had been towed.

Thirty minutes later I'd confirmed that Jed Harrington had bought the .38 three years ago at a place called Ammo and Mercantile, about a mile north of the Mason Falls city limits.

I knew that Mandelle would be speaking to the gun store directly, so I walked down to the precinct lobby. I wanted to run over to the mod garage and see Harrington's car for at least a few minutes while Remy was still there.

As I hurried toward the lobby exit, Hope Duffy hailed me. Hope was the sergeant who managed the intake desk, and the area was full of gift baskets, wrapped in colored cellophane.

"You wanna tell me what to do with all these?" she asked.

I glanced at the pile. Hope was blond and late forties, with the body of a volleyball player. "Most of them are from middle school parents and addressed to you," she said.

It felt morbid to accept a gift for taking a man's life, even if it saved the lives of students.

"I dunno," I said. "Patrolmen's families, maybe? You know who's crushing it on the day shift. Why don't you give them out to your favorite cops."

"Will do, Detective," Hope said, and I moved past the pile and into the crisp September air.

The mechanical mod yard was located around the back side of the same building the precinct was in, but it was faster to walk outside and around the corner than navigate the elevators and hallways that led through the bowels of the hall of justice.

As I turned the corner, I saw the place was hopping with activity.

The two outside bays had black and whites in them, each jacked up into the air. A mechanic worked under the body of the cruiser on the far left, while a second guy installed a new battering ram on the black and white at the right.

In the center spot was Harrington's black 2008 Dodge Magnum, the only vehicle not up on a lift.

Remy was gloved up and leaning over the open hatchback of the station wagon. Beside her stood Carlos Esqueveda, in a blue one-piece canvas jumpsuit.

Carlos had shoulder-length dark hair that was wrapped in a thick red rubber band, and he sported a beard that must've taken two months to grow.

"Jesus," I said. I hadn't seen him since June. "You look like a god-damn terrorist."

Carlos grinned. "Hey, man, don't be racially profiling me. My people have stuck to illegal immigration and drug trafficking for a century. We don't do bombs. Keep us in our lane, okay?"

I smiled. Carlos and I went back and forth like this all the time.

"So what've we got?" I asked Remy.

My partner offered a frustrated look that I knew well. "More like what we don't," she said.

"There's no notes planning any school shooting," Carlos said.

"No other firearms in the car," Remy jumped in.

"And no extra ammo in the car for the .38 he was carrying," Carlos added.

"Huh." I snorted, not understanding the logic of Jed Harrington bringing a loaded .38 Special into a school with no additional ammo, either with him or in the car.

"A buck knife," Carlos offered, lifting the object up. "Six-inch clip blade. Steel."

"Well, he didn't bring that with him onto campus," I said.

"I'll keep looking," Carlos said. "But preliminarily, I can tell you that Jed Harrington recently went to a Waffle House, from the coffee cup in the car. And that he wore a size large, from the clothes in his gym bag in the back."

I stared around. The bay smelled like someone had spilled a gallon of motor oil inside the place. "That's it?" I asked.

"Not much else in his ride," Carlos said. "His glove box has the manual, and nothing else. His center console has some coupons for a juice place. A hundred bucks hidden in an envelope. Probably emergency cash."

"Will more time help?" I asked.

"Always." Carlos nodded. "But I'm not hopeful. How about I tell y'all anything new by two p.m.?"

"Deal," I said.

I told Remy what I'd learned from ATF about the weapon and where Harrington had bought the .38.

She stripped off her latex gloves. "You wanna drive out there?"

"ATF's already doing the legwork, partner," I said. "Plus, we got Ginnie Tanner coming in five minutes. That's why I came to grab you." I wasn't going to do our interview with the wife of the dead teacher alone.

Remy nodded, and looked to Carlos. "Two p.m., C. We need something big," she said.

Carlos nodded. "Then how about giving me 'til end of day?"

8

Ginnie Tanner was in her thirties with jet-black hair and muscular arms. She wore a black blouse and tan pants, the athletic but stocky build of a soccer goalie.

Remy and I sat across from her in Interrogation Room B, and Abe watched from the window. The skin around her nostrils was raw.

We apologized for her loss and got background first. Found out that she and Leaf had met through friends and were married for the last five years.

"I don't know what else you want to know," she said, offering a blank stare.

I'd seen this look a dozen times on the spouses of victims. The pale skin. The resigned attitude. Abe called the ones left behind "flickers," since they were like traces of themselves. Copies of the original.

"I talked to the guy in uniform yesterday," Ginnie continued, referring to Patrolman Gattling. "I told him already. It wasn't any special day. Just another school day."

"Your husband hadn't had any trouble with anyone?" Remy asked.

Ginnie Tanner's eyes were flat and black like buckshot. "Like who?"

"Anyone at school?" I said. "A parent? Another teacher? A coach or administrator?"

"Nope," she said. "Now these reporters are calling all our friends and family. They give some line about honoring Leaf's memory, but they're like maggots, digging through our lives."

"Our press information officer," Remy said. "She may be able to give you some advice on how to handle reporters."

Ginnie Tanner barely heard Remy. "I loved him," she said, "but it's gonna come out. And I'm gonna look like a monster."

Remy reached out and held Ginnie's hand. A good move. "What's gonna come out, hon?"

"We were getting divorced," the wife said. "So naturally I'm confused. I mean, I cared about Leaf, but we argued every day. I wouldn't want him dead. But he was so friggin' mean. Just—all the time. Always some agenda."

"Was he physically violent?" Remy asked.

"No," Ginnie said.

I thought about the prospect of a divorce, and if this changed anything. "Was there infidelity?" I asked.

The wife glared at me. "I know where you're going with this, Detective, because the TV people haven't been shy about it. One of them asked my sister straight up—was Leaf screwing this art teacher?"

We waited a second.

"No way," she said.

"What makes you so sure?" Remy asked.

"*I* had an affair three months ago," she said. "It was a way out for me. Away from him. Then I confessed it to Leaf."

Remy and I waited.

"It didn't go well, but he didn't leave either," she continued. "Leaf would say over and over, 'Maybe I'm gonna screw someone today and tell *you* about it.' So I'm pretty sure if he did, I would've heard."

Remy was typing notes in her laptop, and I was watching Ginnie Tanner's eyes. They were set deep in her face. Two circles of lead, dead of emotion.

"Now he's some kinda hero, and I'm gonna be the mean-spirited bitch about to leave him."

I slid forward a photo of Jed Harrington. "Do you know this man?"

"Nope," she said. "They've been rotating the same three photos of him on TV. I've never seen him before."

We needed more background on Tanner. Something that put him in that art room at 1:54 p.m. "Was your husband friends with other teachers?" I asked.

"Sure," she said.

"Which ones?" Remy asked.

"Pam Gronus, the algebra teacher," she said. "Jessica Lopez. She teaches history."

Both women, I thought. Was Leaf screwing around? Maybe he was and just hadn't shoved it in his wife's face, like she thought he would.

"Putting aside a physical relationship," I said, "did your husband ever mention Kelly Borland? As a professional? Were they friends?"

"Not that I knew of," she said. "But he was that kinda guy. Women liked talking to him."

"Do you know what he usually did during his free period?" Remy asked. "From two to three?"

Ginnie Tanner made a noise with her nose, as if struggling to blow something from it. "Went online?" She shrugged. "ESPN.com?"

The cuticles around the woman's pinkie finger and thumb were red, and tiny splinters of skin stuck out like cilia, the remains of anxious scratches and pickings.

"Sports were an interest?" I asked.

"That and teaching were his only interests," she said.

We went on with Ginnie for another half hour. Where she grew up. Where her husband had lived. Jobs they'd had. Schools they'd gone to. Military service. All of it with one purpose—to search for some overlap between Harrington and her husband.

It didn't exist.

We moved on then. Got a name and address to follow up with the man she'd had an affair with. It didn't sound like a solid lead, but we had to consider every angle.

On the way back to my desk after we sent the wife home, Abe found me.

"What'd you make of Ginnie Tanner?" he asked.

"She's got nothing to do with this," I said. "But Leaf Tanner." I shrugged. "All women friends? That guy you tell your sad stories and secrets to? We've seen that type of guy. He usually ends up getting himself into trouble."

Abe nodded in response. "I just heard back from the *Register*," he said.

I squinted. We had calls out with *The Washington Post* and *The Atlanta Journal-Constitution*. All in case Harrington had sent in some manifesto. The *Mason Falls Register* was the smallest paper on the list. Our local paper.

"They have something?"

"He pitched them an exposé on the school board," Abe said. "How it was selected. Influence in the community. How vendors were chosen when Falls Magnet was built."

"You have a copy?"

"They didn't end up publishing anything," Abe said. "The editor thought the story was leaky." Abe read from his notes. "'Wild theories. Big leaps in logic. Unsound journalism.'"

"What was Harrington's reaction to them passing on it?"

"Nothing, according to the editor. Almost like Harrington was feeling them out for another project. Then Harrington contacted the same editor a week ago. Said he had new information. Something salacious."

I raised my eyebrows, skeptical. "Salacious about how vendors were selected?"

"The editor never found out," Abe said. "Harrington said he needed another week."

I considered this. Was some administrator gonna get exposed? And if so—how the hell did that lead to Harrington with a gun on campus? After all, he was the aggressor.

"This editor give you any background on Harrington?" I asked. It felt like we still didn't know the man.

Abe smiled. "Oh, you'll love his answer on that. He said to read the paper tomorrow. They're putting together an eight-page spread."

"Sure," I said. "That's more important than public safety."

"But this other guy from the *AJC*," Abe said. "He told Merle that Harrington sounded healthier than he had in years. Said he was working on something big. A book, he figured."

"A book?"

Merle came around the corner and waved us to follow him. He steered us into the second-floor kitchen, where the TV was set on the local Fox channel.

A journalist named Deb Newberry was on-screen, a blonde wearing a black pantsuit and a bright orange blazer.

I knew Deb. She was a hard-ass. A smart investigative journalist with deep inroads into the MFPD.

"Jedidiah Harrington lived alone," Deb said to the camera. "Unemployed. Unhinged. With potential PTSD symptoms that he would never receive therapy for, since he never officially served with our military."

The image of the reporter faded, and a picture filled the screen.

It was a shot of Harrington's backhouse, with those boxes piled everywhere. Then a second picture: a close-up of the gun case.

"What the hell," I said. We'd been the only ones on Harrington's property.

"This is just one picture this reporter obtained to paint you a picture of Jedidiah Harrington," Deb explained.

Abe answered his phone, and I could tell it was the chief.

"Boss," he said, "I got no idea how that got out."

Abe looked to me, and I shrugged. "Neither does P.T.," he added.

Abe walked to the other side of the kitchen. Shook his head in frustration. "And you really need to tell that to the mayor?" he asked.

Merle and I glanced over at Abe. His jaw was set hard, his mouth scrunched up and his cheekbones riding high.

The TV moved on to a story about a progressive candidate named Jerome Bleeker who was running against Toby Monroe for the governor's seat.

Bleeker came onto the screen. He was in his forties and Black. "It's pretty clear what happened," he said to a reporter. "Toby Monroe's people went out at night and stole all my signs. We had about a thousand on lawns throughout Atlanta. This morning there's twenty."

Across the kitchen, Abe raised his voice. "So I took the bedrooms and the front," he said to the chief. "P.T. had the backhouse and kitchen."

I shook my head, incredulous that the chief wanted to know who had inspected the backhouse, where the leaked picture was from.

I picked up a bottled water off the kitchen table and began shaking it from left to right, popping my palm against the base, like a smoker prepping a cigarette box.

Abe hung up and kicked at the legs of the kitchen table. The TV moved on to sports, and Merle flicked it off.

"It's okay," I said to Abe. "Does the mayor want me off the case?"

"Yeah." Abe nodded, embarrassed. "And nowhere near the GBI as we hand it off."

I nodded. Between the photos of the fifty banker's boxes on the news, the five guns at Harrington's backhouse, and the excerpts the *Register* would print tomorrow, the public had some part of their "why"—way ahead of Mayor Stems or Chief Senza having a chance to break it to them first.

And that pissed them off.

But was it really an answer—to say that Harrington was just crazy?

I moved back to my office, not sure where this left me and Remy. Or the case itself.

Would the incident move over to the GBI faster than we originally thought?

At the same time, the anxiety that I'd been carrying around for the last day relaxed just a bit.

Harrington was a crazy man, looking for conspiracies where none existed and ready to take the lives of students. And sure, Mayor Stems and Chief Senza would've liked to make that announcement instead of the media breaking it. But I'd gotten it right, taking him down.

Thirty minutes later, Chief Senza sent a group text, informing us that Abe and Merle would finish the investigation on the school shooting, with Remy and me assisting only as requested. Come end of day Friday, every detail about Falls Magnet would be turned over to the state and Feds.

I wasn't sure if the chief was pissed, especially after seeing the picture of the backhouse on the news.

I started my own text chain. Just me and Senza.

How's Avis?

A text came back:

> Everything A-OK. She's with her mother and has stopped
> crying.

I wrote back:

> Are you and I okay? I don't know how those pictures got
> out.

A text came back fast:

> That question came from the mayor. Don't worry about it.

> But did you miss your therapy session?

Shit, I thought. My appointment was first thing this morning, and I'd completely blanked. I explained to the chief that I'd been in with the teacher's wife and that I'd reschedule.

A minute later the phone pulsed and I saw one more text from the boss:

> You saved my girl's life, P.T. But Fuller was right that
> you need to recover. Right now just make those therapy
> appointments. Let your partner assist Abe if he needs a
> hand.

I stood up. My office windows were cranked open, and a smell like medicine had drifted in.

The anise hyssops in the flower bed alongside the building had gotten long and wispy and reeked like an odd mix of carnations and chemicals.

Sometimes, when I'm coming down from the stress of a case, I want a drink. It's a reactive instinct for someone in recovery. A reward for survival. And lately when this happens, I take a drive. Being in motion soothes me in a way that AA meetings don't.

I left work, even though it was midafternoon. Got in my Silverado and drove home. Grabbed my bulldog.

Purvis was eight years old and reddish-brown, with white blotches on his body and a large underbite. He also had a tendency to drool when excited, which he was by the time I unlocked the front door.

I led him outside. Rolled out an old UGA blanket onto the passenger seat of my truck and placed my dog atop it. Within a minute of driving, Purvis was asleep. Apparently being in motion soothes him too.

I pulled over just past a bridge along I-32.

Grabbing Purvis, I climbed out onto a slice of grayish-brown granite that protruded over the edge of the Tullumy River.

There are places in the world with magical value. The religious speak quietly when they enter churches. Sports fans grow silent when they walk the hallowed grounds of their favorite stadiums. And for me, this was my mystic place. A strip of forest with a river that had both saved and ruined me, surrounded by trees that transcended time and the geological diversity of northern Georgia. The truth is that Mason Falls is a place so densely populated with minerals and rocks that the only way to know it is to listen quietly as nature peels back each layer, like a hundred-year-old onion.

Below me, the water was green and dark, and I sat there for an hour, talking to my family. Speaking words into the wind, right at the place where my wife, Lena, and my son, Jonas, had gone into the water. Where the Jeep had left the road and slid down the embankment.

You've gotta let yourself off the hook, P.T.

I glanced down.

It was Purvis. He speaks to me sometimes. In a voice that sounds

just like mine, but with a touch more sanity. And maybe some sar-
casm.

"I've got this itch," I said to my dog. "There's something unsettled."

You always get that itch, he huffed. *Maybe you need that itch to
make yourself feel good. To make yourself feel special. Needed.*

The late afternoon sun flickered through the loblollies that grew
tall by the riverbank, and the air moved through the small hairs on my
arms. I got up ten minutes later. Loaded Purvis into my truck and
headed home.

In the shower, I let the hot water soak into my skin. I got out,
poured a Dr Pepper on ice, and put on the Braves game.

I knew the right thing was to let the case go, but the call from the
governor nagged at me.

Monroe had asked me to shoot a man. And I'd taken the shot.

Had losing my wife and son made me open to drawing blood
whenever it was needed? Had it made me reckless?

And then there were two other questions, the first of which was on
my mind all day.

*Did I take the shot because Monroe asked me, or because Har-
rington was about to unload that .38?*

Whatever the answer was, it was good that the case was over.

I mean—it was over, right?

Because that was the second question.

9

I woke up four hours later to the sound of Peter Moylan on my big-screen TV. A postgame report was under way, and I saw that the Braves had lost to the Phillies 5–9.

Out the front window, it was pitch-black, and I needed to talk to someone about what had gone down at the school. I rang up Remy's cell, but she didn't answer.

After a half hour of waiting on a text, I got in my Silverado and headed to her place. At least I'd see if her lights were on.

Driving over, I decided that if Remy and I were going to be partners again, I needed to lay it all out. To tell Remy how the governor had used his influence to find me the address of a man named Kian Tarticoft this past May. A man who wasn't just the main suspect in our case back then, but who had also driven my wife and son off the road. To tell her how Monroe fed me that address. And how, because of that, I owed the governor a favor.

As I pulled up outside, I saw a light on in the corner unit on the third floor.

Remy was up, even now at eleven p.m. Maybe like me, her head was spinning from the last thirty hours.

I caught the lobby door as a couple walked out, and I headed for the elevator, not needing to bug Remy to buzz me up.

There was a chance this could go sideways on me. A chance that Remy might tell me to go to Senza and lay things out for the chief to decide. What I knew of Kian Tarticoft last May. The deal I'd struck with Monroe. And the call yesterday on the roof behind the school.

All of which could cost me my badge.

I got off the elevator at three.

Walking down the hall, I practiced coming clean to Remy about how I'd lied to her four months ago.

Remember this spring, Rem? When you wondered how I found that assassin we were hunting? Found him so quickly? I had a helper. The same guy who encouraged me to kill Harrington yesterday: Governor Toby Monroe.

I knocked on Remy's door and heard a muffled voice. I was so anxious I paced sideways to keep myself from flying away.

I need to tell you something, Rem. Something that's gonna make you mad as hell. But I gotta be honest, regardless of what you'll do to me.

The door swung open, and I saw Darren Gattling, the blue-suiter who worked with us, standing in a T-shirt and boxers. His dark biceps looked more muscular than when he was in uniform.

Gattling's head dropped. "Aw hell," he said.

Remy appeared behind him, in black leggings and a workout top.

"Hey," she said. "What are you doing here?"

I was ready to spill the beans on my relationship with Governor Monroe. *And my partner was—what? Hooking up with a patrolman?*

Remy was the one who asked the boss to put Gattling on our team yesterday. Which made this a bad look, sleeping with him. Someone of a lower rank, reporting to me and her.

"Sorry," I said. "I was looking to see if—"

Remy looked to Gattling. "Darren," she said. He walked away from the door.

I gave her a look. "Jesus, Rem."

Remy blew air up from her mouth, and it whipped the pieces of her straightened hair away from her eyes, spreading her bangs right and left. "We grabbed a drink, and it just happened," she said.

I nodded, no longer sure I could go through with my speech. Not with Gattling standing fifteen feet away. "I needed to talk to you about something," I said. "I tried to call and text, but . . . tomorrow, I guess . . . would be better."

I turned, and Remy followed me down the hall.

"P.T.," she said.

I put my hands up, spinning to face Remy as I walked backward, away from her. "Between the shit I've pulled that you know about," I said, "and the stuff you don't . . . you're the last person who needs to explain yourself to me."

"It won't happen again," she promised.

I pressed the elevator button, and the door slid open. The elevator had a chandelier inside it. I always liked that about this building.

My silence was more about me losing momentum. My nerve to tell Remy everything was gone.

I got in the elevator and left.

10

When I got home, it was almost midnight.

I walked up to the front door and noticed it was ajar.

Had I left the door open in a rush to go out to Remy's?

My service weapon was in my safe in the bedroom, and I used the toe of my sneaker to push open the front door.

Inside, the house was dark, and I slinked into the living room. No one there.

Moving down the hall with the lights off, I felt my way into the bedroom and rolled back the area rug that extended from under the dresser and covered the floor safe. I pulled my Glock from the safe and cocked it to the ready.

I locked the door to the back and cleared the bedrooms, turning on lights as I moved through each room. When I got back up front, I saw Purvis sitting out on the porch.

I dropped into one of the blue Adirondack chairs outside.

No one was in the house, and I touched my bulldog's skin, trying to tell if he'd been out the whole time, wandering the neighborhood.

But Purvis ran hot, and his coat gave no clues.

I was wired, even as my body was shutting down from fatigue. My mind was still racing through the moments on the school roof, and I craved the taste of rum. Some Papa's Pilar Dark that I could mix with Coke. Keep me focused.

I heard a noise and looked up. Remy's red '77 Alfa Romeo Spider was pulling up to the curb.

My partner came up and took the open chair on the porch.

She didn't say anything for a long moment. Then turned to me.

"So what's so damn urgent a girl can't get an inappropriate booty call with a subordinate?"

She smiled, and we both cracked up, with neither of us saying a thing afterward for a few minutes.

The sounds of the night filled the space between us, the frog-mouths and night herons that did their business after the diurnal animals fell asleep. When only restless detectives with guilty consciences were awake, trying to find words for actions that, in retrospect, felt unexplainable.

I pulled my chair closer to hers. "It was a righteous shoot, Rem," I said. "At the school. I'm sure of it."

My partner squinted at me. "Nobody doubts that," she said. But I put my hand on her forearm, as if to say, *Let me finish.*

"There's something I need to tell you."

Remy listened, and I started back four months earlier, when we realized that the killer we were hunting in May was not a one-time offender. Our suspect was a paid assassin, a man who'd been killing and hiding his tracks for years.

"I know all this, P.T.," Remy said.

"There's parts you don't know," I said. "Remember the last day of the case? I went out to a junkyard? I had a lead on an El Camino?"

"Sure." Remy nodded. "That's how you found Tarticoft. You told me this."

"I left a few steps out," I said to my partner. "Tarticoft drove out of that junkyard in the El Camino. But he drove in a year earlier in a Dodge Aries. The same car that pushed Lena and Jonas off the road."

Remy blinked. "Wait, I don't understand," she said. "I thought you never knew the car that hit them. I thought you weren't even sure if Marvin was—"

"Marvin's the one who figured it out," I said, referring to my father-in-law. Lena's dad. "He'd been working with a P.I."

Remy's face was twisted now. She looked bewildered.

"Rem," I continued, "Tarticoft wasn't just our killer in the Fultz case. He took out my family."

I explained to her that I'd found Kian Tarticoft's business address, but the assassin had abandoned the place three days earlier.

"May eleventh," I said. "I finally found out who drove my family off the road. Problem was—Tarticoft was one step ahead of us."

"No." Remy shook her head. "You found him. I shot him at the cabin."

I stared at her. "You did," I said. "But I had *help* finding him. Governor Monroe. He took some scrap of information I had about Tarticoft being a taxidermist. And a P.O. box number. He used his resources and got me the address of that cabin. *That's* how I found the place."

My partner stood up. "In exchange for what?"

"A favor," I said. "Something in the future. His choice. Anything."

"You gotta tell the chief," Remy said immediately. "Monroe's a snake, P.T. He could call you tomorrow. Ask you to hide evidence—cover up an investigation."

"Rem," I said. "I was up on the roof at the middle school. Ready with the Remington, and Monroe called me."

"No," she said. Shaking her head vehemently. "No, no. Don't tell me the governor ordered that shot."

11

An icy breeze moved over the porch, and Remy muttered to herself, her head shaking.

Maiden grass and yellow tickseed grew wild near the edge of the porch, and my partner had turned away from me. I heard her nervously pull at the leaves of the plants, still processing what I'd told her about the governor's call.

"It was a good kill, though," she said, turning. "Harrington was a murderer. He'd already shot Leaf Tanner."

I nodded, knowing this was true.

"It was," I said. "The art teacher verified the events and the order, including Harrington turning with his .38 toward the kids."

Remy was pacing. Her head bobbing in agreement. But her mind was elsewhere. Racing back and forth in time.

"Jesus," she said. "Why didn't you tell me right away?"

"Fuller from I.A.D. was there."

"No, back in May," she clarified. "Why didn't you tell me about Tarticoft and your family?"

I thought of the moment I'd found out the truth about the assassin. It was a scorching-hot day, and I'd pulled out of that junkyard.

I'd vomited a mix of vodka and quail eggs at the roadside, finding out the truth about my family. Then I made one call.

"You were the one person I *did* call," I said. "But you wouldn't listen. I'd screwed up in other areas. So you just kept telling me you were coming to get my badge and gun."

Remy lowered her eyes, remembering the moment. And now she was embarrassed.

"P.T.," she said. "The governor calling yesterday . . . did you take the shot because he told you?"

"No way," I said. "Harrington had a .38 to the teacher's neck. He turned toward the students and Kelly Borland. All that was true."

"Okay," she said. "So be it then. Harrington brought a loaded gun into a middle school and murdered a teacher. He was about to shoot our boss's kid. You did the right thing."

I was leaning against the house. "I know," I said. "But—"

"But nothing," Remy answered.

I stared at her.

"Forget the call ever happened," she said. "The GBI's taking the case over anyway."

For two years I'd been giving my partner shit for being too black and white in her thinking.

Learn to swim in the gray area, I'd said to her.

If she was letting me off the hook now, this was a new Remy. Drenched in so much gray I could hardly recognize her.

"That's why Monroe said your name on TV," Remy pointed out. "An hour after the shooting."

I nodded. "Make me a hero, and I won't turn on him."

Remy stared at me, her face twisted. "But Tarticoft," she said. "Something's wrong, P.T. He was a paid killer. If he went after Lena and Jonas . . . who hired him?"

"I don't know," I said. "I've been thinking about that since the night you shot him."

"And you got nothing?" Remy flicked her eyebrows. "C'mon, P.T. I know you better than that."

"I thought the attack on Lena and Jonas might be related to an old case," I said. "Someone trying to get at me. But I was only on one investigation when Tarticoft drove them off the road."

"Which was what?" she asked.

This was a time that predated Remy and me working together.

"A robbery at a liquor store," I said.

"And you're thinking what?" Remy asked. "Someone came at Lena to get you off that robbery?"

"I don't know."

"Was it a big heist?"

"Just the opposite," I said. "Thirty-three dollars and a Cherry Coke were stolen."

"It might have nothing to do with your wife then."

"Yeah," I said. "But the manager at the liquor store was lying to me, and I couldn't figure out why. I kept circling back there. Harassing him."

"So do you have a lead or not?"

"I'm not sure," I said. "The liquor store went out of business, Rem. It's been abandoned. But I searched—a month ago—for who owned the property. Thinking I might ask the owner if I could look around the place. You know, re-jog an old memory?"

"Sure," Remy said. "Who owns it?"

"An outfit called FJF Investments."

"Should that mean something to me?"

"It's a partnership," I said. "But when I searched further, I noticed every legal document was authored by Lauten Hartley. Most signed by him. He owns the majority stake."

"I know that name," Remy said.

"The first time we saw Hartley was last Christmas," I said. "A rich guy named Bernie hanged himself in jail. Lauten Hartley was the family attorney. Last person to talk to the rich guy."

"Okay . . ." Remy said, waiting for more.

"Then in May, when that attorney Cat Flannery was suing the police department, a law firm came in to help. They worked pro bono against me and the department. You remember?"

"Johnson Hartley." Remy nodded. "*That's* how I remembered the name."

"Lauten Hartley has made it personal with me, Rem, multiple times. And I don't know why. In May, he tried to have me fired. Then I find out he owns this liquor store . . . ?"

Remy took this in, processing. "Could just be an attorney that hates cops. And him owning that store is coincidence."

"Like I said," I told Remy, "I don't have much."

"P.T.," Remy asked, "you didn't go investigating Johnson Hartley while you were suspended, did you? It's a big law firm. Powerful clients, if I remember. Tell me you haven't been spending your evenings stalking this guy."

I pursed my lips. "I drove out to Hartley's two or three times," I said. "Sat on his house overnight. Followed him here and there."

"Jesus," she said. "What else?"

"Nothing."

My partner leaned against the railing at the top of the front porch.

There is something poignant about the inadequacy of language to explain ourselves. The lack of words to make concessions that truly symbolize our transgressions.

I had lied to my partner: back then and again recently at the school. And while Remy was clearly a better person than me, she'd also abandoned me back in May. Now we were together again and walking through the messy swamp of it all.

"P.T." She turned to me. "I'm sorry about the junkyard. I can't imagine you finding out about the guy who killed Lena, and my response was that I was coming to take your badge."

"Rem," I said, "don't apologize for that. You were doing your job."

She stared at me, nodding.

"I'll see you at work tomorrow," she finally said. "This Harrington thing was a good kill, and it's no longer our case. Doesn't matter what Monroe said."

"Yeah," I said. "I keep coming back to that."

She put on her jacket.

"In between other cases, we'll start peeling back the layers on Tarticoft. This attorney Hartley too. If someone put a hit out on your family, we'll find 'em. But when we do—we *discuss* what to do. Okay?"

"Yeah."

Remy gave me a hard look. "Promise me, P.T. You don't go rogue."

"I promise," I said.

Remy turned without another word and walked down to her Alfa. Got in and sped off.

12

I awoke to the sound of a loud vibration: metal against wood.

My cell phone must have fallen off the side table in the middle of the night and was skidding along the hardwood floor.

"Marsh," I said, leaning a long arm over the side of the bed and grabbing it.

"We got a hot one," Remy said.

I rolled over. Guessed at how long I'd slept by the amount of light filtering through the curtains.

"What time is it?"

"Seven twenty-two, sweetheart," Remy said. "And people are dead."

"Good dead people? Or bad dead people?" I asked.

Which were the opening words of a game Remy and I played sometimes.

"Double murder," my partner said. "I'm fifteen minutes away. Get dressed."

I hung up and jumped in a cold shower. Let the water shock my system before turning on the hot. Tiny bumps on my arms disappeared, and my skin became more malleable under the warm water.

Getting dressed, I popped a K-Cup in the coffee machine and

stepped outside. Lit a half-smoked Marlboro Red that I'd left by the front windowsill.

The last two days had been surreal.

The school shooting. Opening up to Remy about what happened in May.

I felt renewed somehow and took two long puffs before stubbing out the cigarette and leaving it there.

The air was muggy, but you could almost feel the heat burning it off. And you could sense that by afternoon it would be one of those days when you could smell the nitrogen sticks in the flower beds as you drove down residential streets. And that everything would be okay.

I grabbed the coffee and dumped it into my silver cup, seeing Remy's Alfa pull up toward the curb.

As I locked the front door, I noticed my reflection in the window: my wavy brown hair had gotten long, and I wore a dark sport coat over a white button-down and black pants. One of my go-to outfits.

I got in Remy's sports car, and the Alfa guzzled loudly away from the curb, its signature *dugga-dugga-dugga* rising from the back of the car.

"A new case," I said aloud. A little surprised I hadn't been moved to paid administrative leave. "Are we just vetting it, or is it ours?"

"Ours," she said. "I got the call from the chief myself."

I stared at Remy. Of the two of us, she was the junior detective and yet the call had come from Senza directly.

"I assume it came with a request to keep an eye on me?"

My partner's face tightened. With the school shooting still not handed over to the state, Abe and Merle couldn't take this one on.

"It's okay, Rem," I said. "So what do we know?"

"Patrol found a '96 Chevy Caprice," Remy said, "abandoned on the side of SR-914. Driver and passenger both shot to death, execution style, most likely from someone in the back seat."

"Jesus."

Remy glanced at her phone and then at me. "The driver's name is Juan Vinorama. No I.D. on him, but he owns the car. His buddy in the passenger seat is still a John Doe."

Ten minutes later, Remy steered her Alfa to the side of 914, about six miles northwest of Mason Falls. Ahead of us we saw the abandoned Chevy Caprice, a boat of a vehicle. Long and midnight blue, with a tan interior and a back seat big enough to deliver a baby in.

We got out and were briefed by Officers Ford and Atienza before gloving up and swinging the front doors of the Caprice open.

Standing by the driver's side, my feet straddled the edge of the highway. I stared in at the two bodies, while Remy walked around the other way, which abutted an incline full of wormwood.

The guy in the driver's seat was Latin and had been shot through the back of his head. I leaned over, examining his face. There was no exit wound, which meant the bullet must have found its final resting place inside Juan Vinorama's brain. Or maybe its second-to-last resting place. Our medical examiner, Sarah Raines, would dig in there and remove it.

"Safety first, Rem," I said. Tapping at Vinorama's seat belt, which was strung over his chest and still plugged in, even though his keys were up on the front dash, rather than in the ignition.

"Someone they knew?" my partner theorized.

Remy and I looked at the man in the passenger seat, who was Latin like Vinorama, but heavier, with a chest like a keg and thick muscular arms. The big guy had taken a shot to his head, but the bullet had exited somewhere near his right eye, spraying blood and brain across the front and right windshield inside the car.

I examined both men from head to toe. The two wore cheap dress pants and plain white T-shirts. They sported inexpensive black shoes with rubber soles, as if they worked in a restaurant. Nothing about them screamed high-end, except for the fact that they'd obviously been hit by a pro.

"You think drug couriers?" Remy asked. "Maybe they crossed someone?"

Northern Georgia has had its fair share of drug trafficking in two categories: illegal and illegally manufactured. At one point three years ago, when sales were at their peak, the *AJC* reported that over 180,000 Georgians had an opioid problem. Which was like saying the entire city of Macon was hooked.

Remy had the back door on her side open, and I did the same on mine, letting the sunlight stream in. The plants on the hillside smelled of sage and were covered in whiteflies. Some of the insects had migrated over to the car and were stuck, dead, in the blood on the passenger windshield. It looked like someone had taken jelly and dusted it with powdered sugar.

I took a step back.

Behind the driver's side, on the floor, was a pile of four T-shirts, still folded. I held up the top one and saw that they were thin, novelty-style shirts. "Five-dollar shirts," my wife used to call them. The one I grabbed featured an illustration of an anthropomorphized worm climbing out of a bottle of Mezcal. The bubble near the worm's mouth read, *I don't have a drinking problem. I drink. I get drunk. I fall down. No problem.*

"You think these guys were living out of their car?" Remy asked.

On the back-seat floor on Remy's side was an empty bag of Doritos and some Skittles wrappers.

"Looks more like a road trip," I said.

I leaned in and checked the tags on the shirts. "These are all XXLs," I said, motioning at the man in the passenger seat. "Maybe the big guy didn't pack properly."

I sat down in the back seat of the car, directly behind Juan

Vinorama. At a touch over six foot, I could see just above his head, making the driver about five foot eleven. Probably a hundred and fifty pounds. I glanced to his friend, who clocked in at over two bills, but was shorter. He had a hard, rectangular face, from what I could make of it through the bloody mess.

"Bam." I held up my finger like a gun, pointing at Vinorama over the back seat. "Bam," I said again, pointing at an angle at the John Doe in the passenger seat.

Remy sat down in the back seat on her side, next to me. She moved her gloved hands along two lines that ran from back to front, across the center of the back-seat vinyl, in between us.

The two marks were dimpled impressions, each less than an inch wide and ten inches long, right in the center of the seat. Like where a person would sit in the middle, if there were three sitting in the rear.

"Something heavy?" she theorized.

I nodded, agreeing, and my eyes moved to a smear of reddish-brown blood that had stained through the passenger seat, from front to back. Beside the mark, the material that made up the seat back was torn up.

"What do you make of those marks?" I said, pointing at the dark spots on the back of the passenger seat. The lumbar area behind the big guy.

"Probably an errant third shot. Guy bled through from front to back," Remy said. "Bam, bam. And then, bam." She imitated what I had done, but added a third shot through the seat cushion that landed in the passenger's lower back.

"Sure, but why?" I asked. "If Biggee was already shot in the head, why hit him again?"

Behind us, I heard an engine shut off and glanced up at the Caprice's rearview mirror. Sarah Raines, the local M.E., got out of the crime scene van, along with Alvin Gerbin, her tech.

"I dunno," Remy said. "Maybe the first shot was at the lumbar area. *Then* the head."

I climbed out of the Caprice just as Officer Atienza walked up.

"Detective," Atienza said. "Results came back from the prints on the passenger. His name is Miguel Dilmendes," she said. "Thirty-two years old. From Cocoa Beach, Florida, just like Vinorama."

"Brevard County," Remy said, her mind a steel trap. "It's got the sixth-highest drug overdose rate in the state of Florida."

I stared at my partner. The thing you have to understand about Remy is that she not only skipped a grade in junior high, but graduated college in three years. This made her the third-youngest rookie patrolman to come out of the academy and the youngest to make detective in Mason Falls. And while I was downright impressed by both those facts, her parents did not find her occupation to be a source of pride.

They didn't think much of the police and had imagined their daughter could be a doctor or a scientist. Someone who left their community for some time and then returned to Mason Falls, a symbol to others that anything was possible. Instead, she was stuck with me.

"I thought Brevard was the fifth highest for drugs," I teased. "Sixth? You sure?"

My partner rolled her eyes at me.

The two men being from Brevard County probably meant this was just another death in the drug war. Bad guys killing other bad guys.

The M.E. walked up, her blond hair pulled back in a hair tie. She had on booties and a crime scene onesie, today in blue.

"Detectives," she said. "Busy week."

I smiled gently at Sarah. She and I had dated for a few months, until I realized I hadn't been ready to date anyone at the time.

"Yes, ma'am," I said.

Alvin Gerbin, her tech, loped along behind her, a flowery blue XXXL Hawaiian shirt over a white tee.

Remy and I took a step back toward the rear of the Caprice to let Sarah and Alvin get at the bodies.

The Caprice had whitewall tires that looked bleached, and I remembered arresting a guy for robbery back when I was in patrol. He'd been caught stealing five bags from a Dollar General, and all he had to show for it were ten boxes of baking soda and eight packs of those rectangular Mr. Clean erasers. From my interview with him, I learned that those were the secret to beautiful whitewalls.

I stripped off my gloves and turned to Remy.

Most people know that detective work largely happens in the first twenty-four hours after a murder. What they might not know is that most of the early work comes from human intel, not medical evidence. The medical findings come in later and help more in court. In proving out hypothesis and in conviction.

"Let's let 'em get the bodies out of there, Rem." I pointed. "Get the Chevy towed into the mod yard. Print it. In the meantime, you and I can start chatting up these guys' families and friends."

"Agreed," Remy said. "Maybe we can find out what the hell these two were doing so far from home."

"And if they're low-level schlubs," I added, "why did they die in such a high-level way?"

13

By ten forty-five, I was at my desk in the precinct, my head buried in my notes from the crime scene.

Juan Vinorama's license and car were both registered in his Florida hometown, so I'd called up a Cocoa Beach detective from the roadside before Remy and I left the scene. The detective had offered to do a courtesy notification at the address on file with the DMV, and now I stared at my phone, seeing a text come in from the cop in Florida.

> Bogus address on Vinorama, Detective. Same with
> Dilmendes. Sorry. No one to notify.

Remy came in holding up the jackets on our two dead guys. "I got yearbook photos," she said.

But as I glanced over, something bizarre moved in front of my field of vision. Far off, across the squad room.

Chief Senza was escorting Lauten Hartley on a tour.

Lauten Hartley. The lawyer.

The same one who Remy and I had just talked about last night. The guy who I theorized had contributed to the worst day of my life.

Hartley ran a hand through his reddish-brown hair and placed a briefcase down in an empty office on the far side of the floor. The chief disappeared into a stairwell.

"What the hell?" I said, moving past Remy.

I hustled out of my office and across to the opposite stairs. Took them two at a time up to the next floor. Followed Senza into his office.

"Chief," I said, "you got a second?"

"You already got something on your double?"

"No, not yet," I said.

I pulled his door halfway closed as I entered. "Lauten Hartley." I pointed down. Cocking my head.

I was still getting to know Senza, and he had this way of taking a deep breath while he nodded. Signaling that he was following you. "Sure," he said. "So, Vicky Goff is leaving the police oversight board. You knew that, right?"

This was the civilian position. The lead position on the board.

"I heard whispers."

"Well, the mayor's been looking to replace her," Senza said. "You remember Hartley from last year?"

"You kidding?" I said. "How could I forget? He worked pro bono to sue the department."

Senza motioned for me to close his door all the way. Which I did.

"And the mayor's got two thoughts on that, Marsh," the chief said. "One, if Hartley sits on the board, he's conflicted, so he *can't* sue us again. Make your enemy your friend."

"And two?"

"This is what the public wants these days, P.T. It's the age of transparency. Honest reporting. Body cams. So the type of public servant who *would* work pro bono against a police department—just because he believed in a cause—that's the type of guy the public wants running an oversight board."

A *cause*? I squinted at Chief Senza.

The issue that we got sued over last December wasn't a cause. Some degenerate's sister was suing the department for her brother's death. Her brother who shot Remy in the arm. Then held me underwater until I nearly blacked out. Somehow I found the energy to fight back. Which ended in his death, instead of mine.

I did my best to nod at the chief. But the reality was—politics eluded me. Not the simple practice of them. I'd learned long ago how to compliment people's kids and wives. How to play nice at work. But the advanced stuff—the counterintuitive moves where you took one step back for six months to take two steps forward later—I guess I just lacked the discipline to sandbag myself and those around me for some theoretical future gain.

"You're following me, P.T.?" the chief asked.

I hadn't been listening for about thirty seconds.

"Sure," I said. But all I was thinking was that if Hartley was a member of the board, he'd have unlimited access to any case in the department, including anything that Remy and I would find looking into his own movements.

Which might be his purpose here at the hall of justice in the first place.

"I know you're still raw about that settlement against the department," the chief said. "And I am too. But I'll tell you what. Go down there now. Introduce yourself to Hartley. Be the better person. Tell him, 'No harm. No foul. Welcome to the team.'"

"It's okay." I put my palms out. "We don't know each other—"

"Even more reason," Senza said.

I hesitated, looking to the boss's closed door.

Did I want to get into this with Senza?

"That's an order, Detective," he said. "Go on now. Take the high road."

I nodded and left. Headed to the stairwell. As I came down the steps, I found the office where Hartley had put down his briefcase.

I knocked on the open door, and he raised his head.

The attorney had the body of a wrestler. Not as tall as me, but a compact figure and thick, wiry arms. He wore a black suit, cut tight against his strong frame.

"Paul. Thomas. Marsh," Hartley said.

I closed the door behind me.

Hartley stared at me then, saying nothing more. And I said nothing back. A long moment passed. What Remy and I called "S.T.F.U. time." And generally when we shut the fuck up, the other guy talks first.

"I guess you're wondering what I'm doing here," he asked.

His hair was bushy along his temples, and I studied his face. His eyebrows were like unkempt wires in an abandoned house. The color of old copper turned brown. Same as the hair that covered his head.

"You like to work pro bono?" I asked.

Hartley grinned like a cat. "Nope. The truth is, I prefer a paying case. I like money."

He laughed then. A deep and confident laugh. One you'd want to join in on, if you were in on the joke.

"But," Hartley continued, "I figured the department could use the help, so I was asked to join the board. And here I am."

I felt air settle against the dry area at the back of my mouth.

"I hope there's no hard feelings," he said. "From last year and all."

Be cool, Purvis said.

"'Course not," I answered.

"'Cause there's lawyer stuff you gotta do when you're a lawyer, Detective," he said. "Antagonism is part of the game."

Inside, a storm was taking shape. An updraft of energy feeding something unknown. Then a pull-down revealing a front of gray. I knew this guy was dirty.

"That's why I came by," I said. "Clear the decks. Let you know that we're good."

Done, my bulldog said. *Now walk away.*

The area between Hartley's eyebrows came together. Folded to form a crease. His smile curved upward. He didn't buy a thing I was selling.

"Well, I hope we can become friends," he said. "But at the same time, you understand I gotta do my job on the board, right?"

"That's why you're here," I said. "Just like I'm here to investigate crimes. New ones . . . old ones."

He stared at me then, and I wondered if he was thinking what I was. That he was involved somehow with the Golden Oaks robbery. And that I knew it.

"Good." He checked his watch. "So let's start by making sure you don't miss another therapy session."

He got up. Walked closer, his face inches from mine.

And suddenly I was staring into the black waters of the Tullumy River at night. A gurgling sound. Water filling up a 2012 Jeep.

"'Cause, you know," he said, his face serious, "you miss another appointment, and you'll be put in front of the police board. And I run the board now. So who knows what could happen to you."

14

I crossed through the farm of cubes from Hartley's office over to where Remy sat, my mind spinning from back-to-back conversations with Senza and Hartley.

"I gotta take a walk," I said to my partner. "Did Carlos get the Chevy Caprice yet?"

"Yeah." She looked up. "But it's only been an hour, P.T. I'm not sure he's even had a chance to—"

I grabbed the murder book from Remy's desk and headed toward the stairwell to the lobby.

"Everything okay?" Remy asked, following me.

I nodded, but didn't speak. Flipped open the book as I walked, taking out a printout of a photo Remy had shot at the roadside.

Breathe, Purvis said.

"So this was a planned meet, right?" I said, once I realized Remy was following me. I held up a wide shot of the Caprice parked along 914.

In the photo, there were marks in the gravel that indicated a car had parked in front of the Caprice, where the two dead men were found.

"Our pro shooter pulls over in front of them," I said, theorizing. "Gets out. Walks back toward their car?"

We got to the lobby, and my partner pulled out her phone. She showed me other pictures she'd shot at the side of the road. There were skid marks kicking up gravel, like a car had left fast. But the marks could be days old. Or weeks.

"You're thinking someone Vinorama and Dilmendes knew pulled over in front of them," Remy said. "They welcome him into their car. Maybe they thought it was just for a quick second. Hence the driver never undoing his seat belt."

"Exactly," I said.

I moved through the lobby and onto the sidewalk. Outside, the sky was steel-colored, and the clouds looked like a series of white blankets that had been rolled military-tight and placed beside each other, in rows.

"I was thinking about that errant bullet through the back of the seat," I said, walking the long way around the hall of justice. "You think Dilmendes turned? From where he was sitting in the front passenger seat?"

"If it's an ambush," Remy said, "he'd turn when he heard the first shot. The shot at the driver."

I imagined the killer sitting down into the back of the Caprice. Making a few words of small talk before he pulled out a .22 and laid a single bullet into the back of the head of Juan Vinorama. It made sense that Dilmendes would turn suddenly as the gun moved in his direction.

In front of us was the edge of the mod garage, but my partner grabbed me by my arm, stopping me before we entered.

"P.T.," she said. "You want to tell me what the hell's going on?"

I nodded, my lips pursed for a moment. I had walked out of the station and a full block with Remy, all from nervous energy.

"That was Hartley," I said.

Remy looked confused. "The guy setting up in that office?"

I explained about my conversation with the chief and with Hartley, and Remy shook her head. Here and there she asked, "He *said* that?" and then followed by asking, "What did you say?"

"I just tried to stay calm," I said. "Give us a chance to investigate. That's what you told me last night, right?"

"Right," she said, her eyes big atop those curvy cheekbones. Realizing her words in front of my house last night weren't hollow, but the start of a plan. A plan she couldn't back out of now.

No one said anything for a moment, and suddenly Carlos was in front of us. He'd sauntered over while we had gotten into it.

"So yesterday you show up two hours after I get that Dodge Magnum," Carlos said. "Today it's one hour after I get this yacht?"

I held up my hands. "I just needed a walk, C," I said. "Thought I'd check if you had anything early on the Caprice."

"I actually got two things early," Carlos said. "But then you gotta leave me alone. Give me some real time. Cool?"

"Cool," Remy said. "Let's hear 'em."

Carlos walked over to the Caprice, and we followed him. He had all four doors splayed open at once and the car looked like some winged metallic animal, ready to take flight.

"Well, first off, the car's a bit messy, right?"

We nodded.

"Candy wrappers. Haskell's Burger wrappers," he said. "Clothes. Here's the thing, though. There ain't a print inside."

"What do you mean, 'ain't a print'?" Remy asked.

"Zero. Cero. Nada."

I blinked. "Someone wiped it down?"

"Like a professional," Carlos said. He held up an empty Skittles package with his purple gloves. "Even the candy wrappers. By the way,

Wild Berry is my favorite Skittles, in case you ever feel like bringing me a snack as a thank-you."

Remy and I went silent. For the first time since we'd arrived, I heard country music coming from an overhead speaker in the garage. A Cole Swindell song about a girl dancing in a nightclub. Carlos was humming under his breath to the tune, and I remembered something Abe once said to him. That Carlos couldn't carry a tune if it was in a bucket with a lid on it. I still didn't know what that meant.

"What about our two guys' prints?" Remy asked. "Vinorama and Dilmendes?"

"Other than on the steering wheel." Carlos shrugged. "None of their prints either."

I stood back, inspecting the car with a fresh eye. It was odd enough to see a professional hit in Mason Falls. A complete lack of prints was even rarer. Someone had been in that car. Took their time looking around. And then removed any trace of themselves.

"I'm thinking the guys in the car were low level," Carlos said. "Couriers probably."

"Based on what?" Remy asked.

"Their dress," he said. "My point is—the odds are better that they *had* something than they *knew* something."

"You think their killer searched the car for something these two had?" I asked. "Found what it was. Then wiped everything down after?"

"Possibly," Carlos said. "'Cept I don't know about the 'found it' part."

I smiled at Carlos. "You wanna take the car apart?"

"I do."

"You think what?" Remy asked him. "Inside some tube in the engine . . . someone was searching for something they never found?"

Carlos nodded. He had a good instinct for these things. What my father-in-law called "horse sense."

"Make it happen," I said. "We'll clear the O.T. with the chief."

I took a step back and stopped. "Wait. You said two things . . . that you found."

"Yeah," Carlos said. "There's this guy Nick who delivers stuff from the lab. He's got a handful of those same shirts you found in the back. The ones with the stupid slogans on them."

"Okay?" I said.

"So I called Nick twenty minutes ago. Asked him where I could get a shirt like his."

"What'd he say?" Remy asked.

"He told me about some gift store about three miles from where you found this car. Big signs all over it. Ninety-nine cents this. Two for twenty that."

"I know that place," Remy said. "It's not the only thing out there either. There's a liquor store. A bar."

"If these guys were staying in town for a couple days," Carlos said, "that bar might be where they were getting their drink on."

15

As Remy drove north on 914, I thought about what we had so far on the double murder and what open questions existed. But mostly I tried to avoid thinking about Hartley. Which meant I mostly thought about Hartley.

Should I have said more to the man? Less?

Gotten angry?

Demanded more from the chief?

The sound of tires crunching on gravel signaled our arrival, and I stared up at the building that housed Art's Novelties and Gifts. The place was a large wooden structure, with an angled tin roof that had a sign every ten feet or so. One read *T-Shirts $5*, while another shouted *We've got . . . what you forgot.*

I looked around.

When you work in patrol, you get to know every seedy corner of town, and the rural shitholes too. That's why you gotta work patrol at least two years before you can even apply for your detective's badge. But I hadn't been out this way in some time, and the store was new since then.

"What do they call this area nowadays?" I asked Remy.

"East Fork," she said.

My dress shoes crunched underfoot. We were a hundred feet from the edge of 914, and I stared across the highway to the other side.

Two buildings sat across the road, their architecture mirroring the novelty store, except without all the crazy signs. One of the places was a bar by the name of Tandy's. The other was a package store called Lucky's Liquor.

Remy was almost at the front of the gift shop, and I caught up with her.

The door dinged as we entered.

Inside, the place looked like the love child of those temporary seasonal stores and your local ninety-nine-cent place. Along crowded shelves, it was Christmas, Easter, and Halloween, all at the same time. A giant sign suspended on two wires called the shop *The stocking stuffer capital of Georgia.* Never mind that it was still September, last time I checked.

"Christ," I said under my breath, looking at all the crap you didn't need.

A minute later, Remy motioned me over to a stack of tees.

The top shirt had a familiar message, but a different picture. *I don't have a drinking problem,* it announced in a big bubbly font. Below that were four frames, drawn like a comic book. Each square contained a cartoonish-looking man. *I drink. I get drunk. I fall down. No problem,* the panels read.

I walked over to a woman in her late thirties at the register. She had a thin frame and freckles with big eyes set in a small head. She was pretty, but at the same time, like a caricature of someone else. A gaunt princess with two or three features that were unnaturally large. Her name tag read *Nina.*

"How you doing, Nina?" I smiled.

"Better now," she said, her eyes landing on mine.

I flashed my shield and held up the T-shirt. "We're looking for a guy who bought a handful of these."

"Well, they're pretty popular," she said. "You know anything about this guy?"

I pulled out my phone and showed her pictures of Vinorama and Dilmendes. For Dilmendes, I used his DMV photo, but for Vinorama, the driver, I showed her the close-up of him in the front seat of the car.

"Holy shit," she said. "Are they dead?"

A gaunt princess who cut straight to the chase.

"Yes, ma'am," I said.

"Well, they were in here for sure," she said. "Just the other day."

There was an old-timey popcorn machine at the far end of the store, and the smell of imitation butter found its way over to us.

"Do you remember which day?" Remy asked.

Nina widened her stare at the picture. Her eyes were blue and wide with a perfect black circle inside, like a painted doll.

"It was right before closing," she said. "Tuesday night."

This was two nights before the men were killed.

"Were they on foot?" I asked. "Or maybe you remember what kinda car they drove?"

"I think they walked." Nina pointed. "Like across 914."

"From the liquor store?" Remy motioned.

"That or Tandy's," she said. "I couldn't tell ya."

"Which guy bought the shirts?" Remy asked.

This was a test, since we knew the sizes in the car were XXLs. Too big for Vinorama.

The woman took my phone. "That one." She pointed at Dilmendes, verifying our hunch and handing my cell back. "But his friend was interested too. Everything was just too big for him."

I cocked my head, confused. We'd seen Juan Vinorama's body in the car this morning. The medium tee I was holding would fit him just fine. If not that, a men's large.

"What do you mean, 'too big'?" I asked, flicking the photo back to Vinorama and looking at it myself.

"No, not him," she said. "The other guy."

I flicked to Dilmendes, and she shook her head.

"No, the third guy. The little one," she said. "You don't got a picture of him?"

Remy and I moved a bit closer to the woman. A third man with these two very well might be our killer.

"What did the third guy look like?" Remy asked.

"Like them." The woman shrugged.

I flicked my eyebrows at her, and she put a palm out, wanting to correct herself. "Mexican, I mean. But little."

"Ya got more than just the word 'little'?" Remy asked.

"Well," she said. "We don't have kids' sizes, and he kept asking for shirts. I told him he should go lookin' at Walmart. The teens section. He looked pissed off and left. Had a smoke."

"You said it was before closing?" Remy asked.

"Uh-huh."

Remy was typing notes in her iPad. "Do you remember how close to closing? Like what time?"

"Well, we shut down on Tuesdays at ten p.m.," the girl said. "Let's call it nine forty-five."

I looked around the store. Out the crowded front windows and across at Tandy's. If these guys were drug mules, what the hell were they doing hanging in this area for days? I thought of what else was out here, far from the city. At ten o'clock, the bar would be open. The package store. Not much else.

"You got security cams in here?" my partner inquired.

The woman smiled for the first time. "Not even fake ones, sugar," she said to Remy. "We rely on the kindness of folks—and the security of the good old Mason Falls PD."

We both grinned at that.

"And well you should," Remy said. The official response.

"We got people who can draw a picture for you, Nina," I said. "You describe the eyes or nose and they can—"

"I wouldn't know where to start," she said. "All I remember was he was Mexican and his size. Like four foot ten or so. Four-eleven tops."

"Hair color?" Remy said. "Eye color?"

"I'd guess dark and dark."

"How did the big guy pay for the shirts?" I asked.

"Cash."

Remy and I peppered her with more questions. Did she see any car the men might've hung around in the parking lot? No. Did she overhear any of their conversation? No.

"Were they speaking in English?" I asked.

"I dunno. I think so, yeah."

We'd gotten everything we could from Nina and left.

Walking across 914, we found the liquor store manager unhelpful, and the front door to Tandy's locked.

Standing in the parking lot, I stared down the highway, imagining the men crossing this road. The land out this way was flatter than a gander's arch, and largely white and rural. These three would've stood out. Been remembered.

We suddenly heard a garbage truck pull out from the back of the bar, and began crossing the street.

Other than the noise of the truck, the area was quiet and desolate, at noon on a Friday.

From behind Tandy's came the noise of a dumpster rolling. We turned. Was someone working at this hour and had ignored our knocking on the front of the bar?

We walked around to the back of the place.

A rolling steel garage door was pulled open behind Tandy's, and a man was pushing industrial trash cans full of empty booze bottles and crushed beer cans over to a dumpster. Filling it back up.

"How ya doing?" I said.

The guy glanced up for a moment, but kept to his work. He was sixtyish and Black—heavyset with a wrinkled face and graying hair, cut short. He wore a black sweater with a red *O* on it, outlined in white. Ohio State.

"Buckeyes gonna be any good this year?" I asked.

The man sized me up as harmless. "Favored to win the Big Ten," he said. "Hung forty-two on Cincinnati last Saturday."

Remy badged him as we walked closer. "Detective Morgan," she said. "This is my partner, Detective Marsh. You work in the bar here?"

"I'm the manager," he said.

Remy took out her phone, which had the same pictures of the DOAs as mine.

"We're looking for a couple guys," she said. "We heard they were in here in the last couple days."

The man glanced at Remy's phone for a quick second and nodded, moving back to his chore.

"Yeah, they were here."

"You remember when?" she asked.

My partner always began with fidelity: test out one fact that we already know. Then go to other questions. I had come up under a different training: always begin with connective tissue. Find rapport.

"I dunno." The man shrugged. "Two days ago?"

He grabbed another trash can. Started wheeling it away from us and toward the dumpster. Cans rattled around inside, and Remy gave me a "what the fuck" look. The guy was ignoring us.

My eyes glinted at my partner. It's an odd thing—when you're young and time stretches out endlessly across the horizon, your only desire is to will it to move faster.

"I was trying to remember that quarterback's name from 2018," I said to the man. "Was it Haskins? Must've completed seventy percent of his passes last year. You guys lost him, right?"

"Drafted by Washington," the man said. "But I didn't watch the Buckeyes before this year."

This was my own test, and I understood the man better now. I'd seen a number of Ohio State shirts recently on folks in the area. Justin Fields, our backup quarterback at Georgia, had transferred there, under those new rules that let kids leave one school with no penalty and go to another.

"You a Fields fan?" I asked.

"Pride of Kennesaw," he said. "Four thousand yards of passing in high school."

Fields was a local kid from northwest of Marietta, and some fans thought he should've started at Georgia instead of the current QB, Jake Fromm. Now heading into week three of the 2019 season, it was too early to tell.

I walked closer to the man. "Help us out, will ya? These guys are in the morgue."

The man motioned for Remy's phone again, and she handed it to him. A pile of wooden pallets was stacked twenty high against the building that housed the bar.

"From what we heard, there were three guys," Remy said, breaking the silence of the barkeep's inspection of the photos. "The two you see here—plus another buddy. A shorter fella."

"Yeah," he said. "They were in here together a few nights ago. Tuesday night. Maybe again Wednesday. Then last night it was just the one guy."

"The shorter guy?" Remy confirmed.

"Yeah, he came in last night," the man said. "'Round ten p.m. One shot of tequila. Two Dos Equis. Tipped me a twenty and said he'd see me tonight."

"What's he look like?" Remy asked.

"Think he's Puerto Rican. Curly dark hair. Probably twenty-seven or twenty-eight. Real short. He had a thing on his hand. Not a cast. It's more like gauze. Messy, like he taped it up himself."

"Right or left hand?" my partner asked.

The man cocked his head, picturing the customer from his vantage point. "My right, at the bar, so his left."

"And he said he'd be back tonight?" I asked.

The man nodded, but slower now.

"What's your name, sir?" I asked.

"Isaac McGulden."

"You're gonna have a police presence in your bar tonight, Mr. McGulden," I said.

"And what if I don't want one?" He stepped close to me, his body a similar frame to mine, even if thirty years older. "Friday's my best night."

"Well, we won't be in the way," I said. "But if the register runs short, I can always talk to my chief. See if we can help out. A night out here with patrol." I shrugged. "Drinking parties with cops tend to run up the tape pretty well."

He hesitated, not sure what to make of the offer.

"I think it's a fair guess that this man is armed and dangerous, Mr. McGulden," Remy said. "We'll be in plainclothes, so no one'll notice. But we'll park some black and whites nearby."

"All right," the old guy said, even though we weren't asking his permission.

We followed him inside the bar then, and arranged where the best place was for us to wait and what time we'd be back. Made sure he didn't alert any customers.

As we drove back to the station, I was thinking about Lauten Hartley again and whether he'd still be hanging around.

The woman who'd led the police oversight board before Hartley was in that office only ten days a year. It would be the same for Hartley. Today was just a show of force. He'd set up that meeting to intimidate me. To get a reaction.

But why now?

As I entered the precinct lobby, a woman stopped me. She touched my elbow as Remy and I headed toward the stairs.

"Detective Marsh," she said, and I glanced over.

She was in her thirties, pretty, with hair the color of a reddish-orange pepper, tied up in a bun. She looked familiar, but I couldn't place her.

"I'll catch up with you," I said to Remy, and turned to face the woman.

"Can I help you?"

"My name is Kelly Borland," she said.

On instinct, I took out the small reporter's notebook that I keep in my jacket breast pocket. But as I did, I realized that I knew the woman. She was the teacher from the school shooting. The only other time I'd seen her was through my binoculars. That, and on the news.

"Sorry," I said. "Your hair. I didn't . . ."

She smiled gently, and when she did, small dimples formed on each cheek. She was five foot three and white. Attractive, with brown eyes. A curvy but athletic figure.

"I'm trying to lay low." She pointed at the red bun. "Coloring the hair sounded like a good idea when my friend suggested it. I didn't realize how red it would get."

I smiled at the shade. "It worked on me," I said. "Incognito. How are you doing?"

"I'm okay," she said. "I mean, you know, given everything."

I wasn't sure what she was here for, but I could imagine the week that Kelly Borland had had. First, some psycho holds a gun to her head. Then a bullet rips through the glass inches away and lands in the man. Blood in her hair and on her body. And if that wasn't enough, the media started accusing her of having an affair with the dead teacher.

"Listen," I said. "I'm not part of the investigation. So if there's something you've remembered, Detectives Kaplan and Berry are your—"

"It's not that," she said. "I know you and I haven't talked. And Detective Berry has been great," she said of Merle. "I just . . . I went to a therapist today."

"Oh, that's great," I said. "It's good to talk it out."

"I wanted to come by and thank you. For saving my life."

I got it now. Understood why she brought up therapy related to what she was doing here. "Not necessary." I put up my hands. "I was just doing my job."

She squinted at me. "Are you not on the case 'cause you took the shot?"

"No," I said. "There's other cases . . . other cases that need help."

I suddenly remembered that I had my own therapy session to attend to. In about an hour. If I missed it, I could end up facing off with Hartley at a police board meeting.

"In a lot of cultures, I would owe you a life," Kelly Borland said. She smiled as if embarrassed. "I know that sounds hokey, but—"

"Not in my culture," I said. "In my culture, we're even-Steven."

She had been fidgeting with her hair and undid something that made it fall to her shoulders.

"Well, my counselor said it was good to come here, and I did. But I'd also like to buy you dinner. As a sign of my appreciation."

"Again," I said, "not necessary. Really."

She nodded then, as if she'd done what she came here for.

At the same time, it was odd. I could feel an energy between us.

"Thanks for coming by," I said, and she shook my hand. I started toward the stairwell.

"Detective Marsh," Kelly Borland said from the door before leaving. "It was just an offer for dinner. A salad. A plate of food. Not your hand in marriage."

Hope Duffy, the desk sergeant, started laughing at me then, and I smiled. Now I was the one who was embarrassed.

I walked back toward Kelly Borland. Pulled out my card. "I'm on a case now, but try me in a few days. I'd be honored."

She took the card from me and wrote a phone number on the back of it.

"I didn't mean to be pushy," she said. "You call me if you feel up for it."

16

The office of Dr. Gary Cavendish was located in a building just south of the precinct, on the corner of 5th and Drake.

The psychiatrist's place of business was on the same floor that housed human resources and was the place where city employees went to get discount tickets to Amicalola Falls or add a child to their insurance policy.

I waited for the shrink in a red upholstered chair set up in the hallway outside his office. On the walls were prints of coastal Georgia. Tybee Island. Skidaway State Park. The squares of Savannah, hung with moss and covered in tourists.

A minute after I arrived, I heard a door scrape open. Cavendish emerged from the stairwell.

He was slightly shorter than me and slender, with thin wispy strands of blond hair that barely covered his head.

"Am I late?" he asked, checking his watch.

"I'm early," I said. "Take your time, Doc."

Cavendish unlocked his office door and flicked the lights on.

Inside, the place had an artificially floral smell. Like a lavender candle or air freshener was used more often than needed.

"Come on in, Detective. Grab a seat."

I had seen Cavendish two times before. The first was when I was a young detective and had shot a man who had pinned down me and my partner inside a check-cashing place. Then in January, I'd been ordered to see the doc a second time after I'd killed a man who was trying to drown me.

Cavendish was carrying a paper bag, and on the side was a logo from North Street Bread. If you wanted a biscuit with a piece of chicken in the middle, topped with a fried egg and gooped in spicy honey, you couldn't do much better.

"Did I interrupt your lunch?"

"Absolutely not," he said, dumping the bag into a small wicker trash basket. "We're old friends anyway, right? If I was starving, I'd eat in front of you."

He got into his chair, which was a brown leather number with a worn mark, right where his butt sat down. I moved to the center of the room and dropped into a gray lounger. The blinds were lowered, and the place was cool.

Cavendish pulled his chair close. His skin was pinkish-red in places, almost as if he'd been stung by a jellyfish, and his eyelashes were so blond they were nearly invisible against his flesh.

"So how are you feeling?" he asked.

"Never better," I said. "What've we got here—two sessions?"

"Two hours," he said. "Then you're home free."

Unless he says different, Purvis said in my head.

Department policy was that Cavendish had the ability to keep a cop from returning to work. Then again, there was an oddism about this time. Unlike normal protocol, I'd already returned to work. Minutes after the shooting.

When I woke up this morning, I was expecting Senza to put a full stop on my work schedule, but then the call arrived for the double murder along 914.

Cavendish and I small-talked for twenty minutes, mostly about the required process of me coming here and the methods the doc used to get cops to feel comfortable and share. To start talking about their hobbies first. Their favorite college or pro teams.

"Well, you know me," I said. "I'm hobby-less and team-less."

"That's not true," he said. "We've talked about both the Hawks and the Dawgs before."

Cavendish made a comment about a patrolman who'd left the force a month ago, after a different officer-involved shooting.

"Did you know Terry Willard?"

"Sure," I said. "He was in patrol, but we came up together. Same rookie class."

We talked about the incident, in which the senior patrolman had mistaken a screwdriver for a gun and shot a man in the numbered streets.

"Willard was a good cop," I said. "Firing a gun just does something different to each person. For some guys, they don't want to touch the steel again."

The mood had suddenly gotten serious, and it wasn't lost on me what the doc was saying.

"Well, the cops that end up here," Cavendish said, "two times. It's a pretty small fraternity, P.T. Not all of them make it back into uniform like you."

"I guess I'm not like most people."

He nodded, staring at me like I was a part of some science experiment. "And what do you attribute that to?"

"My first C.O. taught me to view violence as a zero-sum game," I said, thinking about my commanding officer when I was a rookie.

"Like this guy with the gun at that school . . . he made a choice to put lives in jeopardy. If we can get to him before he gets to someone innocent—like Avis Senza—then the life he exposes becomes his own."

"An eye for an eye," the doctor said.

I didn't answer. 'Cause it wasn't like an eye for an eye. And maybe I'd walked into the therapy session feeling a little chesty. Like I didn't need to be here.

But that came from the knowledge that the Jed Harrington shooting was a good kill. The ruling wasn't official yet, but I'd been all but told.

"Are we here to talk about other options I had, Doc?" I asked. "'Cause I assume you know there was a man with a gun to a woman's head. A man who turned that gun on kids. Was about to kill them."

"You're right," he said. "Let's talk about something different. What do you want to get out of these two sessions?"

This was a standard Cavendish question, and I'd been thinking about it since I woke up that morning. In fact, I liked the question for its simplicity and purpose. It was good to have a goal after all, rather than just show up and bullshit.

"I'd like a lay of the land," I said. "Symptoms. Stages. What do your studies say I should be feeling? So I can see it coming. Work on it."

Cavendish sat up taller.

"The whole idea is that we work on it *together*, P.T. I don't hand you a playbook."

I went quiet then, and Cavendish scrutinized me a minute. He knew me well. He also knew I was already working, and would be out of his sight after the next session.

"Tell me what you're feeling, Detective."

"Okay." I leaned in a little. "Honestly, at first when I shot him, I felt relief."

"All right," he said. "That's good. You wanted to know about symptoms. We call that first period 'the impact phase.' A lotta cops feel a sense of survival. Relief is part of that."

"I mean, I know it's a righteous kill," I said. "But nobody wants to take a life. Right?"

Cavendish shrugged at me. "If that's what you're feeling . . ."

"I am," I said. "I mean, I was. A few hours after that, I guess I got a bit sensitive. I went back to work. Got a lot of 'atta-boys.' Friends and neighbors heard about the shooting. It's on the news."

"And how did you feel?" he asked. "About the 'atta-boys' . . . ?"

"Maybe I bristled a little."

"Okay," Cavendish said.

"Then I felt a little remorse."

"Remorse?" Cavendish blinked. "Specifically what . . ."

"Guilt." I shrugged. "Self-questioning. Regret. I mean, he's a scumbag school shooter, but he was somebody's son, right? He's got a mom. A sister."

Cavendish was staring at me funny.

"What is it?" I asked.

"Nothing," he answered, shaking it off.

"And now I feel like it's gonna be okay," I said.

"Acceptance?"

"You could call it that," I said. "Like I've realized this was the only way things could've gone down."

A chime sounded from atop Cavendish's desk. Our time was over.

The doctor stood up. "Well, this sounds better than I thought, Detective."

I cocked my head. "I thought so too. I mean, I know it's only been a couple days," I said. "But I feel solid."

I grabbed my phone from where I'd placed it beside the chair. Stood up. "I know we have a time on Monday. Can we pick it up then?"

"Absolutely," he said. "I'm glad you're feeling so confident."

I got up then and walked out. Took the stairwell two steps at a time. When I got to the bottom, I checked my phone to see if Remy had finished prepping for the stakeout at Tandy's.

I also closed the browser window that I'd been studying before Cavendish showed up in the hallway.

It was an article about the "five stages" a cop goes through after a shooting.

There was the impact phase, which Cavendish mentioned. Followed by recoil. Then there was remorse, bargaining, and eventually acceptance. Below the headline was the author: Gary Cavendish. And I knew that the doc was wondering whether I'd read it and was bullshitting him.

But at the same time, if he'd asked and was wrong, he knew he'd be sending me looking for it online.

A catch-22.

I crossed the street and opened the back door of the precinct.

I was fine, and it was time for real police work.

17

In my first three years as a detective, I was a part of five stakeouts, and my then-partner, Miles, who later became chief, was most in his element on a sting.

But Remy had only been a part of one operation of this type, and I felt like I'd done her a disservice by not getting her into more of these scenarios.

While I was in with the head-shrinker, my partner had gone home and changed into a casual outfit that consisted of black tights and a torn white UGA sweatshirt. Her straightened hair fell to her shoulders, and she was back in contacts.

As she met me outside, Remy motioned at a beat-up green Ford 250 Ranger parked at the curb.

"I picked it up from impound," she said proudly.

"These are great trucks," I said, starting a three-sixty around the old beater. "They're worth cash too, Rem," I added, trying not to reveal what a shit-kicker I could become around trucks.

By the time I made my way around the old beast, I was eating my words. The passenger side featured an un-matching door. It was blue in color and the rest of that side had rusted from water damage. "'Course, the ones that have been underwater in lakes . . ."

"Are worth considerably less?"

I laughed at myself. "Does it run?"

"I got it up to fifty. Engine made a racket, but it seemed solid."

"You get me that jacket?"

My partner tossed me an old jean jacket and a T-shirt. She'd swung by my house and grabbed a couple things, to help me dress down.

"Let's do it then," I said.

I got up into the cab and Remy hopped in the passenger side. I fired up the Ranger with a deep thrum and headed toward SR-914, which zigzagged north from the west side of Mason Falls like some wild artery.

In most stakeouts, you're in one of two situations. One, you're trying to collect information to get a warrant. Or two, you already have that warrant and you're trying to catch a suspect.

But we weren't surveilling some drug hole *or* trying to catch a bunch of license plates on camera to work our way through a network. We were searching for a suspect, but didn't even know his name.

"Carlos finished his search of the Caprice," Remy said as I drove.

"And?"

"No secret stash anywhere in the engine."

"He find anything?" I asked.

"There was a semicircle," Remy said. "Burned or torn into the carpet in the trunk. It could've been there for years."

"Well, it was worth a shot," I said.

The sun was starting to fall, but according to the bartender, Isaac McGulden, Tandy's would be empty still. The early patrons didn't arrive 'til after seven.

"Let's go over the basics," I said as we drove. "Egress and ingress."

"Ingress is just the front door at this place," Remy said. "Egress is the front door, plus a fire exit into the alley. And then there's the manager's exit. Through the back office and out that rolling door. Locked unless he opens it."

"Where should we be?" I said, quizzing her.

"You're gonna hold down the booth inside the door," she said. "You're playing drunk and alone."

"And you?"

"I'm gonna sit halfway between the pool tables and the entrance. Booth by the window. Gattling's gonna come in an hour and join me."

I smiled at her. "Me a drunk and you hanging with Gattling like you two are dating. Wonder if we can pull off these scenarios."

Remy didn't answer, and I turned off at an exit, pulling into a Quik-Trip along the roadside. Told my partner I'd be back in a second.

Inside the convenience store, I grabbed a sixteen-ouncer of apple juice and used the restroom to change into the T-shirt and jacket. I walked back out to the truck, balling up my dress shirt and tossing it on the back seat.

I headed up 914 for another mile until we saw the three store-fronts—the package store, the novelty place, and the bar. It was a quarter to seven, and the neon sign was lit, shining a dull orange glow that read *Tandy's* in curving scroll on the tin roof.

I pulled the old beater behind the bar and parked. Rapped on the emergency exit like we'd agreed with the barkeep.

A minute later, Isaac McGulden opened the door and waved us in. He'd taken off his Ohio State sweatshirt. Under it was a white cotton T-shirt. His biceps were thick and defined.

"Anyone here?" Remy asked.

"One regular came early. Already drunk and passed out at a table. Pool of drool under his face."

"Let's get situated," I said to Remy, and we moved inside.

Up on the bar, McGulden had a can of potted meat with a plastic fork sticking from it. Redneck caviar, my father would call it.

"Okay," I said. "Okay."

There are a couple types of stakeouts when you're on the hunt for a suspect. But this particular one was what we call a "dynamic" in Mason Falls. Which means that the rules can change as we go.

In a dynamic stakeout, there's a decision matrix that runs through one senior cop, who's charged with looking at a series of variables and making live decisions. Like, if we saw what car the little guy showed up in, we might decide to hang back and get his license plate. Have patrol pull him over a mile down the road. Which was why Remy had a patrol car parked just south of the bar, ready to intercept.

If we felt like we could strike up a conversation with the guy, we might try that instead. The most likely person to do that was Remy, who I'd seen hit on guys as part of interviews and interrogations for eighteen months now.

The last option was—with a click of a walkie, which I'd keep hidden in my booth—I could have the black and whites outside in a minute. We could spook the little guy on purpose, flushing him out to a pair of unis, who'd arrest him on the spot.

Remy took a soda water from the bartender and walked over to a table. Placed it there and sat down.

I walked behind the bar and took out four shot glasses. Broke the seal on the apple juice and filled each of four cups, positioning them on a waitress tray and sliding it under the lip of the bar.

"You recovering?" McGulden asked.

"I'm on duty," I said.

I walked away. Half the bartenders I knew were ex-drunks. In and out of the bottle at some stage while they worked the bar. Maybe this McGulden guy could smell it on me.

We dug in then, and this is what I remembered most about stake-outs from my early days. The waiting. The waiting with nothing friggin' happening for hours. Sometimes even days.

An hour passed, and the place began to fill up. At eight-thirty, Darren Gattling arrived in casual clothes. He gave Remy a hug. They looked good together, and I wondered whether last night was, in fact, the first time they'd hooked up, like she said.

It's not uncommon for cops to date other cops, although the ratio of women to men in most departments is pretty one-sided.

Plus, it seems safer. The people you meet at work understand the drill and the toll it takes. So you avoid the badge bunnies who are more interested in telling their friends they're dating a guy who carries a gun. Or the women that Remy calls "holster sniffers." Which, if I understand the term correctly, means a woman who flirts a lot, especially with married cops, but has no interest in anything at all.

At half past nine, I heard the rapidly alternating noise of a police siren, and I hoped no speeder was getting pulled over in front of Tandy's. Not when the little guy was headed here and could easily be spooked.

The sound passed us, and the bar noise took over again.

A husky older guy in an army jacket and a white beard came in after that. Looked around and headed over to the pool table. Two college kids were playing, and the guy sat off to the side, watching them.

McGulden took a phone call and then walked back to the bar. Someone had brought a bag of boiled peanuts into the place, and the smell of the salt and garlic powder used in the cooking brine floated over in my direction.

Another ninety minutes passed, and I thought about the amount of time I'd spent in bars in my life. A girl fell over drunk by the juke-box and was helped up by a friend.

I walked over to the bar and leaned in to McGulden. "You said he'd be here by now."

McGulden shrugged while cleaning a glass. No eye contact. I slid over a five spot on the bar. In exchange for it, he handed me the third shot from the tray below the counter.

Bill Withers's "Lovely Day" was playing over the sounds of cracking billiard balls, and there was a haze of smoke that hung a foot below the ceiling.

I walked back to my booth with the apple juice. The tables around Remy and Gattling had filled in with couples and friend groups. Mostly blue-collar types, but a couple peckerwoods from the farms north of here in Shonus County.

By the top of the next hour, it didn't look like our guy was coming, and the real possibility surfaced that he took a night off, and we'd wasted time and resources. But other questions arose in my head.

Had the bartender tipped him off? Called him in the time since Remy and I were here earlier? Maybe the call McGulden got a minute ago was from the short guy.

I slid the walkie closer along the worn red leather of the booth, ready to hit the mic. Tell everyone to call it a night.

And then the door opened, and in came a Latin man.

He was four foot ten or so and good-looking, his thick wavy hair still wet and combed toward the back of his head. The bouncer at the door checked his I.D., since he was the size of a child.

As the man pulled out his wallet, my eyes moved to his left hand, which was wrapped in an Ace bandage. Streaks of dried blood stained the gauze haphazardly, as if it had been wrapped and rewrapped a couple times.

My partner sat more erect, and the man approached the bar.

McGulden shook his hand. They exchanged a few words and then the bartender brought the guy his regular. The short man turned then and faced the place, his back against the counter and his eyes scanning the far wall. He threw back the Cuervo with his left hand, but as he did, the bandage began to unwrap.

The short man cursed something inaudible from my distance, trying to tuck the bandage strap under itself, but the thing was a mess. He started unwrapping it as he headed toward the far side of the bar, where the bathroom was.

Once he was out of sight, I slumped into the darkest area of my booth and brought the radio to my lips.

"All right, people," I said. "Gattling, hang back at the table. Rem, it's go time."

Remy stood up and pocketed her earpiece. She moved across to the bar and waved McGulden over for a drink, in a ready position for when the man returned from the bathroom.

I'd trained Remy from the first day she'd left patrol, and there was no better cop to have in this position. This wasn't just because she was beautiful and strong, but because she was smart and knew how to play a man.

I laid the radio down on the seat and watched as Remy put her elbows along the counter, her butt leaning against the stool, but not sitting on it. She positioned herself right where the short guy had left his beer, which would force a conversation when he returned.

The song changed, and a familiar guitar riff kicked in. George Thorogood and the Destroyers.

I felt excitement move through me. Two hours ago, there was an outside chance of coming face-to-face with our murder suspect. Now he was here in the bar.

But before the man could return from the can, a loud noise came from that direction.

Pop, pop, pop.

A woman screamed, and a man ran toward me from the far side

of the bar. Gattling rose from his seat. He took a gun from his boot, and the three of us—me, him, and Remy—flew across the bar. Customers streamed around us, running the other way. The old guy. The drunk girl. And the bass of the music pumped.

Gattling flipped open the door to the men's room, and I scanned the small space, my Glock 42 out.

Both stalls were empty, but lying across the dirty linoleum was a body.

It was one of the college kids who I'd seen playing pool. Bleeding now from his gut.

"Jesus," I said to the kid. "What the hell happened?"

The kid's breathing was shallow, and his eyes were giant spheres of white that moved up to the window. A space that was probably two feet by four and missing a screen. Laid out in the sink was a mound of Ace bandage.

"Darren," I said to Gattling, looking at the kid's stomach wound. "Get me some clean bar towels."

I looked to Remy—and then to the window.

"I got him," Remy said, and took off. Racing across the bar.

I crouched, grabbing the kid's hand. "What's your name?"

"Jacob."

"All right, Jacob," I said. "You want the good news or the bad news?"

"Good," he muttered.

"The good news is you're gonna be fine. It takes two hours to die from this kinda wound, and our EMTs are gonna be here in five minutes."

"What's the bad news?" he asked through labored breathing.

"It's gonna hurt like hell," I said.

Gattling came back with a stack of seven or eight clean white bar towels, and we peeled back the kid's shirt. Saw the entry wound in his stomach.

"My dad," the kid said. "He's, uh—"

"Shhh," I said. "We'll call your dad on the way to the hospital. Don't worry."

Gattling held the towels down with direct pressure, and I stared at the open window. The room smelled like a mix of Lysol and vomit.

"Ambulance is three minutes away," Gattling said to the kid.

"What happened?" I asked, and the kid looked from Gattling to me, his breathing fast.

"The old man," he said. "He just st-st-started shooting."

"The guy watching you play pool?" I asked, and the kid nodded.

Son of a bitch. He'd run right past me on my way to the bathroom.

"The little guy," Gattling said. "He made it out that window?"

"He pushed me into the old man," the kid said. "Knocked us both over and jumped to the sink." The kid looked down at his own blood, and his eyes went wide again. "Some parkour move. Jumped out the window headfirst."

"The old man was the one who shot you?" I asked.

The kid nodded, and I made eye contact with Gattling. There were two men out there in the night, and Remy didn't know it. The old guy, whoever he was, was after the short guy.

"Go," Gattling said. "I got this."

I stood up. "Direct pressure," I said. "Keep it up."

I left Gattling with the kid and took off toward the fire exit.

I was out back in five seconds and saw Remy, halfway up an incline behind the bar that headed into the woods. She heard the back door slam and turned.

"Little guy's gone," she hollered. "But I saw something."

"Wait." I ran up a slope full of kudzu, my calves burning as I hustled.

"Old white guy from the bar," I said, half out of breath. "Shot at the little guy. That's who hit the kid."

Remy nodded, not at all out of breath.

"Makes sense," she said. "I saw two figures, not one." She pointed at the woods, and we took off, with me following her lead.

My partner ran five miles every morning, and she moved effortlessly around vertical stripes that marked the shapes of ironwood and hickory in the dark.

Up ahead, she came to a stop, and we listened.

There were movements in the forest, but it was dark. The sounds of animals and twigs creaked. Or maybe it was the sound of men.

Clack, clack, clack.

Three shots lit up the forest, but weren't aimed at us. By the third one, we saw there was a man about thirty yards west of us. And no fire came back from where he'd shot.

We moved left, trying to outflank the shooter, but in a minute he saw us coming.

Bam, bam, bam.

Spits of dirt flew up in front of us, and I dove to the ground.

But Remy was frozen. Standing there, right in the glow of the man's flashlight.

"Who the fuck are *you*?" the old guy hollered. He stared at Remy, who looked like a college kid in her UGA sweatshirt.

The man was twenty feet away, but he didn't see me, hidden behind a pile of fallen logs.

I saw the shadow of an arm pass the beam, and I rose up, unsure if he was lowering or raising his weapon.

"Freeze. Mason Falls Police." My gun was trained on the old guy's body, center mass, but I could only see his shape silhouetted in the light.

Click.

The light went off, and I dove for Remy, crashing her to the forest floor.

I heard footsteps fading. The crashing of brush. And in a minute, silence. The old man was gone.

Remy and I got up slowly. Behind us by a few hundred feet were the sounds of sirens. Police cruisers. Ambulances.

Sometimes a shoot-out is clearly defined like in a movie. Good guys on one side and bad guys on the other. But most of the time, it's chaos. Gunfire coming in, and you're not sure who's shooting who.

"Was that his gun that clicked or his flashlight?" Remy asked.

"You're still here, aren't you?"

She took this in, shell-shocked.

"I'm sorry," she said. "For freezing."

"You're okay," I said. "That's the important thing."

Remy walked back and got a flashlight from a blue-suiter. We searched the area then, scanning to the east, in the direction the old guy had shot.

An eastern screech owl flew over our heads, landing on a branch above us, its yellow irises glowing in the night.

"Oh geez," Remy said.

She'd found the short guy, and he'd been hit twice in the chest.

Remy took off her sweatshirt and tried to stem the blood loss, but it was useless. I got on my phone, calling patrol. "We need a stretcher up here fast."

I leaned over the short guy, while Remy held his hand. His eyes were piercing, and he smelled like mint chewing tobacco. "He didn't get it," he mumbled, patting at his leg. Searching for his wallet maybe. "The old fucker. He didn't get it."

He almost smiled then, and his chest shook.

"Hold on, bud," I said. "Just hold on. An ambulance is coming."

"C-café," the short guy stammered.

Remy pressed hard, but the blood was soaking through her sweat-shirt fast, and no ambulance was in sight.

A moment later, there was no shaking, and his body was still.

"Shit," Remy said.

When we finally came down the hill a good thirty minutes later, we saw Gattling sitting on the edge of an ambulance. A tech was checking him out, and his body was rocking back and forth.

"What's wrong with Darren?" I asked one of the patrolmen.

"A kid died in his arms at the bar."

"What?" I said, incredulous.

I hustled over, and Gattling's face was gray. "What the hell happened?" I demanded.

"I put direct pressure like you said," he mumbled. "But by the time the bus came, the kid was barely speaking." Gattling stopped talking and took his big hands, wiped at his eyes.

Jesus, what a mess.

I saw the chief's Audi pull up, and I exhaled loudly. Everything had been running perfectly at the stakeout, until it wasn't. Until I'd crapped in the oatmeal real good.

The passenger door to Senza's Audi flipped open and out came Gary Cavendish. The police shrink.

What the hell was he doing here?

In Mason Falls, the officer-involved protocol kicks in when one of two things happen: one, an officer discharges his or her weapon. Or two, when someone, a cop included, is injured or dead.

But neither of those things had occurred.

"Doc," I said, but he barely looked at me. He headed over to talk to Gattling.

I looked over at Darren. As the shrink talked to him, he nodded, wiping at his face. I wondered whether this is the reaction I should've had after the school shooting.

Chief Senza was by my side, and I hadn't realized he was talking.

"Do you know Timothy O'Neal?" my boss said.

I blinked. The name was familiar. A patrolman. Older. Near retirement.

"I think," I said. "Why?"

"The dead boy is Officer O'Neal's son, Jacob."

"Christ," I said. A cop's kid had been killed. On my stakeout.

And Gattling must've known.

"I need some air," I said, and walked away from Senza. When I came back, I made my report to Abe, who'd come by to help. I was tired and asked for a ride home from patrol.

But before I got in the car, Cavendish met me by the cruiser.

"Did your gun jam out in the forest?" he asked.

"I didn't have a shot," I said.

"You know, Paul." Cavendish used my first name. "You were having so much fun earlier today in my office. Quoting me back to me."

I stared at him.

"I guess it threw me," he said. "I didn't think until now about how impersonal it was."

"I don't follow," I said.

"You taking that shot," Cavendish continued, "at that school from a hundred feet away. It's almost like target practice. Or some video game. It's not like when a guy's ten feet from you in a forest and threatening your partner."

I looked over at Remy, who was talking to the chief.

Her shoulders were turned up, unable to answer a question that I couldn't hear.

"I thought my problem was that I shot too many people, Doc?" I said. "Now I'm not pulling my gun enough?"

"Oh, you don't have any problems, Detective," Cavendish said. "In fact, I'm considering this our second session. So go on—just do what you wanna do. We can all see what's coming for you. You're the only one who can't. But you're the smart one, right? The clever guy, quoting someone's article to the one person trying to help him."

"Doc," I said. "I'm sorry that—"

"Oh, don't worry about me, Marsh. I'm just the one who's gotta counsel a cop's family tonight about their dead son," Cavendish said. "Straight-A student on scholarship to Vandy. Came home to surprise his dad for his birthday."

I swallowed, and Cavendish stormed off. I stumbled toward the patrol car.

Ten minutes later the cruiser slowed outside my house, and I made it up the porch. Opened the door and let Purvis out.

My bulldog climbed into my lap, and I thought of the conversation with Cavendish six hours ago. About that cop, Terry Willard, who quit the force.

Firing a gun just does something different to each person. For some guys, they don't want to touch the steel again.

I ran the night back in my head. From when the short guy arrived to when we got back down and saw the ambulance.

But mostly I thought about that moment in the forest.

The click Remy heard wasn't the sound of a flashlight going off.

The old guy had fired a single shot at Remy, but his clip was empty.

And I hadn't returned fire. I imagined that Remy had guessed at that in conversation with Chief Senza and Dr. Cavendish. After all, how else would the doc suspect it?

I wanted a drink, and it was good that the house was empty. Dry of the poison.

I laid back on the top step of the porch, my back on the cool concrete. What was the first stage called again? Of an officer-involved shooting?

Impact?

I felt flattened. Out of breath, and I didn't want to go back to work. Didn't want to talk to another soul, especially anyone who was a cop.

18

A t first Allie D'Antone didn't understand what she was witnessing. A smear of red paint.

A mahogany-colored handprint that slid along the white wall. Revealing a hand that grabbed at one of the art smocks.

The bell had just gone off, and the words of Ms. Borland were ringing in her ears.

Always use an art smock, *Ms. B would say.* I don't want to hear someone's momma telling me they ruined a perfectly good blouse in art class.

Then it was like slow motion.

Mr. Tanner. What was he doing here?

And why was he covered in paint?

From behind her, Allie heard a noise.

It was Avis screaming, and some part of Allie knew that something was wrong. Because Avis knew things that the other girls didn't know. Avis's dad told her stories. Stories of crime and violence.

Mr. Tanner grabbed at the hook that held the white smocks, and yanked it off the wall, landing on the ground with the pile of smocks atop him.

And then she saw the man.

Standing as if he were catatonic.

He looked like the dad of a cute boy in her French class.

Except that he stood over Mr. Tanner with a gun, as the science teacher fell to the ground, his chest leaking red all over the art smocks.

19

I woke up the next day, still fully clothed in what I'd worn during the stakeout. I loosened my legs from around Purvis's body and rolled over to see the clock by the bed: 10:21 a.m.

I found my phone and looked at my "sent" mail. Confirmed what I'd remembered from last night. That I'd gotten up at two a.m. and sent a note to the chief, telling him I needed to take leave for a couple days.

Of course, his response at eight a.m. read. Get lost for three days. Then check in with me.

I moved into the shower and let it run until the water went cold.

Getting out, I threw on some old jeans and a black Bulldogs T-shirt. I grabbed my cell and rang up my father-in-law, Marvin. Which is to say, my dead wife's father.

His voice was hoarse as he picked up. "What's going on?"

Marvin had been my roommate for two months this summer after an accident, living in Jonas's old room. But he'd recovered now and moved back into his own house.

"I'm taking the day off," I said. "Was thinking of driving up to Schaeffer Lake. Fish for a couple hours. You up for it?"

"Does the pope shit in the woods on a camping trip, like the rest of us?"

I cocked my head. I was pretty sure that wasn't a saying, but I was suddenly unable to *not* see the pontiff in bright white, squatting among a patch of kudzu.

"Pick you up in a half hour," I said.

I got my rod and reel from the garage, along with my fishing vest and a pair of waders. I probably didn't need those if we were going to rent a speedboat. Marvin certainly wouldn't have any. His waders were called blue jeans, but mine were high-quality Frogg Toggs with stocking feet that Lena had bought for me three Christmases ago.

I pulled off 906 at 20th Avenue and coasted into my father-in-law's neighborhood.

Marvin was waiting at the curb in a double flannel and old Lee jeans, a belt pulled tight around his scrawny twenty-nine-inch waist. He laid his rod in the back of the truck and opened the passenger door. He had on clodhoppers, but they didn't have a spit of mud on them.

"Morning, Pop," I said, motioning at a coffee I'd picked up for him along the way.

"Morning, Paul," he said, taking a sip.

His hair, which was normally trimmed short, looked like it hadn't been cut since I brought him back to his house over a month ago.

"What are we working on?" I said, pointing at his curls. "This is like a Questlove look? André 3000 in the Outkast days?"

Marvin blinked. "I'm not sure what those words mean."

"Let me pick something from your time period," I said. "Sly Stone? Pam Grier?"

Marvin chuckled, leaning in to the rearview mirror to stare at his dark skin and thick curls. "I guess I could use a trim."

I pressed down on the accelerator and pointed my truck northeast.

As a kid, I'd learned to fish on a trip with my dad to Lake Rabun when I was eight. We had such a good time that we went for the next five years, until Dad left home. We'd fished across the whole northern part of the state, a few times along the Soque River in Habersham County, but most other times on the Chattahoochee, hunting wild trout.

Last summer, while I was off of work and Marvin was recovering, he and I went back to some of those places. They were great, but nothing beat the simplicity of Schaeffer Lake in September. Forty minutes from Mason Falls, but it might as well be a million miles away.

As we drove, I found the number of a guy we'd rented a boat from before, and called him up. He told us a dock to meet him at, and I handed the phone to Marvin, who listened for directions.

When I was five minutes away, I pulled into a QuikTrip and grabbed some supplies. A bag of ice. Two bags of jerky. A sixer of Dr Pepper and some Doritos. Man food.

I dropped Marvin by the boat dock with our gear and found parking farther down the road. By the time I walked back, I saw Harry Glavis, who owned the boat, helping Marvin aboard.

"Harry." I nodded, motioning at the eighteen-foot aluminum speedboat with two swivel-seats. "This is nice."

Harry was in his late sixties and bald, a former dentist. The boat was a Tracker Pro Team, and was newer than anything he'd rented us before.

"Same price as last time, Detective Marsh," he said.

Harry had an adenoidal accent, and every word was thick and seemed to emanate from deep within his nose. "It's available," he said. "So I figured—what the hell. Law enforcement discount, right?"

Marvin sat down in the seat beside the helm, and I stepped aboard. My father-in-law was wearing what his daughters used to call his high-water pants.

"I got a credit card on file for you. Want me to use that?"

"That's perfect," I said.

The boat was black with a silver pinstripe, and it sported all the bells and whistles. A fish finder, dual rod boxes, and a deep tackle storage area. Stuff that usually didn't come with the boats we rented.

Harry took a duffel that was on the boat dock beside him. Tossed it onto a houseboat that was parked just the other side of the dock. I pressed the button, and the speedboat's engine purred. A hundred-and-fifty horsepower, but whisper quiet.

"That yours too?" I motioned at the houseboat.

I'd heard grumbling that Harry was sort of a boat-carpetbagger in the area. That he'd retired with money and bought vessels from folks for a song when they hit hard times.

"Just got it last night." He smiled proudly. "Some tourist from New York bought a house up here on the lake, but never moved in."

The houseboat was maybe twenty feet long, with space for two people to live, and two tiny decks.

"You wanted the Tracker, right?"

Harry smiled like a cat, and I could feel an upsell coming.

"This is plenty of boat for us," I said, and grabbed a life jacket. Held it out to Marvin, who begrudgingly put the bulky thing over his tiny frame.

We waved goodbye to Harry and throttled off, moving slowly into the big water.

Once we were settled in and had our lines in the water, Marvin turned to me. He was a patient man, but he also knew me.

"You wanna tell me what happened?"

"I was involved in a shooting," I said.

"The one at the school?" Marvin asked.

"That, yeah," I said. "But another one. I didn't kill the guy in the second one, but . . . it went south on me. A cop's son died in the cross fire."

"Jesus," Marvin said. "They pull you from duty?"

"Nope," I said. "But they might still and there would've been some questions. So I beat them to the punch. Told the chief I needed a couple days to sort things out."

"Good," he said. "It's good to regroup, Paul. Take some time to think. Reflect on your actions."

I looked out at the long expanse of Schaeffer Lake. When we left home, there were red smears in the morning sky, but they'd disappeared by now, leaving behind a pale blue canvas brushed lightly with cumulus.

I checked out the gear aboard the boat and showed Marvin an umbrella rig, which was basically a fishing line that terminated into six or eight leads. The end was shaped like a mobile you'd see above a baby crib, with each lead dangling with bait. Marvin and I had seen guys trawling with these and mocked them. But since it was onboard, we thought we'd at least give it a shot. When in Rome, right?

I put my waders on but left the front unzipped and rolled them down to my waist, to catch the spray. Then I let out about a hundred feet of line and motored at three miles an hour, the umbrella rig moving behind us.

We caught four stripers in about ten minutes, each of them around fifteen pounds. But it wasn't as fun as the fishing we were used to, so we threw them in the cooler and slowed the boat down. Stored the umbrella.

Marvin put out his reel, and he told me a story about his best friend, Barry, when he was ten. How they'd go out at midnight and catch crawdads—the cockroach of the sea, as Marvin called 'em. "Mudbugs" was the term his friend Barry used. Then they sold the bugs to folks looking to hook flounders and catfish.

Marvin pulled in another striper, and I grabbed it in the net. "Thank you, Lord," my father-in-law said every time a fish landed on deck.

By three p.m., we had fifteen fish and were sitting in each of the two captain's chairs, talking with no lines in the water. All along the coastline, ravenna grass grew thick. If you wanted to swim to the edge, you'd barely be able to climb through it and onto land.

Marvin sat back for a moment in silence, and his silhouette blocked the light until all I could see was a line of pink around the fluff of his hair. He was a good man. I knew a dozen guys who didn't get on with their father-in-law while their spouse was alive and, well, here I was, sitting with the old man, fishing on my day off.

"Paul," Marvin said to me, "I gotta tell you something."

"What is it?" I asked.

When he moved closer, I smelled Old Spice and Ivory soap.

"This is somethin' you need to listen to. And maybe other folks won't tell ya."

"Okay?" I went quiet.

"You were a good husband to my daughter. But you can't hold on to that forever, y'know?"

I didn't respond.

"Look at these raggedy old bones." He pointed at himself. "You shouldn't be out here with me. You're young. You need to get out and meet someone. You got your whole life to live still."

I stared at Marvin. *Had I been holding back out of respect for him?*

"Okay," I said. "I appreciate you saying that."

We motored back to the dock about fifteen minutes later in silence.

I remembered Marvin seeing me with Sarah Raines, the city medical examiner, who I'd dated for five months earlier this year. He seemed uncomfortable around her, but maybe I'd imagined that. Maybe it was me.

We drove home, and I studied the sights on the way back, the truck creaking quietly with just the sound of the wind whipping across two open windows.

About ten miles northeast of the city, high on a bluff above the road was a sign for a business converting lawn mowers into racing mowers.

"You ever seen one of those races?" I asked, but Marvin shook his head.

"I remember my daddy bringing me to one," I said. "'Look at these great hillbillies, Paul,' he'd said to me." I didn't understand the statement as a ten-year-old. My father was a complex man. In one moment, he was in awe of these men and their skills with a motor. In the next, he saw them as rednecks.

I dropped Marvin at his place.

Helping him in with his gear, I gave my father-in-law most of the fish. Then I drove home and brought everything straight into the garage.

I showered, tidied up, and started some laundry.

Thinking of Marvin's advice about getting out there, I searched my bedroom for the business card where Kelly Borland, the teacher from the school shooting, had written her phone number.

I found it and stared at the card. Beside her number, she'd drawn a small heart. This was probably not the type of woman Marvin had been talking about. A victim in a shooting.

A couple minutes later, I grabbed my phone and called her.

Strange, but I actually felt butterflies.

"Hey there," I said. "It's P. T. Marsh."

A beat passed.

"Detective Marsh," I clarified. "You came by the precinct—"

"Oh, sure. How are you?" Kelly said, her voice cheery.

We small-talked for a minute, and when that went quiet, she cut to the quick. "So you hungry for that dinner?"

"Well, I wouldn't presume you have no plans tonight."

"It's no big deal," she said. "Remember, Detective. Just dinner. No ring."

I laughed at this, and she said to give her two hours and then come by. Gave me her address.

I hung up and poured a glass of orange juice from the fridge. A floating circle of mold dropped down the ribbon of juice and into the glass. Which caused me to promptly toss it down the drain and clean out the whole fridge. I'd wait and have a Coke at dinner.

I took Purvis for a walk and let the laundry go through the cycles while I watched a recording of that afternoon's Bulldogs game against Arkansas State. The Dawgs trounced the Red Wolves 55–0, and it looked like the decision to let that quarterback go to Ohio State wasn't so bad after all. Who knows? The quarterback carousel was a funny one in college football these days. For all we knew, Fields would go on to be a Heisman finalist at Ohio State the following year.

20

By eight p.m., I had met Kelly Borland at her condo, and we'd walked to a restaurant that was six blocks from her place, called Olive and Chive.

Kelly had a striking look—an oval face framed by a mane of frizzy curls that ended just past her shoulders.

The red dye she'd put in her hair was fading, and her natural brown shade was starting to peek through.

At the restaurant, I ordered the Dijon chicken, and she got a Caesar with steak atop it.

She told me about an issue the residents of her condo complex had been having with an older neighbor.

"This guy's eighty-five and lives there with his son," she said, lifting her white wine and taking a drink. "But he sneaks out all the time. Forgets where he is after a few blocks."

I shook my head. "I saw that years ago on patrol. It's as common as missing kids, you know."

"Missing adults?"

"These days, yeah." I nodded, finishing my chicken.

A second glass of wine came, and she lifted it to her lips. I was having a Dr Pepper.

At some point, Kelly reached a hand across and laid it on mine. "Listen, I googled you," she said. "Read about what happened to your family. I figured I'd tell you that, rather than have you wonder. I wanted to say I'm sorry."

"Thanks," I said. "I appreciate that. How are you feeling, by the way?" I asked. "I mean—since everything went down?"

"Well, I'm kinda stir-crazy, to be honest," she said. "We're all on leave for another couple days, but they told me to take three weeks now, so I started painting today."

"Is that like . . . therapy for you? Artistic release?"

"I guess," she said. "But I'm used to working, you know?"

"I do," I said. "I'm on leave too."

Kelly cocked her head at me, confused. "Yesterday you said you were on a new case."

"Yeah, that ended." I chose my words carefully. "So I finally got a chance. For a break."

Kelly lifted the glass. "To time off, even if we don't think we can handle it."

I smiled, cheering her with my glass of soda.

"To time off," I repeated.

The waiter cleared our table then, and Kelly explained how she'd grown up in Tallahassee and moved to Charleston as a teenager. Her mother was an E.R. nurse, and her father worked in a machine shop as a foreman.

After supper, we walked back, and I stood outside her place as she finished her story. It ended with her taking a leap of faith on this new school in Mason Falls. A place that had ten times the resources of her old school.

We hit that awkward moment. *Was she going to ask me up? Did I want to start something with a woman who is this fragile after a school shooting?*

"Do you wanna come in for a minute?" Kelly asked.

"Sure," I said, and she unlocked the front door.

Inside was an expansive room, one that suggested someone had taken down a spare bedroom and made one giant space. Leaning against the walls, but not hung, were bright orange paintings on stretched canvas, most of them hard to make sense of. Across many of the pieces, a few dots or lines sat against a field of color.

"You coming or going?" I pointed to the screws that were sunk into the wall, a few feet above where each painting leaned.

"I took the old art down," she said. "To make way for new stuff."

I stared at the artwork. The paintings on the far wall looked like a splash of flecks to me. Like someone had made a mistake with their brush.

"You don't like 'em," she said, nervously tucking a string of curly hair behind her ear.

"No, I just, uh . . . they're modern," I said. "I'm ignorant of art. Wouldn't know what to look for."

Kelly broke open a bottle of wine. "You want a glass?"

"I don't drink," I said.

"Right," she said. "Dr Pepper. I thought that was about driving home."

We sat down on her couch, and I thought about Kelly changing her whole life to come here for this school. And now the shooting happened.

"These kids in your class—are they talented?"

"Oh yeah," she said. "Your boss's daughter, Avis. Her freehand sketches are amazing."

"And it's that much of a difference?" I asked. "Falls Magnet versus your old school?"

"Oh my God, P.T." She sat up, sipping from her glass. "Back home we were begging the parents to bring in paper towels and using house paint. Here, we have a fifty-thousand-dollar paint studio that rivals a college."

She described all the equipment that Falls Magnet had, most of it in that attached room where the shooter had entered. The one with the kiln and the press. It crossed my mind that there was an elephant in the room.

A man had held a gun to her head. And I was the one who'd saved her life by killing him. Neither one of us had said a word about it all night.

I excused myself to use the restroom. As I washed my hands after, I decided that I'd bring it up. At least to clear the air. I was no saint, and I didn't want her to see me that way.

"Hey," I said, coming back out. "I was thinking that it might be good to—"

I stopped as I rounded the corner to the living room.

Kelly was asleep. She'd kicked off her shoes and curled up on the couch.

I looked around. Thinking about the pathos of a woman who had been this close to taking a bullet. I had been in that situation myself before, and there could be a sense of PTSD.

A trauma that might cause you to drink too much, especially around someone who you know won't hurt you. Who already saved your life.

I covered her with a blanket and turned off the lights. At the front door, I checked the bottom lock to make sure if I turned it, she'd be locked inside and safe.

It worked like I thought, so I left her there to sleep off the wine.

21

By ten a.m. the next day, my phone started ringing while I was about to take Purvis for a walk. I recognized the number as Kelly's.

"Hey," I said. "How are you?"

"Hungover," she answered. "I haven't drank in a while, and I feel a strong urge to know how rude I was. Did I fall asleep mid-conversation?"

I explained to Kelly how I'd come out from the commode and found her asleep. Put a blanket atop her and locked up.

"What a gentleman," she said. "I'm getting a coffee. You told me you're off of work, right?"

"Yeah."

"Tell me your order and where you are. I'm coming by with a caffeine apology."

I gave her my address, and Purvis and I took a walk. As I got back to the house, I saw Kelly getting out of a silver Honda CR-V.

She was wearing black leggings and a scoop-neck blouse. The outfit showed off what a good body she had even better than last night's ensemble.

She met me on the porch and handed me the coffee. Then she leaned over and rubbed the folds of Purvis's face.

"Red brindle and white," she said. "He's gorgeous."

I smiled and sat down. This was how Lena always referred to Purvis. "I call him brown all the time, and true bulldog lovers accost me."

"They're right," she said. "No such thing as a brown bulldog. What's his name?"

"Purvis."

"What are you two doing today?" she asked in cute voice, pulling Purvis into her lap. A string of drool hung from his mouth, and I wiped at it before it landed on her leggings.

"I dunno," I said. I mentioned I'd gone fishing the day before, and she told me she used to go with her dad as a kid.

"We'd fish on a place called Lake Talquin," she said. "I'd kayak around in the mornings, and in the afternoon my dad and his best friend would drink beers and hook largemouth bass and speckled perch."

"Would you wanna go fishing for a couple days?" I asked. It was sudden, and as soon as I said the words, I felt unsure about them.

Kelly's eyes got big, and she gave me a funny look.

"I'm sorry," I said. "Too much, right? It was supposed to just be dinner. No ring, no reel."

She laughed and made crazy eyes. "Don't worry. I have all my stuff in the car, ready to move in. I know the dog likes me, at least."

It was easy talking to her, and a minute later, we were just laughing, the dog between us, and the hummingbirds darting across the lawn and hiding in the hibiscus.

"I don't know that I'm ready for anything, P.T.," she said. "I wasn't even sure I wanted to stay—"

"I shouldn't have brought it up," I said. "Forget that I said it."

"No," she said. "Let's get out of town together. We could probably both use a break."

I nodded, hesitant.

"I just can't promise I'm ready for anything," she said. "Physically. You should know that first."

"We'll just fish and relax," I said. "You can fall asleep mid-conversation, and I'll get the message."

We laughed some more, and then I called up Harry Glavis, up by Schaeffer Lake. He told me all his boats were out except the houseboat.

I mouthed to Kelly—"houseboat"—and she shrugged, mouthing back "sure." He also gave me the number it went for, for a three-day and two-night rental. Then I made him give me the law enforcement discount.

An hour later, we swung by her place to get some clothes and dropped Purvis over at Marvin's.

The morning sky was a silver-blue, and we got on 908, heading northeast. Kelly wore a floppy hat on her head, and she rolled down the window in my truck. The breeze blew at the curly strands of her hair, and I thought about drives up this way that I'd taken for cases. How every highway was a trip to see some suspect or witness. How work had slowly become my entire identity. My connection to every part of this region.

Did I want that to be my future—or could I change?

We arrived to see the houseboat on the dock, its green and white colors playing off the wood trim of the cabin and cockpit.

We pushed off, and Kelly loaded the groceries we'd picked up along the way into the galley, and put our clothes away. We barely knew each other, but it felt okay somehow.

I motored out into the deep water, taking my rod out and locking it into place on the starboard side of the boat.

I piloted around the lake slowly, pointing at waterfront property. Big six- and seven-bedroom places that had been remodeled recently. And more secluded houses from the 1970s and '80s. Older, but on perfect little inlets.

Kelly mentioned that she had fixed up her old house outside of Charleston, three years ago. The place she'd left to move to Mason Falls.

"I scrubbed and painted that house," she said. "Installed the wood floors myself."

"So you're not just artistic?" I smiled. "You're available for weekend work?"

She hit me on the arm, describing how she'd dug up half the front yard in the month before she left town. Planted a hedge of foxglove and a line of purple indigo that led from the street to her front door.

"That's what's nice about renting now," Kelly said. "If I want to, I can just up and go. I've already figured out that I can get everything important in one carload."

The sun rose up into the sky, and I pulled into an inlet. Kelly threw anchor, and I took out two umbrellas. Set them up on the deck near the two fishing chairs.

Kelly went inside then and grabbed Sprite atop crushed ice. She came out with a pack of salami and cheese.

We got a second line in the water and waited, passing the food back and forth.

"Are you close with these kids in your class?" I asked.

"You're not supposed to form personal relationships," she said. "But you do."

"So the girls from that day?" I asked.

"I love those girls," she said.

The conversation went quiet for a second, and far off I could see only one other boat on the lake, motoring along. A solid mile away.

"What was your son like?" she asked.

"Jonas," I said, a smile coming to my face. "He was so curious. So smart." I thought a moment before continuing. "That's one of the things that crushes me still," I said. "Not getting to find out what he would've become. He was reading really early. That was Lena's doing. They read every night and every morning. It was my job to tell him stories."

"Like make-believe?"

"A lot of them were cop stories that were real." I grinned. "But I'd take out the dangerous parts. Like instead of a guy having a gun in his hand, he'd have a donut."

Kelly patted her waistline. "Donuts *can* be deadly."

"I'd tell Jonas it was a really menacing snack. An illegal snack, so Dad had to arrest the guy. He loved that part. Where I cuffed him and took the donut as evidence."

Kelly reached over and put her hand on mine.

"When he was six, he got into these Magic Tree House books where this boy and his sister would go up into this big tree." I furrowed my brow, remembering. "I *think* it was his sister. Anyway, they'd use books to travel through time."

"You remember where they went?"

"Everywhere," I said. "The Middle Ages or the Cretaceous Period. The Wild Wild West. Egypt. Jonas and Lena would read them, and then he'd explain every detail to me. Then he'd tell me about these new endings he'd dreamt up. Alternate endings. And I thought—wow. Maybe we've got a writer in the family."

I fell silent and pulled in my line, resetting my bait, which was gone now.

Kelly climbed onto my lap.

I leaned against the chair back, and she hugged me. She had no bra on under her T-shirt, and I felt her breasts soft against my chest.

I exhaled, and she laughed.

"I'm gonna see if that stove top works," she said.

She went inside and made up a bit of chili. Mixed in some avocado and some fresh tomatoes and came out with a bag of chips.

"Damn," I said. "Did you mix pimento cheese in there?"

"I did," she said, flicking her eyebrows.

I did a twangy voice. "That right there will make a freight train take a dirt road."

Kelly laughed, and I explained that this was an expression my dad used to say about food that was so good you took a different route to get it.

After the snack, we took a nap on the deck, and a warm breeze woke us at sundown. In the distance along the shore, someone was piling firewood by their lakefront home, six feet high and four feet deep.

We cooked a striper and talked.

"This stuff at your job—it doesn't always end right, does it?" Kelly asked.

"You mean do the right people get punished?"

She nodded, her face still.

"Most of the time," I said.

"And when they don't?" she asked. "How do you deal with that?"

"It's hard," I said.

"You never want to take the law into your own hands?" she asked.

"I have," I said. "And it hasn't gone well for me."

She went silent then, not asking for more details.

Kelly had this instinct—when to back off and when to press forward. I wondered how she was coping since the shooting. I wanted to ask her, but inquiring would just open her up to asking me. And I wasn't really sure myself. It wasn't just pulling the trigger on Jed Harrington at the school. A cop's son had been killed at the bar. An innocent.

We stared at the stars, and I saw that Kelly was fading, so we lay down in the bed, each of us in shorts and T-shirts that stayed on all night.

It felt good not to complicate things. To just be with someone.

The next morning I got up and went skinny-dipping. As I swam about in the cool water, I heard a splash around the bow and realized Kelly had dove in the other way.

She swam around my side, and her hair looked different. Wet and plastered back to her face.

She noticed me looking and pointed. "I'm gonna have the craziest frizz about five minutes after this dries."

"I don't mind frizz," I said.

I climbed out by the ladder and grabbed a towel, wrapping it around me. I laid out another one for Kelly and took two more. Draped them across the deck.

"Close your eyes," she said, and I did.

Kelly climbed out, and after a moment, I opened my eyes. The oversized beach towel was wrapped around her, from her thighs up and over her breasts.

She lay next to me, atop the crisscross of the towels. It was a Monday, two weeks after Labor Day, and the lake was empty of all boat traffic, the kids back in school and the tourists all gone home.

Kelly inched closer to me, and I took my finger and traced a line that ran along her cheeks and onto her neck. Her hair fell onto my shoulder. "What do you want to do today?" I asked.

"You," she said.

We started cracking up then.

I hadn't shaved in a couple days, and she took the back of her hand. Ran it down the coarse area along my jaw. "You have a good face," she said. "And there haven't been a lot of good faces in my life."

She closed her eyes and I did the same. Resting there. Thinking nothing.

We got up a bit after that, and Kelly made eggs. I got out the fishing gear, and the two of us joked around, but kept steering away from topics we couldn't handle right now.

After breakfast, we sat out on the smaller deck. The afternoon water was calmer than usual, and a swallow-tailed kite dive-bombed the blue-green water, but pulled up right before he hit the surface. Then he flew back to a tiny island of grass nearby. Stared at us from a thick tree twig. And then repeated the same action all over again.

Kelly donned a Braves tee, tied tight in a knot around her slender waist.

We had drifted into the low water near a shoreline, and a musty sulfide odor from the blue-green algae filled the air. I motored farther out into the deep water.

"I'm gonna go inside and read a book," she said.

"Okay."

After an hour I lowered the bill on my fishing hat and closed my eyes.

When I awoke, hours had passed and I ambled over to the cabin.

Kelly had fallen asleep, a copy of Brian Panowich's *Like Lions* dog-eared on her lap, about two hundred pages in.

I moved up to the main captain's chair on the bow, where I'd been fishing, and pulled out my cell. A handful of texts came in, but I didn't look at them.

Something had been stirring within me since Kelly's question about taking the law into my own hands the night before.

Remy answered on the fourth ring.

"Hey," she said. "I've been looking for you."

"The chief didn't tell you?" I asked. "About my email?"

"Sure he did," she said. "But that didn't keep me from stopping by your house. I wanted to see if you were okay."

"I just needed a couple days."

"Of course," Remy said.

"How's Gattling?" I asked.

"Not good," she said.

I saw this coming the other night. The way he'd been rocking as if in a trance at the back of the ambulance.

"I went by Marvin's, and he said you went fishing."

"I'm sitting on a boat right now," I said. "Staring at the water."

"Well, don't worry about the case."

As she said this, it dawned on me that I hadn't considered the case at all in the last two days. Hadn't thought once about the short man or the old man.

"I was calling about something else," I said. "I made you a promise. That I wouldn't look into Lauten Hartley alone."

"Yeah," she said.

"Tomorrow," I said, "I start looking into it."

Remy didn't answer right away.

"*We* start, you mean."

"That's why I'm calling."

"Okay," Remy said. "But easy, P.T. All right? Easy."

I stared out at the black water. The moon was rising into the sky, a waning gibbous. It shone off the surface and made the still water look like igneous rock.

"Tomorrow night, partner," I said. "You and me." I hung up and stared out at the lake. A striper jumped, and concentric circles formed, more perfect than smoke rings coming off the stage at an old jazz club.

I moved about the boat. Flipping down jump seats and making sure the tackle boxes were affixed in the aft stowage locker.

I went into the galley and climbed into bed beside Kelly. My eyes were tired, and I fell fast asleep beside her.

22

In the morning, we motored back to the dock and met Harry Glavis at the time we'd originally arranged with him. Along the way, Kelly sprayed down the deck and cleaned up the trash. She stripped the sheets off the bed and left them folded atop the mattress.

Once we handed over the boat, we got back in my truck and fired up the engine. Headed down through Ralston and into Oakes Bluff.

As we moved through rural areas, I saw more election signs for Jerome Bleeker than I did for Toby Monroe, even in the traditionally conservative white areas. *Did this Bleeker guy have a chance of taking down Governor Monroe? No way.*

We moved southwest, following the route of the Tullumy River, its water churning parallel to the road that carried us to Mason Falls. The river that had changed my life.

Down in the valley close to the river, a blanket of fog was thick and gray, but as the sun rose, the fog became translucent and misty over the trees, and it disappeared as it hit the highway.

"I'm glad I stayed," Kelly said, the sun streaming in through the open passenger window and the light playing off the tan sheen of her legs.

I stared at her.

"With you, silly," she said. "On the boat." Her brown eyes studied me. "You've been quiet," she said. "Are you okay?"

"I'm good." I placed my hand atop hers. And I *felt* good. A few days clean of the school shooting and the mess that the stakeout had become.

Ten minutes later, I dropped Kelly off and gave her a kiss. Told her I'd call her later.

"You better."

As she walked away, my eyes lingered on her shape, and she turned, shaking her head. Caught red-handed.

About five minutes after that, the phone rang, and I smiled. In three days, I felt like I already knew enough of Kelly's sense of humor. That she'd call me five minutes later and ask if I was ready with the ring. Our running joke.

But it wasn't her at all. It was a man from County.

"P. T. Marsh?" he asked.

"Yeah?"

He introduced himself as Lonnie Fuchs, explaining that he worked for Animal Services.

"There's a note," Fuchs said, referring to a canine he'd been holding. "It says 'Before euthanizing, contact Detective P. T. Marsh.' We've been calling you for two days."

"Geez," I said, remembering now that Remy had asked for a favor for me about Harrington's dog.

"The dog you're planning to put down is Beau?" I asked. Referring to the tan-and-white husky-retriever mix that I'd found in the school shooter's backyard.

"Exactly," the man answered.

"And your facility has a capacity issue?" I confirmed. "Detective Morgan is my partner."

"So you know then," he said. "We can't keep animals more than three days. Are you interested in adopting?"

"Me?" I said, surprised. "Oh no, I can't. Apologies if I slowed down your process."

I hung up and drove another mile, thinking about Jed Harrington, the school shooter. Of what he'd done to Kelly and me. About the tension that entered the police department when the shooting happened. And how it segued into me rooking that shrink and maybe thinking I was in better shape than I was. And how it ended in me not firing on that old man in the forest.

There was a line from Shakespeare that my mom quoted when I was a kid.

The evil that men do lives after them.

Until, of course, something good steps in its way. And stops the cycle.

I called back the number and heard the same guy's voice pick up at County.

"Fuchs," I said. "Give me your address. I'm gonna take that dog after all."

23

By five p.m., I had filled out the necessary paperwork at County, and they brought Beau out from the back.

He had a tan body with a thick white ring that circled his chest, and a white stripe that meandered across his head and nose.

"He looks excited," Fuchs said, selling it hard, even though I'd already committed. Then again, it was true. The dog was over the moon to be out of a cage. He ran to me, wagging his tail and jumping.

I sat down on the lobby floor and took the eight-foot leash into my hand, letting the dog jump into my lap and lick me.

"Okay," I said. "It's gonna be okay."

I called Marvin to bring Purvis back home.

Per my new friend Lonnie at County, it was not kosher to put Purvis and Beau into my truck together, since Purvis's smell would be in the vehicle, nor was it okay to bring the new dog home first and then get Purvis after.

So Marvin met me at the duck pond in the neighborhood and had Purvis leashed up, so the two dogs could meet on neutral turf. I parked outside my house and hustled over. As I turned the corner, I saw Marvin and Purvis, the two wandering around the edge of the water.

Beau saw Purvis and picked up his pace. He arrived and promptly gave my bulldog a good smell from head to butt.

At eight years old, Purvis was slower at avoiding dogs' sniffs, but Beau was only a year and a half old and excited to be outside of the county kennel.

"You catch anything?" Marvin asked as the dogs consorted, both of them friendly.

"Some bass," I said, leaning over and getting Beau to sit so Purvis got a break for a second. "Six or seven striper. That lake's full of striper," I said. "Practically jump into the boat."

Marvin had brought some dog treats with him, and he rewarded both dogs for being nice.

We stayed out there a good half hour, and Marvin never asked about Kelly once. I liked that about him. That he didn't push things. Eventually Marvin told me his legs were aching.

"C'mon, fluffy-butt," I said to Beau, who had two large tufts of white hair on either side of his tail. I pulled hard on the leash. The dog wasn't technically a puppy, but he was hyper as hell.

We brought the two home, but kept Beau on a longer leash, tied inside the house, like my friend at County had advised, while Marvin got off his feet. We talked fishing, and some changes Marvin was making to his yard.

"You're planting in fall?" I asked, and Marvin nodded.

"Black-eyed Susans bloom in fall," he said. "So do daylilies."

As we talked, Beau smelled around the living room, and Purvis, who prefers to drool and sleep most of the time, left the area and went out back. I heard the plastic flap of the doggie door and guessed that Purvis was headed to his favorite area on the lawn out back.

"You stay two days on the lake and then get a dog?" Marvin asked. "You gonna buy a Porsche next?"

"You're the one who said I needed to be open, didn't you?"

"Hey, I'm not complaining," Marvin said. "I've just always wanted to drive a Porsche."

I smiled at my father-in-law, and we let Beau off the leash. He stayed close to us, and when we walked into the kitchen, he followed.

"I didn't entirely think this out," I said to my father-in-law, grabbing a Coke for him and a Dr Pepper for me. I pointed at the new dog, who was full grown at thirty-five pounds. "But they were gonna kill the little guy."

"He's a good dog," Marvin said, leaning over and petting Beau. "You want me to take him for a couple days?"

"No," I said. "I just gotta meet Remy tonight. Can you hang out for a bit and watch the two of them?"

"I thought you were off of work."

"I am, and I'm not," I said. "I promise I'm back by midnight. You can crash in your old bed if you get tired."

"Hold on," Marvin said. He checked the guide on the TV before answering and saw that the Braves were back playing the Phillies again, the first in a three-game stretch. He grabbed his Coke and waved for me to get going.

I took a shower and threw on some dark jeans. A black tee and a midnight-blue hoodie.

When I came out, the game was in the sixth inning, and the two dogs were both asleep on the couch, a foot or so between them. A good first day.

Marvin stretched his left leg out, the heel of his sock up on the edge of the coffee table. He pointed his toes toward the TV and then brought them back again, working the muscles in his calf.

"You robbin' a bank or something?" he asked, staring at my clothes.

I shrugged. "Porsches don't come easy."

I grabbed my keys and drove to the address that Remy had texted me.

24

I sat at the counter at Scala's, a full mug of Pabst Blue Ribbon in front of me.

The place was a neighborhood bar, and in not such a good neighborhood. The numbered streets, 20th and Pike to be exact.

I'd been to this bar for a cop's retirement party. But it was years ago, and my policy back then was one beer and home to the wife.

The owner of Scala's had been a boxer, and he'd decorated the walls with images of famous boxing moments—some from movies and others from the yellowing extracts of sports sections. All of them were housed in black frames that plastered every wall.

I sat at a counter facing the street, my view a handful of empty storefronts along 21st Street. A shuttered hardware place. An abandoned liquor store. A barber shop that was still in business, but closed now, at ten p.m.

The bar smelled like stale beer and pretzels. When I heard the chime on the door, I glanced to my right.

At work, Remy Morgan dresses up. So other than at a stakeout like the other night, it's all professional-looking skirts or pantsuits. Nice jackets. But now she had on gray leggings and a black T-shirt that read *Extra* in black letters.

A waitress came by as Remy climbed onto the stool next to me. "What'll you have, hon?"

"Ginger ale," she said, looking from my beer to me.

After the woman left, I pushed it farther away. "A prop," I said. "If I wanted to start drinking again, it wouldn't be PBR."

"Sorry I'm late," she said. "Was following up on a lead."

"Everything all right?"

Remy nodded.

Tomorrow I was expected back at work, per a text I'd gotten from Chief Senza. So I'd be back on the case Remy was working late on. With four dead bodies and counting, I'd have to be ready to go whole hog.

"The short guy," she said. "I went back over the area outside of Tandy's in the daylight on Saturday. Specifically the route that Shorty took out the bathroom window."

"You find something?"

"In the weeds outside the window," Remy said. "A motel key card."

"What motel?"

"The Garden Palms," Remy said. "Although the card was generic, so it took us a day to figure that out."

"I know that place," I said. It was a crap bucket down the road from Tandy's. A one-story motel. The kind of joint that put stickers on the front door reminding guests not to enter with guns.

"And?" I asked.

"Me and Abe spent Sunday there. Short guy's name is Thiago Carilla."

"You find a weapon in his place?" I asked. "He didn't have a gun in the forest, or he would've shot back at the old guy."

Which meant his weapon might've been left in his hotel room.

"Abe said the same thing," my partner said. "But no. No weapon. We found six spools of Ace bandages. Vaseline. Two boxes of gauze." Remy did an imitation of Abe. "'Rem—it looks like a damn Eckerd's exploded in here.'"

I grinned at this. "And you told him, 'Eckerd's stopped exploding ten years ago. Those are all called Rite Aid now.'"

"Pretty much," she said. "But judging by the amount of blood loss this guy was dealing with, we're thinking Carilla's hand injury might've been a bullet wound, P.T. A graze."

"Well." I shrugged. "The M.E.'s got the body. What does Sarah say?"

"Inconclusive," she said. "She did note a divot at the proximal end of the wound."

"A divot?" I repeated. "Did it have a parallel mark next to it, right before the abrasion?"

"Exactly," Remy said.

The M.E. before Sarah had once explained to me about the odd relationship between the yaw of a bullet as it caromed off human skin. Pressure waves were generated, and the skin buckled. It's sort of like a plane's nose, touching the ground and then bouncing off it. There's a notch in the skin where the bullet first connects, then two parallel marks and a shallow abrasion that follows.

I sat back, thinking about how this might change our theory of the crime.

The two dead men in the car were killed execution style, and the truth was that we were still guessing as to how the short guy and the old guy were connected.

Remy's drink came, and behind us the music changed to "Light My Fire" by the Doors. Ten minutes later, the sound of shuffleboard stopped, and so did the music.

"We're closing up, hon," the waitress said.

I dropped some cash onto the counter and pulled on my hoodie. The night air was brisk, and Remy and I left, walking out onto Pike.

As I headed out, I glanced back to confirm that the beer on the counter was still full. Not a touch gone.

We headed into the alley beside the bar, and I lit a Marlboro Red.

Remy confirmed that we were here to check out the liquor store across the way, but were waiting for the street to clear. The bar was the last place open on the street every night, which was why Remy asked to meet there.

"We also found a throwaway cell phone in the short guy's hotel room," Remy said.

"Anything good on it?"

"An interesting text. 'Need more scratch,' it read. Sent to another throwaway cell phone."

"More scratch as in he wanted more money?" I asked.

"Yeah," Remy said. "Sent on Wednesday."

This was two days before the short guy had been shot out in the forest behind the bar. I put out my cig, and we moved to my truck, our eyes on the employees inside the bar cleaning up.

"Hey," I said to Remy. "You don't have the final medical report on Dilmendes on your phone, do you? The guy in the passenger seat of the Caprice?"

"No," she said. "Why?"

"That other bullet he took. Through his back."

"Oh yeah," she said. "There were no other bullets, P.T. The head-shot was his only injury. A through-and-through."

I took this in. *Then where the hell did the bloodstain on the back of the passenger seat come from?*

"We'd been thinking that the short guy—"

"Carilla," she interrupted.

"Carilla." I used his name. "That he was our shooter, but there's another possibility, Rem. The bullets in the gut of the college kid and Carilla were both .22 slugs, right?"

"Yup."

"Well, we know the bullets in the two dead guys on the roadside were also from a .22. If the slugs match, that could mean it's the same gun. Meaning the old man from the forest is our killer on the side of the road."

Remy nodded. "So under that theory, the old man enters the back seat of the Caprice."

"Driver's side." I pointed. "Back door."

Remy nodded, agreeing. "Two guys that are soon to be dead are in the front."

We each thought about this for a second, and I pictured it.

"I've been stuck on that blood," I said. "The bloodstain on the back of the passenger seat."

"'Fixated' is a better word."

"I've been fixated," I agreed. "But here's my new theory. There's *three* guys in the car. Driver and his buddy in the front. And Carilla, also a buddy, in the back seat, passenger side."

"Okay . . . ?"

"Old guy gets in. Pops Vinorama, the driver. Pops Dilmendes in the passenger seat. He turns to shoot Carilla, but by this time, the short guy has the door open and is on the run."

"He grazes him in the left hand with a bullet," Remy said.

"Exactly." I nodded. "That's why he had the gauze on his hand."

"And all those medical supplies in his motel."

"The shot nicks him," I said. "And after that, the old guy's searching for Carilla—because whatever he killed the other two men for, Carilla's a witness to it."

Remy's eyebrows went up, and I could tell from the look that she liked the logic.

"If that's the case, P.T., then the blood on the Ace bandage will match that blood on the back of the seat. Both would be Carilla's blood. That's easy to test."

"And then," I said, "maybe you won't refer to me as fixated, but astute."

Remy smiled, and we went silent for a moment, scanning the stores. The bartender and waitress from Scala's were gone, and I turned to my partner.

"So . . . you said to meet you here." I glanced around. "What's the plan?"

"Well," she said, "two days ago, I started researching that partnership you told me about."

"Lauten Hartley's partnership?" I asked, referring to the company that owned the liquor store. "FJF Investments?"

Remy nodded, and outside a single car passed us. A beat-up Hyundai Santa Fe.

"The Golden Oaks liquor store." She pointed across the street. "If you believe the filings, the store was making good money. Lottery tickets and hard liquor mostly. And then it just shuttered. Out of nowhere. Right past Christmas two years ago."

I stared over at the façade that once read *Golden Oaks*.

I still couldn't explain why I'd told my wife that I was too busy to help with her battery problem at the roadside back in December of '17. I'd been consumed with this robbery and asked Lena to call her father, Marvin.

Marvin arrived at the side of I-32. But as he spoke to his daughter at her window, a car struck Marvin's vehicle into Lena's. And down the hill my wife's Jeep went. Into the Tullumy River, where Lena and Jonas would drown in minutes.

The empty space I stared at across the way had no sign on it. The windows that were once crowded with liquor bottles were blocked with bars. And behind them, someone had placed plywood with the words "out of business" spray-painted on the wood.

The words "Golden Oaks," which used to sit on a horizontal sign above the front door, were gone, as were the words "Liquor," "Fine Wine," and an illustration of a yellow oak tree.

The only remnants, in fact, that it had been a package store at all were the vertical letters that spelled *LIQUOR* attached to a concrete spear that stuck up into the sky and was probably too expensive to remove.

"Are you okay?" Remy asked.

I'd felt a curious calm in the last day or so, not just because I'd taken time off, but because I get this sort of focus when I chase a lead. And no lead mattered more to me than this one.

"Yeah," I said. "Are we breaking in?"

"I prefer to call it exploring," Remy said.

25

We walked across 20th Street and passed the front of the Golden Oaks. Moved past the package store and turned down Pike to an alley behind the place.

A rolling gate stood between the worn asphalt of the alley and the back of the store property. It was my height roughly, but above the gate was a string of razor wire, formed into a series of loops.

I took off my hoodie and swung it atop the sharp wire, pulling the fabric down so it formed a barrier above the razor to grab on to.

Remy found a foothold and climbed over, disappearing out of sight.

I went next, landing on a fenced-off rectangle of blacktop behind the liquor store, an area that was empty, except for two angled white streaks denoting parking spaces. One of them still held the faded blue markings of a handicapped sign, painted onto the ground.

I stared at the rear of the store. In front of us was a steel door, and off to its right a window.

I tested the door, pulling on the latch, but quickly realized that it wasn't going anywhere.

"Your plan . . ." I whispered to Remy.

"Sure." She nodded. "You didn't hear something inside?"

I blinked. Thinking I knew where she was going.

"I mean, anyone could be in there," Remy said. "And we have a responsibility to investigate."

I smiled at this, but also thought through the machinations of this deception. My partner was talking about us going through the place, and then reporting it. Saying we heard a noise. Then getting a patrol car down here, to document anything we found. This held more risk than usual, with Hartley's position on the police board.

Remy walked back to the six-foot-tall fence. She grabbed my hoodie and wrapped it around her fist. Approached the window.

Without warning she punched at the glass.

I'd seen Remy hit plenty. Both out in the field and at her kickboxing gym.

The glass shattered fast, and she took a flashlight from her back pocket. Looked inside.

I wondered how much of this Remy had thought through before she met me at the bar. Her moves were something I'd do, and it usually wasn't good to be working off the P. T. Marsh playbook.

Remy took her right boot off then and used the metal heel to clear the rest of the window, sending glass shards down into the store.

Knocking out the remaining glass with the toe, she shined her flashlight inside again, and we saw it was a small bathroom. Through the open door at the far side of the tiny room, we could make out the empty liquor store.

"Age before beauty," my partner said, spreading the hoodie over the edge of the window.

I laid my right foot inside the hole, and then my left. Turned on my stomach and eased myself backward through the two-foot-square space.

I thudded to the ground, noticing a piece of glass had sliced at my right hand on the way in.

My blood was smeared onto some shards on the floor, and I carefully picked up the red glass and placed it in my back pocket.

I flicked on my own flashlight, raking the darkness with light. In the quiet, rats scurried, and Remy landed behind me.

We moved into a storeroom, standing in the middle of two aisles with empty wooden racks. From the different heights of the shelves, I could imagine which ones once stored six-packs and which ones were for "fine wine," as the sign outside had originally advertised. More like Two-Buck Chuck.

But nothing lined the shelves now except an inch of dust.

When I first came to investigate the robbery in December 2017, I'd met a man named Christian Pelo. He was a new employee, a few days into the gig, when a man in a ski mask walked in and demanded everything in the register.

Pelo was in training, and his boss, a store manager named John Adrian, had just left for the bank. Adrian left Pelo shorthanded, with only thirty-three bucks in the till.

If you were a crook, it was the definition of shitty timing. Then again, I hadn't arrested a lot of Rhodes scholars while working in burglary or homicide.

Pelo showed the thief the safe, which was empty, and he opened the register too. Full transparency to try to save his own life.

The robber cracked Pelo with his rifle, took the thirty-three dollars, and filled up a Cherry Coke. Fountain drink, not bottle. And that's what got me fired up about finding the shitbrick back in 2017. The nerve to stop and fill his drink with ice. Then soda. Take his time leaving.

The event also reminded me how much the numbered streets had fallen into disrepair since I'd been on patrol. Part of me thought the blame for that fell on us, in MFPD, for choosing to ignore calls and not make obvious arrests. "Why arrest them?" I'd once heard a blue-suiter say. "Let the animals kill themselves." It was exactly the wrong philosophy to come from any cop if our goal was to ever come together as a city.

Within a day, Christian Pelo was gone from the job at the Golden Oaks.

When I came by to get more information from John Adrian, the store manager, he never seemed to be able to tell me where Pelo lived.

"Do you have his employment paperwork?" I'd asked Adrian, trying to get a valid address for the short-term employee. "His I-9 form?"

At every turn, gathering information was like peeling cat hair off duct tape.

I got railroaded. Ignored.

But I'm a stubborn person. And proud of my record on cases back when I worked robbery full-time. So even though I was just covering for guys in that department, I stuck by the case. Came by again and again over the next week. A couple weeks after that, on December 21, the accident with Lena happened.

In the days that followed, I dropped the Golden Oaks robbery. I later learned that it was closed as unsolved. With only thirty-three dollars missing, no one seemed to care.

Remy and I fanned our flashlights across the place, and dust moved through the rays of light. We walked into the main area of the store and out toward those plywood boards that covered the windows facing 20th.

With Remy digging through details and not liking them, I felt recharged. I wasn't some crazy guy who lived in the past with a talking dog and invented details to fit the case. I was Detective Marsh, from the old days. The guy with gut instinct. The guy you went to when the hair on your arms stood up.

But now that I was standing here, I wondered what the hell I was even looking for.

I stood by the door where I'd come in and talked to the manager.

"Tell me what you remember," Remy said.

"Adrian was nervous," I said.

"He was the guy who got robbed?"

"No," I said. "That was Pelo."

"Right," Remy said. "Adrian was the manager."

I nodded, picturing John Adrian. Five foot ten. Wild, curly black hair. "Adrian felt more invested than an employee, Rem. But there was something else. It always felt like he was pushing me to talk outside."

"To not stir up customers?" Remy asked. "Having a cop there?"

"That was my guess back then," I said. "But now I dunno. Maybe he was avoiding something that I didn't notice. Something illegal, hidden among the liquor bottles? Something . . ."

I walked over to the counter of the store, remembering my conversations with the manager.

"The store looks different now," I said.

Presently, the counter was shoved against the far wall, opening up a giant space in the center of the store by the front door.

"Years ago, customers lined up here," I said, motioning at where we were standing. "Made impulse buys of lottery tickets and rolling papers. Cheap cigars."

As I stepped toward the counter, I heard a squeak. The kind of thing you only hear when a place is dead empty. A weak floorboard maybe.

I stepped forward and heard it again. *Ehhh.*

Back again. *Ehhh.*

Remy crouched, wiping at the dusty wooden floor with the back of the arm of her sweatshirt.

When she got the area a little cleaner, we noticed that a few of the planks didn't match the others around them.

"This area would've been behind the counter, Rem," I said. "Back then. On the cashier's side."

I crouched down and moved from board to board, feeling along the wooden floor. After a dozen pushes, one area popped back out at me, a spring-loaded door.

Remy grabbed at the edge and opened a hole about two and a half feet square, on a hinge. Propped it open upon itself.

Shining my flashlight into the hole, I stared down a set of concrete stairs. As I stepped down into the area, cobwebs covered my face.

"Jesus," I said. Pulling the mess from my hair and mouth.

I shined the light around and saw a concrete room, maybe twenty by twenty, with three or four card tables set up in the center, and shelves lining each wall.

Remy followed me down, and both flashlights scanned the place.

If the upstairs felt like a land locked in time, so did this space. Except dustier. It smelled like dead soil and ammonia, and I heard Remy cough. She held her sweatshirt over her mouth.

I walked over to the shelves and saw only one item left behind. A busted money-counting machine.

What was someone doing down here that you couldn't find out about? Purvis huffed in my head. *That was worth killing a cop's wife and son over?*

My bulldog's voice was raspy when it came to what happened to Jonas. He'd lost his best friend after all.

"So John Adrian . . ." Remy said, her voice trailing off.

"Yeah," I said. "The manager must've been aware of what was going on down here."

"And Pelo, the clerk, wasn't," Remy said, finishing my thought.

I stared around.

The subflooring was made of worn plywood and all around it were fresh scratch marks from some animal.

I pointed toward a wooden shelf at the far side of the room. It had a solid back to it, and none of the rest of the shelves did.

"That's odd, right?" I said.

I walked over to it and ran my hands along the dusty wood. To my right I saw a set of two industrial-strength L-brackets mounted on a blank wall. The kind you might hang something heavy on.

I reached my hands around the sides of the shelves and lifted.

Off it came, a lightweight wood.

I carried it to the hooks and hung it there.

"Wow," Remy said.

Behind where the shelf had just stood was a door.

"So if anyone came down here, looking around . . ." I said.

"They wouldn't see a way out," my partner answered.

We opened the door and found an angled stairwell. Followed it up into a tiny entry area maybe ten square feet wide with two more doors. One was locked, but by the direction, presumably led into another storefront. The other was a metal door that swung out onto a loading dock in the same alley we'd been in ten minutes ago.

"Huh," Remy said.

We walked outside into another area cordoned off by a fence. But it was clear that we were behind the hardware store now, two doors down from the Golden Oaks.

"The partnership owned this place too," Remy said. "I saw that in the paperwork. They shut down the hardware store the same week as the Golden Oaks."

I left the door ajar, but glared out at the loading dock.

The exit was one of those kinds where the driveway angled away from the store. So you could step right into trucks from our level. Load boxes right from this back door.

"So someone running an illegal operation under the liquor store," I said, "could use this as a way to ship—"

"To ship what?" my partner said. "It could be anything illegal down here, P.T. Anything."

"Yeah," I said, my flashlight cutting through thick dust that came off the stairs.

"What did you find out about the guy who robbed the liquor store anyway?" Remy asked.

"That's why I kept coming back," I said. "I figured the key was talking to this clerk Pelo, but he went MIA. I never saw him again."

We walked back down the stairwell from the loading dock and into the big dusty room below the Golden Oaks. Above us, I could hear a rat moving with something clinking behind him. Some part of his body was probably caught in a trap, and he was carrying it with him.

As I scanned the shelves more carefully this time, I noticed three or four empty cardboard boxes, each lined with a plastic bag of some sort. The bags were empty, but had traces of powdery white residue on the inside.

"Drugs?" Remy asked.

"I dunno," I said. I opened my wallet and found a parking receipt on hard card stock. I scraped it along the inside of the bag, collecting the residue. Then folded it upon itself and saved it in my pocket.

In movies you always see a cop taste powder he suspects to be drugs. Which always drives me crazy when I see it. I mean, would you put some unknown foreign substance in your body? You wouldn't.

"It could be construction materials," Remy said about the powder.

"Yeah." I nodded. Concrete and plaster were placed in bags, and shipped in boxes. I looked for markings on the sides of the boxes, but there were none.

"So they were moving something illegal . . ." I said, my voice trailing off.

"Only problem is—there's nothing down here now," Remy said. "Other than the rats."

Remy was right, and we spent the next thirty minutes confirming it. Inspecting each shelf and empty carton for evidence. First down here. And then upstairs after. But for Lauten Hartley, who owned this place, there was no crime to chase him over, unless failure to dust was a felony.

"Let me ask you a question, P.T.," Remy said after we'd searched every shelf.

"Shoot."

"Where do you think this is going to lead anyway?"

"What do you mean?" I asked. "By 'this,' do you mean us sneaking around?"

"Yeah." She nodded.

"We're gonna get to the bottom of this old crime," I said.

"And then what?" my partner asked. The look on her face was legitimate curiosity.

"Put these guys away," I said. "Hartley. Whoever he's with."

"When you called me last night, you were sitting on the deck of that houseboat, right?" she asked. "That's what you said."

"Uh-huh." I nodded.

"Where was Kelly Borland?"

I stared at Remy. Had she been spying on me? Or more likely, had Marvin given me up? Described the woman I was with when I dropped off Purvis?

"She was inside," I said. "Asleep."

"By herself?"

I wasn't sure where Remy was going with this. "Yeah."

"Why weren't you with her?"

I sneered at my partner. "It's none of your business who I do or don't sleep with."

"I just want to understand how this ends," my partner said. "Let's say we find the guy who hired Tarticoft to take out your wife," Remy said. "What then?"

"What do you mean?"

"Well, I was gung ho before," she said, pausing to look around the dusty rat trap. "But . . . will it be over for you?"

"Are you for real?"

Her voice softened. "I need to know, P.T., if this is just another mission to distract you from the rest of your life."

A flare of anger shot through me.

We were back under the liquor store, and I balled up my fists. Climbed back up the ladder. "You have no clue what you're talking about."

"Really?" Remy asked. She followed me up.

"You're a single person running around, having fun," I said. "You wanna sleep with a co-worker, you do it. A subordinate at work? Even better. You have no idea what it's like to commit to someone and make a family and then have that taken away from you."

"And you have no idea what it's like to watch someone torture themselves," she said. "Someone who's full of regret that they did something wrong—even though they just worked late one night."

I moved closer to Remy's face. I was mad enough to chew nails. But I just turned and climbed out the back window. Over the fence and out to my Silverado.

I crossed the dark street ahead of my partner, but sat in my truck for a moment. My body shook with anger, and I heard Remy's Alfa start up in the alley.

I waited until she was gone, fired up my truck, and drove home.

26

*E*aston Pappas had always been one of the popular kids. A favorite of the girls and envied by the boys. He was picked first in sports. And by now, in eighth grade, he was king of the campus. On the verge of high school cool.

Easton had been known to brag. He talked trash while playing point guard for the middle school basketball team. And at the debate for eighth-grade president, he ran circles around this smart, nervous girl from the honors classes.

Which was why it was odd that Easton had dropped his backpack now and stood, speechless, outside the art class.

"You okay, bruh?" a younger kid asked.

Easton nodded, but didn't speak. The smaller kid flipped the door open and hustled into math class, two doors down, the bell for the next period about to ring.

The man Easton had seen inside the art room wore a green flannel shirt and jeans. And hiking boots. Expensive ones.

He also held a .38 toward Mr. Tanner.

Mr. T, who Easton had last year for Life Science.

Easton blinked, a wave of nausea rising inside him. The eighth grader who'd won the election in a landslide was suddenly reduced to a gesturing monkey. And no one was paying any attention to him.

"Mrs. . . ." he croaked to a teacher passing by.

"Shouldn't you be in class, young man?" the teacher asked, heading in a nearby door.

He found the fire alarm then. Smashed the glass and reached inside. Pulled.

A bell walloped into action, and the same teacher from a moment ago emerged from her classroom.

"Are you okay?" she asked.

And Easton finally found his voice.

"Gun," he screamed. Pointing at the art class. "Man with a gun in that class."

27

The morning sky across northern Georgia bore a streak of blue, the kind so pure you could paint a nursery with it. Except in the distance, there was an orange band that signaled rain might be coming.

I had been gone for three days, and although Remy had partially caught me up in the alley last night, I needed a full download on our double murder—and quick.

I pushed through the lobby and nodded at Hope Duffy. Hustled up the stairwell and found my partner. We hadn't exchanged a word or a text since last night.

"How about we get coffee?" I said. "I'm buying. You can officially catch me up on the case."

Remy stared at me, her dark eyes searching my face. Wondering if I was still angry about the argument last night. But the reality is—I don't have a ton of people in my life that I trust. And some days, it seems like Remy, Marvin, and Abe are the only ones. It was too short of a list to write any of them off.

"Sure," she said. "Let me grab my iPad."

We walked down the steps to the first floor and out the door. There was a guy who set up in the park down the block and served Italian coffee from a cart.

"So what's the latest on our old guy?" I asked. "We never discussed that part."

"We've had a BOLO out on him for three days now, and no reports. Patrol's been canvassing."

"You said last night you picked up a motel card from the guy who escaped out the window. The one who got shot."

"Thiago Carilla," she said. "We've also gone through his phone records. I told you about the text we saw, right?"

"He wanted more scratch."

"Exactly," Remy said. "We also found earlier texts to Vinorama and Dilmendes. So we know for certain they were all buddies."

We walked across this spongy material on the playground and over to the coffee cart.

"And what's the latest on them?" I asked. "The two dead guys in the car."

"We still suspect they're drug couriers," Remy said. "From Carilla's texts to them, it's obvious they're friends. He told them he had something to deliver and could pay them a grand for their trouble. Were they up for a little road trip?"

"They said yes?"

"'*Por supuesto*,' is what they said." Remy did her best Spanish accent. "Of course."

We got to the coffee cart, and I ordered an Americano.

"For you, honey?" the coffee cart guy asked Remy.

"Fior di Zagara," she said.

I paid the guy, and he got under way with making our drinks.

A mom and her son were flying a kite in the distance, and a green dragon flipped and danced against the sky. It smelled like fresh-cut grass outside.

"P.T.," Remy said. She hesitated, her brow a mess of lines. "Last night—"

"Don't worry about it," I said.

I grabbed my coffee. "So the two guys up front in the Caprice both have charges for drug possession," I said. "And Carilla referred to them as drivers. Can we assume this whole thing is about drugs?"

"Or drug money," Remy said. "Or what Abe and I were working on. Which is drug equipment."

"Meaning what?" I asked.

"A pill press," she said. "We figure that's what left those lined impressions in the back seat of the Caprice."

"So the theory from outside the liquor store last night?" I said. "About Carilla and the old guy in the back of the car?"

"Works out perfect for this," Remy said. "That might be what the old guy was after. Plus, I asked the night shift guys to hit the Caprice with Luminol. In case the shooter cleaned up after Carilla ran out of the car."

"And?" I asked.

"And this is what they found." Remy showed me a picture on her phone.

The photo was shot in the dark and showed smears of a bright blue color across most of the back seat of the Caprice, where someone had cleaned up. Except there was a rectangular void across the middle of the back seat with no chemiluminescence.

"So something was on that seat when the old guy shot at Carilla," I said. "Something the shooter took with him?"

"Exactly," Remy said. "Abe thinks it was a pill press. A desktop unit. The same folks who used to run Oxy up here a couple years ago . . . a lot of 'em are now running other pills. Seemingly legal, but not."

"Fakes of legal drugs," I said.

Remy nodded. "Filler mostly. Stamped with a die that makes it look like real pharmaceuticals."

Remy grabbed her tea drink, and we turned toward the precinct.

"You're talking about a small tabletop pill press?" I asked. "The kind you set up on a dresser in a bedroom?"

"Exactly." Remy nodded.

"Rem," I said. "You know I go out with the narco squad once in a while, right? On raids. Neal and I over there have been buddies since the academy."

"Sure," she said.

"Well, I haven't done it in six months, but I'm on a text chain with those guys. They seized a pill press last month. It's probably still in the evidence room."

Remy saw where I was going. "We can test this theory," she said.

"Exactly."

I texted my buddy in narco and asked for a heads-up to the guy who ran the evidence room.

We came in through the front of the precinct then. Passed through the lobby, but didn't go upstairs. Headed instead down to the basement.

When we got to Evidence, I saw Ed Udall, who had to be seventy this year and still working. He'd been eligible to retire when I was a rookie.

"Ed," I said. "You get a heads-up about a pill press we wanna check out?"

"What business is it of yours?" he asked. Classic Ed, which is to say hard-ass. "Not your case, Marsh. Not even your department."

I explained how Remy and I wanted to test out a theory, and Ed made a couple calls, even though narco had already given him the green light.

Ten minutes later, Ed wheeled out a pill press on a rolling cart.

"Wow, it's small," Remy said as she saw the machine coming toward us.

This particular press was made of aluminum and sat twenty-four inches high. The base of the apparatus was affixed to a square piece of steel three inches thick and the shape of letter-sized paper.

At the top of the machine was a feed port or funnel to pour whatever powder formulation into, and along the side was a hand crank.

"So it requires no electricity?" Remy said as Udall had me sign for the item.

"Exactly," I said.

That was the main advantage of these presses. The lowlifes who used them could set up in some abandoned house or a rural structure out in the woods with no power.

I pointed at the spout. "You fill up here," I said. "Your die lives right in this column. That's what stamps the letter or word onto the pill so it looks legit. Like Bayer Aspirin has an '81' on it. And then you crank it like this." I turned the hand crank one revolution, and the column jammed down. "The pill comes out there." I pointed at the smooth base of the machine. "You hit this to eject it and wipe the area clean for the next pill. And on you go."

Remy lifted the machine and turned it on its side. Staring at the column that stuck up twenty-four inches into the air. It had two rails, and she was mentally lining them up with the two marks on the back seat of the Caprice.

"It's close." I nodded. "But let's get it down there and check. Take some pictures and make sure."

Remy and I took the elevator down to Basement 2, and we were off like a herd of turtles through the bowels of the building. We pushed the cart down yellowing hallways with rooms where case files were stored. When we finally got to the end, we took an elevator all the way up into the vehicle mod yard.

As we got there, Carlos had just arrived for his shift, and he saw us rolling the pill press toward him.

"Oh shit, CSI's in the house," he said. "Is this Vegas or Miami? The women were hotter in Miami."

"You can't say stuff like that anymore," I said.

Remy and I rolled the cart over to the Chevy Caprice and gloved up. Then we grabbed the pill press and carried it carefully toward the car.

The back seats of American cars from the '90s are huge, and Remy got in from one side, while I pushed from the other.

Carlos handed me the press, and I placed it on the seat, positioning the two rails right into the dimples left on the seat.

"Perfect match," Carlos said.

I got out and went around to Remy's side. Inspected the indents. Carlos was right. It *was* a match. But I scrunched up my face, mentally playing through the action.

"What's wrong?" Remy asked.

"Can I see that picture?" I said. "The one you showed me with the blood smears."

My partner handed me the shot done with the Luminol spray, and I glared at the square void on the seat.

"Well, I don't doubt that a press like this was in the car," I said. "Enough times to make those impressions."

"But not this time?" Remy asked, anticipating from my tone.

"Well . . ." I compared the picture to the size of the actual pill press in front of me. "Even though this is a small pill press, it's still two feet high on its side, Rem. It would've blocked more of the blood spray."

"Aww shit," Carlos said, seeing it himself.

"Plus, if this press was in the car at the time of our double," I said, "I don't think the old man could've gotten off that shot at Carilla."

I sat down in the back seat, mimicking the shooter's action.

"Bam." I pointed at the driver in the front seat with my finger. "Bam." I pointed at the front passenger. Then I reached out to where Carilla would've been seated and my hand smacked against the pill press.

"He coulda side-armed it," Remy said.

I held the gun like in a gangster movie, cockeyed, my hand extending in front of the machine.

"The other problem's the spray," I said. "It wouldn't have gotten all over the back of the seat with this big-ass machine in here."

"Truth," Carlos said.

My phone pulsed in my jacket pocket. Heard Remy's ring at the same time. But I ignored the noise, focusing on the task at hand.

"Let's get it out," I said, and Carlos grabbed the pill press from one side, while I held the other.

Once the press was back on the cart, I leaned into the back seat again, from the left side.

"Something was back here all right." I motioned at the back seat of the car while grabbing Remy's phone and holding the picture out. "It's yea high. Maybe six or eight inches."

"And goes out to here." Remy tapped near the front edge of the seat.

"Hold on," Carlos said, and walked over to the recycle bin.

He came back with two empty Amazon boxes. He placed the first one on the seat, and I shook my head. But the second was pretty close. I got out of the car, leaving the cardboard box in place. Remy and I stared in then, comparing the box to the picture with the void in the blue smears on her phone.

"A case of some sort," she said, taking back her cell and snapping a picture of the cardboard box on the seat.

"The sort not found when patrol came upon the car with the two bodies," I added. "So if Carilla ran—"

"The old man took the case with him," Remy said. "After he cleaned up the car."

My partner glanced down at her phone and nudged me to look. The text we'd both gotten was from Dispatch. A patrolman had found the hotel where the old guy had been staying.

"We gotta go," I said to Carlos.

I pointed at the press. "You mind returning that to Ed in Evidence?"

"Mean-ass Ed?" Carlos asked.

"The same." Remy smiled.

"Oh yeah, he loves Mexican guys with long hair. My pleasure, P.T."

28

Remy and I hustled to the parking lot across from the precinct, and I told her I'd drive.

"What's the place?"

"Homewood Suites. Out on 909."

I knew this hotel. It was one of two that was put up in about six months' time, a few miles west of my father-in-law's house.

We left the city and drove toward Bergamot, passing County Records. Ten minutes later we pulled off 909 and found the hotel about two blocks from the highway.

The place was made of prefabricated concrete that had been trucked into Mason Falls at night in sheets eight inches thick and twenty feet wide.

A blue-suiter named Ingram met us out front. He was waiting by his cruiser, parked in the turnaround.

"Jesus, Clint," I said to Officer Ingram as we pulled up, staring at the patrolman's facial hair. He was midthirties, with a baby face and a brown moustache that looked like a caterpillar.

"Is it Movember already?" Remy asked him.

"No, I just—" Ingram touched the tiny fur ball above his mouth. "I thought it looked good."

"That's what matters." Remy patted him on the shoulder. "What *you* think."

"What've we got here?" I asked him.

"The manager rented a room five days ago to a Stanley Creiss." Ingram held up the sketch of the old guy that was composited from five accounts of him at Tandy's.

"Is he a hundred percent sure it's our old guy?"

"A hundred and ten percent were his words," Ingram said. "But there's no one in the room, P.T. Plus, the I.D. and credit card are stolen. Stanley Creiss is actually eighty-six and lives in the West Cobb area of Atlanta. Retired helicopter pilot."

Ingram walked us inside then, introducing Remy and me to the manager, who was five foot three, with tiny arms that emerged from a short-sleeved dress shirt. His eyes were closer together than an earthworm's, and his name was Robert Riggs.

"Like Bobby Riggs, the tennis player?" I asked.

This drove my partner crazy. That I always found a famous name to compare to the person we were interviewing.

"Robert," he said, adjusting his glasses. "Not Bobby."

"Did you personally rent the room to Mr. Creiss?" Remy asked the manager.

"I did," Riggs said. "One week. Flat rate. He asked specifically not to bother him. No maid or towel service either."

Officer Ingram led us up a flight of stairs, and we entered the second floor. As we approached Room 203, we saw Ingram's partner, Officer Glenda Yantsy, standing at an open door.

"This is the room Creiss was in," Ingram said. "Or whatever his real name is."

Remy and I moved past Yantsy and stood just inside the door.

We took a beat, studying the place. The old guy had killed four people in the last few days, one of them a cop's son. The scene was not to be treated lightly.

"There's no luggage inside," Ingram said. "We saw that much and then cleared out."

The hotel room was nice for Mason Falls standards. To my right, just inside the door, was a small kitchenette with a white melamine counter that had a sink and a small Frigidaire. The counter curved to face out into a living area, and a chair was tucked underneath, making it a desk for work from the other side.

The common area was quaint, with two chairs and a couch that faced a thirty-inch TV and a door that led into the bedroom and bath area.

"I'll take in there," Remy said, moving into the bedroom. I started in the kitchen, gloving up and going through each of the four cupboards. They were bare, except for some essentials. Salt and pepper shakers. An extra coffee cup, wrapped in plastic. A travel-sized bottle of Dawn liquid soap.

In the trash can, I found a handful of sparkly flecks, enough to sit two inches high on your palm. I carefully collected them in a clear evidence bag and held up the bag. They looked like speckled shavings of some sort.

Placing the bag on the counter, I noticed two brownish scuffs on the melamine, each about four inches long. I took a picture of them with my phone and then wet a single gloved digit, wiping at the edge of one of the scuffs. The mark came off fast.

I moved out to the living area and pulled the drapes wide, letting light pour into the area big enough for three adults to sit and watch TV.

The couch was slate-gray and rigid, and the armchair bore a pattern of gray and blue diamonds.

I lifted each couch cushion out, one by one, but found nothing under them. It was as if no one had ever spent time in the area.

After another ten minutes, I glanced in at the bedroom.

The bed was left unmade, and Remy was lifting a brick-red dust ruffle and examining the area under it.

"Anything?"

"Nada," she said. "You?"

"Something in the trash, but I'm not sure what."

My partner came out and inspected the evidence bag. "Is it paint?"

"I was thinkin', yeah," I said.

She moved back into the bedroom, and I did round two in the kitchen, getting up under the sink.

Outside I heard the loud pop of a transformer blowing, somewhere down by the highway.

"Is there a safe in there?" I hollered to Remy.

"Yes, and left open," she said. "Empty."

Under the sink I found a paper coffee cup. I bagged it, but couldn't tell if it had been there for a day or a month.

I stood near the melamine kitchen counter, staring at the shiny filings in the evidence bag. The room smelled like coffee grinds and stale air.

I turned to Yantsy, who stood by the open door that led out to the carpeted hallway. "Yantsy," I said. "You didn't move anything, right?"

"We cleared the place and stood sentinel, Detective. I've been right here while Ingram went outside to call y'all. Nobody touched a thing."

"All right," I said. "I appreciate you."

I turned and opened the evidence bag. Picked up a few of the filings between my gloved index finger and thumb and let them fall back into the bag.

My dad had a wood shop when I was a kid, but often he worked with metal too.

"These particles from the trash look like steel," I said to Remy, who was in the bedroom. "But they don't feel like it."

The pieces had fallen back into the evidence bag, and I sealed up the top.

Out in the hall I heard Yantsy shift her weight from one hip to the other, but when I glanced over, she was looking away from me, down toward the elevator.

I turned and stared at the fridge. I'd already checked inside when I first searched the kitchen, and it was empty. I opened the tiny freezer area. Felt a wave of cool come at me. Opened the main door again, but didn't feel much at all. When I checked the dial, it was at two out of ten.

Remy had come out from the bedroom and was watching me.

"I can see the little hamster running in that big brain of yours," she said. "Burning off the dust bunnies."

This was a line a man said to me once, right before he and his friends kicked the shit out of me. I'd told Remy the story, and she thought the line was pretty cool. To be honest, I remember thinking the same thing right before the first punch.

"Well," I said. "We got metal filings." I motioned at the evidence bag.

"Check."

"The counter is scuffed. And the fridge is turned down. Maybe you're doing some metalwork here. Then you gotta store something, but temperature control it? I dunno."

"Something like what?"

"Remember Carilla told us there was something the old guy didn't get."

I reached for Remy's iPad and found her notes from the aftermath of the stakeout at Tandy's. The final moments of Carilla's life.

I scanned through them, paging down with a gloved finger.

"Three shots were fired from west to east," I said.

"That was the old guy shooting Carilla," Remy said.

I nodded. "Then the old guy saw you and took off. When we found Carilla barely alive, he patted his leg and said, 'The old fucker. He didn't get it.'"

"Then started mumbling about some café," Remy added. "Bled out a minute later."

I held up my own notebook. Old-school. Six-by-nine spiral bound.

"We both have slightly different notes, but those details are the same. Patting the leg. What he said."

"Guy in patrol heard three shots too," Remy said. "I interviewed him during your vacation."

I scrunched up my brow at the word "vacation." I'd been part of a school shooting, back-to-back with a kid dying in the bar. I took three days off. Cops. The way we talked to each other sometimes.

I stared at the paper cup in the evidence bag. Then turned to Remy. "You wanna take a ride?"

"We're not finding much here," she said. "You got someplace in mind?"

"I do," I said, letting Yantsy know we'd be back in an hour.

Out in my Silverado, I asked Remy to get out my patrol light, and she tossed it onto the dash so we could haul ass. We drove northeast on small rural highways that crossed 906. Off to our left I could see an area of deforestation that led out to the Condesale Gorge, where Remy and I had faced off with assassin Kian Tarticoft this past spring in a blaze of smoke and fire.

As we kept cutting northeast, the area became more rural and the elevation dropped. Some farmland was here and there, with a dozen or so cows dotting the horizon. But most of the area contained deserted properties.

On several parcels of land, I saw signs with demarcations on boards stuck into the dirt. The signs rose six or eight feet high, with dates spray-painted on them, all in the 1970s. Of a time when the area had flooded, over and over again. Eventually the Army Corps of Engineers stepped in and dammed off the water that flowed here from June Lake.

Now the opposite effect had happened. The lack of precipitation had killed the region.

We crossed 914 and moved closer to the area where we'd found the Caprice at the roadside.

About five minutes later, we were standing at the front office of the Garden Palms. Thiago Carilla's motel.

The place was a notch above an Econo Lodge, but well below the level of the Homewood Suites, where we'd just come from.

The manager had shiny black hair with one lock of bangs that hung over her left eye. She wore bright red lipstick and sported a V-neck that sat low, with a solid inch of lacy pink bra showing, choreographed right along the V of the shirt. Her nametag read *Lady*.

I hadn't met her before, since I was on leave when Abe and Remy had gone through Carilla's motel room.

"I love that," I said, pointing at the name tag. "Is that your birth name?"

"It was either that or 'the Tramp,'" she said, flicking a set of huge fake eyelashes at me. "My mom chose Lady."

I grinned, wondering how many times she'd stared a man down and said that line.

"What can I help you with, Detective?" she asked, her hands clasped together, showing off her matching red nail polish. "I aim to please."

"Room Eleven." I pointed out the door.

She held on Remy, before moving her gaze back at me. "Tell me you're not gonna make the same mess that this one did?"

"No, ma'am," I said. Guessing that Remy and Abe had torn the place apart after the shooting at the bar.

"All right then."

Lady grabbed a set of keys off the counter and clipped them to a shiny blue carabiner clip that hung off her wrist. "We've had cleaner visits from the fire department than y'all."

She locked up the office with the keys on her wrist, and took out a plastic master. Led us down the sidewalk.

The motel was made of cinder blocks that looked like they'd been painted by a lazy drunk. All along the windows, the caulking was thick with paint. I could make out the clerk's perfume as she moved, some mix of a woodsy scent, laced with citrus.

"How many guests have stayed in that room since my colleagues left, Miss . . . ?"

"Lady," she said. "Just Lady. And the answer is one."

She walked toward the room then. Or maybe "strutted" is a better word. Her clothes fit tighter than a pregnant bride's.

The numbers on the doors we passed were all odd: 3, 5, 7.

At number 9, I saw a dent in the shape of a foot in the lower half of the door. Someone had drawn a rectangular shape around the hole in Sharpie, and I guessed that a kick-plate was being installed. Hide the hole, rather than replace the door.

We got to Room 11, and Lady used her plastic master key to unlock the door.

I stood on the concrete strip outside the room for a moment. Examining the place for the first time.

"The room ain't gonna search itself, handsome," Lady said.

I smiled at her and moved inside. The room was simple. A queen bed, covered in a white quilted comforter with a gold throw blanket draped long-ways across the base of the bed. It matched a single gold pillow that was placed in between two bulging white pillows at the head of the bed.

"You looking for something in particular?" the manager asked.

"I am," I said.

Beyond the mattress stood two dressers, both made of a fake wood laminate, done in a red oak. Atop one of them was a black Mr. Coffee machine. Single cup hotel style. It was set on a plastic tray that contained a paper cup with a stirrer, a packet of sugar, and a single plastic container of creamer.

I walked over and lifted the machine up, examining it. The air in the room smelled stale, and I was guessing that the window-unit AC had mold in the water circulating inside it.

"This work okay?" I asked about the coffee machine.

"Damn well better," Lady said. "It's brand-new."

"What do you mean, 'brand-new'?" Remy asked.

I don't think my partner appreciated Lady's comment about the fire department, because these were the first words that Remy had uttered since we arrived.

"The one guy who stayed here complained that nothing was working. So that's a new one. Grabbed it from our stockroom this morning."

"Café," I said, and Remy made a noise with her nose.

"Shit," Remy said. "Carilla was saying 'coffee' in Spanish."

"Where's the old unit?" Remy asked.

"Dumpster." Lady pointed to the parking lot.

Remy turned and headed out the door.

My partner's hand whipped to the back pocket of her slacks, where she always carried at least two pairs of gloves. The second set was usually for me.

A black dumpster stood in the parking lot. It had a gray, hard plastic top that flipped on a swivel. My partner grabbed the top and pushed it up, spinning it on its hinge. As she did, Lady and I caught up with her.

The thing was about half full. About a hundred small clear bags full of crap that people toss in hotel trash cans.

I was pretty sure chain of custody had blown the need for gloves, but I put them on when Remy handed them to me. On the far right, I could see a black Mr. Coffee machine.

"Right there." I pointed.

Remy wedged her shoe into a slot on the side of the dumpster and took a step up, grabbing the machine.

She handed it over, and I walked a few spaces down from the dumpster to my Silverado. I opened the back door and grabbed a shop towel from my truck.

I placed the coffee maker on the hood of my truck with the towel under it.

Flipping the machine over, I stared at the screws that held it together. All four were nearly stripped.

"You got a screwdriver in that office?" I asked Lady.

She glanced at me, perhaps considering a smartass comment. Turned to the office instead. "Coming right up."

While we waited for her, I turned to Remy.

"You know what I can't understand?" I said to my partner. "Why the hell was Carilla still hanging in this area?"

"After his two friends are shot, you mean?" Remy asked.

I nodded. "His boys get killed Thursday. He got shot in the hand. Yet he circles back to the bar. Shows up at Tandy's Thursday night. Friday too, when we see him. Why?"

"Abe asked me the same thing. The only idea we had is that he's waiting."

"Waiting for what?"

"I dunno," she said. "He sent another text to that same throw-away cell."

I blinked. "What?"

I was still playing catch-up from being gone three days.

Remy checked her tablet and pointed to something in her notes.

Thursday morning's gonna come fast, and you're still
gonna need what I got. Let's talk.

"Jesus, what the hell?" I said to Remy, my eyes narrowing. "You never told me that."

"Sorry."

"And that was sent when?" I asked.

"Five p.m. Friday," she said. "Same day we saw him at Tandy's. Presumably he was referring to the following Thursday."

I was frustrated that I was getting this piecemeal, and I needed an hour free to go through all of Remy's notes from the three days I took off.

Lady came back with the screwdriver then, and I thanked her.

After she left, I pressed the Phillips-head hard into the screws, knowing they were stripped, and I might only get one shot at removing them. Slowly, each turned and fell, popping with a metal clink onto the shop towel sitting on my truck hood.

I removed the bottom panel of the coffee maker then, and Remy and I glanced inside.

Carilla had removed the entire motor, leaving an open shell inside for hiding items.

And something *was* hidden there. Taped inside.

29

I carefully peeled back a strip of silver duct tape. A piece of what looked like metal was inside. But it was an odd shape.

I handed the item to Remy, pointing at a second piece, also taped inside. This was a square metal box, the size of my palm, and I gingerly pulled it away from the tape that held it in place.

I put the housing of the coffee machine down on the ground beside the truck and stared at our two findings, laid atop the shop towel.

The first piece I removed was about six inches long, with a squared-off flange down one end and a circular ring down the other.

"The hell is it?" Remy asked.

She laid the object across her palm, easily lifting her hand up and down, in a demonstration of its weight. Because although the piece looked like metal, it was light, like balsa wood.

"It looks like one half of the front of a set of eyeglasses," I said. I ran my finger around the circular shape. But down where it would become the bridge, if it were a set of glasses, the metal-looking material terminated in a squared off blunt shape.

"It's painted," Remy said. "To look like metal."

I turned to the second piece then, which was a small box, also plastic, about four inches by two inches by one inch. It had a curving piece of what looked like metal coming out the bottom of the box, and another one from the top.

It was hard to be certain what the hell we were looking at, but I had a thought.

"Do they fit together?" I asked.

Remy messed around with the two parts, trying to fit one to the other.

"Nope," she said.

I pointed at the curved metal piece that protruded from the bottom of the box. "I think this might be a trigger."

"To a gun?"

"A plastic model of one," I said.

Remy took the box from me and pushed the metal flange that protruded from the top back and forth. "If that's a trigger"—she pointed at the bottom—"then this thing might be the safety. And not a good one," she added, pushing the flange back and forth. It didn't lock well into place.

I took the box back, noting again how light it was.

"So it's a toy?" she asked.

"Seems so," I said. "Except for one thing."

"The trail of dead bodies?"

"Make that two things," I said. "The trail of bodies. And the fact that Carilla hid these two things inside a coffee machine and told a couple cops about it with his dying breath."

I thought about the hotel room. Not this one, but the old guy's. The Homewood Suites.

"The old guy could've shaved a piece like this down," I said, turning over the box in my hand. "Could've created that pile that looks like metal filaments we found in his kitchen at the Homewood Suites."

"Maybe," she said. "But neither of these two pieces have any paint missing or rubbed off."

This was a good point, and I turned it over in my head. We had two pieces of some puzzle, but we were missing the other parts. And a lot of context.

"So going back to the roadside," Remy said, trying to put the story together.

"The old guy shoots the two guys in the front seat."

"Vinorama and Dilmendes," Remy said.

"Then he turns to shoot Carilla, but only hits him in the hand."

"Carilla takes off," Remy said.

"Let's say whatever's in the case between them," I continued, "not all of it *is* in the case."

"What do you mean?"

"Carilla didn't trust the old guy," I said, holding up the pieces we'd taken from inside the Mr. Coffee. "Maybe he didn't trust the meet itself. So he held back these two pieces in case things went south at the roadside. Now the old man needs these two, whatever they are, and the short guy's got leverage."

My partner nodded, but it was just theory until we knew what the hell the two pieces were.

Lady let us go back through the room then, and we searched through other areas where Carilla might've hidden additional pieces. We looked for a set of screws on the back of the TV, but found none. Shone our flashlight inside accessible AC vents and checked up under the sink and inside the commode tank. Nothing anywhere.

Back in my Silverado, we knew that cross-traffic would be busier at this hour and took a different way back to the Homewood Suites.

Moving across a local road that housed a marble refinery, we tracked white chalk dust down the highway. "8 Hour Drive" by Lynn Miles played on the radio, and I told Remy about a friend named Chester Gardner who owned a gun shop.

"Yeah, you've talked about him before," she said.

"What do you say we send these two pieces his way?" I asked. "Give him a few hours with 'em."

"It's too light to be a gun," she said.

"But if it's a trigger to something," I said, "Chester'll know."

Remy agreed, and we hustled back to the Homewood Suites.

As we arrived, we saw Alvin Gerbin from our crime unit, who'd come by while Remy and I were gone and was printing the inside of the room. We were still trying to get an I.D. on our old guy.

"Anything so far?" I asked, knowing a print would go far in terms of identifying the man who had killed four innocents, including a cop's son.

"Not yet," he said.

Alvin's normally pink cheeks were flushed, and his face was a little pastier than usual.

"You all right?" I asked.

"I had some bad Indian for lunch."

"I need you to dust these," I said, producing the two pieces found inside the coffee maker.

Alvin placed them on the counter and photographed them first. Then dusted them.

"No prints," he said when he finished the work.

"Shit."

I handed the two pieces to Patrolman Yantsy to rush over to Stock and Barrel, the gun shop that Chester Gardner owned east of town, between Falls West and Burna.

Remy and I headed back inside the hotel room then, wanting to go through the place one more time.

We reversed roles, with me taking the bathroom and bedroom this time, and Remy the common areas. After an hour of finding nothing new, we left Alvin there, and headed out to the gun shop ourselves.

30

By the middle of the afternoon, Remy and I had taken SR-906 east and gotten off at the exit for Ferris.

In the corners of the afternoon sky, a pinkish-red color was dancing. In the distance beyond it, thunderheads were rising, the second day in a row with wind and the threat of rain but no payoff.

We parked in a gravel lot that served a plumbing supply store and housed a line of orange-and-blue trucks. Pickups mostly, F250s and Tundras with camper shells covered in vinyl wraps advertising parts from Moen or Delta. To the left of the storefront that read *L&M Plumbing* was a western-themed sign that read *Stock and Barrel: The Finest in Weapons and Ammunition.*

We crossed the lot, with dust and gravel trailing behind us. As we entered the gun store, a small bell hooked to the door dinged. *Bing bong.*

Inside were three waist-high glass display cases that ran the length of each of the walls. The first contained Glocks and Berettas, since Stock and Barrel was a dealer for those manufacturers. The second held ammo, shotguns, and AKs, while the third was a clearance and surplus section, with everything from knives and scopes to cleaning kits and Mace. The far back wall bore an American flag with the words "In God we trust. All others pay cash."

I spotted Chester Gardner from the door and headed over.

Chester is a big man—white, six-four, and two hundred eighty pounds—with an unkempt brown beard and a wide chest. He wore a pea-green army jacket over a Black Flag T-shirt.

"There's my dog," he said, pulling me into a bear hug that I couldn't prevent if I wanted to. We'd grown up together and had gotten into trouble since we were kids.

"Chess," I said. "This is my partner, Remy Morgan."

"The one with the good shot," Chester said. "Appreciate you keeping this guy around."

Remy nodded. She had saved my life by putting a bullet in someone's forehead earlier this year, and I had told that story to friends a half-dozen times.

"You get my package?" I asked.

He nodded. "I keep thinking you're gonna send me something I can keep. You know—five-finger discount from the evidence room, like on TV."

"You think the evidence guys trust him?" Remy asked.

Chester grinned. "I like her," he said to me. He surveyed his store, which had one customer talking to a clerk in the handgun section.

"Tommy, you're it," Chester said, and turned to face us. "Let's talk in back."

We followed him over to a door that looked like a storage closet, which he unlocked with a key from around his neck, but didn't open yet.

"She knows we met in third grade, right?" Chester said, his eyes moving from Remy to me.

"No one's here to go through your secret stash, buddy," I said.

He pushed the door open then, and we stepped into a room that was about fifteen by ten. A work space, with shallow tables around the perimeter and stools pulled up here and there. Each area of table was marked with a white towel, covered in gun parts, as if four simultaneous projects were under way.

All along the walls were pegboard, strung with a mix of two types of weapons: old or valuable—and most of them were both. An eighty-year-old Parker shotgun was hung on the far wall. Beside it was a Winchester 1873 and a Colt 1911 that had been used in Vietnam. The place smelled like Hoppe's No. 9 bore cleaner.

Chester locked the door behind us. He set an alarm, and flicked on a series of screens so he could monitor the store. A half-dozen grenades hung on loops near the TVs.

He moved over to one of the tables then, and we followed him.

There, laid out on a towel, was the first part we'd found inside the black Mr. Coffee machine at the Garden Palms. The piece that I thought looked like part of a pair of eyeglasses.

"Okay," Chester said. "Let's start with the simple stuff. This part here is a trigger guard, like you figured."

"All right," I said. "Except it's not part of a handgun, and it's light, man. We couldn't tell—"

"Just bear with me," he said.

Chester crossed the room and came back carrying a massive gun. An M24 sniper rifle. Because of his chest and girth, it almost looked small in his hands.

He proceeded to take it apart, piece by piece, while we waited.

The M24 is a bolt-action rifle preferred by many of the world's best snipers. I'd shot one last year, at a gun exhibition that Chester had dragged me to. In an expert's hands, an M24 had a range of twenty-five hundred feet. In mine, a pretty decent shot, maybe eight hundred.

"The trigger guard," Chester said, removing it from the massive weapon he'd brought over, "is the bottom-most part of a gun like this. The hole in your piece is where you thread your finger through in order to shoot."

"So that attaches up under the body?" Remy confirmed.

Chester nodded, and I pointed at the two small holes on the underside of the piece we had found. "Except the holes in our piece aren't even threaded," I said.

"Yeah," Chester said, holding out the two matching pieces: the one that we'd found and the heavier piece that he had just removed from the giant rifle.

"When I first saw what you sent, I assumed that's 'cause it was a toy. Or a 3D-printed model that guys paint and put on their wall. You don't need a screw if it's a model, you know? You can just put a dab of glue there."

"So it's a toy?" Remy confirmed.

"Well, you may know this already. There ain't no 3D-printed assault weapons that work more than two or three minutes before falling apart. That's the edge of 3D technology right now. AKs that fall apart. That's what these 3D printers are all trying to make."

Remy and I had discussed this on the drive over. That 3D gun printing may be part of this story.

"So sniper rifles are well beyond anything in process?" she asked.

Chester leaned in closer. He smelled like kerosene. "That's the going knowledge," he said.

"What about the other piece?" I asked. "The box?"

Chester walked to the table at the far side of the room. "That piece had a pin inserted to hold things in place," he said. "Hope you don't mind. I took it out so I could look inside."

I stared at a number of tiny parts laid out. Whitish, unstained plastic pieces. One circle looked like a ball bearing. Another was the metal flange we'd seen sticking out. Also a tiny plastic clip.

"This doesn't make sense," I said, swinging over a magnifying arm from nearby.

Chester was nodding, and his face had grown serious. "So you see now," he said.

"What?" my partner asked.

"This box has a half-dozen discrete parts inside, Rem," I said. "You wouldn't make those if this was just a model or a toy. Models are *empty* inside. You don't need the guts of something to hang it on your wall or put in a case."

I exhaled, shaking my head.

Because suddenly I realized why all these bodies were piling up. I also knew what had been in that case on the back seat of the Chevy Caprice.

This crime wasn't about drugs. And this wasn't a plastic model of a gun or some toy.

"You're saying it might work," I whispered.

Chester's eyes met mine, and he held his hand out, warning me. "So far all we got are two pieces, Paul."

Remy swiveled the magnifying arm her way, glancing from the tiny pieces to Chester. "I thought you just said the edge of the technology was assault rifles. That these 3D makers couldn't even get the assault rifles right."

"I said that was the going knowledge." Chester ran his hands through his curly hair. "So I called up a friend who builds models. I mean really intricate shit. Most of it 3D-printed."

"He looked at the two parts?" Remy asked.

"Five minutes before you got here."

"What'd he say?"

"I told him you were coming, and he took off. Doesn't like cops."

I walked over to one of the monitors and saw a man, sitting on the edge of a lowered, black pickup truck, two parking spots down from my Silverado. He wore a big coat, but even in black and white, I could see he was bone thin.

"This guy," I said, almost as a question. "He hasn't left, Chess. What's he want from us?"

Chester smiled at me, staring at the monitor that covered the parking lot. "You always were the smart one in the group, Paul. He's got a warrant. Going eighty in a fifty-five."

"And he didn't show up in court?" Remy asked.

Chester shook his head.

"Tell him if he helps us out, we'll clear it," I said. "Get him in here."

Chester walked outside then. A minute later, he was followed in by a skinny white guy in his late twenties. "This is Lowell M. Forster," he said. "You'll need that name to clear the warrant. But everyone I know calls him Wolf."

Wolf's eyes were sunken, and his skin was sallow. A meth addict was my first thought. But he looked sober. He took off his jacket, and underneath he wore a gray tank top with an image of Chewbacca on it.

"Take us through what we're we looking at, Wolf." Remy pointed to the gun parts.

The skinny guy looked to Chester and back to us. He carried all a hundred and thirty pounds like a gangster, dipping his shoulders as he moved.

"Well, first thing y'all should know," Wolf said, "is that this shit ain't manufactured. That's straight-up number one."

Up close, Wolf wasn't bad looking. His oblong face was unshaven and he had green eyes and hair that he'd purposely shaved short. Definitely not high. Just unusually thin.

He took a kit the size of a shaving bag from his jacket and removed a series of instruments. Miniature screwdrivers and something that looked like forceps, but were smaller.

"Okay," I said. "Meaning what?"

"It's handmade, yo. It's a one-off. Custom."

My face must've given a "so the fuck what" look, because Wolf glanced from Chester to me.

"Take your time," Remy said, calming the skinny kid.

"People like me print these," Wolf said, picking up the trigger guard. "Piece by piece. Once you dry 'em and sand the edges, you paint 'em with a polyurethane. The black parts—a gunmetal acrylic stain. I mean, no one wants a plastic-looking gun, amirite?"

"Sure," I said flatly. "It doesn't look cool."

"'Xactly," Wolf said. He grabbed the box and carefully placed the white ball bearing and flange back into place. The plastic clip. Then he popped the pieces back into the box, using the two plastic dowels to hold them.

"In a real gun"—he held up the small box—"you'd call these pieces inside the stop release and the detent ball—"

"They're all part of the trigger assembly," Chester finished his sentence.

"'Xactly," Wolf said. "So guys like me—we've made 3D handguns. And it's expensive, yo. Cheaper to get a black market gun if you really wanna shoot. Plus, my boy Snake—you've met him, Chester—he shot a 3D Beretta last year, and it exploded in his damn hand on the first shot. Homeboy's got permanent burns."

I looked to Chester. *Were we learning anything here?*

"But here's the thing," Wolf said. "How that ball was made. How this guard piece functions." He held it up. "Someone done skipped *over* the Holy Grail of Assault Weapons. Went to the next level."

Wolf was smiling now—mostly at Remy, who was holding the trigger assembly.

"'Cause what you got there, girl," he said, "are pieces to a prototype. You're holding parts of the first functioning, 3D-printed M24 sniper rifle."

"We knew that before you walked in," I said. Grabbing the piece from him.

"Sure," he said. "But that's 'cause I'm the one who told Chester. And he told y'all while I was outside."

I smiled at this. The kid was right.

"Okay, tell me something, Wolf," I said. "If you had the rest of this rifle and you lost these two pieces, what would you do?"

"That depends," he said. "If I got the plans and a printer, I'd just make another two pieces. But that ain't always the case."

"Why not?" Remy asked.

Wolf explained how 3D printing worked. How architects or engineers designed CAD, or computer-aided design, plans. Sometimes the ones for weapons were published online for free, and 3D printers could use them to make any product. And sometimes they purposely weren't published online, because of their value.

"You know a federal judge shut down a website last year for putting out handgun designs, right?" Wolf asked.

I nodded. We'd been briefed on this at work. The Liberator was the name of the gun.

Wolf explained how the printing process worked, by a machine printing tiny layers of plastic atop each other, slowly forming the intricate curves and edges of whatever the CAD plan dictated. It could produce a toy. A household object. Even a gun.

"So it's possible someone *can't* replicate the same gun twice?" Remy asked.

"If they don't own the plans," Wolf said, "they definitely can't make the two replacement parts."

"Or maybe they're just struggling to replicate it," Chester said.

"With assault rifles, these guys in Alabama produced four M4A1 carbines," Wolf said. "But each time some piece broke off on the gun as they took the first shot. Something different on each weapon too. Usually after thirty seconds, they flat-out fell apart."

"Like *literally* apart?" Remy asked.

Chester jumped in again. "These are guns made of plastic, Detective Morgan. So like anything that's machined, there's tolerances before the plastic gives way. Plus, guys like Wolf paint 'em and sometimes that throws off the tolerance. You gotta shave the pieces down, just to fit 'em together."

I blinked hearing this. Found the evidence bag in my satchel. The one holding the tiny pieces of paint that I'd found in the trash at the Homewood Suites.

Wolf shook the clear evidence bag, so the tiny filaments separated. He grinned, showing off a metal-capped incisor. "Now you're getting it, boss," he said to me. "So if you were making a rifle from 3D-printed parts, you'd print each piece one at a time. Then paint 'em. Then put the pieces together. But sometimes—as cool as it is to have a resin or stain on a piece—it can mess with how the parts fit together. You follow?"

"Sure," I said, staring at the bag of filaments. "Someone put part of this sniper rifle together. But they had to sand a little paint off some pieces to make it work."

"'Xactly," Wolf said.

"But tell me something, Wolf," I said. "Knowing this rifle will fall apart—"

"And with a high-velocity rifle," Chester said, "it probably will after one or two shots."

"Then who the hell would buy it?" I asked.

"Someone like him." Wolf pointed at Chester.

We all looked at my friend since third grade. "Hey, man." Chester held up his hands. "Okay. Sure, there'll be a market for this, and I'd be interested."

"You mean a collector?" I asked Wolf.

"Sure."

"Disregard a guy like that," I said. "I don't care about someone who has a room like this to show off to their friends. Who else wants one?"

"Someone who only needs to shoot once," Wolf said.

"Meaning what?" Remy asked.

"Someone principled," Wolf said. "And angry. A cause in mind."

I squinted at Wolf.

"A guy who buys this," Wolf said, "he wants to pull a trigger from a half mile away and kill someone. Then take his time packing up and go home to his family. Tuck his kids in bed. Like nothing happened."

"Why not just get a gun like that one?" Remy asked. Pointing at Chester's real M24 rifle.

"That might fall under the category of making a statement," Wolf said. "Lately the bullets are even different in 3D guns. So when cops like you find a body—you're gonna know." Wolf made a gun with his hand. "Pow, I got you with a ghost gun."

I swallowed.

"And if he's real careful," Wolf added, "he'll melt the gun so it never existed. 'Cause some dude in Britain figured out how to trace 3D guns using plastic polymers. So the non-traceable thing—that just got harder."

A synapse in my brain fired.

I took out my case notebook and paged backward, to my notes on the Chevy Caprice.

Carlos had told Remy that there was a ring in the shape of a semicircle on the trunk carpet. A mark where something had eaten away at the fabric of the trunk.

"So if I sold you this gun," I said to Wolf, "but also included a vat of acid, that's a good pairing, right?"

"For sure," Wolf said. "Drop the gun in that after and go home to the wife. Poof goes the proof."

I nodded, seeing the story from start to finish. Then I told Wolf his warrant was clear.

31

It was chilling to hear Wolf describe it, but a story line was emerging. Someone had engineered plans to make a 3D-printed sniper rifle that was untraceable. Unregistered. And disposable.

A prototype was made, most likely for a one-time use.

I stepped outside while Remy went back through the details with Wolf and Chester. Meanwhile, I called Abe and asked him to double the canvass around the Homewood Suites. To trace anywhere that the old assassin might have gone.

Now Remy and I were in my Silverado, headed back to the Homewood.

"Twenty-four hours ago," Remy said, "I was sure our double was linked to drugs."

I shook my head. "And now it's about a damn ghost gun."

"When you stepped out to talk to Abe," Remy said, "Wolf made this statement. Like he wanted us to know. These guys are makers, P.T. Craftsmen."

"I'll tell you what they're crafting, Rem. Goddamn weapons."

"Sure, but they're not all nuts, P.T. A lot of these guys are pro-freedom. Pro-open-source. Pro—"

"Don't tell me you've got sympathy for Wolf," I said.

Remy shrugged and went quiet for a minute. *Had my partner somehow gotten liberal in the time I'd been suspended?*

"Let's get water-tight on our current theory," I said.

"Sure." Remy nodded. "So Carilla was hired by some unknown person to carry a 3D-printed M24 sniper rifle up to Mason Falls for some meeting."

"Check."

"He had two buddies who ran drugs up here, and they knew the routes," Remy said. "Carilla decides to make a road trip of it with them. He gets protection. They know the area and he cuts them in."

"Copy that," I said.

"We know from transactions on Vinorama's debit card that the other two stopped near the Georgia–Florida line," Remy said. "Crashed for the night at a Comfort Inn."

I changed lanes and got off 909, heading back toward the Homewood Suites. A sleeping bag lay discarded in the grassy median between the north and southbound sides of the highway.

"Vinorama and Dilmendes picked up Carilla and his package the next afternoon," I said. "Drove up here. But they're early for the drop. They go drinking at Tandy's Tuesday night. Buy those T-shirts. At some point along the way, Carilla opens the case."

"He realizes that what he's carrying is worth a whole lot more than he's being paid," Remy said. "And he gets greedy. Sends that text on Wednesday that we found in his phone. To the unknown cell number. Asking for a pay bump."

"More scratch," I said, using Carilla's words.

Remy nodded.

"Whoever he texted," I said, "they called the old guy to come get the gun and get rid of Carilla and his two buddies. But Carilla got out of the car. He escaped."

"That's when the old guy opens the case," Remy said. "Goes back to his hotel and puts together what he can of the M24. Realizes he's missing the trigger assembly and the trigger guard."

I nodded. It all tracked.

"So what would you do next?" Remy asked. "If you're this old assassin."

"If I'm him, the whole situation has gotten hotter than I probably anticipated. A sting at a bar? Cops chasing me and Carilla out into a forest? If I'm that old guy, I'm thinking that I didn't get paid enough for this shit."

We turned onto Tanus Road toward the Homewood Suites, and I slowed, seeing Abe's Lexus SUV parked alongside a cruiser in front of a Cracker Barrel about four blocks down from the hotel.

I turned into the lot, and Remy and I got out of my truck.

Was there a lead on the old guy?

We headed inside the restaurant, passing through the gift area that sold knickknacks and candy. By the far side of the restaurant, Abe was standing with Patrolman Ingram. He saw us and walked closer, meeting Remy and me by the hostess stand.

"I was just about to call you," Abe said. "The old guy was here. Came in around ten-thirty today after the breakfast rush. Held down an area and tipped heavy."

I noticed Glenda Yantsy, the blue-suiter from the hotel, was sitting in a booth with a blonde in her late twenties. The woman wore the white short-sleeved dress shirt and brown apron that I'd seen on every Cracker Barrel waitress in my life.

"That's who waited on him?" I asked.

"She's a little shook up to discover that he was a killer," Abe said. "The old guy gave her a two-hundred-dollar tip. Told her he wanted to sit in a specific section that was closed."

I eyed the woman. She was white with freckles, her face as plain as homemade soap. Her apron had three gold stars on it, above which was her name: *Therese*.

"Video?" Remy asked.

"Manager's working on pulling it up. Ten minutes, he says."

Remy flicked her eyebrows at me and turned to Abe. "I say we let golden boy here chat her up."

Abe turned to me, his palms out. "Then we wait on your charm with bated breath."

I walked over, and Officer Yantsy looked up. She introduced me to Therese Kuth and heaved herself out of the booth.

"Therese," I said, "this is that moment you've seen on TV. Where the second cop comes over and you gotta repeat all the stuff you said to the first cop. You okay with that?"

"Sure."

"I could use a cup of coffee," I said. "How about you?"

"Yes." She smiled faintly. "Let me get—"

I held out my hand. "You relax," I said. "You've had a tough enough day already."

I turned to Remy, but she'd already heard me and was heading toward the hostess stand.

Therese proceeded to tell me how the older guy came in and requested to sit in an area that had just been mopped and was closed.

"I said no." Therese shrugged meekly. "But he offered me two hundred bucks. Gave me an extra hundred for the shift manager."

Remy laid down a tray, and Therese instinctively grabbed the jug of coffee. Filled my cup first.

"He had this case with him," she said, motioning with her hands spread about four feet apart.

I figured this was a gun case, but wanted to be sure. I took the tack of going the other way. "Like a guitar case?" I asked. "Musical instrument? Luggage?"

"No, it was rectangular," she said.

I'd once owned a Pelican gun case that was two feet by four. About eight or ten inches thick.

"Was it black?" I asked. "Looked like a hard plastic material? Like a carbon finish?"

"That's the one," Therese said.

"So you sat him where he wanted," I said. "What happened next?"

"He drank his coffee," she said. "Black, two sugars. No cream."

"Where?" I asked.

Therese motioned at the far side of the restaurant. A corner booth that looked out the window onto a side parking lot.

I pulled my phone out and showed her the sketch of the old guy. "You're a hundred percent sure it was this guy?"

"Oh yeah," she said. "The other cops already asked me twice."

Remy and I had seen the old guy in person, but it was in the dark inside Tandy's. And dark again in the forest behind the bar. I wanted to know if anything had changed.

"He still have a beard like in our picture?"

"Uh-huh." She nodded.

"Seventy-ish?"

"Yup."

"He look distinguished?" I asked. "Look like somebody's uncle?"

"He looked like somebody's grandpa," she said. "If Grandpa was in shape."

"Okay." I nodded. He was fit.

I hadn't heard the old guy speak more than five words in the forest. "You hear an accent in his voice, Therese?"

"Not anything specific," she said. "Not like us. Not like up North. Somewhere neutral."

"What happened next?"

"Nothing for a good half hour," she continued. "I brung him two refills. Then some guy joined him. I didn't even see the second fella come in. He was just there. I came toward the table, to see if he wanted a drink, you know? Or maybe they both were gonna order food now that the second fella was there. But the old guy waved me off." She held her palm out at me, as if to demonstrate.

"So you didn't get to the table, but you saw something."

"Not much," she said. "But the guy who joined him was white. Black hair. Younger than you."

"Okay . . ."

"This new fella brought out a paper bag," she continued. "Grandpa looked in it and then went to the restroom. When I looked up, Grandpa was heading back and the young guy was gone."

"Back from the bathroom?"

"Uh-huh." Therese nodded. "No paper bag anymore. Just that black case he came in with."

Somewhere in the distance, someone was laying on a car horn. Over and over again.

"He took the black case to the bathroom with him?" I confirmed. "You sure?"

"Yup."

"So he's back at the table. What's the next thing you remember?"

"He seemed antsy now. Squirming in his chair like a kid. In comes these other two men, maybe twenty minutes later. One of them's real big. Like a football player. Tank top showing off his muscles. White. Dark hair. The other guy . . . I dunno. Shorter. Not memorable."

"The unmemorable gentleman—white? Black?"

"White," she said. "Grandpa leaves them two the case, and he gets up himself. As he does, the football player grabs his arm. You could almost see there's gonna be a fight. But then the unmemorable guy says something and the football player lets go. And out goes Grandpa. Two minutes later, the two men take off with the case."

Therese had gotten to the bottom of her coffee cup, and Remy leaned in and refilled it. As she did, my partner's eyes moved to me and then toward the back of the store. I thanked Therese and got up. Told her we'd be back in a sec.

As we walked toward the back, I leaned in to Remy. "I think someone might've brought our old assassin those missing parts."

"Yeah, I was listening," Remy said. "The paper bag?"

"The trip to the bathroom was probably to make sure they fit."

"So these two new guys have the gun now," Remy said, heading with me into the back of the restaurant. "The football player and the nondescript guy."

"With the missing parts in the case," I said. "The old guy just turned it over to the buyer, Rem."

In the back room, a man in a Cracker Barrel apron with the name York on it stood with Patrolman Ingram. The place was a tiny box, and I leaned against the doorway, the last open space available. A video was queued up, and Ingram hit *Play*.

We saw the older man enter the restaurant and stand there. His back was to us, and his hunting jacket was zipped tight around his collar. A baseball cap sat low on his head, his wavy light hair coming out the back and sides. He pointed to an area in the restaurant and the waitress shook her head.

The rest of the video went exactly as Therese had explained. I couldn't see much of the man with the paper bag, except to say he looked white or Latino and was in and out fast. But when the other two men arrived, they came in a different door from the parking lot.

The man Therese called the football player wore a tank top that was too small and showed off his hulking arms. Even in black and white, you could see he was ripped.

"Bodyguard?" Abe asked.

The football player was followed by a shorter man. Both men sat down opposite the older guy.

The two men got up after Grandpa left. As they headed out, they grabbed the case from the opposite seat in the booth. Ingram paused the video. We had a solid image of them.

The bodyguard was white. Six foot with arms like granite. His friend—or more likely his boss—was smaller. Five-six and late thirties, a wiry build. He wore a designer polo and slacks. He had piercing dark eyes.

Remy took a shot of the paused image with her phone.

I looked to Ingram and the restaurant manager. "Our assassin sat facing the parking lot," I said. "We got cameras outside?"

"We were just going through 'em before you walked in," Ingram said. He used the controls on a desktop computer to pull up a different camera.

"The guy who came with the paper bag," the manager said. "He mustn't have parked in the lot. But them final two . . ."

Onto the screen came a shot of the bodyguard getting into a Cadillac Escalade. Black or dark blue. The wiry guy got in the back seat, but he opened his own door.

"The first four digits of the plate look like 5DUT," Ingram said, jotting the number and letters on his hand with a Sharpie from off the manager's desk. "Let me go outside and run it."

He left. And Remy, Abe, and I asked the manager if we could have the place to talk. The manager nodded and took off.

"The ideal situation would be to surveil these folks," Abe said once he left. "Track that car. And wait."

"Especially if they can replace the gun parts that fast," Remy added. "'Cause what we really want here are the 3D plans. More than the gun."

I nodded, but my mind was somewhere else. On the message that Carilla sent to the throwaway cell.

"Carilla's text," I said. "It referred to something happening Thursday morning, right? He was trying to press the buyer into paying up."

"He said, 'I know you're still gonna need what I got,'" Remy said.

"Well, it's Wednesday afternoon now," I said. "If those were replacement parts for that gun, then someone rushed them up here for a reason."

"You think something's going down tomorrow?" Abe asked.

"It's a sniper rifle, guys. *Someone's* going down. And when you shoot from that distance, it's hard to know who even took the shot. We need to call ATF and fast."

32

By the time we reviewed what else was found in the canvass and got back to MFPD, our friend Mandelle Clearson from Atlanta PD was there, acting in his capacity for the Bureau of Alcohol, Tobacco, Firearms and Explosives.

He and a Fed named Quarles had set up in our conference room, and Clearson smiled when he saw me. "You hillbillies can't seem to stay out of gun trouble, can you?"

I didn't return the smile.

"I'm kidding, buddy," he said.

"What do we know?" I asked.

"The bodyguard's name is Anton Sedonovich," Clearson said, opening up a file on the guy that the waitress called the football player. "He grew up in Louisiana, got a scholarship to wrestle at LSU, and dropped out his sophomore year. After that, he picked up a charge for domestic abuse that was reduced to a misdemeanor."

"The shorter man's name is Nolan Brauer," said Quarles, the other agent.

Quarles was late forties like Clearson. Black, with gray in his side-burns. "Brauer was Army," he continued. "Iraq War vet, and a helluva sniper from the records we're allowed to read."

Quarles had soft features and his shoulders were rounded. He looked more like an insurance actuary than a guy packing heat for the FBI.

"He's been on a federal watch list for three months," Quarles continued.

"Based on what?" Remy asked.

"Some comment he made online. Agents interviewed him, but didn't find any reason to do more."

The Fed had an accent like Abe's, but different. More twangy. Like someone from the cuff of the boot of Louisiana. Or from Mississippi.

"He's not just a great shot," Clearson said. "He's got resources."

"How much?" Remy asked.

"Brauer's granddad apparently patented most of the car bumpers originally designed in this country," Quarles explained. "Sold those rights to the Big Five automakers in the 1960s. Took the money and invested. The family owns three golf courses, about a dozen high-rises in Atlanta, and a franchise of paintball ranges."

"And Nolan Brauer is the grandson?"

"And sole living heir," Clearson said. "He also runs a blog called Patriots of Fort Pulaski."

Fort Pulaski was a Civil War post in what's now Savannah. Cock-spur Island to be exact. The South had lost that battle. Maybe Brauer was still sore about it.

"Do we know where Brauer lives?" I asked.

"He owns five houses," Clearson said. He walked over to a map of Georgia that was tacked to the conference wall. The hotel and Cracker Barrel were marked in red Sharpie, and a perimeter was drawn. A circle about a hundred miles around. Too big to search. Too big for anything. There were five black *X*'s, one on each of Brauer's houses.

"Officers are on their way to all these addresses," Clearson said. "We can assume he had two hours' jump on us, and we've put every jurisdiction in this range on alert."

"That's gotta be twenty jurisdictions," Abe said, walking into the room.

"Twenty-four," Clearson answered. "But if your dead guy Carilla was right about the timing of something Thursday morning, then hopefully it's just a matter of time before someone picks him up."

Remy and I exchanged a glance. It was five p.m. and there was a possibility that a sniper rifle would be used tomorrow morning. *A matter of time?*

"How can we help?" Remy asked.

"The FBI has fifty men on this, as of ten minutes ago. Three different federal agencies are scouring every pro-NRA email, gun blog, and right-wing database. We're in touch with the governor. The GBI."

"Great," I said, repeating what Remy had said. "How can we help?"

Clearson looked at Quarles and then at Abe. "We're guessing he's long gone from Mason Falls, P.T. So I think we're good without local help."

Clearson said "local help" like it was a slur.

"So nothing?" I asked.

"We already talked to your chief," Clearson said. "I'd say go home and get some shut-eye. Maybe Abe stays here. P.T., you or Remy come in the morning for relief."

Remy and I glanced at each other. Clearson was usually a good guy, but when he put on his asshole Fed hat, voilà, he sounded a lot like an asshole Fed.

"I'll take the first shift," Abe said. "Why don't you come back around five a.m. I'll be dead on my feet by then."

I stared at Abe. I'd been the senior guy on the totem pole for so long that I had to remind myself that it was his job now to make these choices.

"All right," I said.

We moved outside then, to where I'd double-parked my Silverado.

I dropped Remy at her place and rolled down the windows of the truck, letting the cool air in as I drove past downtown. In a few minutes, I passed 10th Street and was about to turn south to pick up 906. To go home and crash.

But I didn't turn south. I was restless and kept driving.

Plowing ahead into the numbered streets, I passed 15th Street, 18th.

At 20th, my truck almost unconsciously steered to the curb, and I stared across at something that made no sense.

Remy and I had been inside the Golden Oaks liquor store less than twenty-four hours ago, but now a green fence surrounded the entire block and a wrecking ball hung from a rig.

The vertical sign that read LIQUOR was gone. The giant one that I'd assumed was too expensive to tear down. And the building was half-demolished. Some partial walls stood, but most of the place was a pile of rubble, ten feet high. A rolling mountain of concrete debris.

I took a picture and texted Remy.

A moment later, a message came back:

WTF? Is that the Golden Oaks?

I told her it was, and my mind scrambled through a number of scenarios.

Lauten Hartley knew we'd been inside his place.

He must've been.

The building had sat dormant for almost two years. Now a day after we found the basement, the place was destroyed, rendering any revisit useless?

Had there been an alarm system? Cameras that Remy and I were caught on?

I started up my truck, but my mind was spinning. I got on 906, but saw Remy's number blinking across the screen in the truck.

"I'm not searching the liquor store property," I said as I picked up. "Don't worry."

"I'm not calling about that," she said. "I've been thinking about Brauer and that bodyguard. You okay just sitting this one out?"

"We can't search fifty square miles, Rem."

"Sure, but I don't want to wake up tomorrow and find out about another school shooting. Or some dead elected official."

I thought about the liquor store and the school shooting. About action and regret.

"Well, the Feds' assumption was that the best way to chase this guy is to pick up digital scraps," I said. "Some chat room or blog. The dark web. They're probably right, Rem."

"Sure," she said. "But if this is about 3D printing and guns, we might know people who have better ears on the ground than the Feds."

"Who? Wolf?" I asked.

"'Xactly," Remy answered, imitating the way Wolf talked. "He didn't want himself or his maker buddies to get maligned. Well, they're about to. Anyone with a 3D printer is gonna be on an FBI watch list by tomorrow if someone innocent is shot."

"Call him," I said to Remy. "If he bites, let's see if he can introduce us to this community he bragged about."

33

One of the interesting things about living in modern times is how people of strange interests connect and find their own kind of people. You collect Victorian coins? So do a hundred other folks. And those people eventually want to meet "IRL," as it's called.

In Real Life.

So I guess if you make complex 3D models, same goes.

Remy and I parked behind a place called Cells and Vipers on Green Street, just up toward the north end of town. My partner had called Wolf, and in fact he did bite. Then I swung by and grabbed her.

I'd grown up in Mason Falls, and I knew the northern side of town pretty well. But I'd driven by this particular mini mall a dozen times and never noticed. It had a nail salon in it, a pizza place called Mr. Sauce, and the game place.

From what Wolf had told Remy, Cells and Vipers was a business that sold games and hosted games, both analog and digital. They also sold electronic parts for robotics and had two meet-up areas, one in a room behind the retail area and the other in the basement.

Wolf texted us to meet him in the alley behind the place, and I pulled my truck close to a dumpster by a metal back door that was painted orange.

A minute later the door scraped open, and Wolf came out. Walked over to us.

"Y'all are comin' on my turf now, so you're gonna be cool, right?"

"Of course," I said.

"And you brought something?" he said. "Something to offer?"

I pulled out five business cards. On the back of each I had written, *This individual is a close friend of Detective P. T. Marsh. Please call P.T. immediately.* My cell number was written below.

Wolf looked them over.

"These are not 'get out of felony' cards," I said. "But they are 'get out of misdemeanor' cards."

"Meaning what 'xactly?" Wolf asked, flipping them back over to the fronts.

"You get in a stupid fistfight with your buddy," Remy said. "You're going eighty and you're about to spend a night in jail. You call P.T. He makes it better."

"A'ight," Wolf said. He asked us to wait in the alley a few minutes more. He took the five cards and went inside. Ten minutes later the back door opened again, and he waved us in.

We entered a room that had eight or nine worktables, atop them mostly plastic bins full of metal parts. Gears and motors. Young men in their twenties were huddled in groups of two or three around each table, building something. They wore hoodies and sported barely any facial hair.

"Over here," Wolf said, pointing to a set of stairs that led to the basement.

We clanked down the metal steps and into a subterranean room.

The place was cramped and done in a greenish-blue color. Paint peeled off the ceiling. It felt like the inside of an old submarine. There were tables and old furniture spread throughout the space, but there was also machinery. A 3D printer sat at the far end of the room.

Twenty men and two women hushed up as we reached the third rung from the bottom, where Wolf stopped. This group was older than the one on the floor above. Thirties and forties. Everyone stared at me and Remy.

Wolf cleared his throat. "These folks are the cops I talked to y'all about," he said. "They got something to say—maybe it's lucrative for someone here."

Lucrative?

What angle had Wolf presented to these people?

"Fuckin' cops," I heard someone say, but I couldn't tell who.

"Nolan Brauer," I said. I passed a photocopy of the man's picture to Wolf, who stepped down and handed it to another guy. Brauer was the man who the Cracker Barrel waitress had called unmemorable. "He's got a 3D-printed M24 sniper rifle."

"Bullshit," someone said as the photo passed among the group.

"No, y'all," Wolf said. "I saw some of the damn parts. And not the easy ones to make. The inside of the trigger assembly was tight as fuck."

Murmurs moved through the room.

"Guys," I said. "He's gonna shoot someone tomorrow, and there's a couple rooms full of Feds looking everywhere online to see who it might be. But I think you guys have places that you hang out that the Feds don't know about. We need to know where this Brauer guy might be. And who he might hate enough to kill."

I stepped backward and looked to Remy. "You wanna add something?"

Remy stepped forward, and the place went quiet. Maybe it was my own bias, but I was guessing some of these guys didn't get laid too often. And here was this cop who was drop-dead gorgeous and packing heat.

"Guys," she said. "We need you. We need your help. And we need it fast. 'Cause if someone dies tomorrow morning, a world of hurt is gonna fall on anyone who owns a 3D printer."

Wolf nodded and pointed us back up the stairs.

"That's it?" Remy asked as we trudged back up.

"I think the way it works," I said, "is now we wait."

"That's right," Wolf said as we got to the top. "'Cause the folks inside are just a small portion of the community. You gotta let 'em work. Text and chat with their people."

We moved back to the alley then, and the night sky was a purplish-black. The air smelled clean here, just four miles north of the numbered streets.

I grabbed a pack of Marlboro Reds from my truck, and Remy grabbed her iPad.

As I smoked, I found myself thinking about Kelly Borland.

I considered what Remy had said last night when we argued. How it was part of my mission to keep myself unhappy. Was it a line my partner said to get a reaction out of me? Or the Gospel that I had been denying?

My phone pulsed, and I looked down.

It was Abe.

> The Feds got something. An assemblyman from Alabama. He received harassing mail from Nolan Brauer ten days ago. Turned it over to the police, but it's just been sitting on someone's desk.

I picked up the phone and called Abe, putting him on speaker.

"Clearson is getting on a copter and heading to Birmingham," he said. "From there, it's a one-hour drive to Downey."

"What's in Downey?" Remy asked.

"Some fundraiser tomorrow morning," Abe said. "I'm going with him, so no need to be here at five a.m."

Remy and I looked at each other, but didn't say anything.

"So that's it?" I asked.

"The assemblyman's got a pancake breakfast tomorrow morning outside his headquarters. There's a five-story hotel a block away. It's the only building over one story in the town. We assume that's Brauer's base of operations."

I stubbed out my cigarette and looked to Remy. This was a good thing. And at least we'd exhausted all means, trying to talk to Wolf.

"So they got some confirmation on this?" Remy asked. "The Feds?"

"That's what they told me," Abe said. "They've contacted the governor, who called his counterpart in Alabama. Everything's whisper quiet so we can catch this son of a bitch setting up at that hotel."

The metal door to the back of the game place scraped open, and Wolf pointed at me and Remy with his bony fingers, beckoning us inside.

"All right," I said to Abe. "Stay safe."

Remy was already moving ahead of me. Before I could tell Wolf that we didn't need his help.

I hung up and squinted at Wolf, who was standing with two nerdy-looking dudes. One was white and had legit mom jeans on. Like high-waisted, early '90s numbers, into which he'd tucked a collared shirt. The other guy was Black and wore thick glasses and a white button-down over shorts. For the first time, I realized that Wolf was probably the hippest guy in this crowd.

"This is Ladrell and Malcolm," Wolf said.

The two men stared nervously at Remy—their eyes moving from her chest to the asphalt and then back.

"Wolf," I said. "Sorry, I don't think it's—"

"Just hear them out, Marsh," Wolf said, reading my look on the pair.

Malcolm, the Black guy, spoke first. "So, a lot of the guys downstairs make models, you know? LOTR characters—that sort of thing."

I looked to Wolf, who quickly translated that LOTR stood for *Lord of the Rings*.

"Or Darth Sidious figures if you're into Star Wars," Ladrell said. As if that clarified something about their culture.

"Point being," Malcolm said, pointing at the basement below, "they aren't gonna be able to help much. But with us, it's different."

I suddenly noticed Malcolm was holding three of my business cards and Ladrell was holding two. These guys had scored the full set.

"We don't print those things," Ladrell said. "We make guns, me and Malcolm."

He swallowed. Waiting then, as if I might arrest him.

"Okay," I said. Trying to wear a friendly face even though the guy had just admitted to producing ghost guns.

Remy cocked her head at Ladrell. "Have you heard something?"

"I didn't take it seriously," Ladrell said. "But there was like . . . I don't know how to describe it . . . an RFP that was put out."

"A request for proposal?" I asked.

"An online challenge," Malcolm said. "A million bucks for the first person who can make a 3D-printed M24."

"As a model?"

"No," Malcolm said. "There's already models. I got two of them. You get the million bucks if you can prove it works. One test bullet fired and posted online. And the gun still intact."

"We figured it was a prank," Ladrell said. "The plastic couldn't withstand the power."

"But there's new plastics this year," Wolf said. "Metallic powders in them. They mimic metal."

"And did the person putting out the RFP say why they needed the gun?" Remy asked.

"No, but there's been chatter," Malcolm said.

"Is the target someone in politics?" I asked. Trying to connect the maker of the weapon to the man who Abe and Clearson were flying to Alabama to protect.

"In a way," Malcolm said. "There's this foundation that some of our friends have been watching. A guy named Saul Goldberg started it. He was some Wall Street type, but not a trader. Came from the tech side and made hundreds of millions. His sister's kid was a victim in a shooting. So four years ago he started something called Not in This Town."

"It's an anti-gun group," Wolf said, this time with no affect in his voice. It suddenly dawned on me that Wolf's whole style and vernacular might be a put-on, all the "yo" and "girl" shit.

"The idea is to fight the NRA their way. With money," Ladrell described. "This Goldberg guy put in fifty million to start the foundation, but now they got a ton more money from Democratic donations and fundraisers."

"So Goldberg works with politicians?" I clarified.

Malcolm nodded. "And in two districts so far, they've beaten the pro-NRA candidate at election time."

I looked to Remy. This was all coming together. Verifying what Abe and Clearson had said.

"So you've heard chatter on the politician who's the target?" Remy said, looking for fidelity.

"Well, we caught wind of something, but we're not sure it's legit."

"Is it at an event in Alabama?" Remy asked.

The two looked at each other and shook their heads. "No. What we heard is in Atlanta," Malcolm said. "Eight a.m. tomorrow. Outside the Georgia Aquarium."

I cocked my head, confused.

I asked the guys to hold a second and stepped over to my truck with Remy. Decided to call up Mandelle Clearson myself.

"Hey," I said. I could hear a chopper behind him. "We might have a lead here. How sure are you on this Alabama thing?"

"Who's your lead from?" Clearson asked.

"You don't know him," I said. "But listen. Have you heard of a group called Not in This Town?"

"Yeah, we know the guy who runs it," Clearson yelled. "Pain-in-the-ass loudmouth from New York. He thinks he's doing our job getting guns off the street."

"Have we considered if someone in his group is the target?"

"We know who the target is, P.T."

"This group has an event in the morning," I said. "In downtown Atlanta."

Clearson's voice became more distant.

"Mandelle?" I asked, but the phone disconnected.

Remy looked at me. "What'd he say?"

"I think he hung up on me."

My phone pulsed a moment later, and I stared at a message from Clearson:

> We got this, P.T. Stand down. Get some rest. You're
> grasping at straws.

I handed the phone to Remy, who stared at the text.

I had been wondering all day what I used to like about Clearson.

I couldn't remember.

"So?" she said.

"Where's the place in Atlanta that this function is at in the morning?" I asked.

Remy had the foundation's website open on her phone.

"The National Center for Civil and Human Rights," she said. "It's located between the Georgia Aquarium and the World of Coca-Cola."

I considered the symbolic nature of this. "Can you think of a more iconic act by some nut who calls himself a patriot?" I asked. "Taking out someone at a place named the National Center for Civil and Human Rights?"

"Intimidating," Remy said. She held up her phone. "And check this out. The speaker in the morning. It's Jerome Bleeker."

This was the candidate running against Toby Monroe for governor. He was speaking on the topic of 3D guns.

We walked back over and found Wolf, Ladrell, and Malcolm, all huddled in a group outside the back door of the game place.

"What'd your boss say?" Wolf asked.

"He's not our boss," Remy said.

"He's a Fed," I clarified. "And he said he knows better. But we're gonna check out your lead."

"Nice," Wolf said.

"The problem is, where the ATF is looking is some tiny suburb in Alabama," I said. "One tall building in town. If you're right—and this Brauer guy's as good as we think with a sniper rifle—he could be in one of fifty buildings in Atlanta. Too many to check in one night."

"Then we'll need to look at trajectory," Ladrell said, more to Malcolm than us. "Angle from roof to street."

I looked to Remy.

We? Did I black out and someone deputized the nerds? Then again, without the Feds' help, we were dead in the water. Just the two of us and no way to consider this many buildings.

"I got a buddy," Malcolm said. "He's got a perfect one-to-five-hundred scale model of Atlanta. He's probably ten minutes from here. If we want to check out trajectory, we could go old-school."

"String?" Ladrell asked.

"I was thinking laser pointer," Malcolm suggested.

I glanced at my phone. It was past midnight.

"And this friend of yours is up at this hour?" I asked.

"For a couple more of these?" Malcolm held up my cards. "Zach'll wake up."

34

The 3D model of downtown Atlanta was in a house just north of the city limits.

We left Ladrell behind and followed Malcolm and Wolf there. My Silverado trailed behind Malcolm's Chevy Blazer, while Wolf and Malcolm called their buddy Zach and gave him a heads-up.

As we drove, Remy did some phone research on the Not in This Town website, seeing that their 2020 platform wasn't directed only at 3D-printed guns. It had a very specific angle.

The group wanted to make the development of engineering plans equal to the manufacture of the guns themselves.

Which would legally corner anyone putting plans online, unless they had a federal firearms manufacturing license. Which none of these rogue guys designing 3D guns in their basement did.

I thought about what Wolf had said when we were in the back of Chester's gun shop. About the reason someone might use a 3D sniper rifle.

That might fall under the category of making a statement.

What better statement could you make against a potentially

onerous 3D-printing law than to take out the people pushing for that law? And do it from a half mile away, using a 3D weapon.

"Shit," I said to Remy. "That's a game-changer if it becomes law."

Malcolm's Blazer slowed outside a large ranch-style home with confederate jasmine curling along a white picket fence that ran along the edge of the property.

Remy and I got out. Followed Malcolm and Wolf over to the door, where he introduced us to his friend.

Zach Obernick was white and six foot tall, with a neatly trimmed black beard and wavy hair. His wife, Flora, was Black and wore hospital scrubs that featured a pattern of tiny bears against a pink field.

"You're a nurse?" Remy asked the wife as we walked through their home.

"I'm a pediatric neurosurgeon," she said. "Just got off a late shift. You're the detectives?"

"Yes, ma'am," Remy said.

Her husband opened their back door, and we followed the couple from the home out into a huge backyard.

In the center was an all-glass room, about fifteen feet by fifteen feet.

"A greenhouse," Remy said, just as we approached the structure.

"And wouldn't that be nice," Flora said. "Some beautiful flowers inside maybe."

The husband, Zach, came around with a key and unlocked the greenhouse door.

But we didn't see a garden full of daylilies or trays of hothouse tomatoes. Instead, we stared at a 1:500 scale replica of the city of Atlanta, set up on a mahogany ten-by-ten table, about four feet off the ground.

"Wow," I said. It was a city of white plastic structures, perfectly molded to show off every window and rooftop pool, but not painted.

In between the buildings, which were labeled with their addresses on tiny signs, were gray roads painted on the table.

The whole city stood about ten to twenty inches high off the board, depending on the actual height of each building.

Wolf and Malcolm were the last ones in the door, and Malcolm moved around the far side of the table.

"Right there's the Georgia Aquarium." Malcolm pointed. "Here's the World of Coca-Cola." Malcolm's finger moved back to the courtyard. "And right here is the Center for Civil and Human Rights. That quad outside is the spot of Bleeker's speech."

I knew Atlanta okay, and I recalled spending time in this specific area. Lena and I had taken Jonas to the aquarium when he was six. I remember going on the behind-the-scenes tour and learning this was the only place in the country where whale sharks lived.

Remy moved around the far side of the table and was doing the same thing I was. Her eyes flitted from building to building near the center. Studying trajectory like a sharpshooter.

"Laser pointer?" Wolf asked Malcolm, who produced one.

Wolf handed it to Remy, and she pointed the pen from the top of the miniature SunTrust Plaza.

"That works," I said, watching as my partner aimed the red light down onto the open quad area in front of the civil rights building.

"There's one possibility," Remy said.

We did the same for the Westin Peachtree.

I stared at the row of structures set along Centennial Olympic Park Drive NW. "Any of these condos you could take a shot from."

I pointed at a set of three buildings with tiny unpainted pools at the top. "The Children's Museum of Atlanta. Also the Coca-Cola place itself. The parking garage for the aquarium."

We moved with the laser from building to building, each time assessing where a shot could come from. When we finished, there were sixteen buildings in question. Maybe eighteen if you were a perfect marksman. And we knew Nolan Brauer could shoot.

"It's a lot," Remy said.

"Well, you have a bunch of officers, right?" Wolf asked. "You said there were a couple departments of Feds working."

This was part of our spiel at the game place where we found Malcolm and Ladrell an hour ago. Then again, those agents all worked for Clearson, not us. And they'd all headed to Downey, Alabama.

"Let's jot down these addresses, Rem," I said. "Get out of these nice people's home."

Zach leaned in with a rectangular magnifying glass. He read off each address from the tiny buildings, while Remy typed them into her iPad. When she was done, I took a photo of the list with my phone, guessing we might have to split up.

We thanked Zach and Flora and pushed out into the cool night.

Outside, Malcolm moved toward his car, but Wolf hung back for a second. "You got more bodies than just you two, right?" he asked.

"You did great," Remy said to Wolf. Knowing we had to get going.

"Yeah, I feel you on that," Wolf said. "But answer my question. It's more than just you two?"

"No," I said. "But we're gonna hustle, man. I promise you that."

"I could keep helping," Wolf offered.

My partner glanced at me. I knew we could use a couple extra bodies. But there was a pro on the loose. An expert marksman, hauling around a lightweight sniper rifle and protected by a bodyguard with a background in hand-to-hand combat.

"Against regulation," I said. "And Remy and I—we've gone against regulation enough times to know."

"I can call Chester," Wolf said. "Me and him take half the buildings."

"You've helped enough," I said, and we shook hands. "We'll stay in touch. Tell you how it goes."

"Okay," he said, and caught up with Malcolm.

I turned to Remy after they left, the two of us standing by my truck.

"We got seven hours and no warrants," I said.

"Just out-of-town badges and an expectation of cooperation."

"Okay then," I said. "We go light and fast. You split up the list of buildings as I drive. When we get to Atlanta, let's be sweet as pie to any building security."

35

By six-forty a.m., I had checked six buildings off my list, starting with SunTrust Plaza, at the tallest.

I'd badged security and night watchmen, and so far, each had shown me the roof, or their security center. Some had even helped me search it.

As I walked out of the W Hotel, I thanked the guys in charge and told them to keep up their vigilance.

My phone rang and it was Remy, who had taken the structures along Centennial so she could work on foot, going building by building, while I explored the places that were farther away and required the truck.

"I've cleared six so far," I said to Remy on the phone. "I'm heading down near you, by the plaza. Check the Coca-Cola building and the parking garage by the aquarium."

"Ten-four," Remy said. "I'm walking up to Ivan Allen Jr. Blvd."

There was a crest of orange on the morning horizon, and I was thinking what I'd thought the night before when I got Abe's note about the shooter being in Alabama. That it would be good to be

wrong. That I'd rather be tired from searching these rooftops in Atlanta than sorry that we hadn't explored them and something bad had
happened.

When I got down near the Coca-Cola building, I talked to security and they inspected my tin.

They assigned me this old-timer named Cecil, bone thin and
white with wavy hair.

"How long have you worked here, Cecil?" I asked as we walked.
The guy was older than dirt.

"This location, ten years," he said. "But for Coke—a half century."

Cecil moved like a turtle, and I pulled up alongside him. He
smiled at me, but didn't accelerate. He'd been around so long he probably knew the secret recipe for Coke.

We took a freight elevator up to the roof.

The top of the place was enormous, but I could immediately see
that there was no one up there.

"Where to next?" he asked.

"What about the parking garage?"

"That's not technically part of Coke, but we can go over there. It's
closed now, you know."

"Let's do it."

Cecil's left leg started getting gimpy, and it slowed us down more.
We walked what seemed like a football field before getting to another
elevator. Took it up to the fourth floor. Another cavern.

There were no cars parked in the lot, but we weren't at the top
level. "What's above here?" I motioned at the concrete ceiling.

"It's closed off right now."

"Can we check?" I asked.

Cecil found a stairwell, but he looked at me. "The alarm's gonna
go off if we push this open."

"Will it turn off after we close it?"

"Sure." He nodded.

I pressed the bar to open the door, and the sound was deafening. "C'mon." I motioned him inside.

The walloping ended, and we took the stairs up to the top, but Cecil was right. Nobody in sight.

I looked out from the rooftop toward the courtyard where the civil rights building was. The event was in less than two hours, and I could see uniformed staff rolling out circular tables and setting up an elevated stage for the speech.

My phone buzzed, and I took it out. The number was Wolf's.

"Wolf," I said. "We don't know anything yet. Let me call you in a bit."

"P.T.," he said as if he didn't hear me. "I think I just saw the big guy."

"Big guy who?" I asked.

"The bodyguard. The one in the picture with Nolan Brauer."

"In Mason Falls?" I asked.

"No," Wolf said. "Uh . . . Chester and me came down here. Help out, you know?"

I moved across the parking garage toward the edge that looked up toward Centennial. "You're in Atlanta?"

"Chester said, 'If you can't run with the dogs, stay on the porch,'" Wolf said. "So we thought—"

"Where did you see the bodyguard?" I interrupted Wolf.

"He was leaving some hotel," Wolf said. "Midtown Suites, I think. I can't find him now. Or reach Chester."

I pulled up the picture of the list of buildings on my phone. *Shit*, I thought. What the hell had Wolf and Chester been thinking—coming here?

"Is everything all right?" Cecil asked.

"That's one of Remy's," I said to Wolf, bringing the phone back to my face. "I'll call you back."

I hustled across the top of the parking garage in the other direction until I could see over the edge toward Ivan Allen Jr. Blvd. Diagonally up the street from me was the top of the Midtown Suites.

I took my binocs from my back pocket and scanned the roof of the hotel.

Remy had just come out of a door and was threading her way in between giant air conditioners.

I scanned left, across the rooftop, to see if it was empty.

That's when I saw a man dressed in black pants and a long-sleeved black T-shirt.

"Shit," I said. It was Nolan Brauer.

He pushed aside a gun case and lifted up the M24.

I could see the two replacement pieces, top and bottom, in unpainted white, as part of the gun.

"Remy!" I yelled instinctively, but she couldn't hear me. She just kept walking. Maybe twenty yards from the guy. With neither of them seeing each other.

I pulled up my phone, but didn't want the ringing to distract Remy or be something that Brauer heard.

Cecil came up behind me. "Do you see something?"

I nodded, moving a few feet toward the edge of the parking garage. "Go find a phone, Cecil. Call 911."

I typed a quick text to Remy to watch out, and waited.

But Remy didn't look down at her phone.

In between us was Ivan Allen Jr. Blvd. One busy lane in each direction, and my partner a block up.

I couldn't get there in time. Nor could I reach Brauer with a bullet from a Glock 42.

I scanned back to my partner and saw her moving across the roof.

Then, fifteen yards away, dust kicked up, and Brauer ran toward Remy.

It seemed like slow motion. Him heading toward her—and her not seeing until it was too late.

She pulled her Glock as he tackled her, and the gun skittered away from her.

They went down together, rolling along the roof until they slammed into the edge of an AC unit, its turbine spinning away. I saw a hand go back, and Brauer swing hard, right at Remy's face. But she shifted her shoulder blades and Brauer hit his hand onto the edge of the AC box.

While he was stunned, Remy pushed him off and got up, running for her gun, but not knowing where it was.

I glanced down onto the boulevard. Then over at the hotel.

If you run for it, you'll never get there in time, Purvis said. *Worse, you won't know what happened.*

Remy found the gun case, but Brauer had already removed the weapon, placing it in between two air-conditioning units.

He dove at her, knocking her off her feet.

They squared off then, and I found myself talking aloud. Powerless.

"C'mon, Rem."

Brauer landed a hard punch to Remy's face. Motioned her to come closer.

She moved in, faking with her left and then coming with her right, landing a hard hit to his jaw.

Then she roundhouse-kicked Brauer, but made contact with his hand or the rifle instead, coming down funny on her leg.

Remy didn't get up right away, and Brauer turned.

He grabbed the M24, a gun designed to be shot from long distance, and pulled back the action, aiming it at my partner.

I shifted my binoculars to Remy. She was crawling away, but something was wrong with her leg. She dragged her body across the roof, and I could hardly breathe.

Am I going to watch as someone murders my partner?

Am I forced to look on as someone else I love dies?

Brauer aimed the rifle at her from twelve feet away—and *bam*.

36

Jed Harrington saw the middle school campus ahead of him.

The main structure at Falls Magnet Middle School was a wide, one-story building with a façade of charcoal-colored bricks, interrupted only by strips of stacked stone that ran vertically, every thirty feet or so, from the bottom of the building to the roof.

The place had a look that split the difference between time periods—half colonial Georgia and half contemporary. A compromise in design that projected that the ways of the old South were a thing of the past, an architectural memory only.

Harrington pulled his Dodge Magnum slowly past the building on the far left side of the campus and shook his head.

"Motherfucker," he said aloud.

He glanced around then, and maybe it was all the time he'd spent with the military, but he noticed the solitary road he'd just used to get onto campus.

One way in. One way out.

He pulled into a parking spot then and got out. Stood sentinel for a good minute before exhaling and pulling his long flannel over his jeans.

Am I really doing this? *he wondered.*

Am I really stepping into this?

And then he put his head down and plunged forward.

37

An explosion came from the roof where Remy was. A huge puff of smoke floating through the frame of my binoculars.

A car alarm went off, and a black cloud covered the rooftop.

Go, Purvis said, and I took off, down four flights of stairs without looking.

Crossing the street, I sped down the sidewalk. One building. A second building. I crossed the busy street without looking and burst in through the front doors of the Midtown Suites.

I moved through the lobby of the hotel, and my heart was in my stomach.

"I need access to your rooftop," I said to a guy at the front desk, badging him. "Now!"

"Excuse me?" he said.

"Now." I banged on the counter.

The clerk ran with me over to an elevator. But I could see from the dial that the two cars were both on high floors.

"Stairs," I demanded, and he pointed me the way.

Up I went, the clerk in tow for the first two flights.

As I headed around the turn at three, I saw Chester Gardner, crumpled in the stairwell corner. His face was as purple as eggplant.

"Chess," I said.

"The bodyguard." He pointed up. "I'm sorry. Go."

I jumped over Chester and raced up to the fifth level. The sixth.

I pushed the door open at the roof and heard the emergency alarm chirp on and off as the fire door closed.

I looked across at the parking garage where I'd left Cecil. Tried to judge where to look from where the aquarium garage was, and then moved right.

As I came around the corner, I could smell the pungent stink of nitroglycerin in the air—mixed in with blood. The smell of a weapon freshly fired.

And I stared at something strange.

The body of Nolan Brauer, except without the top of his body. The man's head was gone, as was part of his upper chest.

And that's when I saw Remy.

Her leg was twisted at an odd angle, and her body was covered in blood and guts.

38

I splashed water on my face, and wiped the dirt from it with a cheap hospital paper towel that broke apart in my hands.

It had been four hours since EMTs had ferried my partner down from the roof. Four hours since Wolf had steered Chester and me to Emory University Hospital about a mile away from the hotel, following the ambulance that held Remy.

I walked into the room where my partner was.

Darren Gattling stood by Remy's bed. He was holding her hand, and he let go when he saw me.

I hadn't seen Gattling since outside of Tandy's bar, six days ago, and now he was in street clothes. A light blue sweatshirt and dark jeans clung to his muscular frame.

"I'll let you two talk," Gattling said, and turned. Headed out to the hallway.

I stared at Remy. Her face and arms bore a dozen cuts, but she looked better than she had on the roof when I found her, covered in the skin, blood, and intestines of the man once known as Nolan Brauer.

"How long you been up?" I asked. The room smelled of Mercurochrome and bacitracin.

"I dunno," she said. "Why?"

"I came by a half hour ago, but you were asleep. I got close. Made sure you were breathing."

"Creeper alert," Remy said.

I started laughing, and so did Remy. Then she stopped.

"Oh my God, don't make me laugh, P.T. I think I cracked a rib, and the doctors haven't figured it out yet."

I looked Remy over. When I found her atop the Midtown Suites, I quickly put together what had happened.

Brauer and Remy had fought, and she had landed a roundhouse kick in his direction.

He'd stopped the kick with his hand. Which was holding the M24.

Except what Brauer didn't realize was that Remy had dented the plastic of the rifle just slightly when she made contact.

He aimed the barrel at Remy's face, ten feet from her, and pulled the trigger. And the gun had backed up on itself. Kinda like Wolf's friend, who had burned his hand with a 3D-printed gun. Except much, much worse,

"I'm sorry, Rem," I said. "That I didn't go to that hotel instead of you."

"Oh my God." My partner shook her head. "Of all people—*you* cannot pull that masculine shit on me, P.T. *I'm* the one who told you we should go see Wolf. Meet the whole Dungeons & Dragons crew and go after these guys."

"I was on the top of the aquarium parking garage," I said. "I haven't felt that helpless since—" I stopped talking and Remy nodded.

"I know," she said.

"I saw you kick him and then a minute later—boom."

"When I came down from that kick," she said, "I felt something in my leg snap. But I also had a feeling that I'd fucked up that gun."

"You basically created a grenade," I said. "You blew him up when he pulled the trigger."

"Pretty badass, huh?" she said.

"Pretty badass," I agreed.

"You talk to the Feds?" she asked.

"A bit," I said. "They have about fifty guys scraping Brauer off that roof. I didn't think they needed any 'local help' with that."

Remy went quiet then, probably thinking about the life she'd taken.

"C'mere," she said, and I pulled over a chair. "I'm gonna be laid up for a couple weeks," she whispered. "Doc said it's a day here before they transport me home. But at home I'm gonna be out of work. In a boot, first. Then on crutches."

"It's okay," I said. "The case is over. I'll cover stuff."

She shook her head then. As if I wasn't following her.

"The case with Lena," Remy said. "Under the liquor store. I said I'd go all the way with you. But I can't now."

"I'll wait," I said.

"No," Remy said. "After this. And the school shooting. You're never gonna be as high as you are now. And you're gonna need to break some rules to take down Hartley."

I stared at her, our faces close.

"Maybe I don't need to," I told her. "Like you said, maybe I just need to ignore the past. Stop chasing ghosts."

Remy put out her hand to quiet me. "That's important," she said. "All that shit I told you when we were under that liquor store."

"But?"

"But Hartley took out that building the next day because we went there," she said. "We visited an abandoned building, and he blew it up. So you're gonna have to be smarter than him, P.T. One step ahead of him."

I held my gaze on her. "Yeah."

"And you're never gonna have more equity to burn than you do now," she said. "So I want you to do something for me, okay?"

"Anything."

"Go home. Walk the dogs. Rest that big brain of yours because we've been up for twenty-four hours, P.T. But then get up. Tell Senza you need a couple days off. And go like the wind, partner. Find out who hired Tarticoft. What they were doing under that liquor store. How Hartley's involved. And fucking get 'em all."

"Okay," I said. "Yeah."

But I could tell Remy wasn't done.

"Somebody needs to tell you that you're worth betting on, P.T. That you deserve good things."

I nodded.

"So maybe it's the drugs talking—but I gotta be straight with you. You listening?"

"Yeah."

"You're not at fault for that shit that went down with Lena. You worked late, P.T. You took a case. You worked late a million other nights. It's what we do."

I could feel a tear moving down my cheek, but Remy kept going.

"If you attracted the wrong type of attention, it was 'cause you were trying to help someone," she said. "And Lena knew that about you. Probably why she loved you."

I sniffed now, my nose clogging up.

"So you find these fuckers, P.T. But then you gotta be over with it. Y'understand?"

"I do."

"All right," Remy said, giving my hand a squeeze. "So what are you still doing here?"

I tapped the edge of her bed and took a step back. Turned and left.

Out in the lobby I crossed the room toward Darren Gattling.

"I know what you're gonna say." He put up his palms. "When you came in. You saw us holding hands."

He stopped talking and stared at me. My face was probably still covered in tears.

"Take care of her, Darren, okay?"

I patted him on the shoulder and left.

39

I stepped out of the elevator and crossed the lobby of the hospital, trying to remember where I'd stowed my truck when I'd arrived in a panic.

Standing in front of me were two giant men. They were Black and built like S.E.C. tight ends. Each at least six foot tall and ripped. Pure muscle they couldn't hide, even in a two-piece suit.

"Mr. Bleeker would like a word," the man closest to me said in a baritone.

He steered me toward an E.R. waiting area, and I noticed a man I'd seen only on TV.

Councilman Jerome Bleeker was five foot ten, with a few extra pounds around the middle. He was in his forties and dressed in gray slacks and a white dress shirt. A tie, no longer around his neck, was laid out atop a magazine copy of *Atlanta*, on a chair beside him.

"Detective Marsh." He stood up as I approached. "I understand I owe you and your partner a debt of gratitude."

"Councilman." I shook his hand. "It's our pleasure. If you have a moment, Detective Morgan is on the third floor, in recovery."

"That's my next stop," he said.

He scanned me, stopping at a red mark that was probably Nolan Brauer's blood on my shirt. And I stared at him. He had a kind face and unusually large brown eyes.

"From what I hear-tell, your partner nearabout died."

"Yeah," I said. "I guess that's true."

"Are you a religious person, Detective Marsh?"

"I grew up going to church," I said. "My father was religious. I don't go now."

"Well, I only know one person well in Mason Falls," he said. "A preacher by the name of Reggie Webster. He speaks very highly of you."

I smarted, almost embarrassed. Remy and I had worked a hate crime against Webster's son, Kendrick. But we came onto the case after the boy had been killed. Too late to prevent the catastrophe.

"I'm curious how you knew someone was going to shoot me," Bleeker said.

"We worked a lead," I replied. "Sometimes it's more gut than science. I'm just glad everything turned out okay."

The councilman nodded, studying me.

"And you're the one that Governor Monroe praised on the news," he said. "You live a complex life, don't you, Detective?"

I stared at Bleeker for a spell. I hated that I sounded like Toby Monroe's boy. "I work for the Mason Falls PD, Mr. Bleeker. Not Governor Monroe."

"And thank God for that," he said.

He put out his hand, and I shook it again. "All right, I'll go see your partner. You get some rest. Your eyes are bloodshot, Detective."

I headed out the door of the hospital, and after a minute I located the doctor's parking lot where I'd stowed my truck.

I'd already sent Wolf and Chester back home. As it turned out,

Chester had gotten his ass kicked, but wasn't hurt too badly. Mostly cuts and swelling on his face that needed ice and time.

"Detective Marsh," a voice said as I walked under the ER's portico.

I turned and saw Quarles, the Fed from the day before. Jesus, I just wanted to go home.

"I've been asked to bring you over to the Midtown Suites."

"I'm tired, man," I said. "I'm going home to crash."

"Detective Clearson said you might say that."

I turned and stared at Quarles. The starchy white shirt and dark blue coat. Were all these guys issued the same suit as some uniform?

"Detective Clearson wanted to make sure I passed on his gratitude," Agent Quarles said.

"His gratitude?" I blinked.

"For your part in the multi-agency approach. You were the third leg of the chair—as he just announced at the press conference. Federal. State. And locals, all working together."

I smiled at Quarles.

So teamwork—that's the story we're going with?

"My pleasure," I said.

"Yourself and Detective Morgan will be properly acknowledged once she's better."

"Sure," I said. I turned toward the parking lot, but the guy kept walking alongside me.

"We did have a question about this man," he said, holding up a photo.

I stared at a shot of Chester Gardner. The angle was from above. A hotel security cam, and it showed Chester and the bodyguard in a face-off.

"We've got an APB out on the bodyguard, Anton Sedonovich," Quarles said. "But it appears that *this* man tried to slow him down. Do you know him?"

"Yeah," I said. "That's the fourth leg of the chair, Quarles. Civilians. It's who you count on when the first leg of the chair sends you a text that says 'Stand down.' Tells you that you're grasping at straws."

"Right." Quarles nodded.

I clicked the fob and unlocked my truck. Pulled the door open.

"So do we need to take care of this gentleman?" he asked. "Make sure he's clear on his story? Reward or acknowledge him in some way?"

"He did his civic duty," I said. "He'll be bragging about it at barbecues. That's enough for him. And I get to hear as the stories get better each year. In ten years, *he'll* have kicked Sedonovich's ass."

The Fed smiled at this.

"You wanna be clean with me?" I asked. "Not have any PR problems, right?"

"It's like you're reading my mind," Quarles said.

"The old guy we were hunting." I looked at him. "He killed a cop's son in Mason Falls. Why don't you put the same attention on finding him as you did on Brauer? All those agency resources you talked about. Find us something, and I'll say whatever words you want."

"Done," Quarles said.

And I got in my truck and drove off.

40

By two p.m., I'd made it home and saw Purvis in the window, wagging his backside. Beau quickly scooted in front of him, his youth an undying engine. He placed his front two paws up on the window, and the glass shook with excitement.

I took both dogs for a walk, their leashes twisting around each other as Beau ran in circles like a kid hopped up on Easter candy.

"C'mon, puppy," I said to him, untangling the cords as I walked.

It had sprinkled in the neighborhood overnight, and water pooled unevenly in the street. A neighbor was circling the duck pond with a set of Yorkies, so I took my time getting there, and she saw me with my two wild beasts and headed in the other direction.

At the pond, I let go of Purvis's leash, and he walked slowly around the perimeter. There were no mallards today, or Beau would've gone ape shit and yanked himself out of his collar.

I sat on the grass at the edge of the pond, even though I immediately felt the wetness of the Marathon sod soak into my pants.

I pulled Beau into my lap, calming him down by putting my arms around him and rubbing at the tufty area that ran from his neck down toward his stomach.

After a minute, he was restless, and I got up, barely able to stand with fatigue.

Back at the house, I filled both of their bowls and stepped out onto the porch, hearing the scuffing of aluminum against tile as each of the dogs scarfed up their food, pushing their bowls with their faces until they clacked against the molding at the two corners of the kitchen.

Where the hell did the last day go?

My eyes grew lazy, and I realized that, other than the time with Kelly on the houseboat, I hadn't gotten a good night's rest in days. I had also been up for thirty hours straight.

I moved inside, closing the doggie door to lock the dogs in the house with me and keep the barking down. I closed all the drapes and turned the AC low, getting under the covers and letting the stress of the last week disappear.

Get some rest, my partner had said. *And then get going.*

When I awoke, seven hours had passed, and it was night. Maybe nine or ten p.m. Beau jumped onto the bed and walked straight across Purvis's body to lick my face.

"Okay," I said. "I'm up, boy."

I took a hot shower while Beau ran laps around the house, chasing an imaginary foe.

I could hear him slam against walls as he cornered, and I wondered if we had chosen each other because of common DNA. Dead ends were my specialty too. But maybe with my mind clear, I could find some new string. Some tiny thread that would lead me back to Lena. Back to my past and this robbery and maybe even to a crash along I-32, two Christmases ago.

Coming out in jeans and a sweatshirt, I realized that Beau had accidentally closed the bathroom door on himself and panicked. Locked inside, he'd scratched half the stain off the door.

I let him out and stared at the damage.

I'd ask Kelly about it later. She was a painter. She'd know how to fix scratches on a stained door.

I moved into the dining room and took a weathered manila folder off the shelf. The one that had everything I knew about the Golden Oaks robbery on December 12, 2017.

I hadn't put quality time into this case in months, but tonight I felt a fire in my belly.

My phone pulsed and I grabbed it. I was thinking it might be Remy, but I was wrong. It was Kelly Borland. Funny, I'd just thought of her.

> Doing anything tonight?

I typed back.

> Working on a case. Sorry. Miss hanging out with you.

The three dots blinked and a new text appeared.

> Me too. Soon then? After your case is over?

I typed back:

> For sure.

I switched my phone off, going back to the opening of the case in December 2017. To what was stolen and how patrol first got to the liquor store.

I unclipped the case extract, breaking the file into pieces, mimicking the normal sections that make up a murder book. Even though the case was a robbery and not a murder.

Separate sections for witness statements.

For detectives' notes.

For evidentiary matter.

Organize the information in a fresh way. And start from zero.

For this case, that began with a call on December 12 to 911.

I stared at the transcript, which was typed and pasted into my notes from two years ago.

OPERATOR: 911, what's your emergency?

CALLER: A guy just came in here. Fuckin' robbed us.

OPERATOR: I see your address is 2016 Pike Street. Is that correct, sir?

CALLER: Took his fuckin' time after he hit me too. Got a damn Cherry Coke.

OPERATOR: Sir, is anyone seriously injured or shot?

CALLER: No. Thank God. But son of a bitch, my heart is rac—

OPERATOR: Sir, can you still see the <*inaudible*>?

CALLER: No, he's gone.

OPERATOR: Good, are you in a safe place, sir? Are you okay?

CALLER: He hit me in the fuckin' head, so no. I'm not okay. He had a gun to my face.

OPERATOR: Officers are on their way, sir. Can I get your name?

CALLER: He was a white guy. He had a single bro— <*inaudible*>

OPERATOR: What was that?

CALLER: —tattooed.

OPERATOR: You're cutting out, sir. Can I get your name?

CALLER: Christian.

OPERATOR: Christian what?

CALLER: Pelo. Like yellow, but with a *p*.

OPERATOR: Can I confirm your address is—

CALLER: Yeah, like you said before. The Golden Oaks. Pike and 20th.

OPERATOR: Officers are on the way. Would you like me to stay on the line?

CALLER: Not if someone's coming this <inaudible>

OPERATOR: Excuse me?

CALLER: What?

OPERATOR: I'm sorry, sir, what did you—

I flipped the page forward and saw that the call ended. I remembered Christian telling me he hung up in frustration. At the questions the woman was asking. How he couldn't hear her. How his head was throbbing from the hit he'd taken.

On the next page were the notes taken by Emmanuel Bastian, the first patrol officer who responded to the call. Bastian was an older guy, and I'd been to his retirement party last year.

At the top of the page, the report listed the address of the Golden Oaks, along with the type of incident, which was first-degree robbery and assault, along with criminal codes 16-7-1 and 16-5-20.

Below that, Patrolman Bastian had written his case summary:

On December 12 at approximately six p.m., Mason Falls Police responded to a 911 call on the 2000th block of Pike Street of a potential 211 in progress at the Golden Oaks liquor store. I arrived at the store at approximately 6:14 p.m. and found no suspects present.

Per Christian Pelo, the store clerk, an unknown male had entered the package store armed with what appeared to be a bolt-action rifle. The suspect approached the checkout register. He held the weapon to the right temple of Pelo. Then the suspect demanded all the money in the store.

Pelo opened the cash drawer, revealing the contents as thirty-three dollars, broken into the following denominations: one twenty-dollar bill, one ten, and three singles. The suspect struck the clerk in the head with the butt of his rifle and quickly ran to the clerk's side of the counter. The suspect told Pelo he knew there was a "fuck-ton of cash in this joint" and to "give it up"—tapping the butt of the rifle on a safe that was obscured behind a series of liquor bottles along the back counter.

Pelo opened the store safe, but it was empty, as his manager had one hour earlier headed to the bank. At this point, the suspect became irate and struck Pelo a second time, knocking him to the floor behind the counter. The suspect grabbed a plastic drink cup from behind the register and told the clerk to stay down.

Taking the thirty-three dollars from the cash drawer, the suspect asked the clerk if his fountain machine dispensed Cherry Coke, to which Pelo, from the floor, affirmed that the machine did. The suspect then filled the cup with the beverage and left, telling Pelo to count to fifty before he got up.

Pelo reported the suspect wore a black ski mask over his face with one oval hole for the eyes and nothing where the mouth was. From the skin he could see, Pelo reported that the suspect was white and about his height, which was five foot ten.

The report was signed by Bastian and dated December 12, the day of the robbery.

I sat back, noticing that Purvis had settled atop my right foot. A line of drool hung from his mouth and across my sock, ending on the hardwood floor.

"I don't know what you're expecting, here, buddy," I said to him, looking from the file to my bulldog.

Just work the details, Purvis said.

I flipped to the next page, but I remembered well what happened after that, because that's when I came onto the case.

Dispatch called robbery, who said they were backed up, and a request went out to Miles Dooger, who was the police chief at the time.

Miles called me at my desk and asked if I could help.

The next page contained my interview with Pelo from the day of the robbery.

This was the only time I'd spoken with the clerk, since in subsequent visits, I had instead spoken to the day manager, John Adrian, who insisted that the establishment didn't want the incident followed up on, and that Pelo had abandoned his job in distress after the robbery and left no forwarding address.

When I pushed for a home address where I could speak to Pelo, Adrian told me he didn't know how to find the clerk and that the address line on Pelo's job application had been inadvertently left blank.

"What about his I-9 form?" I'd asked, and Adrian went into the office at the rear of the store. Came out five minutes later and apologized. Told me *Christian* hadn't yet filled out his I-9.

"You're a real hustler," I remember Adrian saying to me. "Thirty-three bucks and a drink and you've been back here three times. My view of the whole Mason Falls PD is changed for the better."

I slipped my foot out from under Purvis. Got up and grabbed a hard rubber ball that I'd bought for Beau.

Pacing around the dining table, I bounced the ball, trying to shake the rust from my memory of those days. Across the room, Beau lifted his head, but then dropped it, falling back asleep on the couch once he realized I wasn't playing with him.

John Adrian, the Golden Oaks day manager, was always wanting to talk outside. This was something I'd told Remy recently.

"You mind if I smoke while we chat?" he'd say, and let one of his employees take over the register.

At the time, I read this as nerves, which a lot of folks get when talking to a cop. But now I figure he might've been trying to get me away from the hatch that Remy and I had found behind the register. The hatch that led under the store, to whatever illegal activity was going on back then.

I thought of the powder that Remy and I found inside the empty boxes under the liquor store.

I'd never had it tested, but had transferred it to an evidence bag two days ago when I came home from the liquor store. The next time I headed into the precinct I had to figure a way to have Alvin Gerbin test it.

Staring at the short interview I'd done with the clerk, I thought about Christian Pelo on that first day. He had just begun working at the liquor store and told me he didn't really fit in so far. That maybe the robbery was a sign to find something new to do.

Pelo was from southeast of Atlanta, and I wondered if he had left the area and gone home.

I went online and joined one of those research databases that P.I.'s use, finding one that took my credit card, but promised a free three-day trial. Within minutes I was perusing public records. Of course, we had tools like this at work, but they left a paper trail behind. A trail that someone like Lauten Hartley could follow.

I began by looking into all men named Pelo in the southeastern United States.

Was it possible that Christian was living in Georgia still? Or Florida or Alabama?

As I found the number of each man named Pelo, I wrote it down on my yellow legal pad. And when I found a woman named Pelo, I wrote it on my white legal pad. Maybe Christian Pelo was married now, and a phone or address was under his wife's name.

Or maybe I was searching for a needle in a needle factory.

An hour later I had two pages filled in yellow, and one in white. I began calling. Yup, at this hour.

The truth is that sometimes it helps when doing this sort of cold-case work to call late at night. To wake people up at eleven p.m. as they climb into bed, unused to solicitors calling at that hour. You piss them off, sure. But you also get their attention.

"This is Detective Merle Berry," I'd say. My standard way of doing business, in case anything went south. "I just have a quick question for Mr. Pelo."

If there was any possibility of a lead, I'd circle the name, get what I could, and move on. If it proved to be nothing, I'd cross it out and one less possibility.

"He's been gone, almost two years now," a woman said. I'd only been half paying attention and scanned to my white pad. Saw the name Laura Pelo. An older voice.

"And this is Christian we're talking about?" I asked.

"Uh-huh."

"This is your son or husband?"

"He was my son," she said, a Latin accent coming clearer in her voice. "Is my son?"

A statement first. Then a question. Past tense. Then present.

"Do you know where he went?" I asked.

"We assume maybe he's dead, but no one knows," she said. "Who are you again?"

"My name is Paul," I said, now using my real name. "I met a Christian Pelo at his job. He worked in a liquor store that got robbed."

"The guy who drank the Coke," she said. "Mason Falls."

I sat up straighter. "Yeah," I said. "Cherry Coke."

"That was it," she said. "Cherry Coke. I've never had it. Are you a police officer?" she asked.

"I am," I said. "And I tried to follow up with Christian, but he disappeared. I was concerned, way back then, that something had happened to him."

"I spoke with my son the day after that robbery," she said. "At first he was scared to death. But then he won the lottery."

"The Georgia Lottery?"

"No, not the real one," she said. "He just called it that. Because his boss was going to give him a thousand dollars as breaking-off money."

"What do you mean, 'breaking-off'?" I asked.

"It's called something else," she said. "Money to never work some-place again."

"Severance, you mean?"

"Yes, severance."

Except that two years ago John Adrian told me Christian no-showed for work. He called it job abandonment. There was no sever-ance paid. In fact, since Pelo disappeared his first week on the job, he had never even received his first paycheck.

"He was happy about it," the mother said. "Because he didn't want to go back after that robbery."

"So they paid him off?" I asked.

"He was gonna meet them somewhere. Then we never heard from him again. We went to where he was staying, but it wasn't his place. He was sleeping on a friend's couch. His friend said he'd been talking about leaving town all week. Finally he did."

"Do you remember the guy's name he was meeting with?" I asked.

"He had two names," she said. "Two first names. But I don't re-member what they were."

"Was it John?" I asked. "John Adrian?"

"Yeah," the mom said. "Yeah, that was it."

And there it was, I thought. Sitting back.

Evidence that the feeling I'd had almost two years ago at the li-quor store was justified. Adrian had lied to me.

"And how about where the meeting was?" I asked the mom.

"I think he said it was at his boss's house," she said.

"John Adrian's place?"

"Yeah."

I thanked the woman and hung up. Sat there, with Purvis asleep against my foot again.

I needed to find out where John Adrian lived two years ago. If the liquor store was hot after the robbery, it would've been wise for Adrian to take the meeting with Christian Pelo off-site.

The adrenaline was pumping, and it was one-thirty a.m. And I wasn't gonna find that info slogging through names like a P.I.

I needed the tools we had at work. I threw on my jacket and grabbed my keys. Headed to the precinct.

41

I pushed open the door to the lobby, and Hope Duffy at the front glanced up from her computer.

Hope had been a hard-ass cop on patrol for nearabout a decade until she went over a wall too hard and screwed up her leg. Since that day, she's run the intake desk up front, and works late and early shifts.

"If it ain't the big hero," she said. Hope used a hand to pull a strand of blond hair behind her ear. "Or is it Loverboy Hero?"

I glanced at her. Hope had earned the right to talk smack from her time in the field. I just didn't always understand her.

"That woman stopped by again," she said by way of explanation. "The same gal who asked you out in front of me."

Meaning Kelly Borland, the teacher.

"When?" I asked.

"Six p.m. maybe," she said. "She asked about you."

This was before Kelly had texted me, so I'd already responded. I grunted in acknowledgment.

"What are you doing here?" Hope asked. "I heard what happened in Atlanta."

"Yeah," I said. "My sleep schedule's a mess."

I eyed Hope's terminal. I needed to look up John Adrian's info, but didn't want to do it with my own log-in.

"I went home and crashed," I said. "Just got up and realized I needed to finish some paperwork."

"Well, you're in the right place for paperwork."

I plopped into one of the big chairs across from Hope. Our lobby, like the rest of the building, had been remodeled in the last year. The idea was to make it more welcoming for folks walking into a police department for the first time. This included furniture that was actually comfortable, like the chair I was in.

I glanced at the sign about tomorrow's police fundraiser. An old picture of me was plastered front and center across the foam board.

If I hadn't come in here, I probably wouldn't have even remembered I was set to accept an award for my role in the school shooting.

"How's your son?" I asked. Hope had a boy who was a local star in football. A two-way player, receiver and safety. An eighth grader.

"Good," she said. "They're getting ready for the Best of the Best State Championships. It's over winter break at Georgia State."

"Wow," I said. "At fourteen? They play at the old Turner Field?"

"You should see the size of some of these fourteen-year-olds," Hope said. "Damn near three hundred pounds and six foot in junior high."

"You got recent pictures of Daniel?" I asked.

"In my pocketbook." She shrugged. "Back in my locker."

"Let's see 'em," I said. "I'll cover the front."

Hope got up and stretched her bad leg. "Take your time," I said, and sat down in her chair.

As soon as she rounded the corner, I punched in John Adrian's info.

There were six Adrians listed in Georgia, and three of them were in zip codes that placed the men within an hour of Mason Falls.

I pulled up the DMV photo of each one, quickly narrowing to the man I remembered from two Decembers ago.

John Vincent Adrian was five foot eight and white. Thirty-one, with black hair. An address listed him in Glubb County, south of Mason Falls, but his driver's license was expired.

I selected Adrian's DMV and criminal records and picked a printer upstairs. Hit *Enter* to print all current and past addresses.

The truth was that Adrian didn't have much of a criminal record when I interviewed him back in December of '17. So if I wanted to dig for dirt, I'd have to start as I would on any cold case. By gathering background info and a lot of it.

Knowing I was still under Hope's I.D., I did a quick search on Lauten Hartley too. What the hell, right? I sent a list of his previous addresses to the printer. Information on some ticket Hartley had gotten in 2016. Even an altercation with a cop back in 2004.

I heard a noise in the stairwell and closed all the windows on the computer.

Hope swung open the door, her head turned down toward her cell.

She handed me the phone, and I got out of her chair.

"Oh, he's bigger than when I saw him last," I said, staring at the photo of her son, Daniel.

"Five foot nine," she said. "Gonna be taller than me before he starts high school."

"And how's he playing?" I asked.

She took the phone and swiped left through her photos. There was a video of the team, breaking through a paper banner and rushing onto the field. The camera followed Daniel and zoomed in before cutting out.

"Six receptions," she said. "And one pick six. Some guy from a Catholic high school in Atlanta talked to us in the parking lot. Asked us if we were tied to a high school in Mason Falls or would we consider commuting."

"That's a helluva commute," I said. "Have you been on those highways headed south at seven in the morning?"

Hope and I chatted a minute more before I told her I had to get to work.

Upstairs, I swung by the printer and grabbed the pile of paper.

I got settled at my desk and sorted the stack, starting first with the information on John Adrian.

In 2017, Adrian's Ram 1500 was registered at 124 Penescue #1 in Mason Falls. If the meeting with Christian Pelo to get his severance had been at Adrian's place, my starting point would be to visit his old stomping grounds. Knock on some doors and talk to neighbors.

Two a.m. was too early to start looking for background on Adrian in person, so I searched county records online. Found the database and punched in the address at 124 Penescue.

The building was an apartment complex. Multi-family housing that looked to have nine or ten units. But I shifted in my seat as I saw the owner of the building where Adrian had lived.

FJF Investments.

Hartley's partnership.

And not just that. Specifically the same joint venture that owned the Golden Oaks.

"Son of a bitch," I said aloud.

Hartley's partnership hadn't just employed John Adrian in 2017. They'd given him housing.

I looked back at the other addresses I had on John Adrian, seeing that he no longer lived at 124 Penescue. He'd relocated south of here into Glubb County.

I logged in to my own account and checked who currently resided at the address on Penescue where Adrian had once lived. A woman named Maria Evans lived there now, although she was also listed as living in #3 at the same address in earlier years.

I sat back. Out my office window, the sky was an inky black, the trees outside barely an outline. I grabbed the rest of the papers and got up. Walked to Alvin Gerbin's desk and left him that evidence bag with the powder that came from under the Golden Oaks. I placed it under his keyboard with a note that read, *Off the record favor . . . what is this?—P.T.*

Then I plotted the address on Penescue into my phone.

The apartment was ten minutes from the numbered streets in an area called North Heights that had been getting nicer through gentrification.

I had a feeling something was on the horizon. The next clue. The next lead. It was out there, waiting for me. All I had to do was grab it.

42

I woke to the sound of a moped buzzing past my truck's window. It was eight-twenty a.m., and I remembered putting my seat back and grabbing some z's in my Silverado around two a.m.

I rubbed at my face and sat up. Adjusted my seat.

The moped that woke me was a baby blue Italian number. That brand with the curving backside. It sped past me and past the address at 124 Penescue that I was sitting on.

I thought about coffee. Black. Extra sugar. I was about to put my keys in the ignition when a red Dodge Charger pulled up in front of the address. Same model as Marvin's, but four decades later.

A teenager got out. He wore skinny jeans and a long-sleeved T-shirt and had one of those winter caps on that looked more like fashion than function.

He walked cautiously up the stairs. Leaned in to ring the bell and then thought better of it. Knocked instead.

The door opened, and a woman stood there in one of those silk-type Japanese robes. It was yellow with purple hyacinths on it, and she glared at the kid. Asked him something. I couldn't hear them from across the street, but the kid grabbed at his wallet. Pulled it out and handed her a single something.

His identification?

She shut the door, and the kid turned, but didn't leave. His eyes raked the street, and I grabbed binoculars from my glove box.

The door opened again, and I held the binocs to my face, scanning the front porch.

If the woman was Maria Evans, she was late fifties with olive skin and unkempt brownish-gray hair. A small sign stuck into the dirt outside her door read *Manager*.

The woman made what looked like small talk with the kid, who just nodded. Then she pulled a number ten envelope from the pocket of her kimono. The kid looked inside.

His head started bobbing, and he grabbed something from his pocket. Handed it to her.

My eyes moved to the woman then, who counted a wad of cash. Fives and tens. Maybe a hundred bucks in total.

There was no paperwork exchanged, so it didn't feel like how you'd take an apartment deposit.

Opioids? The epidemic had been declining, but wasn't over. Then again, you didn't see drugs being delivered in business envelopes.

I reminded myself that I had to be careful here. The fact that the Golden Oaks had been demolished meant that Hartley knew Remy and I had been down there. I couldn't have Hartley find out that I came here next.

The kid walked down the steps to the muscle car. He fired up the Charger, and I did the same with my truck, letting him pass me before I turned the corner and began following him.

Two blocks down, I grabbed the portable siren from my glove box. I tossed it onto my dash and flicked it on, hitting an air horn that I'd installed when I bought the truck.

The kid slowed and pulled over.

I walked along his driver's side, real slow like, sweating him.

As I came by his window, I held my badge out. Told the kid to keep both hands on the steering wheel.

"Was I speeding?" The kid looked up, a chin pocked with acne.

Closer now, I could see he was seventeen at most. Lanky arms that took up space, but were skinny. Wavy blond hair poking out of his ski cap. Freckles. The envelope was lying on the passenger seat three feet to his right.

"What's in the envelope?" I asked.

"Just, uh—some mail."

"Mail you got from that woman in the kimono back there?"

The kid's face fell, and his hands relaxed off the wheel.

"Whoa, whoa, whoa." I backed up a step, my hand to my waist, where I was packing. "Keep your hands on the wheel, bud."

"What is this—some setup?" the kid asked.

"You're gonna wanna take your right hand," I said. "Reach directly across—and hand me the envelope. Then put your hand back on the wheel."

I needed to know what kind of shit this woman was peddling. Specifically, so I could use it against her. To get her talking about what she might know of John Adrian.

The kid did as he was told, but all that I saw inside was a driver's license.

I glanced at the date of birth. Which showed him to be twenty-one as of last month. "Let me see your real I.D."

He took it out of his wallet, and I saw how good the fake was. It had a professional laminate like a real driver's license. That hard coat and thickness. A holograph of the state seal of Georgia in the far background, with a ripe peach in front of it, a miniature image of the kid's face across the fruit.

We'd just had a new license design come into play in the last year, making the I.D. up to date. Even future-forward.

"Have you been arrested before, Mr. Meyers?" I asked, reading his name off both licenses.

"No," he said, his voice scratchy. "My parents are gonna kill me."

"Well, let's see what we can do then," I said. "You wanna tell me about the woman back there?"

"My friend Leo gave me her email address. Her name is Maria. You send her a picture, and she makes a perfect . . ." He stopped then, and I nodded.

"If I were to let you go . . ." I said.

"That would be awesome," the kid answered.

"You don't want to have this on you, though." I held up the fake I.D. "I mean, it's illegal."

"Keep it."

I hesitated, mostly to scare him.

"Okay, I'm gonna hold on to this, Dave," I said, lifting up the I.D. "Problem is—you tell anyone I went easy on you, I gotta come find you. Y'understand?"

The kid nodded, and I told him he was free to go.

Then I turned and drove back to the woman's address.

When I parked again, I saw Maria Evans locking up her front door and moving over to an attached garage off to the east side of her place. She started sweeping the dust out of the room. Then left and went back into her house, leaving the small door to the garage ajar.

I left my truck and crossed the street.

Entering the apartment complex from the next building over, I moved in between the two structures. Each building looked to contain three apartments, one on the ground floor and two smaller ones on the second level. All around the white stucco edges were blackberry lilies, planted in small boxes. Marvin had these in his yard, and I remember him keeping Jonas away from them. The flowers were pink with spirals of red in the leaves, and they were poisonous.

I came from behind apartment number eight and threaded my way back toward the open garage door.

Inside, a small graphics studio was set up. A Mac hooked to a pile of hard drives. A large industrial Epson. And a laminator, about twenty inches wide.

Along the far wall, blown up poster-size, were images of licenses from Georgia and Alabama.

On the table were three envelopes. Each with a driver's license in it bearing a birth year of 1998, making each kid magically twenty-one years old this year.

I took a couple pictures of the place and of each I.D. before stepping out and moving around to the front door. Knocking on it.

The same woman opened the front. She'd ditched the robe for cutoffs and a yellow Georgia Tech tee.

"Can I help you?" she said.

"Are you Maria Evans?"

"Yeah."

I flashed her some tin and introduced myself. Told her I was following up on a previous tenant.

"What's the tenant's name?" she asked.

"John Adrian," I said. "You two both had the same address here. Number one."

"Yeah." She nodded. "Adrian managed the place before me. I lived in number three for five years. Then the owner asked me to take over when Adrian left."

Fidelity, Remy would say. So far this checked out with what I already knew was true.

"What's the owner's name?" I asked.

"What's this about?" she asked back.

I almost smiled. Innocent people, when asked a question by a cop, rarely responded with another question. But the guilty . . .

I turned my head in the direction of the garage. Its door was still open, her illegal I.D.-making lab fifty feet away. She didn't want me looking over there, and her mouth started moving.

"It's a management company," she said. "FJF Investments."

"And who is John Adrian to you?" I asked. "Did you live together?"

"No." She smiled. "You got this all wrong. Adrian was the guy who first rented to me when I was in number three. He managed the place until I took over."

"So you two weren't a couple?"

"I'm fifty-six, Detective." She laughed. "Adrian must've been twenty-nine back then. Thirty tops."

Back then, she said.

"So he lived in number one *before* you?" I asked. "He managed the apartments?"

"If you call it that," she said. "The place was a mess. No one could even live in number one back then."

I waited for her to explain.

"There was this whole mold abatement thing going on in number one and number eight. Which are here—and the unit behind me. You couldn't live in this building at all," she said. "So when I knew him, Adrian lived in the basement below number four." She pointed at the structure next door to us.

"What did you think of Adrian?"

"He was a scuzzball. Drank too much. Had a bunch of degenerate Mexican friends."

I stared at her.

"Hey, I'm Mexican," she said. "I can say that."

"You know where Adrian lives now?" I asked.

"Nope."

"Forwarding address?"

"He's been gone almost two years, Detective."

The sound of an airplane was in the sky. Far away, but in our silence, we could hear it.

"Still, I'd like to look around," I said, knowing this was a trigger for her to talk more.

"Adrian would come home drunk," she explained. "Gamble with friends from the liquor store he worked at. Make noise. If you complained about it, you'd never get shit fixed in your apartment. I changed that culture."

"With the ownership?"

"Yeah," she said.

"Is that Lauten Hartley?" I asked.

She cocked her head then. "Do you want to come inside? I can get the management company on the phone."

"When's the last time you saw Adrian?"

"The day he moved out," she said. "He didn't tell me shit about how to run this place, and I was pinging him with all sorts of questions. He left me with this leaking septic thing to handle."

I was still standing out front. "He lived in that building?" I pointed to my right.

"Yeah," she said. "But there's nothing to see anymore. There was a septic tank issue. The management company literally filled in the basement, which was part of his apartment. To keep the smell down."

"With what?"

"Dirt," she said. "Like I told you, I was transitioning to manager then. So I was just a resident during half this time, but we were all happy about it."

"Happy about what?" I asked.

"They house-bolted the place. One of those old brick septic tanks got punctured or something while they were under that building."

"I'm not following you."

"There was a bad smell," she said. "Where Adrian lived. Under the house. It got filled in with dirt."

"A smell like what?" I said. "Feces? Manure?"

"More like rotten eggs," she said. "There were flies. That's what I remember most."

"Show me."

43

Maria grabbed a set of keys, and we moved across the small apartment complex. As she walked, she pulled her cell phone from her back pocket.

"I'm gonna need to call the management company if I unlock this for you, Detective," she said. "I've seen TV and all. Warrants and such. I think you need a warrant to be looking around here."

"Traditionally that *is* what I'd need," I said. "Are they pretty involved? The management company?"

"Intimately," she said.

"Mr. Hartley himself?"

"He shows twice a year maybe."

"So he'd object then?" I said. "To having a manager run—say—an illegal graphic design business in the garage? Making fake I.D.'s for underage kids?"

Maria stopped cold in her tracks, a foot from the door. She cocked her head and her grayish-brown hair clumped to one side.

"What do you want?" she said.

"Your full cooperation."

She stared at me, at first expressionless. Then a half smile. "Well, lucky for us, I'm in the cooperation business."

Maria unlocked a side door that led under the building next to hers, and I pointed for her to go in first. She reached a hand inside and flicked on a light.

"Leave your cell phone by the door," I said, and she did.

The place was a box, maybe twenty by fifteen. It was dry-walled and painted in a butter-yellow color and had wood laminate floors. To my right was an open door with a bathroom and a standing shower. A toilet bowl and a small pedestal sink.

I glanced around the room. A couch was turned up on its side, a space heater beside it. The air smelled stale but clean.

"Adrian lived down here?" I asked.

She nodded. "He had it done up nice, but it was temporary, while the mold got fixed."

"I thought you said it was all dirt?"

"Next room over," Maria said, pointing at a single thirty-by-eighty-inch door on the far side of the room. "This structure is built on a hill," she said. "So that's the real basement. This is the basement apartment."

"Open it."

The door swung toward us, and I pointed my flashlight inside. It was another box of a room, but this one had a concrete floor, and the walls only went up about halfway. Above that, you could see the crawl space under the building. Could stare in at the wooden studs that protruded from the foundation and held up the structure above us.

"Y'ever come down here?" I asked.

"Not much of a reason to," she said. "But my old place was . . . over there." She pointed. "Above, I mean. If we could keep walking."

But we couldn't keep walking, at least not without ducking our heads, because dirt covered half of the concrete floor and the room itself. At first, on the side by the door, the dirt was an inch high. But as you walked across the giant substructure, the dirt got thicker and you had to scrunch down, so as not to hit your head on the bottom of the building above. Eventually the dirt reached all the way up to the studs.

"Over there was where the smell was." She pointed at an area piled with three or four feet of dirt.

"So what happened to Adrian when they closed this up?"

"He left."

"Just like that?"

"He didn't seem to care." She shrugged. "Maybe the owner paid him some money. He was packed already."

I pointed back at the main room. "So John Adrian lived out there—in the finished room?"

"For a few months, yeah."

"And this dirt area was what?" I asked. "Before it got filled in."

"Kinda like storage, back then, if you owned or ran the place. Machinery. Plumbing and electrical supplies. I mean, there wasn't a big-ass pile of dirt here back then."

"Where do you store those things now?"

"They put one of those Tuff Sheds in when I took over," she said. "Out by the alley."

I crouched, close to the ground. There was no smell, except if you counted the musty stink of dirt. "Bring me a couple shovels."

"Of course."

I pointed to her cell on the ledge outside. "Don't go calling anyone."

She came back about two minutes later, a pair of garden shovels in hand. The kind with a strong neck that you can put your foot into.

"Should we be digging?" she said. "Like—is it safe?"

"Well, if it's an old septic tank that got filled in with sludge or soft dirt, there's no issue," I said.

I made the shape of a box with my hands. "I don't know what you were told, but a lot of the really old septic tanks are made of brick. Someone hits 'em doing construction and it opens up a hole. The bricks fall in. If that's what happened and they put dirt or sludge down there, that would seep up any smell pretty quick. But the reality is— most of these tanks are so old that everything in 'em already seeped down into the ground or the soakaway decades ago. The real problem is they're dangerous because they're empty holes under the ground."

I took one of the tools and started digging then, right where she'd pointed. I went for five minutes, moving in a grid pattern and digging holes about three feet down each time. The ground wasn't like the hard dirt that filled my backyard, but instead loose material. Soft and easily lifted.

"This would go faster with two people," I said.

She grabbed the other shovel and we both dug, working in silence. After twenty minutes, the dust was so thick in the air that I could hardly see.

It also became clear that there was no concrete subfloor in one area, for a rectangle of about eight feet by ten feet.

Tink.

Maria stopped moving. She stared down at the noise. Which came from her shovel, buried about three feet into the ground.

"Back up," I said. I took a pair of gloves from my back pocket and got down on my knees, using my hands to push away the dirt that was near the head of her shovel. Then I pulled the tool from the ground and reached in.

My hands grabbed at something hard and oblong, with a bulbous end. I didn't pull the object out—just followed it—making rough measurements that told me it was about two feet long.

"What is it?" she said.

My hands sifted more dirt, and I felt a curvature. Kept moving south with my hands buried two feet deep until I came to what I was looking for.

And I pulled a human skull from the dirt.

"Oh shit," she said.

I sat back with my butt against the backs of my shoes. The smell. The flies. The ex-manager who didn't mind moving out. There was never any septic tank issue down here.

Things lined up in my head. My next move.

"You're gonna call the coroner's office," I said. "I'm gonna give you a direct line to the head dog. So you can talk straight to her."

"I assume I was down here alone?" the manager speculated. "Needed some dirt for a . . . planter or something."

"That's a good story."

"That you were never here?"

"Right," I said.

"And the management company?" she asked.

"Let the police call them," I said. "But even the call to the coroner to get things going. Wait five hours after I leave before you make it."

"Okay," she said.

"And, Maria," I said. "I'm gonna hold on to that I.D. I took from the kid. But let me give you some advice on your business."

She stared at me.

"You got a big trunk in your car?" I asked.

"Yeah."

"Big enough for that Mac and a couple hard drives? 'Cause cops might start looking around after they find a body."

"Done," she said.

I held up the skull. Pointed at a hole in it that I could tell was made by a .45. "When you talk to the coroner," I said, "make sure you tell her that the skull you found—it's got a bullet hole through it."

Maria swallowed.

We went upstairs then, and I washed up in her sink.

Maria's place was cute. Her living room was decorated with pictures of northern Georgia that I guessed she took herself. Amicalola Falls from the footbridge. The head of the Appalachian Trail near Ellijay. And downtown Dahlonega around Christmas.

I was exhausted from sleeping in my truck and wanted to get home. Grab a couple hours of rest before the banquet honoring my role in ending the school shooting.

Maria grabbed a bottle of rum and took a shot. "Is that John Adrian's body down there?" she asked.

"I don't think so," I said.

"So it's someone he killed?"

"More likely," I said. "Do you remember exactly when they filled that in?" I pointed at the building.

"December of that year," she said, referring to two years ago. "A couple days before Christmas. Maybe the twenty-first or twenty-second."

Which jibed perfectly with the robbery at the Golden Oaks on December 12. Christian Pelo probably met them out here around the eighteenth. By the twenty-first, the smell might've made the place pretty ripe if Pelo hadn't been buried right.

"Did Lauten Hartley show up for that?" I asked. "When they filled in the dirt?"

"Yeah," she said. "He was here."

"With Adrian?"

"No, Adrian had left town a couple days before that. Some family thing. I remember I was officially manager, even though I didn't know shit yet and wasn't taking over 'til January."

"So just Hartley by himself?" I asked.

She shook her head. "No, he came with this other guy. A guy he comes with still once in a while. He's the one who wheel-barrowed a lot of the dirt down there."

"Muscle?" I asked, but she stared. Unclear as to what I was saying.

"A bodyguard," I clarified.

"No," she said. "I mean, he's muscular, sure. Blond guy. Younger than Hartley. They work together. You can tell they're familiar."

"This guy got a name?" I asked.

Maria shrugged. "He doesn't talk much, but—I think Hartley calls him Iron or something. They come here together."

"Iron?"

"It's not that," she said. "But I can't remember what it is. It's a nick-name, not a real name."

I dried my hands and had her recite what she had to say and do.

"You're gonna do great," I said. "Might even get an award."

I turned to head out then.

"What's your name again?" she asked.

"Does it matter?" I said.

"No, I guess not."

I moved down the steps and out to my truck.

44

Six hours later I pulled my Silverado into valet and handed my keys to a college kid parking cars for the event.

All around me were cops in their formal blues, holding the hands of wives and girlfriends in expensive evening gowns. I wore my blues too, and you could tell a citizen from an officer at a hundred feet.

I tipped the kid who took my car keys and moved into the lobby. On a table outside the large ballroom were two pieces of foam core—each with a photograph on them. The one on the left was of yours truly, a photo from five years ago when I was younger and more photogenic. The other was of a kid from the fire department who'd saved two lives when a bus crashed off 902.

In my head I recounted the number of students in the art room at Falls Magnet. Plus Kelly Borland. I had the firefighter beat by two live citizens. Not that anyone was counting or being competitive. Plus, a fireman? At a police benefit? I hated political correctness.

A photographer caught me with a blast of white, and I moved inside the room.

The ballroom was set up with about thirty circular tables, each with eight or ten chairs around them. Flower centerpieces sat in the middle of the tables like at a wedding, and music was being played by the Bagpipers of Falls West. Which sounded more like noise than music to me.

Around the perimeter of the room were three bars, crowded with people. On a raised stage at the front, a podium was draped in the seal of the city of Mason Falls.

A pair of eyes caught mine. Or maybe it was the curvy and petite body attached to them. Kelly Borland.

"I wondered if you were going to show," she said, walking closer.

Kelly was in a purple dress. Simple and beautiful.

"You didn't see the picture outside the room?" I smiled, leaning in and giving her a kiss on the cheek. "I'm kind of a big deal tonight."

"Yet last night you dodged me," she said. "Working hard on a case. Not the school shooting again, I hope?"

"A different matter," I said.

She glanced over my shoulder, and I followed her eyes.

"And here's another distinguished gentleman I recognize," Kelly said.

Merle Berry leaned in and gave Kelly a hug. He and Remy had stayed on-site the day of the shooting and interviewed her. Merle was her lead contact.

"You both look so handsome in your formal uniforms."

"Thank you," Merle said, beaming.

From across the room, I saw Lauten Hartley, by the bar.

"How are you doing?" Merle asked Kelly.

"Much better than the last time we talked, Detective," she said.

I excused myself and let them chat, moving slowly across the room as a dozen bagpipers filed off the stage with their instruments and threaded through the crowd.

Straining to get past them, I found myself ten feet from Lauten Hartley, who turned, a drink in hand.

He smiled, and out of the corner of my eye I saw Chief Senza, watching us.

"Detective Marsh," Hartley said. He wore a dark blue suit and a red tie. Politician power colors. "If I had known you were coming over, I would've grabbed you a drink from the bar."

"Oh, I gave up the stuff," I said. "I just wanted to take a moment to see if you're fitting in okay. Continue to bury the hatchet. Bygones be bygones and all."

Hartley's head cocked about ten degrees. "Well, I don't believe you for a second, Detective." He paused. "About the drinking, I mean. I swore I've seen you in a liquor store recently. Maybe in the numbered streets?"

Inside, my heart stopped for a beat, but I kept calm on the surface. People crowded close to us, and Hartley moved away from the bar and closer to me.

"I'm sure you're wrong," I said.

Senza walked up then, probably coming to make sure I wasn't creating conflict.

"Wrong about what?" he asked.

"Crime rates being up," I said. "Mr. Hartley has a passion about crime in the numbered streets. But not just that. He's got tentacles out into other areas of the community. Like north of town. He's a better asset for our department than I originally thought."

"I agree a hundred percent," Senza said. "And crime is down in the numbereds, Mr. Hartley. Last four months straight."

But Hartley was stuck on my comment about "north of town." I could see the curiosity on his face.

"Well, I've got to mingle," I said, patting the two men on the shoulders.

As I walked off, my heart pounded, and I wondered if Hartley had me on camera breaking into the Golden Oaks. His comment about the liquor store. I was okay falling on the sword, but I didn't want it to stick into Remy.

And no sooner had I thought her name than I saw my partner. Being wheeled out to the balcony by Darren Gattling, who spoke to her for a second and then left.

I moved across the room, and out into the night. Onto a large terrace that overlooked 5th Street. There were two buildings from the 1930s that were getting a facelift, and metal scaffolding rose four stories into the air beside us.

"I thought doctor's orders were to stay at home," I said. "Watch Netflix."

"And waste this dress?" Remy motioned. She was wearing a black-and-white striped number that cut off at the thigh. In a wheelchair it looked even shorter. "You know how many chances I'm gonna get to come to one of these things and not have to wear my blues?"

I gave her a hug. As I did, I whispered in her ear. "Hartley knows we were inside that liquor store."

"So what?" Remy said.

I stood up and stared at my partner. She was becoming more fearless by the minute.

"What's he gonna do, P.T.? Report us? You know how guilty he'd look? He demo'd the damn building the next day."

This was a good point.

"Tell me what you've found," she said. "I'm jonesing to hear about the case."

"Well, I went looking for Christian Pelo, that clerk who got robbed," I said. "I got lucky."

"You found him?"

"In a manner of speaking," I said. "I found his tibia. And then his skull."

"Holy shit," she said.

A bell dinged, and an announcement was made. For everyone to take their seats for the banquet. I gave Remy more of the details. Of digging under the apartment complex.

"The manager should've called it in a half hour ago, Rem. Direct to Sarah. But I haven't told you the best part."

"Spill it," Remy said.

"Hartley owns that property," I said. "So I think he might be conflicted running the police board."

Remy smiled. "You mean with us investigating how an employee of one of his businesses wound up shot and buried under another one of his businesses?"

"'Xactly," I said. Our new shorthand. Wolf style.

"So what's your next move?" she asked.

"I dunno," I said. "I was thinking about a leak."

Remy motioned with her head at someone behind us.

I turned, just in time to see Deb Newberry, from the local Fox affiliate. She was dressed in black slacks and her go-to Clemson-orange blazer. Below it was a blouse with a plunging neckline.

"The stars are out tonight," Deb said. "But they're all hiding on the balcony."

"Deb," I said tentatively. "How are ya?"

"If I was any better, I'd be twins."

"Two of you would be a lot to handle," Remy said.

Deb ignored the jab and moved in. I smelled coffee on her breath.

"I was just talking to Chief Senza about an exposé on you two," she said. "You know—different ways of thinking. Old school versus new school."

I tried not to roll my eyes. We'd been burned by Deb so many times that it was tough to believe a thing she said.

"You mean Black versus white?" Remy asked.

"Maybe it's old versus young," I said to Remy, playing like I had a cane.

Deb gave us a look. "This would be a serious piece."

Remy glanced at me, a glint in her eyes. "You want a lead on a story, Deb?" she said. "I'm off of work, but P.T.'s got a big one."

Deb turned her focus on me. "And you're just gonna hand it to me, Marsh?"

"I could give it to Raymond Kirios at the *Register.*"

"He *is* a good writer," Remy pointed out.

"Nobody reads anymore," Deb said.

I looked to Remy, who shrugged. "A body was dug up," my partner said.

"A skeleton of a murder victim," I added. "I could give you the address, but you can't say where you got it from."

Deb looked unenthusiastic. "Is it in the numbered streets?" she said with a whine. "Some drug nobody? 'Cause I think I hit my annual quota on bodies in that zip code back in May."

I looked to Remy. "She's not the right person for it."

Deb looked insulted. "All right," she said. "Hand it over."

"I'm not sure you're tough enough," I said.

"Moi?" Deb looked shocked.

"This one could get political," Remy said. "I mean—let's say the person you have to investigate is in this room. A bigwig. Tight with the police. You sure you got the salt for that, Deb?"

"And the pepper, Detective Morgan," she said confidently.

I took a pen out and asked for her hand. Wrote the address on Penescue on the crook above her thumb.

"Two years ago," I said. "That's when the story starts. Find out who lived in number one. But the real story is who owns the building."

"Who owns it?"

"You gotta work a little here," I said.

"The question is," Remy jumped in, "could the owner have known there's a body under his building? Is he connected to the man who died? And, Deb," Remy said. "Word is that the skull's got a bullet hole through it."

Deb's eyes were full moons, and she stared at the address written above the crook of her thumb.

"This is in North Heights," she said. "Not the numbered streets."

"You probably got an hour or two lead on the others." I pointed around. "If you're quick, you could research the story and be back here for an interview with the right person by dessert."

Deb turned and scampered off.

Gattling came back then and wheeled Remy into the ballroom. Found us a table off to one side with a few empty chairs, which I pushed out of the way for my partner.

The lights came down then, and the place went quiet. The mayor walked up onto the stage and took a sip of water.

"Tonight is one of my favorite nights," Mayor Stems said, standing at the podium in a black tux. "Because I get to honor the real heroes who live and work in our community every day."

I looked to Remy, knowing it would be a long night. She held up her wineglass, toasting my water. "You picked the wrong year to quit drinking, partner."

We sat there, Remy and me and Gattling, enjoying a meal without having to say a word. The chief awarded Rookie of the Year to a kid who grew up in the numbered streets but made it out without falling to gangs or drugs. Then there was the award for the fireman. Good guy, it turned out. You could tell from his speech.

Then a series of rich men went up onto the stage and urged other rich men to take out their checkbooks. Literally. Like take them out, write checks to charity, and pass them to your nearest waiter. Which they actually did.

Finally, it came time for me to go up and receive what they were calling the First Annual Community Hero Award. I took the plaque and looked out at the crowd, a big spotlight on me.

"My partner, Detective Morgan, is in the audience." I held my hand to the light so I could find her. "She's temporarily in a wheelchair from taking down someone as bad as the guy I took out. In the same week too." I looked around. The room was silent. Waiting on me. "I don't do big speeches; so, I'm glad no kids were hurt at Falls Magnet. And I'm sorry I had to take a man's life to make the school safe that day." I held up the plaque. "Thanks for the recognition."

The cops in the audience started clapping first, and then the whole place got to their feet. I didn't think the speech was much, but maybe that was the point.

I hung out a little after, and Kelly Borland strolled over. She'd been sitting at the chief's table as his guest.

"Keeping it simple up there, huh?"

"Short and sweet," I said.

While we were talking, a number of cops came by. Each of them slapping me on the shoulder and checking out Kelly.

Men. Men that were cops. Sometimes we were more predictable than criminals.

From across the room, I saw Deb Newberry reenter the ballroom in that bright orange jacket. Her eyes scanned the place, stopping on Lauten Hartley. She met him halfway across the room.

Hartley smiled at her, and Deb turned on the charm. I was guessing she was asking him what he thought of the event. Or of his new position on the police board.

This was classic Deb. To throw a setup punch first. A compliment.

Then his face fell after a follow-up question. A question that must've been about a body found. About his property. Hartley glanced around. *Was he looking for me?*

Darren wheeled Remy over. "You taking responsibility for this one?" he said, motioning at Remy.

I looked to my partner, and Darren explained that he was headed to work. The night shift now. His first day back since the shootout at Tandy's.

"Absolutely," I said. "Ms. Borland." I turned to Kelly. "I've got to take my partner home."

"Of course," Kelly said.

"You see it?" Remy asked about Hartley, once we were a few feet away.

I nodded. "I forgot to tell you. I called Christian Pelo's mom on the way here. Told her to show up at the station with something with Christian's DNA on it. A hairbrush. A toothbrush. I told her to ask for Sarah Raines. Then demand to wait until Chief Senza arrived."

Sarah, being the local M.E., would do a bang-up job on that skeleton. And she'd do it without worrying about who Hartley was.

"And people say you don't know politics." Remy snickered.

As I wheeled my partner out of the ballroom, a man stood by the door, his eyes on Deb Newberry. He was a reporter for the *Mason Falls Register*. A guy named Raymond Kirios, the writer we threatened to give the story to.

"Don't you two know not to feed wild animals?" he said.

Remy and I blinked.

"You gave something to Deb," Kirios said.

"No idea what you're talking about, Kirios," Remy said.

"Print journalism, Marsh and Morgan. It's still alive and available for a good story. Usually, it's the best way to tell it."

I wanted to remind the reporter how Abe had asked Kirios's editor for information on Jed Harrington the day of the shooting. How we'd been directed instead to read the paper the next day. But I kept my mouth shut for a change.

The reporter followed us out the door.

"Whatever it is, we got no comment," Remy said to him.

But Kirios held out a business card. "I'm actually here to give you two something," he said. "I owed a favor to a Fed named Quarles," Kirios said. "Apparently, he owed a favor to you. So via three-way, we're all clean."

I stared at what was written on the back of Kirios's business card.

It read:

> *Alistair Zalinsky is in our custody.*
> *—Quarles*

"Who the hell is Alistair Zalinsky?"

The reporter nodded, as if expecting the question.

"Quarles said to tell you he found a single print on the inside of the trigger assembly, left over from some exploded rifle," Kirios said. "Does that make sense?"

I stared at Kirios.

"He said to let you two know," the reporter continued. "Your cop's gonna get some measure of justice for what happened to his son."

Zalinsky was the old assassin.

The one who'd shot the two drug couriers in the Chevy Caprice and killed Carilla out in the forest. More important, who'd killed Officer Timothy O'Neal's son, Jacob, inside of Tandy's. The Feds had him. Which meant they got him on other charges and were taking first crack at the guy.

I thought about what the waitress at the Cracker Barrel had told us about the man she called "Grandpa."

When the old guy went inside the restroom to inspect the replacement gun parts, he must've inadvertently left a print on an unpainted piece of the 3D-printed M24.

"Thanks, Kirios," I said. "I appreciate the message."

45

By ten p.m., I had dropped Remy off and was back at my house. I walked the dogs down to the pond and felt tired. The full moon had faded in the last week, and the last quarter moon would be in the sky tomorrow.

I thought about Christian Pelo's mom and hoped that she'd followed my instructions. That things were under way that would complicate Hartley's connection to the police department. That would make it difficult for him to be on the board while owning a property where the skeleton of a cold case was found.

As I got back home, I saw Kelly Borland's Honda CR-V, parked outside of my house.

Kelly was sitting on the steps.

I was still in my blues, but she'd dressed down.

I came up with the dogs. Mostly with Beau, since he was leashed. Purvis was lagging behind us.

"Hey," she said. Then she stopped. Stared at Beau and then back at me.

"Is everything all right?" I asked.

"Where's Purvis?"

I turned, revealing my bulldog trailing behind us.

"Oh, I was worried something happened to him," she said. "I know you said he was eight."

I nodded. Bulldogs typically didn't live that long, and people who know the breed are aware of this.

"Yeah," I said. "But he's a survivor."

Beau had been skittish around Marvin a bit, but Kelly was a natural with animals.

"His name's Beau," I said. "I, uh—adopted him from County. He was gonna get euthanized."

Kelly let him smell her hand and then rubbed him as I opened the front door. "Hello, Beau-Beau," she said.

She followed me in, and I wondered if this was what I thought it was. What Remy would call a "booty call."

Kelly wore black leggings and a scoop-neck tee. She held a Kroger grocery bag in her hand, which she put onto the counter.

She pulled out a Dr Pepper and a bag of ice.

"I know you don't drink," she said. "So instead of dropping by with a bottle of wine . . ."

"Let's break it open," I said.

She uncapped it and poured two of them. We went into the living room, where I took a seat in the La-Z-Boy and she sat on the couch, diagonally across from me.

Kelly had seemed tense at the banquet, and more so now.

"Are you all right?" I asked.

"I couldn't tell if you were avoiding me at the dinner," she said.

"It's not that," I said. "With all the press there, I didn't want a big story made out of it. You being where you were, on one side of the gun. And me on the other. And someone guessing we might be seeing each other now."

Beau came over and sat near Kelly.

"So what does that mean about us?" she asked. "I'm always gonna be the girl on this side of the gun. I can't change that."

I hesitated. She was right. And it wasn't her fault that she was an art teacher, caught in the cross fire at a school shooting.

"He likes you," I said. Motioning at the dog. "So do I, I mean." I hesitated. "I got some stuff I'm figuring out right now. A case."

"I figured you were off of work. After what happened in Atlanta."

I thought about the argument Remy and I had down inside the Golden Oaks. About what was holding me back. And if I couldn't allow myself to care about a woman again.

"This isn't for work," I said, wanting to be honest with Kelly. "This case is personal," I said. "It involves what happened to my wife. There's been a break."

"Oh wow," she said. "That's good, right?"

"Yeah," I said. "It's just—until I solve it . . ." I looked at her and then flicked my eyes downward.

"It's hard for you to concentrate on us," she said.

I nodded, and we went quiet then. After a moment, I noticed she was studying me.

"Are you sleeping, Paul?" she asked, using my first name.

"No," I said. "No, I'm not."

"Then sit back." She motioned at the La-Z-Boy.

She moved behind me then and started rubbing the areas right by my temples. Then she moved her fingers along my skull, and by the fleshy areas above my neck.

"Holy moly," I said.

"My magic massage," she said. "If I keep going, you're gonna zonk for ten hours."

"Ten hours is too much," I said.

A few minutes later, she kissed me on the cheek, and I heard her say "goodbye."

46

By ten a.m., I had parked and was heading across the street from the overflow lot toward the precinct.

I was still officially off of work, and had slept most of the night in the armchair where Kelly had left me. But it was Saturday, so it was a perfect time to sneak in and do a little personal research.

Ahead of me, I saw Hope Duffy, from intake, heading out from the nightshift. Ten a.m. was late for her to be getting off, and she lifted her head when she saw me. Adjusted her course in my direction.

"Hey," I said.

"I was hoping I'd see you."

I slowed as she approached. Hope's hair had lost its usual bounce, and her eyes looked bloodshot. Something had dilled her pickle.

"Want to guess where I just spent the last two hours, Marsh?" she asked.

I shrugged. There are things you don't raise your hand for in life. Just in case you're right.

"With my C.O. and a detective from vice," she said. "You wanna guess why?"

I stared at Hope.

"Apparently," she said, "I made a computer inquiry about a man named John Adrian."

"Oh shit," I said.

I'd made that inquiry on Hope's account.

Had Hartley tracked it down and caused trouble?

"What did you say?"

"Well, I was very careful in my phrasing." She raised her eyebrows. "The kinda language I can go back on later, you know?"

"Yeah," I said. But I didn't know what she meant.

Go back on later?

"Like whenever you discover whatever it is that you're looking for," Hope said. "Get another one of those awards . . ."

I stared at her.

"And then you can tell my C.O. how we were working *together* on the case," Hope said, "the whole time."

"Together?" I squinted.

"Well, you wouldn't want anyone pulling records from the lobby camera, would you? Seeing you log in at my terminal."

"Just a thing partners like us do," I said, changing my tune.

"Good," Hope answered. "Then you should know that John Adrian's not our problem anymore. He's dead, Marsh."

"What the hell?"

"Apparently vice has been trying to turn him as a C.I. for some case up in Shonus," she said. "But three a.m. this morning, patrol found their potential confidential informant dead at some flophouse. Ten points of black tar in his arm. The needle still hanging there."

Ten points was a full gram. And a gram of heroin was enough to kill two men, especially if it was cut with fentanyl, which we'd been seeing a lot of in Mason Falls these days.

But more than that, my brain was swelling because of the timing.

Last night Hartley had been cornered by Deb Newberry from Fox 11 about that property where Christian Pelo was found.

Hope turned and moved past me to this little yellow Fiat she drives.

"Good luck, partner," she said. "Do us proud."

I stood there, feeling nervous and numb.

If Hartley had the kind of nerve to go after my wife, it wouldn't take much more to kill someone like Adrian on his own crew. Poison him before he could be flipped by a cop.

Had I gotten arrogant? Moved too fast at Hartley last night?

47

Instead of going into the station house, I got back in my truck and drove to Remy's place.

She buzzed me up, and I took the elevator to three. When I got there, she had left the door ajar and was on the couch in her living room, her foot in a boot.

"You're not gonna believe this," I said. "Last night we corner Hartley, right? Connect him to Adrian. Thinking we'll smoke out Adrian and he'll give us dirt on Hartley?"

"Yeah."

"Adrian's dead, Rem."

"What?" she said.

"Overdose," I told her.

"Hartley," she said. "The fucker got to him."

I stood up and started pacing, not sure if I'd made the wrong move last night talking to Hartley at the police function.

"I'm not sure what our next play is," I said. "Adrian was our link back to 2017. Back to the liquor store."

"Then we find another link."

"Yeah." I nodded, moving in circles like a shark around Remy's dining table. "Except I don't have any other leads, Rem."

"P.T.," Remy said. "Hartley's like this ghost architect, you know? Moving behind the scenes. The problem is—he's seeing the whole chessboard, and we're not."

"Sure," I said, grabbing a chair from her dining table. "You got an idea on how we see more?"

"I've been thinking about what you mentioned—how Hartley interjected himself in the Meadows lawsuit with the department back in May. Why'd he do that?"

"To take me out," I said.

"Yeah, but why *then*?" Remy asked.

"We don't know."

"Maybe we do," she said. "And we just haven't tied it all together."

"What are you thinking?" I asked.

"In May, Marvin and his P.I. were stumbling around in Burna," Remy said. "That's what you told me, right?"

"Yeah."

"They met that lady who got her car stolen."

"Grazia Lauroyan," I said. "Her car is the Dodge Aries that ended up killing Lena and Jonas."

"So Marvin's P.I. tracked that car back to where Lauroyan worked."

"Check," I said.

"Then what?" Remy asked.

"The P.I. probably talked to the neighbors. He went next door to Lauroyan's upholstery shop and ran straight into Kian Tarticoft, our hitman, whose taxidermy business was next to her shop. The P.I. asked her about the car. And inadvertently, he spooked him. Tarticoft up and cleared out."

"Which is not good if you're Hartley," Remy said. "'Cause you think, here's this assassin you hired to kill a cop's family. And now the cop's father-in-law and his P.I. are getting close to that assassin. And that kinda crap's gonna lead back to you."

"Shit, Rem." I ran my hands through my hair, realizing something about the timing.

"The day Tarticoft cleared out his machine shop," I said. "It's the day before Johnson Hartley joined the suit against the department. Agreed to work pro bono."

Remy flicked her eyebrows at me. "So now we're seeing the whole chessboard like him. Tarticoft didn't just disappear from *your* radar. He disappeared from Hartley's radar. And Hartley had to do something about it. He had too much to risk if Tarticoft talked."

I thought about this. About my father-in-law, Marvin, being on a trail that could lead from Tarticoft, the assassin, right to Hartley. The next day Hartley joined in on the lawsuit to get me fired.

"Yeah," I said. "That tracks."

"So Hartley tries to marginalize you," Remy said. "To get you fired by suing the department. But instead, they don't fire you. And I kill Tarticoft."

"Hartley's loose end is tied up," I said. "And I'm suspended."

"His problems are over," Remy said. "Except you don't go away after May. You got demoted, but you're still sniffing out Hartley. Camped outside his house. Following him. So he gets a new idea. Maneuvers into a place to run the police board. Figures P. T. Marsh'll do something stupid sooner or later. And then he'll have you out on official grounds."

"Hartley's making moves to counter moves we don't even know that we're making."

"We know we're making them," Remy clarified. "Just not against him."

"So what now?" I said. "Adrian's still dead."

"Sure," Remy said. "But Hartley can't be pulling all this shit off by himself. Especially if that powder under the liquor store was drugs. He's gotta have a crew, P.T. You got any leads on who else works with him?"

I pulled a pile of paperwork from my satchel. The stuff I'd printed at the precinct the other night when I had Hope's log-in.

Remy saw me scanning a police report. "Does Hartley have a record?"

"No," I said. "But he had some altercation with patrol back in 2004. He was young, but . . ."

I stared at a particular paper, making a connection.

"There was a passenger in the car with Hartley," I said. "During this beef he got into."

I paged through the old police report. "Hartley is twenty-eight back then. The other guy in the car is eighteen."

"Family?" she asked.

"Different last names."

"A friend?" Remy asked.

"I dunno," I said. Moving to the next page of the police report.

"A special friend?" my partner continued, stretching her booted leg. "Hartley's twenty-eight and this guy's eighteen?"

"The passenger's name is Steele Vankle," I said, finding what I was looking for. "Nowadays he'd be in his thirties."

I paged back through my six-by-nine notebook. "The lady at the apartment complex where Christian Pelo's skeleton was found. She said Hartley comes by with a muscular blond guy. His right-hand guy. She said he had an odd nickname. 'Iron,' she thought."

Or Steele.

Remy sat up. "So Steele's known Hartley for fifteen years then?"

"And he was working with Hartley in 2017 when Pelo's body was buried," I said. "According to Maria, the apartment manager, Steele was the one who wheelbarrowed all the dirt into that basement to cover up Pelo's body."

"So if we're thinking John Adrian killed Christian Pelo two Christmases ago," Remy said, "Steele may have done Hartley's dirty work and killed John Adrian last night."

I flipped my chair backward and sat down, leaning over the back and thinking this over.

"It's a unique name," Remy said, her eyes on her phone and her thumbs moving fast.

Remy handed her cell to me. On it was Steele Vankle's Instagram page.

I flicked through the images. He was midthirties like we thought. White and handsome, with blue eyes and blondish-red hair that fell to his shoulders.

Half of the pictures were of him, training at a gym. The cowbell thing. The big rope. There was also a low-quality video from 2005 of Vankle wrestling in some homemade octagon. It was in the shape of an old four-by-three TV screen. Must've been uploaded to Instagram years later.

In the last shot, Steele Vankle stood in front of a red Camaro from the '80s. I stared at the caption below the photo. *Always wanted one of these since my bro let me drive his to the prom,* it read. *Vintage and cherry red.* The post was from eighteen months ago.

I zoomed in on the license plate.

"Well, we got a plate," I said. "If we run it, we'll have an address."

"Sure," Remy said. "But then Hartley might know you're coming again. What you need is a way to find this Steele Vankle guy. But off the books. A hundred percent off the books."

"I got an idea," I said.

48

I was back at the precinct in fifteen minutes, but entered the building through the mod yard and took the elevator down to the bowels of the place. Threading my way through a series of corridors, I got to a small glassed-in office with the words "Data Collection" stenciled in white type on the window.

D.C. was a group that had begun last year with two employees, both named Joan, each of whose title was "police records specialist." Their current job was to assist patrol and detectives with data-based research. To enter warrants into the system and help with protection orders and other paperwork that kept cops sitting behind a desk instead of out on the street.

"Hello, Joans," I said, entering the office.

Both women were blond with brown streaks in their hair. One was in her early thirties and donned a conservative pantsuit and blouse, while the other was late forties with spiky hair and a lot of handmade jewelry. Remy constantly accused me of not knowing which one was Joan Snow and which was Joan Reinhardt. Until I confessed that my partner was right, Remy wasn't giving up the answer.

"There's the big hero," the older Joan said. "And gracing our little basement office."

She got up and gave me a hug, and the younger Joan followed after.

"How's our girl doing?" the younger Joan said, referring to Remy. Every woman in the building loved my partner.

"She's recovering nicely," I said. "I think she's gotta take a few months off of running, but she's in a boot as of this morning. I'll tell her you were asking."

"What do you need, hon?" the older Joan asked. "You on your own while Rem's off?"

"I am," I said, grabbing a black rolling office chair and sitting down. "I wasn't sure if you'd be here on the weekend."

"You're in luck. We back up all the servers, once a quarter on a Saturday. What can we help with?"

"Well, I got a weird question for y'all." I hesitated. "You know that unpopular license plate scanner program we had going last year?"

"You mean the original reason we have jobs?" Older Joan smiled.

Under the old chief, the city had invested in technology that installed scanners mounted to four police cruisers. The cops who drove those black and whites went about their day like normal, but while they worked, three high-def cameras mounted on their roof took photographs of every parked car they passed: the vehicle, their passengers, and the plates. The system was even smart enough to package the pictures together so you had a location on the car, its profile shot, and the license plate, all in one folder.

The original plan was that if a car's plate came across as stolen, an officer was alerted and a squad car dispatched into action. Through tickets and impounds, the program would pay for itself in three years.

"We're not still running that, are we?" I asked.

"The program got shut down," the older Joan said. "I thought you knew that, P.T."

"No, that's what I thought," I said. "I remember some privacy group found out how much personal information the system was compiling."

This included pictures of citizens, and not just the guilty. The cameras were basically documenting a day in the life of our city. Seventy-five hundred photos every day.

"But the database still exists, right?" I asked. "I mean—it was running for over a year. You must have two or three million photographs burning a hole in your server."

"Why do you ask?" Younger Joan said.

"I've got a person of interest who's proving hard to find."

"You know his name?" she asked. "We can put a BOLO out on him."

"Well," I said. "This is a unique case. I've got reasons I don't want the search to be on official channels."

For most cops, this might cause a room to go quiet. When you imply that you couldn't trust other cops with information.

But after the school shooting and the incident in Atlanta, I was above reproach.

"What time period are we talking?" Younger Joan asked.

"Well, there's an initial incident back in December of '17," I said, holding up a close-up of the Camaro with the license plate showing. "But I'll take any locations you have on this car."

Older Joan smiled, sliding her chair behind Younger Joan's station. "I think we can make an exception for an exceptional police officer."

They booted up the program then, and Younger Joan grabbed my phone and typed in the plate number from the picture.

Within a minute, seven hits came up.

These didn't represent anything Steele Vankle had done wrong. Which is why the program had been so controversial. Vankle hadn't committed any crimes related to the pictures taken. He hadn't even gotten parking tickets. In fact, he'd just parked.

"Well," the younger Joan said. "Four of the seven locations are on 31st. And all bunched pretty close together. Within four car lengths."

The older Joan slid her chair sideways over to her computer and typed the longitude and latitude into Google Maps.

Under "Street View," a picture came onto her screen. A non-descript tan building with a logo on it: Personal Best Fitness.

This was the same logo on the wall behind Vankle in the weight-lifting pictures on Instagram.

"Does that tell you time of day?" I asked.

"Yup," the younger Joan said. "Those four pictures are all Saturdays. Between three and four p.m."

So today was Vankle's go-to workout day, at least a year ago. I checked my phone for the time now, and saw it was one p.m. I might find Vankle there soon.

"What's the fifth location?" I asked.

"Fifth and sixth are an apartment or condo," she said, squinting at map view. "Eight ninety-one Burke Street."

Maybe Vankle's apartment.

"And the last one?"

Joan brought it up on-screen, and we zoomed out.

It was a rural area, and it took Joan more time to page left and right to figure out where the hell we were.

"Georgia Wild and Free," she said.

I knew the place. A gun range northeast of town, off SR-908.

I thought of the bullet hole in Christian Pelo's skull. A .45 most likely.

Would I find that the folks who ran this range knew Vankle? And that he shot a .45?

I thanked the Joans and made my way out to my truck, driving fast toward the nearest entrance to 914.

49

I pulled into a gravel parking lot and got out at Georgia Wild and Free. Beyond the lot by about fifty yards was an outdoor range. I'd shot here with a buddy about four years ago.

These types of gun ranges are almost self-serve, and are usually manned with only one employee. I walked through the bushes and came out into a clearing.

In front of me was a series of wooden benches where folks could set up on either side under a slatted cedar pergola and shoot in the shade during summer.

Off to the left was a short range for handguns, and to the right was a long range for rifles. A sign directed patrons farther west for clays.

"Can I help you?" a man asked.

He was Black and slight of build with a face the shape of an upside-down balloon. The man looked to be in his midsixties and had a full beard. He told me his name was Will Jackson.

I flashed some tin and introduced myself. The place was nearly empty. "I'm looking for a guy named Steele Vankle," I said. "I understand he shoots here."

Jackson directed me over to a table behind the wooden benches and took a load off. I handed him my cell with a picture of Vankle on it.

I heard a cease-fire interval being called, and the three shooters lowered their guns and placed them onto the tables.

Folks took their ears and eyes off, heading down-range together. In this particular place, targets were strung between horizontal wires pulled taut down-range. Beyond them a sixty-foot-tall dirt embankment was located maybe a hundred feet past the target and on each side.

"I never forget a face," Jackson said. "So yeah, I seen him. Comes here a lot actually. Shoots a Ruger Precision."

"A rifle," I said. "You remember the last time you saw him?"

"A week ago or thereabouts."

I took back my phone. A horsefly circled us like a plane running low on fuel, its buzzing stopping only as it landed on Jackson's arm for a moment before it took off again.

"He come alone?"

"No, he usually comes with a buddy."

I found Hartley's picture on my phone and held it up. "Him?"

"Nope," Jackson said. "From their body language, the other guy works for him."

I flicked through my phone again until I found a photo of John Adrian.

"That's the fella," Jackson said.

"And what's he shoot?" I asked about John Adrian.

"A Colt .45."

I sat up a little taller.

The two-year-old case was coming together. A .45 was the weapon that Christian Pelo was most likely shot with. Which made Adrian a good suspect for the murder like I thought.

I took out my card. "I need to speak with Mr. Vankle," I said. "And I'd prefer not to spook him. Think you can give me a shout next time you see him?"

"Or the other guy?"

"The other guy is dead," I said.

"Okay then." The old-timer nodded. "I understand the urgency."

I got up then and thanked him. I knew I had to hustle back to get to the gym by three p.m.

"Incidentally, where do you shoot?" Jackson asked.

In the distance, a volley of shots rang out. The range was clear, and folks were shooting again.

"The Georgia Safe, mostly," I said.

"Ahh. Cooz's place," he said, referring to the retired patrolman who owned the Georgia Safe gun range. "He's got the monopoly on all you cops, based on his background of course. But he ain't got nothing outdoor there 'cept two clays. Maybe I help you out here, and you put in a good word with your chief. We could arrange a whole day out here. Just for po-lice."

"Sure," I said. "Send me an email and I'll reco it to the chief. The address is on my card."

"Appreciate that." He nodded. "By the way, I recognized you from the newspaper. Congrats on that award."

"Thanks."

"That girl can shoot too," he said. "The one on the front of the *Register* with you."

"She saved my life," I said, proud of Remy.

He beamed at me. And I headed through the turnstile.

I needed to be on the road.

If Vankle's schedule held, I had about thirty minutes to get over to Personal Best Fitness.

50

When I got to the address for Personal Best, I saw Vankle's Camaro parked two doors down.

But before I went in, I did a loop around the gym, seeing that it was just a storefront facing 30th Street with no back door.

I parked about eight cars down and pulled out my binocs.

Scanning through a propped-open front door, I saw Steele Vankle, talking to a woman at a tiny desk inside the door. His blondish-red hair was pulled back into a pony, and he held a duffel over one shoulder.

I got out of my truck. Crossed the street and entered the place. I wasn't sure yet how I was going to play this.

Could I use what I knew about him and Pelo, and he'd sing about Hartley?

The door closed behind me, and I glanced straight ahead. Vankle stood with his back to me. Up close I could see he was about five-nine with a muscular body—a tank top and athletic shorts on. His hair was slightly redder than in his picture online.

"Mr. Vankle," I said, and he turned. He'd put down his duffel already, and his blue eyes darted to the door behind me.

"I just want to—"

Vankle picked up a medicine ball. One of those heavy types about eighteen inches in diameter. He tossed it at me.

"Jesus," I said, ducking out of the way. The ball hit me in the side, and Vankle charged at me, knocking me off balance.

The two of us landed messy, and I rolled him like I was trained. Reached back for my bracelets and cuffed him. Left hand first. Then as I reached to wrap up his right, he wriggled free and rolled away from me, the cuffs hanging off one wrist.

He brought himself to his feet and flew out the door that I'd just come in through.

"The fuck?" I said, chasing the guy out the door.

We ran down 30th toward Barston Street, with Vankle about twenty feet ahead. At the corner, he turned. He was in good shape, but I brought my arms to my sides, pumping them and keeping him close.

Around the next corner I saw him take to a ladder that ran up the side of a building.

The cuffs clanked off each rung, and he hustled, arm over arm.

I did the same, giving chase.

Up on the roof, Vankle stood about thirty feet ahead of me. The building was older, and he was cornered.

"I just want to talk, Mr. Vankle," I said. Two dozen feet between us. "I promise."

Vankle's hair had fallen from the tie that once held it, and he looked a half bubble off plumb. His cool blue eyes were huge, and a mane of messy curls framed the perimeter of his oval face.

"No way, Marsh," he said, using my name for the first time.

Had I told him my name?

The edge of the roof was ten feet behind him, and beyond it was another building. Lower by a floor, but with a break in between roofs. Had to be ten or twelve feet that separated the two structures.

Vankle took a handful of steps toward me and then turned the other way. Ran as fast as he could toward the edge of the roof and leapt through the air.

"Shit," I said. Running to the edge in time to see Vankle's shoulder land, and then his body hit too, right onto the concrete molding that encircled the edge of the next building over.

He stood up but was hurt, a gimpy gait as he moved his leg.

"C'mon, Marsh," he said, taking a step backward. "Your turn."

But there was no way I was making it over there.

We stared at each other. Vankle's face was pocked with gravel and his hair was sweaty. My cuffs dangled from his left hand.

He limped over to a door and went inside.

I hustled down the ladder again, but by the time I got to the next building over, Vankle had disappeared.

Walking back to the gym, I saw that his Camaro was still there. I looked around. Didn't realize that when Vankle had tackled me, we'd knocked over the water cooler in the waiting area.

The woman from the front was using the *Mason Falls Register* to blot up the water that had spilled, and she looked pissed when I stepped inside the place.

"What the hell was that?" she asked.

"Sorry," I said. "Let me help you."

The place reeked of sweat, mixed in with some sort of vinyl cleaner.

Crouching over, I wiped at the water. That's when I saw my face on the front of the Metro Section of the paper.

The picture showed me with Kelly Borland, standing at the opening of the banquet room at the event last night. A candid, taken by some photographer.

I blinked, staring at the wet version of myself.

"Is this today's paper?" I asked.

"It *was*," the receptionist said.

In my gut, a strange feeling was tingling.

I stood up, staring at the wet photo. Turned and headed out to my truck without finishing the cleanup job.

On the way there, I found the number for Georgia Wild and Free. Rang up Will Jackson, who I'd met an hour ago.

"Hey," I said. "It's Detective Marsh."

"What's up?"

"You mentioned the woman with me in the paper. You meant Remy Morgan, my partner, right? Not sure which paper you saw the picture in."

"I don't know her name, but—"

"Twenty-eight?" I said. "Black woman. Straightened hair to the shoulders. Pretty."

"The one I saw was pretty all right," he said. "But she was white. No bigger than a minute. Brunette. Figured when you said that gal saved your life, you were speakin' more like an expression, since in the picture you two were dressed up. Looked like a couple who might be—"

"You said, 'She can shoot,'" I interrupted him.

"Well," he said. "She's been out here. It's been a bit, but I never forget a face, like I told you earlier. She had another boyfriend then."

"What'd she shoot?"

"A .38," he said. "Gun was his, I think."

I swallowed, pacing by my truck.

"I'm gonna send you a picture," I said to the old-timer, finding an image on my cell and sending it to Jackson.

I heard a ding on his end of the line.

"Yup," Jackson said. "That's the guy."

I thanked him and hung up.

Stunned.

Stunned into silence.

51

Kelly Borland heard a rapping on the side door that let in from the courtyard, and she told Leaf Tanner to hold on for a second.

Leaf was in the middle of a story about a kid in his Life Sciences class. Kelly had been listening while filling an empty trash can with paintbrushes that were too stiff to be reused.

The storage room, which was normally tidy, had turned into a mess of boxes, art books, and supplies. Kelly had been cleaning up. Putting things into piles. Using empty boxes as trash cans. And once she was done today, the place would look just like it had the first day she'd arrived at Falls Magnet. A clean slate.

"Nervous energy?" Leaf had asked her when he first arrived ten minutes earlier.

"Something like that," she'd said.

A loud banging came again at the side door. Kids, she thought. Screwing around.

The metal door opened inward, and Kelly unlocked it. Swung it toward herself.

She stared at the man framed in the entrance.

Jed Harrington wore a green flannel and jeans, and his hair was uncombed.

Kelly stepped backward, and Leaf poked his head around her.

"Can I help you, buddy?" Leaf Tanner said to Jed.

"I doubt it," Jed replied. "And I'm not your buddy. Apparently, I'm not hers either."

52

I hung up the phone from talking to Will Jackson at the gun range and stared down at my phone.

The picture I'd sent him was of Jed Harrington.

Kelly Borland and Jed Harrington.

Together, at a gun range.

My mind was spinning to a specific thought. That I had always known something was wrong. That somehow that's why I hesitated sleeping with Kelly.

But they'd dated? Shot together?

Which meant what? He was a crazy ex, infatuated with her? Then he unexpectedly showed up at Falls Magnet Middle School?

"Jesus," I said aloud, thinking how I'd gotten involved with her.

Stay focused on Vankle, Purvis said. Purvis in my head again.

I took a knife from my utility box. Crossed the street and quietly slashed the back two tires of Vankle's Camaro.

"That oughta slow you down," I said.

I wandered back to my truck then. Called Kelly up, but got her voicemail.

"Hey," I said. "I just had the oddest conversation with a guy at a place called Georgia Wild and Free." I stopped. "It's a gun range, Kelly. But I think you know that. Call me."

A few minutes later I got a text from Kelly.

Had my phone off. Can we meet in person? Twist Coffee on Sunrise?

I texted back that I'd be there in five minutes.

As I drove, I thought about Beau. The way he had sidled up to her so naturally last night. And more than that—the way Kelly's face had gone pale when she first saw the dog, outside my house.

Jed's dog. She recognized Beau. And he recognized her.

I pulled to the curb and saw her, sitting by herself on the patio of the coffeehouse. Her body looked tiny in her chair, and I thought of the dresses we'd seen in Harrington's place. We'd assumed they were his sister's, but each was a small. Kelly's size.

I got out of my truck and walked over. Her face was gray, and her cheeks were wet with tears.

"Hey," I said.

My head was swimming with crazy thoughts. I mean, I'd shot a man at the school. A man we all thought that nobody knew.

"Before you say anything," she said, "can you let me explain?"

"Sure," I said. Standing there. Going over in my head how I'd shared things with her. Personal things that I hadn't told anyone. Stories about Lena and Jonas.

"Will you sit down?"

"No," I said.

"I dated Jed, okay?" She held her hands up, palms out.

"Jesus," I said.

"I figured you knew," she said. "Not the rest of the cops. But you. I figured that's why you were hesitating getting involved with me."

"Kelly," I said, leaning against a metal railing that separated the patio from the street. "You lied to the police. To the school. To me."

She touched my arm. "A teacher was dead, P.T. Kids would've been shot if you didn't stop him."

"I did stop him," I said. "But do you know how much time we spent trying to figure out why the hell he went there?"

"It wasn't fair," she said. "Don't you see? I would've been that woman who some guy shot up a school for. I didn't know he was capable of violence."

"So why *did* he show up?" I asked.

"How should I know?" she said. "We dated for five weeks. That was nine months ago. He was the first person I met in Mason Falls."

"And you hadn't seen him in nine months?"

"No, I'd seen him," she said. "But we were over. Long over."

There was something wrong. Kelly was trying harder to convince me about her lack of relationship with Harrington than her lack of connection to a crime. *Did she think she was salvaging something that we had?*

"So why'd he shoot Leaf Tanner?" I asked. "Jed had no history of violence."

"I don't know."

"Did they know each other?"

"No."

"Were you and Leaf involved?"

"No, I promise."

I thought of the guys at the GBI who now held this investigation. And I'd gone out with Kelly. Jesus, I'd look like a rook.

"I would've been ruined, P.T.," she pleaded. "One of those women who get *Law & Order* episodes made about them."

"No," I said.

"My name would've been a national joke," she continued. "On late-night TV. And for what? It wasn't going to bring Jed or Leaf back."

I considered this. Was Kelly right?

"We wouldn't have allowed that to happen to you," I said.

"You couldn't have stopped it. How did it go for you?" she asked. "The media—around your wife's death?"

A particular image flashed in my head. A photographer who'd jumped the back fence and was taking pictures of Jonas's empty swing set in the backyard. And me—destroying his camera equipment. I remember planting my hands around the photographer's neck. And Marvin, who was there at the time, dragging me backward through the crabgrass, my right arm swinging wide.

"I'm calling for a patrol car, Kelly," I said, pulling out my phone. "This isn't my case. At a minimum, it's obstruction of justice. But more than that, I can't be the one you're telling this to."

She grabbed my hand then, her eyes intense. A single streak of resistant red in her hair hung across her cheek.

"I got caught up in something," she said.

"Apparently," I said. "Your ex came to the school with a gun."

"No," she said. "Something bigger than that."

"What do you mean?"

"Don't call the cops, okay? If you do, I'm not gonna tell you anything."

"Anything about what?" I said.

She was silent for a moment, and I waited.

"I came upon this guy, okay? He was spying on Jed. Outside his house."

"What guy?" I asked.

But inside, I was thinking one word: *bullshit.*

"I went to Jed's," she said. "A couple weeks ago. Outside was this guy, binoculars in hand. Camera with a zoom lens. He had a gun tucked inside his jacket."

"A guy you knew?"

"No."

"He threatened you?"

"Not exactly," she pleaded. "But a few days later, he showed up at my place. He told me I had to take Jed's papers."

I blinked. "What papers?"

"Jed was always talking about publishing some great piece, but he never did. He just talked and talked and accumulated paper after paper. I didn't think he would even notice they were gone."

I stared at Kelly.

Was she making this shit up as she went? Abe and I had looked through all of Jed's papers in those boxes.

I bent my head. "And who was this guy?"

"He never told me his name."

"What did he look like?"

"Handsome." She shrugged. "White. Dark hair."

"A handsome white guy?" I said. Half of Georgia fit that description. "Why didn't you call the police?"

"I dunno," she said. "He surprised me outside on the street. And in my house."

"What kind of car did he drive?" I asked.

"I don't know," she said. "Some SUV. Dark."

"So you did what?" I said. "Stole Jed's research? For what reason?"

"I was scared."

"This guy offer you something? Pay you?"

"No."

I squinted. "Nothing?"

"I didn't think anyone would get hurt," she said. "The guy made it seem like Jed was a danger."

"To you?"

"To himself." Kelly raised her voice.

"But you just said Jed *wasn't* dangerous."

Kelly's eyes flitted left. *Was she lying?* None of this made sense.

"Jed never did anything with this research," she said. "He was fanatical. And then that day at the school, he showed up."

"The day of the shooting?"

"Leaf and I were talking in the back room during our free period, and there was a knock on the door."

"*You* let Jed in?"

"I opened the door, and there he was. This crazy look on his face. I told him I didn't have the papers anymore."

I pictured Jed Harrington, unhinged.

"Things escalated," Kelly continued. "Leaf told him to take it easy. 'Chill out, Cochise,' Leaf said. And Jed took out a gun. And shot him."

Kelly went silent then, but tears ran down her cheek.

Was she faking?

Was she pathological?

"I don't want to lose what we have," she said to me. "That's why I stayed."

"*Stayed*" meaning what?

I stared at Kelly.

Was any of what she was saying true? I mean, we'd been together for three days at Schaeffer Lake, and she never mentioned any connection to Jed.

"So that's your story?" I said. "Dark-haired white guy in an SUV asked you to steal from Jed. Jed got mad and shot Leaf with a gun he brought to school."

"It's the truth."

"And you thought you'd be in a *Law & Order* episode if you told us."

Kelly's face was angry now, and she violently wiped at the tears on each cheek.

I wasn't sure what to believe. Maybe *she* shot Leaf Tanner. Maybe she and Jed planned it together. And then I'd shot Jed, leaving her to invent any story she wanted.

I pulled out my phone. Called for a black and white to take her to the station house.

"Are we finished?" she asked. "You and me?"

I wondered when and where I'd missed something. At the lake, Kelly had mentioned how fast she could leave town. Pack everything in one carload.

"We never got started," I said. "This whole thing was built on a lie."

I walked out to the street and called Abe. Let him know what had happened.

"Jesus H. Christ on a grain of rice," he said.

It was impossible not to look like a fool on this one. But it wasn't just me. Kelly had been the chief's guest at the police banquet. She'd sat between Chief Senza and Mayor Stems. Abe and Merle had interviewed her. Even the GBI in the last week. And poor Leaf Tanner, who we initially had suspected of being involved . . . he'd done nothing.

A black and white rolled to the curb as I finished up with Abe.

I helped Kelly into the squad car. Told the blue-suiters that Abe Kaplan was waiting for her on the other end.

The patrol car left, and I knew there might be charges against Kelly. Obstruction. Theft maybe. The D.A. would have to decide on all that. It was hard to tell right now.

After they'd gone, I fired up my truck and sat there for a moment, trying to refocus on Steele Vankle.

There was one other address that the two Joans had given me. Presumed to be Vankle's home address.

I drove over there and parked behind the condos, my eyes scanning the street. It was six p.m. and the sun was low in the sky.

Kelly, I thought still. What a mess.

Clear it from your thoughts, Purvis said. *Focus.* Purvis in my head again.

I loped around to the front of the complex. Under an open portico, I found mail with Vankle's name on it, along with a #4, which was a ground-floor unit on the corner. I banged on the front door, but no one was there.

Walking around back, I jumped a small fence and found myself in a ten-by-ten yard that had a single flower planter and two patio chairs.

From the back, I could see into his place. A one-bedroom, furnished in a contemporary style. A small combined living and dining area. All of it looked empty.

I'd announced my presence to Vankle at the gym, but not given my name. And yet he'd called me "Marsh" on the roof. He knew me.

I made my way back to my truck and started it up. Finding a more strategic area to park, I watched the place. Grabbed an old Taser from my glove box.

This would be the way I'd take Vankle down.

Non-lethal force. To keep the nut from running with my cuffs on again.

53

It was close to eight p.m. by the time a noise woke me.

I had dozed off in my truck, and the buzzing sound was a text from Alvin Gerbin, from the crime scene unit.

Stuff in evidence bag is Oxy.

I stared at the words. The text was in regard to the bag of powder that I'd found under the Golden Oaks. Now I had a good idea of what was going on under the store. And it matched with the drug trafficking trends from 2017.

The sun had gone down, and all the residents at 891 Burke Street had their lights on. That is, except for Vankle, whose ground-floor unit was dark.

I was tired, but I didn't want to go back to the precinct. Didn't want to hear any bullshit about Kelly Borland and me.

I got home by nine and wandered the house, a nervous energy causing me to clean a full sink of dishes and put all my dirty clothes in the laundry.

The dogs moved underfoot, not barking. Even Beau, who was like a puppy half the time, sensed my mood and was somehow subdued.

I rang Marvin up, but got his answering machine.

"I need to get out of town," I said to my father-in-law's machine. "Go somewhere. Take a few days."

I hesitated, trying to sound unaffected by the fact that the one woman I'd fallen for in the last year was a liar. "I was wondering if you can come by, Pop," I continued. "Grab the dogs and watch 'em while I'm gone."

I hung up and flipped open the cabinets where I used to keep the liquor. Nothing. Cleared out months ago by me and Marvin.

When I finally stopped moving, I went outside and sat on the porch. Beau was clawing at the front window, so I tied his longer leash to a pole out front and let him sniff the entirety of the porch. Eventually he settled down and sat a few feet to my left. His eyes were always on me, a protective stare, and I thought of Jed Harrington.

A loose thread had been scratching at the inside of my brain for the last hour, and a row of questions were lining up, not all of them with answers.

Kelly Borland had lied, sure.

But I had also known something was off about her.

I had avoided getting involved with her physically, and it was more than just about Lena.

Kelly's story about the papers at Jed's place, and the photo of the boxes that leaked out to the media.

Could Kelly have been the one who leaked that shot out to Fox TV? And if so, why? To seal Jed's fate as a crazy person?

I remembered going through those boxes in Jed Harrington's casita the night of the shooting. The empty ones. Wondering if something important might have once been inside of them.

The few reporters that Merle had interviewed said Harrington had had a rough year, but had recently settled into a new rhythm. He was writing something big again. Two of them guessed it was a book.

Opening my satchel, I went through my notes from the night that Abe and I spent at Harrington's house after the shooting.

I read through a list of everything I'd catalogued from his backhouse, scanning down to the last note I'd written when channel eleven broke the story and released that picture of Harrington's place. The one that marked him as crazy.

On my home computer, I found the article by Raymond Kirios in the *Register*, from the day after the school shooting. It detailed everything that was known at the time, from Harrington's past embedded with the military, all the way up to the moment I shot him.

Reading it with fresh eyes, I stared at the photos inside his backhouse that first appeared on channel eleven. Of the gun rack and the banker's boxes.

And I noticed something.

The boxes marked *G.U.* on the sides—in the picture in the *Register*—they were piled in a neat line, parallel to the grout lines, and they sagged with weight.

But when I got to the backhouse, those same boxes were empty.

I stared up at a crack that ran across my dining room ceiling. It curved around the area where the chandelier hung, and I remembered a hundred promises to Lena to patch that crack.

Purvis lay on the floor nearby, and I paced in a circle around the dining room table, tossing that rubber ball from one hand to the other.

The only possible answer has got to be the truth, my bulldog huffed.

The photo from the *Register* must've been taken at some earlier time.

Before the shooting.

Like before Kelly cleared out those boxes, if I believed her story.

I remembered seeing the letters *G.U.* on the boxes, and then searching for a similar reference in Harrington's Rolodex.

All I'd found was a chicken scratch of two paw prints.

I typed "GU," "writer," and "Jed Harrington" into my Web browser and hit *Enter*, looking for an exact match to those expressions, all in the same web link, if it existed.

As usual, a lot of hits came up, but only one entry had all three items perfectly as I'd written them.

Clicking on it, I was brought to a conspiracy theory website, one that specialized in politics in the southeast, mostly Georgia and Alabama.

I searched within the page and found multiple references to "GU," each of them referring to the two letters as if they represented some website or blog.

When I searched within the website for "Harrington," I found a single entry hidden in a back-and-forth between two folks on a comments page.

Do you think that a reporter might be the author of the Government Unrest blog? Someone not working right now, like Geno Sommers or Jed Harrington?

I didn't know who Geno Sommers was, but my eyes lit up seeing Jed Harrington's name. I also wasn't familiar with a blog called Government Unrest. But now I realized what "G.U." stood for. Was this Harrington's blog?

Finding it on my browser, I scanned the blog's articles. The author was listed as "Anonymous," but he or she took on every level of government and tackled multiple issues, from voter fraud to bribes taken to unfair state bidding practices.

And in ninety percent of the blog entries, the author, who went unnamed, targeted one person more than anyone else.

Governor Toby Monroe.

I hadn't breathed in a minute, and I forced air in and out of my lungs.

"Shit," I said aloud.

When Governor Monroe had called me on the roof at the school, he'd acted as if Harrington was some unknown madman.

Could Jed Harrington be the author of this blog?

The articles were highly speculative. They made jumps in logic that were not too different from how the editor of the *Register* had described the work Harrington had submitted.

But the blog also alluded to a trove of support documents in an archive, all at the author's ready. Was this real? Or some bullshit threat?

Looking around the home page, I saw a tiny red period down at the bottom, nearly hidden in a field of black. When I hovered my mouse over it, it became a clickable link.

Selecting it, a window popped up, asking me for a password.

I stared at the box.

I'd taken a security course last year in Atlanta, and there had been a lecture on the most commonly used passwords by Americans.

I typed in "123456," and hit *Enter.* The box went blank.

I typed in the word "password." Not that either.

Then "welcome."

Then "admin."

Harrington was unmarried. No kids. No girlfriend. I thought of the dog and typed in "beau." A warning came up:

```
One more attempt before password locks
```

"Damn it," I said aloud.

I wore another circle into the floor around my dining table, staring at the award for heroism that I'd received for the school shooting, which was parked in the center of the table.

Had that award kept me from pursuing any doubts I had in the back of my mind?

I walked over to my computer, which had gone to a screen saver of me and Jonas in Key West by the Mile 0 marker.

My son had a short reddish-brown Afro that was a combination of his mother's beautiful black curls and my wavy chestnut hair.

Hitting the mouse jogged the computer back to life, and the screen flashed the same message as it had earlier, below the password box:

```
One more attempt before password locks
```

I thought about what Harrington valued.

I'd already put in the name "beau." But I thought of how Kelly had referred to the dog. And the broken frame I'd found in the drawer. The one with the two *B*'s. The *G.U.* index card in the Rolodex also had two paw prints drawn on it.

I typed "beaubeau" into the box. I stared at the nonsense word and hit *Enter*.

The computer beeped, and a list formed onto the screen.

A list of forty or fifty folders.

Two hours later, I'd reviewed all of Jed Harrington's backup documents, each carefully annotated in a process he'd probably learned at places like the *Atlanta Journal-Constitution* or *The Washington Post*.

There was enough hard evidence to keep Toby Monroe out of office or trying to fend off bad press or jail for the rest of his life.

And I hadn't just killed a school shooter. I'd done the governor's dirty work and taken out an enemy.

I moved into the hall bath and threw up.

Shit.

Of course Harrington wasn't innocent. He had come to a school with a gun. Had shot a teacher. But he had been lured there by Kelly Borland's actions.

And none of that changed the fact that Monroe knew who he was.

The governor had called me with a lie that he was concerned about public safety. And I'd executed the governor's nemesis. I'd shot a man for him.

I needed a drink, and the house being empty wasn't gonna stop me anymore.

54

I sat at the small counter at Scala's that faced out onto 20th Street, and a woman brought over a pint of Terrapin Rye.

I lifted the sudsy mix to my lips. The liquid felt cold going down my throat.

I exhaled, staring over at the rubble across the street that used to be the Golden Oaks.

Four nights ago I'd ordered a beer like this one as a prop. I'd committed myself to never drinking again and sat here, a PBR in front of me for a half hour until Remy showed.

And it could happen, I thought. I could stay sober.

I'd been dry since May, after all.

But I felt the old warning light go on, and I didn't care. I knew that when that light flashed, there was no stopping for anything except violence or the type of sleep that others call unconsciousness. I could see the self-loathing out there on the pink of the horizon, and I welcomed it.

I motioned for the waitress, telling her to bring me a double of Dewar's with two cubes of ice in it.

"You got it, hon," she said.

Balls on the pool table clinked, and the door chimed. The music changed from something young and poppy to a song by Led Zeppelin. "Kashmir."

"Jesus, Lena," I said to a window that was shined so clean all I saw was my own reflection. "The only type of woman I can fall for is a friggin' criminal. That's how shitty my brain works since you've been gone."

Outside, cars passed and sirens wailed. The numbered streets were never gonna change.

"And now I got played by Monroe," I said. "And I got no idea what to do about it."

I saw a glass arrive beside me, but it didn't look like Dewar's.

"Your buddy settled your tab," the waitress said, picking up my empty beer glass. "He bought this for you."

The glass held seltzer water, and the buddy, now walking closer, was Darren Gattling, in full uniform.

I eyed him, and he put his hands up, palms out.

"I don't want trouble, P.T.," he said. "But I can call a bunch of cops to help me get you outta here if I have to. Remy told me you might come here. After this mess with Kelly."

Kelly.

This wasn't even about her.

"Can you drive?" he asked.

"I've had twelve ounces of beer so far. So I'd say yeah. But why don't you get the hell of here, Darren. Go back to your shift."

He lifted up his walkie. "Like I said, I can call others. I got a lotta friends in patrol."

I stared at Gattling.

I knew why he had been moved to the night shift. It was because he'd agreed to help out with my undercover sting at Tandy's and had been unlucky enough to have that kid die in his arms. I had messed with Gattling's career, and he never said a bad word to me about it.

I stood up and passed him, walking toward the exit.

"I'll follow you home," he said. "Make sure you don't stop at a liquor store along the way."

I got in my truck, and Gattling got in his black and white.

I could ignore him. Ignore a legion of blue-suiter friends of his. But I saw Gattling's lights go on, and I accepted my police escort, all the way into my neighborhood.

At a stop sign a block from my house, he pulled up next to me. "I think I'm gonna hang out here for a bit."

"Go back to work," I said. "I'm in for the night. I promise."

"You know if you break that," he said, "Remy's gonna be pissed. And I'm not the one she's gonna say disappointed her."

I thought about his words.

"All right," I said. "Hold a sec. I'll be right back."

I pulled into my driveway. Walked back the six or seven houses to where he was parked. And handed him my car keys. "Bring these back at the end of your shift. If it looks like I'm asleep, drop 'em in the mail slot, will ya?"

With my car keys safely in his hand, Gattling pulled away, and I walked down the street to my house.

As I came in the front door, I heard a racket. A barking noise, accompanied by the sound of fur against wood.

Had Beau closed himself inside the bathroom again?

I moved toward the hallway to open the bathroom door, but I caught sight of something shimmering in the low light of the dining area.

My cuffs on the table.

"Don't even think about going for your weapon," a raspy voice said. "You'll be dead before you draw."

A light turned on in the living room, and a man was sitting on my couch, holding a .45.

Steele Vankle.

55

Kelly Borland's eyes sensed a warmth that meant sunlight, and she woke, glancing around without moving.

Jed was still asleep.

As she lifted his long, muscular arm from atop her naked chest, she smelled his scent. A mix of machine oil and body odor. He was a photographer and a writer. Why the hell did he smell like an auto shop?

Kelly slipped out of bed.

"The magic massage," she'd called it with a few boyfriends.

She gave a man a massage along the temples. Around his ears and along his cranium. Then her pliant hands moved farther south, down his back.

Within minutes, every man melted.

For Jed, his sleep was so deep she could bang pots and pans, and he wouldn't wake up.

She moved to the kitchen. Dressed out there and drank a full glass of water. She heard a noise and stopped. Beau-Beau came out from the spare room where he liked to sleep. Where he could hear every noise and protect Jed from strangers.

She grabbed a couple garbage bags from the kitchen drawer. A small *slice of sunlight was entering the yard, and she walked with Beau-Beau out to the back.*

Kelly had met Jed a month after she'd arrived in town.

Harrington was a brilliant thinker and writer. But he wasn't turning anything in for publication. He was simply amassing stories of corruption like a Senate committee. Filling boxes with reams of paper, but no longer ambitious about doing anything with it.

Five weeks into the relationship, she ended it.

And that had been the last time Kelly spent any significant time with Jed in nine months. Until last night.

Kelly stared at the white file boxes grouped together in the backhouse. The ones he was always raving about. Jed was never gonna publish these.

She thought of the man she'd caught spying on Jed. The same man who surprised her at her apartment.

If she left the boxes as is . . . would Jed even open them and know the papers inside were gone?

She saw the letters G.U. on the box tops and sat down beside them. Dumped the contents of each of them into three black bags and then placed the empty boxes back—right where they were before.

With the bags full, she moved across the yard and out to her car.

She got in her Honda and drove then, getting on the highway and moving north.

About ten minutes later, she parked by a dumpster in an empty lot off 20th.

Jed would still be asleep, she thought. Wondering why she'd come by last night. Wondering how he'd gotten lucky.

She heard a noise behind her, and a black SUV pulled in beside her Honda.

A man rolled down his passenger window, and his eyes met hers. The same man she'd met twice now.

She popped the hatchback of her Honda CR-V, and the man got out. Walked around back and inspected the papers inside the bags. Loaded them into the back of his angled Italian SUV.

Kelly appraised the man in her side mirror as he worked. Dark hair, slicked back with product. Tall and muscular under that shirt.

He shut her hatchback and came up alongside her Honda. Close to her window. "You're not thinking of leaving town, are you?"

"I'm headed to work," she said. "It's just another day at school."

The man motioned at the bags he'd transferred to the back of his Maserati Levante. "And Harrington doesn't have a digital copy of all this?"

"Jed?" She smiled. "He's old-school. Paper, paper, and more paper. He probably won't even notice it's gone for a month."

The man handed her an envelope then, about four inches thick.

Then he got back in his SUV and took off.

Kelly exhaled nervously.

She could go home right now. Load up the car and be gone. But his question about leaving town had spooked her.

So she decided to head to school. She'd spend time in the storage area before her first class began. Maybe even at her free period at the end of the day. Take the time to clean the place up so it looked as good as it had the first day Kelly took the job at Falls Magnet.

Life was looking up. This creep she'd given the papers to would be out of her life. And Jed wouldn't even know what happened.

Today was a good day. A new day.

And tomorrow, the start of a new adventure.

56

The ruckus down the hall continued, and I realized that Steele Vankle must've locked Beau and Purvis in the bathroom.

I stared at what had originally caught my attention on the dining table.

"I appreciate you coming in person to return my cuffs," I said.

"Your weapon," Vankle said softly.

I pointed to my waist, where I kept my Glock tucked. Took it out slowly and dropped it on the ground.

"Toss it out the front door," he said. "And close the door afterward."

I placed the gun onto the concrete of the porch and shut the door.

As I moved toward the couch, he shook his head. Directed me instead to the far wall.

"Now ease on down," Vankle said, the .45 trained on me. "Hands behind your back."

He watched me drop to the ground and held his cannon on me. Never shaking. Never looking nervous.

"Don't you want to know who I am?" he asked.

"I know who you are, Steele," I said.

The sound of Beau slamming against the bathroom door changed. A different tone. More muffled. Softer. The dog had worn himself out.

"What I didn't know until recently was that you were running Oxy under that liquor store."

I stared at Vankle, holding the gun on me. If I was to die here, what did I still want to know? I knew about Christian Pelo. Could guess at John Adrian's fate.

"My wife and son," I said, my voice gravelly. "Why?"

Vankle exhaled. "Your wife was supposed to be an accident," he said. "Nothing more than a bump to her car to get you off our backs. I mean, you're a cop after all."

"Meaning what?"

"No one was supposed to die. We were just trying to scare you. And believe me, it created so much damn trouble, I wish I never called him."

"Called Tarticoft, you mean?"

"You don't know the half of it," Vankle said. "The nerve of him coming back afterward. Trying to charge us more money. Just 'cause she went off the road and died."

I swallowed, hearing how callously he talked about Lena and Jonas. I wanted to strangle him.

"*Us*," I said. "Meaning you and Hartley?"

Vankle stood up then, a resigned look on his face. "Close your eyes, bud. You're gonna be with your family real soon if you believe in that sorta thing."

There was a small noise then. A wisp like plastic flapping in the wind.

And down from the bedroom came Beau. He must've snapped open the window frame from the bathroom and jumped into the backyard. The wisp I heard was the doggie door.

Beau ran into the room, and it was just enough to distract Vankle. Just as the dog flew through the air and attached to his leg.

I leapt for the gun, and knocked it from Vankle's hands.

The .45 skittered across the floor, and I tackled him just as Beau bit at his leg.

But Vankle was fitter than me, and he rolled out from under my weight, connecting hard with a fist into Beau's side.

Vankle went for the gun, but I kicked it away, under the couch.

I dove on him again, this time hitting him in the shoulder where I knew he'd come down hard on that rooftop.

"Gahh," he screamed, and I punched him a second time. And a third.

I thought about my Glock. About where I'd left it, outside the front door.

Vankle landed a right cross that stunned me, and I felt my mouth split open. Blood ran down my chin.

Before I could recover, he hit me again, and Beau bit at his arm.

"Damn dog." He swiped with his forearm at the animal, throwing Beau against the fireplace.

I remembered what Remy and I had found on Instagram. That video of Vankle, wrestling in that octagon-style cage. I had to get out from under him, but as I wriggled free, he jumped forward, landing on top of me again.

His fists landed with abandon on my face. Blood poured from my eyes.

"Jesus," I said under my breath. Pushing his body so we rolled again.

I heard the gun clatter against the wall. His hand reaching for it.

The sound of metal scraping along wood. Vankle gripping the .45 under the couch.

We were locked in a death vise.

Then he kicked me hard in the chest, and I fell backward just as he backed up and lifted the .45.

"Time to meet that little Black wife of yours," he said.

I squinted with the one eye I could open, the .45 three feet from my face.

And then the front door opened, and a figure stood there.

Vankle looked over.

A voice said, "What did you just say?"

A light went on then. Blinding me. Someone firing once. And then again. Multiple rounds struck Vankle in the chest and his body fell forward, landing on top of me.

His blood began soaking into my shirt, and I pushed the dead-weight off of me.

In front of me I saw my father-in-law, Marvin. He dropped my Glock, and it hit the wood floor with a thud.

"Did he kill her?"

I sat up, disoriented and bloody.

"My baby girl?" he continued. "And Jonas?"

I was confused as to when Marvin got there, and remembered suddenly. I'd called him to come get the dogs. A few hours ago when I wanted to leave town.

I looked at Vankle, bleeding out fast, and my training kicked in. I grabbed a blanket from the couch, balling it up and trying to cover a hole in his chest.

"Jesus," Vankle mumbled. "What are you doing?"

I was tired of people dying on my watch.

"I'm saving you, you asshole."

"Oh my God." Vankle gasped. "I don't want to go to hell."

The blanket was sopping up the blood fast, and I hollered at Marvin.

"Pop," I said. "Get me a towel."

But Marvin's eyes were glazed over and his body lay against the far wall, immobile.

I pulled out my phone. Dialed 911 and identified myself. Gave them my badge number.

"Ambulance is five minutes away," I said to Vankle. "Just hold on."

The operator stayed on the line and was giving me updates. "Four minutes away," I said to Vankle.

"You must hate me for what I did." He slurred his words. "But it wasn't me. I promise. I just did what I was told."

"Just try to breathe," I said. "Nice and slow."

"It was my brother," he said. "The whole time. It was always my brother."

I heard sirens in the distance, but from the noise I could tell they were MFPD cars and not ambulances.

I glanced over at Marvin and realized I had a second situation to deal with.

"Kick that gun away from you, Marvin." I motioned at the Glock. "Kick it away and sit down over there in the corner. Patrol is gonna arrest you. At least until they sort things out."

Vankle's body started shaking then, and I knew from enough crime scenes that he was going into cardiac arrest. "No no no," I said, but his body stopped moving, and I knew he was gone.

The area around me was a pool of blood, and I reached my hand under Vankle's back, feeling a second exit wound.

He was dead.

I stared over at Marvin, who'd scooted a few feet away from my Glock.

I had run down Tarticoft, and Remy had killed him.

I had Hartley on the defensive after finding that skeleton under his property.

And now Marvin had taken out Vankle.

It had been a long two years for me since Lena and Jonas were killed. Two years alone, but the people around me had done the dirty work that they knew I couldn't do. That I wasn't able to. They gave me time to heal. To think.

And right now I was just thinking about one thing.

Vankle's statement about his brother.

Because a new question haunted me.

Who the hell was Steele Vankle's brother?

57

I sat back against the couch and waited as officers came up the steps.

Beau had snuggled beside me, and I could see his leg was cut. He barely barked when patrol busted through the front door and saw me bloodied up.

"Officer down," Patrolman Atienza said into her shoulder mic. She moved across the room and kicked the gun farther away from Marvin.

"You okay, Marsh?" her partner, Ford, said as he moved toward Vankle's body and saw the .45.

"Given the circumstances," I said.

Atienza got Marvin to his feet. "My father-in-law," I said. "He shot this man with my service weapon."

Atienza moved Marvin out onto the porch without messing with the scene, and Ford leaned over, checking Vankle's pulse to confirm he was dead.

"Let's get you up," Ford said.

"Only after you get someone on the line from Animal Control," I said. "This dog saved my life, and he's cut badly."

"I promise," she said. "Why don't you grab him, and we'll go out to the porch?"

By the time I got outside, there were three squad cars there, and Marvin sat in the back of one of them. I had someone check the bathroom and they found Purvis there, locked inside. Vankle must've put both the dogs in there while he waited for me.

"Is Marsh okay?" I heard a voice ask.

It was Chief Senza.

"He's just beaten up," Patrolman Atienza said.

A bus arrived, but I told them I wouldn't go unless they loaded Beau in with me, so after some delays, they agreed.

Senza tapped on the hood, and the ambulance took off, headed to Mason Falls General.

Lonnie Fuchs from County Animal Services met us out front. The same guy who'd helped me adopt Beau.

I handed him over, and he told me he'd fix the puppy up real good.

Most of the bruises were on my face, and a doctor gave me something to help me rest. But before I dozed off, I grabbed the doctor's arm. "Find my partner," I said. "Tell her to listen to the 911 tape."

By three a.m., I woke up in a hospital room, disoriented. Remy was sitting there, with that big-ass boot of hers up on the bed.

"You're wearing the same clothes as yesterday." I squinted. "That boot must be stinky."

"Didn't get a chance to shower." Remy smiled. "And I got real close to you while you were out—just to make sure you were still breathing."

"Creeper alert," I said.

We laughed for a bit and then Remy got that serious look in her eyes.

"What is it?" I said.

"Do you remember the Instagram post with the Camaro?" she asked. "Vankle mentioned his 'bro' lent it to him for the prom?"

I nodded.

"I had this gut feeling," Remy said. "So right away I checked all the makes of cars Lauten Hartley drove. Going back since he began driving."

I lowered my head. "They're brothers?"

"Half-brothers," she said. "And with the 911 tape, Abe got a warrant. Hartley's in custody, P.T."

I stared at my partner. "So it's over?"

Remy nodded, and the doctor came in. Checked some of my vitals.

"It's hard to look at you, by the way," Remy said. "You're not as pretty as you used to be."

"It's hard to hear you walk with that peg leg," I said. "You're not as light on your feet as you once were."

The doctor stared at the two of us, and Remy started laughing. It felt good to lighten the mood after all that had happened.

"I think he's ready to go, Doc," she said.

A few minutes later, I stood up wearily, and a patrol officer drove Remy and me back to my place.

At five-thirty in the morning, it was only Abe who was on the scene. He was sitting in my dining room, a chair turned backward, staring in at the living room floor. The place was covered in yellow crime scene markers.

"Steele Vankle," he said as I came in. "Cool name."

"It *was*," I said.

"It's a cool enough first name to stick in my memory," Abe said. "Like after we raided that cabin, down in Three Barrels."

I blinked. "Tarticoft's cabin?"

This was the house of the hitman we'd been hunting. Tarticoft. The same man hired to drive my wife and son off the road. The one who Remy shot. "You told me months ago that there was no mention of Lena there in any of his files," I said.

"There wasn't," Abe said. "And Tarticoft kept so much data on the folks he took out. Cash he sorted in envelopes. Research. The folks he killed—he tracked them for months."

"So . . . ?"

"So one of those envelopes," Abe said, "it just had a single Post-it inside. It said 'Cash from Steel.' No *e* on the end. Never knew what to make of it."

"Tell me you're not lying," I said.

"Nope." Abe shook his head. "The cash with it was a little light relative to what the others paid for a hired kill. Only five grand."

And there it was. Nearly twenty-one months after the worst day of my life, I had the last piece of evidence.

"It wasn't supposed to be a hit if you believe what Steele told me tonight," I said. "Just a little bump. A car accident."

Remy sat down next to Abe, and I thought about the robbery at the Golden Oaks in December 2017. I had gone into that liquor store one too many times and disrupted Vankle's Oxy operation.

I stared at Abe. "Did Marvin get released?"

"Back home a half hour ago," Abe said. "There'll be questions, but he'll come out the other side. No jail time."

Abe stood up then, his eyes still on the crime scene. He had been a great partner to me for years. Always analytical on a scene.

"So I assume you're headed to Marvin's house?" He ran his hands through his hair, which he'd cut short recently and looked patchy. "This is an active crime scene, P.T. You can't be walking in here."

"I was gonna shower." I pointed toward the back of the house. "I know it's not protocol, but—"

"Go." Abe nodded. "Then be off to Marvin's."

I nodded, but didn't leave the room just yet.

The body was already taken, but someone had drawn white chalk marks on my wood floors.

"I think if you test-fire that .45," I said, "you're gonna see it goes with that injury to the skull found under the apartment in North Heights."

"Christian Pelo?" Abe asked. "His mom's been waiting in the lobby for a day now."

"He worked at the Golden Oaks," I said. "Back in 2017. If my theory holds, John Adrian killed Pelo with that gun. And then Vankle killed Adrian with an overdose, to close the loop."

"You're gonna need to testify against Hartley," Abe said. "You know that, right?"

"I'll be ready," I said. "Anything else?"

"Not on this case," Abe said. "*This old case* . . . is finally closed. Just a lotta paperwork to do."

I moved to the bathroom then, slowing peeling off the dressing that had been placed on my wounds in the hospital.

In the shower I let the water soak into my wounds and closed my eyes, as hot lightning danced under the pinks of my eyelids, the water pouring deep into places that touched my nerves.

After I got dressed in my bedroom, I rolled back the carpet and took the pile of papers from my floor safe. The ones I'd printed from Harrington's file but never finished reading before I'd left for the bar.

I could hear Remy and Abe in discussion about Vankle and Hartley out in the living room. Apparently, while I was knocked out in the hospital, Abe had done the notification of Vankle's mom. She was also Lauten Hartley's mom.

"'One son worked hard and the other hardly worked,' the mom said." This was Abe's voice.

"That's it?" Remy asked.

"Mom said Lauten loved his little brother. And he'd been cleaning up for him his whole life."

"And little brother had probably been doing dirty work for big brother *his* whole life," Remy said.

I came out with my duffel, and the two went quiet.

"I got a text from Lonnie at County that Beau is in great spirits," Remy said, breaking the awkward silence.

"Well, that's a piece of good news," I said.

I turned to Abe. "Don't mess up my house."

"Don't come back and mess up my crime scene," he said in response.

I grabbed Purvis from the yard, walked down the steps, and got in the car. Headed to Marvin's.

As I drove over to my father-in-law's place, I thought of the craziness of the last ten days. Of the school shooting and the sting at the bar that had gone south. But mostly, I found myself thinking of Kelly Borland.

Had I been too hard on her?

A man had threatened Kelly with violence, and she'd agreed to do what she thought was best in order to survive.

Was it more than that?

Could I forgive her?

Or, like Remy said, was I making it impossible for anyone to live up to the bar set by Lena Marsh?

58

Kelly Borland dropped her keys into the blown-glass bowl near the front of her apartment and used the back of her left high heel to push the door closed.

It was a Friday night, and she laid a dress she'd just picked up, still in its dry-cleaning plastic, over the back of her favorite armchair.

She moved into the kitchen.

"Jesus," she said, her voice caught in her throat.

The man she'd bumped into outside of Jed's place. The one she'd caught spying on Jed. He was sitting in the dark in her living room.

His figure was half shrouded in darkness, his hair slicked back with product. He wore a gray shirt and dark pants, a black blazer over it.

"How the hell did you get in here?" she asked.

"Sometimes I use a five-in-one tool and go through the molding," the man said flatly. "But that can leave a mess of wood shavings." He pointed toward her bedroom. "You should lock your back windows more often, Ms. Borland. It's a dangerous world out there."

"I'm calling the cops."

"No you're not," the man said.

She stared at him, her palms pressed against the white kitchen counter to steady her nerves. He had a handgun when she'd seen him outside of Jed's place. Did he have that gun on him now?

"I need to get into Jedidiah Harrington's house," he said. "Except I cannot be on camera. I cannot be photographed."

She stared at him. She could feel her heart beating fast against her blouse.

"Do you have a key?" he asked.

"No."

The relationship between Kelly and Jed had never risen to that level in the five weeks they had dated. And now it had been nine months. A couple texts exchanged. Pleasantries.

"Too bad," the man said.

He stood up and flattened the wrinkles on his shirt with his hands.

Kelly glanced down at her car keys. She moved the Honda key between her index and middle fingers. Protruding out like a weapon.

The man turned toward her then, and Kelly's mind raced. What had she done to deserve the luck she'd had in the last five years? First with her art, which had shown such promise, but didn't sell. And then with men. Losers. Drunks. And here in Mason Falls . . . Jed.

"He's not stable, you know," the man said to Kelly. "Sooner or later, it won't end well. Especially if these crazy lies he's been writing get out. The people I work for—"

"Jed's just a talker," Kelly said, her knuckles white around the car key.

"You don't know that," the man said.

He stopped five or six feet from her. There was a bulge at his waist. Right side. Under his blazer.

"He's not my boyfriend," she said nervously. "He's nothing to me."

"But if you had a key, you could help him."

"I don't, though."

"Or, if you could figure out some other way. Some way to get me what I need . . . it might be worth a hundred thousand to you."

Kelly's breathing calmed, and her eyes widened.

"Dollars?" she clarified.

59

I found Marvin asleep on the couch, a cup of tea on the table in front of him.

The hall clock read four a.m., and I found my way into the guest room that was once my wife's room when she was growing up. Threw my duffel on the ground and fell onto Lena's old pink comforter.

They'd cleaned me up real good at the hospital, and I'd caught two hours of sleep there, but I was fading fast.

I closed my eyes, and in a minute I was high above Mason Falls.

As I soared through the clouds, it was daylight and I saw the high walls of Condesale Gorge and the rocky canyons below it.

Like a bird, I followed east to where the water had been dammed up years earlier. Farther along the plain, I saw the red clay pits that were famous in this area, the burnt sienna color a residuum of what's left when chemical weathering erodes the calcite and dolomite.

In my dreams I heard Jonas's voice. Telling me it was okay to sleep. But only if I got through the rest of my work first. Only then could I move on. Could I let go.

"Look further," he said. "Look further, Dad," he repeated, and I woke with a start.

Purvis had found a place in the corner of the room, and he sat up, alert and staring at me.

I pulled my feet off the bed and touched the cold hardwood floors of Marvin's house. Stared over at my duffel.

Taking the bag up onto the bed beside me, I grabbed the pile of papers that I hadn't finished going through from Harrington's stash. The stuff I'd gotten from my floor safe before I left home.

As I carried the pile out to the dining table, I noticed that Marvin had relocated from the couch and was now asleep in his bed.

I turned on the lights in the dining room and spread out the last few papers I had not yet gone through before I left to get drunk.

The first ten pages were a journal of sorts.

Jed Harrington had tracked where Monroe had gone for a period of weeks. He'd followed the governor to Atlanta and over to Macon. To Athens. And then up north into Tennessee.

The next two pages were black-and-white printouts of pictures.

The photos were shot at night and were grainy. Pictures of someone taking pictures. At first I didn't understand what I was looking at.

But as I got to the last one, I recognized a man. He worked for Monroe. A nebbish-looking administrative aide that I'd seen at some event.

In the picture, the aide sat in a sedan, a camera in hand, his driver's side window down.

If Monroe had suspected that Harrington was the author of the blog I'd found, the governor might've sent one of his trusted guys to check out the reporter. To take pictures. And this guy had become the subject of a picture himself. Because Jed Harrington had caught him on camera.

I considered what happened next. Because if the governor suspected that Harrington was onto him, then Monroe would send someone more serious than an administrative aide. More dangerous.

This triggered a thought, and I grabbed my cell. Called the front desk at the precinct. Hope Duffy picked up on the second ring, working the night shift again.

"Hey, partner," I said. "It's P.T."

Hope made a noise with her nose. She was still waiting for the payoff of being my partner.

"Hope," I said. "Was Billy Walker there tonight? He's a sketch artist we use."

I wanted to know if someone had sat with Kelly Borland and drawn a picture of the man she'd claimed to see outside of Jed Harrington's.

"Yeah," she said. "He left maybe two hours ago."

"The sketch," I said. "It's probably taped up in Abe's office. I need a shot of it."

"I can't leave the desk for a half hour," she said. "But if it's taped up somewhere, I'll text it to you."

I hung up and looked at the rest of the paperwork I had on Monroe.

The pages at the bottom of the stack were a list of investment holdings.

First, a series of partnerships. And then, when it wasn't clear what percentage Monroe owned of the partnership or who else owned it, Jed Harrington had painstakingly broken that down.

I traced my finger down the list, but they meant nothing to me.

Some REITs. Some trusts. Some LLCs.

It wasn't until I saw the last investment that the hairs on my arm stood up.

And when they did, I grabbed my keys and that single piece of paper at the bottom of the stack. And I walked out the front door.

I had to talk to someone, and I knew exactly where they were for the next few hours: the Mason Falls jail.

60

When Lauten Hartley saw it was me in the visitation room, he turned to the guard, as if to refuse the visit. But I'd given the patrolman a heads-up that he would probably do that. And this particular blue-suiter was a friend.

Patrolman Cole pushed Hartley forward, attaching one of his bracelets to the ring on the table, and forcing his body down into the chair.

I remembered seeing Hartley just ten days ago at the precinct. He looked so calm and self-assured. Now his wavy copper hair looked wild, reflecting off the orange of his jumpsuit.

"What do you want?" he said once the officer left.

"A favor."

He blew out his nose and shook his head, his curls dangling over his forehead. "From me?"

I held his eyes and took the paper from my back pocket. The one I'd just found in Jed Harrington's treasure trove of research.

Hartley looked down at what I'd brought. Saw the name of his partnership. The name of his partner.

"You're like a damn junkyard dog, aren't you, Marsh? You just can't help yourself when you get that smell."

I didn't say anything. After all, Hartley was right. My obsessiveness was at the core of this tragedy in my life. I had thought about that more times than I wanted to admit.

I stared at him. "Did Monroe know?"

"The partnership held a liquor store in the numbered streets," Hartley said. "And two apartment complexes. And it made an eight hundred and twenty percent margin. You think he didn't know what we were doing?"

Hartley tried to get up, but the chain pulled on him. "Guard," he yelled.

I grabbed at Hartley's arm. "Did Monroe order the death of my wife and son?"

"He didn't have to," Hartley said. "We knew what was at stake when we took Monroe on as a partner. The choices we'd have to make."

A different uniformed officer unlocked the gate behind us, and I let go of Hartley's arm.

The patrolman got him to his feet, but Hartley kept muttering under his breath. How he'd been beaten by a friggin' junkyard dog.

I sat alone in the interview room for some time. Folded the paper and put it away.

My blood was pounding in my temples, so loud that I could hear it over the electric din of the cheap fluorescent panel above me.

And then I heard another noise. The buzzing of my phone.

I pulled it from my back pocket and stared at the text that Hope had sent me.

It was a picture. The composite that Kelly Borland had described to our sketch artist of the man she'd bumped into outside of Harrington's place.

And as much as I didn't want to believe a word Kelly said at that coffeehouse, the picture was clearly of a man I'd seen before.

Had met in fact.

A man who'd handed me a packet of papers that helped me locate Kian Tarticoft months ago.

Kelly had said she was scared when she stumbled upon the guy, but until now it hadn't crossed my mind that she could be telling the truth.

I thought of the empty boxes in the backhouse. The ones Kelly said she cleaned out. And I wondered if she had supplied this man with the photo of them. The one that eventually hit the news.

And as I thought of this . . . of everything I'd discovered today . . . it left me just one option.

Just one thing I had to do.

61

It was almost nine a.m. when I left the jail and walked outside.

The sky was an iridescent gray that looked like the shine off a pearl.

Getting in my truck, I headed south and let the music play. Turned off my phone and rolled down both windows, not wanting to pay attention to where I was going.

It was Sunday, and I shifted the stations from country to rock to indie. In one minute, Blake Shelton was belting out "God's Country." In the next, the Cordovas were singing "I'm the One Who Needs You Tonight."

When I got to Atlanta, I switched onto 278 for a mile and then got off the highway.

As I approached the 900th block of Piedmont, traffic was backing up. I parked on a side street, threw a police placard on my dash, and huffed it on foot.

After a few minutes, I'd reached the address I was looking for: a converted mansion from the 1890s that served as the campaign headquarters of Governor Toby Monroe.

The porch of the house was set up as a stage, festooned with red, white, and blue balloons. Below it, on the curving lawn, someone had built a platform out of plywood and painted it white, a big square area for reporters and cameramen.

"Can I help you?" a deep voice asked. I had arrived at an ornate gate that let in from the street.

The voice belonged to one of the governor's security men. A muscular Black guy with a bald head and a body like a keg of beer. His name tag read *Sampson*. A shorter white man beside him held a clipboard.

"Can we get your name and see your credentials, sir?" Sampson asked.

I sized the two men up. They weren't state police. Or GBI. They were private security.

"This is my press pass," I said, holding up my badge. "I'm here to see Toby Monroe."

"The governor isn't taking any appointments today," Sampson said. "If you'd like to set a time to talk tomorrow, we can certainly get his secretary to check his calendar."

The guy was big enough to go bear hunting with a switchblade and no friends. But I was in a crazed state, and I didn't care. "Tell Monroe it's P. T. Marsh," I said. "When he chooses not to see me . . . bad things happen to him."

Sampson walked away, his phone to his ear. His shorter colleague moved into his place, blocking the gate. The smaller man puffed out his chest. And behind me, two men waited, one of them holding an enormous tripod.

Sampson came back a minute later and waved me in. I walked with him, up the steps and onto the porch. A foyer inside the door held four white couches. Beside them were tables topped with antique glass, hand-painted with silver fleurs-de-lis.

"Through that door." Sampson pointed across the room.

I walked across the foyer and into a small room where Monroe sat in a director's chair. He wore a dark blue suit with a red tie, and his salt-and-pepper hair was trimmed short and had more pepper than usual.

A blonde in a black smock was brushing powder onto his face.

"Detective Marsh," Monroe said. "I knew you liked politics, but I didn't count on your attendance at the announcement of my platform. Welcome."

The makeup artist smiled at me, and I leaned close to the governor.

"Jed Harrington," I said.

"That was a good kill, Detective. I'm sorry I was unable to get to the banquet in your honor."

"He was working on an exposé of you."

Monroe offered a sharklike smile. "Jeanine," he said to the woman. "Do you mind if I speak with Detective Marsh alone for a moment?"

"Of course," the woman said.

She left, and Monroe's smile faded. "Harrington was a journalist, so if he was writing an exposé, I reckon that's his right."

"I have all of it," I said. "Every word."

The door Jeanine left through opened, and Monroe's assistant stuck her head in. "Sir, we're gonna be live in ten minutes. Fifteen tops."

A smile was plastered on Monroe's face. "Thank you, Tammy," he said, his voice ringing with confidence. "Just give us a few minutes."

The door shut then, and I turned to him. "Harrington had a digital backup."

"A backup of what exactly?" he asked.

I shook my head at him. "You sent that ghost of yours to get Harrington's files, but you didn't get the only copy."

"I'm not sure if you know how you sound, Detective." Monroe smiled. "*That ghost?*"

I pulled up my shirt and turned in a three-hundred-and-sixty-degree circle. "Just in case you think I'm wired," I said. "This is just you and me. Like on that rooftop at the school. When you asked me to kill a man who was your enemy."

Monroe got up from the director's chair and took off his jacket.

"Well, you did pull the trigger, Detective."

"And you gave the order, Governor. But the crazy thing is—what I found is bigger than Harrington."

"Whatever you *think* you know, Marsh—"

"Voter fraud," I said.

"Oh, please."

"Unfair state bidding practices."

"There is no proof that—"

"Highway contracts," I continued. "Bribery. Corruption. And not just you. Your nephews. Your father, Cliff," I said. "Your guy has the papers on all these. He got them from Kelly Borland, the art teacher. So I don't know what game you're playing denying this. I have them all."

The governor's blink rate had tripled in the last minute, and his mouth was open. I could see his eyes, doing the math on this and not liking what the calculations said.

"Harrington wasn't writing an article, Governor," I said. "He was writing a book. About you."

Monroe was gripping the back of the director's chair, and his knuckles were white. "I can make this right," he said.

"I don't think so."

"You and I have always come to an agreement. After that mess last December, we made great progress on race relations. I had corporations reaching out to Mason Falls. Donating time. Staff."

"You know what?" I made a hissing noise with my nose. "Three hours ago, I wouldn't have even given a shit. You think any of what you've done surprises me?"

The governor squinted. Trying to comprehend what had changed.

"I don't understand," he said.

"I got to the end of Harrington's pile of shit on you . . . and found your holdings," I said. "Your investments. He broke down every partnership." I held up the piece of paper. "Fifty percent ownership in FJF Investments."

"I don't know what that is."

"Let me refresh your memory," I said. "You own part of a liquor store."

A knock at the door.

"Tammy, just wait," the governor hollered.

"The Golden Oaks," I said. "From what I understand, it posted quite a profit in 2016. And in 2017. Not so much after the drug sales stopped."

"Detective, if you think I know every investment in my—"

"Jesus, you cannot stop yourself. Trying to lie your way out of everything."

I pulled out my Glock. Laid it on the counter near the makeup. I wanted him to see my weapon. To understand what I was capable of.

Now Monroe glanced at the door, perhaps worried that he had shooed everyone away.

"It's always about pressure with you," I said. "And you had Lauten Hartley under your thumb, just like you had me."

"Who?"

I looked at my Glock, and Monroe held up his hands, palms out. "I didn't know about it when it happened, okay? I promise."

So the murder of my wife and son was an afterthought to him? A detail he'd discovered and was holding on to. A piece of data to be leveraged at the right time.

"When *did* you know?" I asked.

"After," he said. "Much, much after."

"A week after they died? A month?"

"Six months. But it was just a guess. The investment wasn't performing like it had been—back when . . . you know . . ."

"Back when the store was selling drugs?"

"They said it was better if I didn't ask. Okay? So I didn't. But my guy, the one you call a ghost—"

"He told you?"

"After we gave you the location on that assassin, Tarticoft, my guy did some work. Put it together."

I sat down on a bench near the door where Tammy had come in, my head in my hands.

Monroe had known about Lena and Jonas. I didn't owe him any favor on that roof. He owed me, out of basic decency.

"You have two options right now, Monroe," I said, my head still down. "Number one is to walk out there and resign. Make up whatever excuse you want. But it's effective immediately. You're out, for good. No more politics."

"Or?"

"Raymond Kirios." I said the journalist's name. "Do you know him? Because he's gonna torch you."

"I'm thinking of a third option," Monroe said. And as I looked up, I saw that he was holding my Glock.

"You're gonna shoot a cop?" I asked. "I'm sure your platform involves supporting law enforcement."

"You came in here." He came closer to me. "Unhinged. Causing trouble. There was a scuffle."

"No," I said. "I'm gonna open that door." I pointed. "And the world's gonna see you holding that gun."

Click.

No ammunition. I'd made sure that one bullet wasn't even in the chamber.

When I made that decision out in the car, it was to make sure *I* didn't lose control and kill Monroe.

I shoved him back into the chair and grabbed my Glock. "A year and a half ago, this is how I would've handled you. See, I had this idea in my head back then."

"Do not walk out of here," Monroe said, grabbing at my arm.

"An idea," I said, "that I could play judge, jury, and executioner."

"I can make you rich, Marsh," he said. "You can retire. Rest of your life. Go fishing. Maybe get a place up on Schaeffer Lake."

I stared, incredulous. *How the hell did this guy know I go to Schaeffer Lake?*

"Or wherever you like," he corrected himself.

I decided to take a shot at something. Something that had been itching at my brain for the last day.

"You mean rich like Kelly Borland?" I asked.

The governor hesitated. Blew air out of his nose. "Well, obviously that wasn't money well spent," he said. "If you're here."

My heart sank.

Shit, I thought. *Kelly got paid.*

Maybe she started off scared of Ghost, but in the end, money was offered, and she took it.

Something about the word "stay" was what tipped me. She kept talking about staying versus going. She was really speaking about leaving town with a pile of cash.

I held up my Glock. "I realized before I walked in here, Monroe," I said. "If I use this, you win again. If I trade you *anything*, you win again."

Monroe blocked the door then. His makeup was caking. "Well, what the fuck do you want?" He pushed at me, finally losing his cool. "Name it."

"There's a letter I've already written," I said. "It goes out in two hours if I'm not back. Along with four hundred pages of damning evidence on your father. Your cousins. You. Those nephews of yours who got the contract for the on-ramps along 285."

I opened the door. "And if anything happens to me . . . well, you better hope I drive safe every day."

"Don't leave," he said, his voice barely a whisper.

"You told me something once," I said to Monroe. "You said that influence is like gasoline. The more you use, the less you got left."

Monroe squinted. "Did I say that?" Nodding, as if he agreed with the sentiment. Wondering where I was going.

"Your tanks are all empty, Governor," I said. "You hear me, you son of a bitch? You're slap out of fuel."

62

I turned and left. Walked off the property and back up Piedmont to where my truck was. I grabbed a coffee at the Flying Biscuit and turned on the news as I drove north out of the city.

I thought of everything that had gone down over the last twelve days.

As I pictured it now at the school, Monroe's guy Ghost had gotten the papers from Kelly early the morning of the eleventh and probably circled back around to sit on Jed's house. See if Harrington even noticed she had stolen from him.

Then, when Jed realized the papers were gone and drove to Falls Magnet Middle School, I imagine that Ghost probably followed him. Called Monroe when he got there. The governor must've thought he'd hit the lottery.

Jed, a school shooter.

And me, a cop in Monroe's pocket who owed him one and could take Jed out.

The press conference was delayed, but when it came on, it was a short one. Monroe announced that he'd recently met with his doctor, who told him he was not well.

"The stress of the job has worn on my health," he said. "So after a long discussion with my family, I've made the decision to step down immediately as governor. And not to run for reelection."

A cacophony of noises from the assembled press. Questions about what specific condition he had. *Is it life-threatening? And when had he made this decision?*

I flicked off the radio and drove the rest of the way in silence, thinking of Lena and Jonas. Of a moment when I came home early to surprise them years ago and found the pair on the front porch. Jonas was asleep atop his mother in the hammock, and two discarded pints of rocky road lay on the concrete below them.

Drunks, like gamblers, rarely keep winning.

Yet every day with Lena and Jonas had been a miracle.

I'd been lucky to have over ten years of miracles with her—and eight with him. And somehow since then, I had been even more fortunate to stay alive amid the pain of recovery.

When I got to Mason Falls, I exited 906 and headed to Marvin's place.

I sat on his porch with Purvis, and my bulldog stared at me. "Nothing to say about what I did?" I asked.

But Purvis was silent. After all, he was a dog. What was I expecting?

I heard a noise. Marvin had picked up the puppy from Animal Services.

"Beau-Beau," I said as he came out.

"Let's take a walk, guys."

I grabbed their leashes and told Marvin I'd be back in twenty minutes. As I strolled through Marvin's neighborhood, I called up Remy. Asking her what she was doing.

"There's a get-together in an hour or so," she said. "People that

Gattling and I know. We do extreme mud runs and that sorta thing with them. You wanna join us?"

"Are they millennial types?" I asked. "They wear hipster winter beanies in summer? Ironic T-shirts?"

"Don't forget the craft beer drinking," she said. "Small-batch stuff. We sit around discussing the type of hops. Very few intense detective types, P.T. You'd probably hate it."

"Wow. You make that a pretty tempting invitation," I said.

Remy laughed.

Then her voice changed. "P.T.," she said. "I'm not sure if you heard. Or got any calls in the last hour from anyone downtown?"

"No," I said. "About what?"

"Hartley hung himself in his cell."

"What?" I said, incredulous.

"Two hours ago," she said. "I asked if he had any visitors. They said *you* were there."

"Yeah, we talked," I said. Now, trying to replay our short conversation in my head.

"I guess, after you left, some lawyer named Granton came by," Remy added. "Apparently he and Hartley talked for five minutes. Then Hartley went back to his cell. No one noticed 'til he was dead."

I was stunned and silent.

"The DA said your phone just went to voicemail for the last couple hours."

"I went to see Monroe," I said. "Not sure if you caught the news. He retired from office."

"Just like that?" Remy asked.

"We might've talked first," I said. "What did the DA want?"

"I dunno," Remy said. "She was mystified. Apparently she and Hartley had talked last night. He said he had something to trade. In exchange, he wanted five years in minimum security. She wanted to know what you two talked about. If her conversation with him came up."

"No," I said. "It hadn't." But I understood now why Hartley had helped me. He was about to make a deal.

That is, until someone influential heard about it. Perhaps threatened something that Hartley cared about. His family. Their fortune.

We went silent for a moment, and I turned with the dogs back toward Marvin's house.

Vankle, who had paid for the accident that killed Lena and Jonas, was dead.

Hartley, who had tried to cover it up and run me out of office in other ways, was dead.

And Toby Monroe, who had known about it, was finally out of office.

I hadn't yet had a moment to process all this. To think about the justice I'd been searching for . . . for so long.

And just maybe, if Jerome Bleeker got into the governor's office, things in Georgia might be looking up.

"So all the bad men we know are gone," Remy said.

"There's always new bad men," I said. "That we don't know."

"True."

Remy's voice changed then. "So . . . what do you say? You gonna join us?"

I thought for a moment. I needed to start getting out there. Not every story in my life was going to mirror my past, for good or bad.

"Sure," I said.

"I'll text you the address," Remy said, and then hung up. I walked back into Marvin's and let the dogs get at their water bowls.

"You mind if I borrow your car?" I said to Marvin. "I feel like taking a drive. And not in a truck."

"If you can handle it." He smiled slyly.

The day before, Marvin had drawn thirty grand off his military pension. That, plus a trade-in of his old Charger got him a 2012 Porsche 911.

Apparently he wasn't joking when he said he always wanted to drive one.

I fired the beast up and headed out.

ACKNOWLEDGMENTS

First off, I would like to thank all the people who read *The Good Detective* and *The Evil Men Do*—my first two books—and those who wrote notes of encouragement via email or social media. To that end, I love to meet readers and get emails. So if you like the book (or have a note or suggestion), don't be a stranger. Shoot me an email at McMahonJohn@att.net and you'll be the first to know when the next one is coming out or read advance excerpts. Or just say hello.

My friend and workshop coach Jerrilyn Farmer continues to be a source of inspiration and great criticism, and for this book, she gave me the title. If you're playing the home game, my editor Mark Tavani and I have been doing an alternating "good" and "evil" thing with book titles. So this is where I would normally tell you to look out for another book with the word "evil" in the title by spring or summer '22. But I'm working on a new book, and I may let P.T. and Remy grab a short breather. Not sure as of this writing. If you're on my email list, you'll be the first to know.

I would like to thank Noah, Maggie, and Zoey for being my first three editors and the biggest sources of encouragement in my life. A couple folks to recognize on the "second round" edit team for their help from geography to legal to firearms to continuity: Ryan Loiacono, Suzanne Miller, Kerry

Archbold, Allison Stover, Bette Carlson, Andy McMahon, and my great agent, Marly Rusoff (and Michael).

A shout-out to my people at Putnam: Mark, Ivan, Sally, Danielle, Ashley, Ashley, Dan, Emily, and all the others who work behind the scenes. It's one thing to arrange words on a page, but someone's gotta market this book, sell it to the folks on the sales team, get a cover done, proof the thing, get it to stores, and arrange all the publicity and marketing to let the world know it exists. Appreciate you guys!

The following booksellers hosted me on my tour for *The Evil Men Do*, and their stores are great places to buy a book: Doug at Eagle Eye in Decatur; Cynthia at the Vero Beach Book Center; Rebecca, McKenna, and John at Murder by the Book in Houston; Barbara and Patrick at the Poisoned Pen; and Anne at Book Carnival. The coronavirus laid waste to my visit to Vroman's in Pasadena and Clues Unlimited in Tucson, but I know they would've been great stops. Another big thanks to everyone at the Savannah Book Festival—and to all the writers I've met over the last three years. The only community as welcoming as crime writers are the fans who follow their writing. One other shout-out of gratitude: to Marilyn Stasio of *The New York Times* for giving an unknown writer great publicity.

Last, there's the writing life. And then there's the work that supports you as you get better at your craft. In the latter, there's a handful of folks who were like lanterns in the night, helping me survive over three decades when I was younger. This sometimes came through advice or a job. Or even a place to stay. None of this relates to writing books, but it kept the engines running while I got better at my craft. So I thought I'd give a shout-out to three folks who helped me at pivotal times: Linda Filep, Hahn Lin, and Jeremy Kaplan. Thank you.

I've ended the last two acknowledgments saying that "this is not over" and "P. T. Marsh will be back." I'll just say here that there're more stories to tell with P.T. and Remy. Either way, at some point, you will meet my next hero, Gardner Camden. If you like these stories, you will love Gardner as much or more. Talk to y'all soon and happy reading.